International Perspectives on Gender and Higher Education

International Perspectives on Gender and Higher Education: Student Access and Success

CHRISTINE FONTANINI

University of Lorraine, France

K. M. JOSHI

Maharaja Krishnakumarsinhji Bhavnagar University, India

SAEED PAIVANDI

University of Lorraine, France

emerald PUBLISHING

United Kingdom – North America – Japan – India – Malaysia – China

Emerald Publishing Limited
Howard House, Wagon Lane, Bingley BD16 1WA, UK

First edition 2021

British Library Cataloguing in Publication Data
A catalogue record for this book is available from the British Library

ISBN: 978-1-83909-887-1 (Print)
ISBN: 978-1-83909-886-4 (Online)
ISBN: 978-1-83909-888-8 (Epub)

Printed and bound by CPI Group (UK) Ltd, Croydon, CR0 4YY

ISOQAR
REGISTERED
ISOQAR certified Management System, awarded to Emerald for adherence to Environmental standard ISO 14001:2004.

Certificate Number 1985
ISO 14001

INVESTOR IN PEOPLE

Table of Contents

List of Figures

Chapter 9

Chapter 12

Chapter 13

List of Tables

List of Contributors

Shirin Abdmolaei	Western University, Canada
Kinjal V. Ahir	Sardar Patel University, India
Rumana Ahmed	Monash University, Australia
Tom Bekers	KU Leuven, Belgium
José Beltrán Llavador	University of Valencia, Spain
Chiara Biasin	University of Padua, Italy
Elisa Chaleta	University of Évora, Portugal
Gina Chianese	University of Trieste, Italy
Jorge Correia Jesuíno	University of Lisbon, Portugal
Miriam E. David	University College London (UCL), Institute of Education, UK
Kurt De Wit	KU Leuven, Belgium
Christine Fontanini	University of Lorraine, France
Daniel Gabaldón-Estevan	University of Valencia, Spain
Aldo Hernández-Barrios	Konrad Lorenz University Foundation, Colombia
Nelia Hyndman-Rizk	University of New South Wales, Australia
K. M. Joshi	Maharaja Krishnakumarsinhji Bhavnagar University, India
Tamas Kozma	University of Debrecen, Hungary
Georgia Eleni Lempesi	University of Patras, Greece
Mariele Martins Torquato	Campeche College, Brazil
Yukari Matsuzuka	Hitotsubashi University, Japan
Alejandra Montané López	University of Barcelona, Spain
Yasmin Nadir	CNRS, France

Céline Sidonie Koco Nobah Epse Kacou-Wodjé	Ecole Normale Supérieure, Côte d'Ivoire
Saeed Paivandi	University of Lorraine, France
João Pissarra	University of Lisbon, Portugal
István Polónyi	University of Debrecen, Hungary
Goli M. Rezai-Rashti	Western University, Canada
Ione Ribeiro Valle	Federal University of Santa Catarina, Brazil
Silvana Rodrigues de Souza Sato	Federal University of Santa Catarina, Brazil
Georgios Stamelos	University of Patras, Greece
Lina Uribe-Correa	Konrad Lorenz University Foundation, Colombia

Foreword

Feminist Imaginings Challenging the World of Academic Capitalism for Gender Equality in Global Higher Education

Miriam E. David

Introduction

The twenty-first century has witnessed major global changes in economies, higher education, political systems, and social structures. A key transformation is the involvement of groups other than traditional upper and middle class men in universities and other higher education: groups such as women, disadvantaged, poor and working-class men, racialized, Black, Asian and minority ethnic (BAME) groups, those with physical or invisible disabilities and diverse sexualities, as students, faculty or academics, and staff. Globalization is the term most commonly associated with these international transformations, although there are significant differences between countries, particularly those of the global south as compared with the global north (Connell, 2007). The question of whether these various and varied changes lead to greater equities, equalities, or inequalities between groups or social classes is a question that is taxing many social researchers, as well as politicians (Burke, David, & Moreau, 2019; David, 2018; David, Burke, & Moreau, 2019).

The worldwide changes for both students and academics in higher education have been enormous (David, 2016a, p. 50; David & Amey, 2020). In the United Kingdom alone, there are more than 2 million students in higher education, making for a massive increase in participation, such that females are in the ascendance. The worldwide increases have been fivefold, making higher education a major component of global economies. Women account for a majority of students in most countries, and this is part of an increase of around 500% in enrollments over less than 40 years (1970–2009). UNESCO commented that

> …the capacity of the world's education systems more than doubled—from 647 million students in 1970 to 1,397 million in 2009 …[and] from 33 to 164 million in higher education.
>
> (UNESCO, 2012, p. 9)

They went on to say that

> ...female enrollment at the tertiary level has grown almost twice as fast as that of men over the last four decades. The colleges, schools, and universities to which students now go vary greatly, as do the students themselves.

There are, however, major methodological and theoretical issues to be resolved over how to interpret these developments. On the one hand, the statistical approach to assessment or evaluation of changing forms of participation in higher education, now known as metrics, has been increasing and used as a policy tool internationally. On the other hand, this methodological approach has been critiqued by feminists as "misogyny masquerading as metrics" (David, 2016a). All theoretical approaches involve personal and political values, relating to views about the family, gender, political, and social structures of society. Very often, however, the underlying values are occluded or relate to the traditional social and political order. Taking a feminist perspective foregrounds women as integral to the analysis (David, 2018). This could lead to the question of whether it is possible to single out the impact of these various changes on how well girls or women do in relation to access to, involvement, or participation in higher education and subsequent family and employment, including employment in higher education. How important is an intersectional analysis to this: in other words, are issues of social class, Black, Asian and Minority Ethnicity (BAME) and/or race, religion, gender, family, and sexualities interlinked in this analysis? Intersectionality as a methodological approach was first proposed by the Black American feminist legal scholar, Kimberley Crenshaw, over 30 years ago, about various forms of stratification and their intersections and social and cultural effects (Crenshaw, 1989/2017).

Taking a feminist methodological approach to studies in higher education draws on the political project of feminism. This arose out of the civil, social, and human rights movements of the last third of the twentieth century (especially initially in France and the United States) and was closely linked with the growth of student participation in higher education. One aspect of this ongoing feminist project has been to try to transform women's lives toward gender and social equality into the twenty-first century. As I argued:

> ...this is fundamentally an educational and pedagogical project: to understand how the current gender, sexual and social structures have come about and to develop the knowledge and wisdom to further that understanding and to transform such relations in the direction of what has become known, in the twenty-first century, as gender and social justice. It has been a project increasingly in universities, as higher education has expanded, with changing socio-economic and political systems globally.
>
> (David, 2014, p. 1)

The overarching question about the nature and character of the expansion of global higher education has engaged and troubled scholars for over 75 years, given that, in 1945, there were only 500 universities and in 2019 there were over 10,000 according to UNESCO (Redding, Drew, & Crump, 2019, p. vii). This expansion has been considered the massification of higher education or the creation of massive universities versus universities for the masses (Langa Rosado & David, 2006, pp. 343–365). Rosado and I considered that "the masses" were groups of people, women included, who had previously been excluded from elite forms of higher education, namely the prestigious universities. In our case, we considered universities in Spain and the United Kingdom. There are now, internationally, very large institutions, catering for large swathes of students from a diversity of social class, ethnic and racial backgrounds, and gender or sexualities, but these institutions remain stratified by their elite and privileged status (Langa Rosado & David, 2006). The majority of students in elite and traditional universities come from the middle classes rather than the poorer or working-class backgrounds (Archer, Hutchings, Leathwood, & Ross, 2003), even though there has been an expansion of provision for women students.

There are many explanations for these transformations with agreement about globalization and the technical revolution in information and communication technologies (ICT) (Redding et al., 2019). Whether or not this can also be considered "academic capitalism," a term coined by the American feminist scholar Sheila Slaughter, with colleagues Larry Leslie and Gary Rhoades, is more contested, calling into question changing political values around corporatization, individualism, marketization, and neoliberalism (Slaughter & Leslie, 1997; Slaughter & Rhoades, 2004). Slaughter and Leslie (1997) illustrated how the expansion of higher education was intertwined with the developments in capitalism and the particular political forms of neoliberalism. The thesis was that the expansion of the university together with economic development was not about increasing equality but about the growth of new markets and new social relations within economic development. In their analysis, this constituted a major shift from the post–World War II emphasis, in the majority of industrial countries or those now known as the global north, on public investment in the expansion of education, including higher education, as a means of developing social equalities and social mobilities. They went on to show how rapidly this transformation was taking place not only in the United States but also internationally. In a subsequent study Slaughter with another colleague Gary Rhoades wrote an extended analysis entitled *Academic Capitalism and the New Economy: markets, state and higher education* published in 2004 that illustrated quite how advanced the new system of capitalism entwined with higher education had become internationally.

They also argued that equality, fairness, and social justice as political values have been downgraded in the pursuit of more business or corporate approaches to global economies. There is also the question of the impact and influences of the changes on socioeconomic and structural factors including the participation of women and people from disadvantaged groups such as those in poor regions, Black and minority ethnicities (BAME), social class, and other diversities and sexualities. These latter are not a dominant consideration, despite the international policy changes to increase access and participation from disadvantaged groups. The policy changes arguably for increasing equality and social justice have therefore had complex implications despite the exponential growth in overall participation in some form of higher education (David, 2018). It can, in fact, be argued that the expansion of global higher education in the twenty-first century has led to increasing inequalities between countries and regions, social classes, gender and sexualities, and other diversities.

Student Access to and Participation in Higher Education: Issues of Gender Equality

Widening access to and participation in higher education emerged as a major policy concern for the UK New Labour government (1997–2010), as in many other countries mainly of the global north, connected to longer histories over struggles for the right to higher education, to concerns for greater fairness in society, and to try to ensure that higher education is more equitable and inclusive (Burke, 2012). It also wanted a different approach to expanding higher educational opportunities to fit with global economic expansion. Thus, major political contentious debates were set in train about academic excellence versus educational achievement, which had implications for how to implement fair access and widening participation. It also meant that the question of which kinds of student to include was debated: and the criteria for choice.

Widening participation in higher education was not a new policy mantra in the twenty-first century. Indeed, ideas about how to make educational opportunities more equal or equitable for various groups such as those in poverty, economically or socially disadvantaged, or on the basis of being working class, from an ethnic or racial minority, and according to gender, had been a policy theme throughout the second half of the twentieth century. Initially, though, it was a theme applied to reconstructing secondary and compulsory education, rather than access to, or participation in, higher education. Widening access and participation was also shaped by the growing diversification of student groups that have resulted from higher education expansion over the later decades of the twentieth century. Widening participation, often shortened to *WP*, gained discursive hegemony, and this discourse has gained momentum internationally. However, the discourse is highly contested within and across different national contexts, and there is no one agreed definition. There are also different associated policy discourses, such as equity, social mobility, social inclusion, and social disadvantage.

For example, Reay, Davies, David, and Ball (2001) observed how applicants to higher education from working-class backgrounds often stress the importance of locality and community in their decision-making process and the sense of security, comfort, and familiarity generated through these localized expressions. Ball and Vincent (1998) highlight how students from middle-class backgrounds are often able to draw on both the formal forms of "cold" or official knowledge available as well as "hot" knowledge—the knowledge available through informal social networks. Students from working-class backgrounds usually do not benefit from access to "hot" knowledge about higher education and therefore must rely on official forms of "cold" knowledge, which might be challenging to access and decipher (Burke, 2015, 2017).

In the aftermath of the UK Labour government's specific policy to expand and regulate undergraduate student access to and participation in different types of higher education, through the 2004 Higher Education Act, studies were commissioned (David et al., 2010). These were because of the acrimonious debates surrounding the questions of access to and widening participation in higher education, whereby the aim was to ensure 50% of the relevant age cohort participated in higher education. The UK Government through its Higher Education Funding Council for England (HEFCE) and the Economic and Social Research Council (ESRC) with its major educational research program—the Teaching and Learning Research Programme (TLRP)—committed £2 million funding for the research and I was appointed to direct the studies (David et al., 2010, p. 14). We wrote (David et al., 2010, p. 13):

> Over the last forty [1970–2010] years, the overall numbers of undergraduate students participating in some form of higher education has quadrupled from half a million in 1965, to two million in 2005–6 (HEFCE 2005a). As Hayward and colleagues go on to argue: 'educational participation beyond the compulsory school age has increased in the UK since 1945, with a massive increase in full-time provision between 1985 and 1994'. Moreover, over the years from 1996–7 to 2005–6, in absolute terms, women outnumbered men and are 60 per cent of full-time student population in UK universities with some variations in English, Northern Irish, Scottish and Welsh forms of access and participation.

We elaborated this (David et al., 2010, pp. 7–8):

> The UK government, during the first half of the first decade of the twenty-first century, has been eager to develop and extend learning opportunities for both young people and adults, across their life course, *to ensure that the education and skills base of the UK economy is internationally competitive*...Deploying new ideas about forms of governance and what have been called new managerialism or neo-liberalism has meant that a variety of new and innovative approaches to education and individual or personal learning opportunities have been tried and tested...

Understandings of the meanings of fair access and widening participation were extremely eclectic and not at all concerned with altering existing power relations. There was contestation between meanings of educational achievements and "fair access." Seven studies were commissioned through the TLRP ranging from statistical to qualitative studies of diverse participants in higher education and including one study of a community where adults did not necessarily participate in higher education. The main aim was how to improve learning by widening participation to higher education. The studies all focused on questions of "transforming institutional practices and on developing appropriate and sustainable pedagogies for social diversity and learning across the life course" (David et al., 2010, p. 180).

The implication for the future which came out of these seven fine-grained and sensitive policy-oriented studies was to "argue for the centrality of educational opportunities across the life course to ensure that they are aligned to men and women's changing socioeconomic and family circumstances" (David et al., 2010, p. 180). An array of inclusive and personal pedagogies was suggested that might engage students of the future in educational courses and new or innovative subjects, going beyond the twentieth century. This also had implications for social mobility and how to change circumstances for underrepresented groups in an entirely new light. We stated (David et al., 2010, p. 201):

> Finally a vision for fair access, equity and diversity in participation in the global academy would surely incorporate the uses of critical and connectionist pedagogies, including developing inclusive and yet personal pedagogies to ensure people's lives across the life course were enhanced and improved...If we value inclusion, teachers, practitioners and policy-makers should maintain high expectations of all students as learners, whilst recognising the diversity of their needs, cultures and identities.

This was but one policy-related program of research to consider how to engage and involve different kinds of students from the more traditional 18-year-old white male student in higher education. Only one of the considerations was the question of involving more women students, and that was not a paramount consideration. Together with Burke and Moreau and others, I have considered how the changing context and transformations of higher education have implications for equity, social, and gender justice. Policy reforms driven by intersecting political forces are profoundly reshaping global higher education (Burke et al., 2019; David et al., 2019). Burke, Moreau, and I also considered the international statistical and social evidence to show how white middle class male privilege remains entrenched in complex ways in new forms of higher education. We have written extensively about the impact of such changes on equity in higher education and on women in particular (see for example Burke, 2012; Burke, Crozier, & Misiaszek, 2017; Burke et al., 2019; David, 2014, 2016a, 2016b). This has included attention to gendered and sexual violence (David, 2016b).

We also explored this in relation to ongoing structural inequalities and how patriarchal discourses work with neoliberalism to reproduce continuing, and generate emerging, forms of difference and inequality in and through higher education (David et al., 2019). This takes place in a context in which structural inequalities, such as gender, class, and race, are seen to have been erased and symbolic inequalities, that are associated with women and femininities, are made invisible through discourses that assert a logic of gender neutrality (Stambach & David, 2005). We also discussed how being caring and having caring commitments are dispositions that carry little value in the often seen as gender-neutral institutional spaces of universities. This is shown most clearly through the pursuit of an uncritical notion of excellence and the approaches to pedagogies. Explorations of, for example, how student parents are treated "carelessly" or without care, as are how the majority of academic staff have become precarious workers, while privilege remains for White middle-class men in power (David, 2016a; Moreau & Kerner, 2015).

Women and Gender Equality among Academics and Researchers in Higher Education

The massive expansion and transformation of global higher education has affected both the institutions that provide teaching, learning and research, and who becomes a student (Archer et al., 2003; Shavit, Arum, & Gamoran, 2007). Inevitably, this also affects who becomes an academic, across changing subjects and/or disciplines. Very little commentary has been made of the specific gendered and linked social characteristics of the students, their teachers, and the institutions. However, equality or the obverse, inequality in higher education, is still largely considered in gender-neutral terms. For example, as recently as October 2017, Roger Brown defined inequality in higher education as income inequality, relying on studies by the OECD (2011), to support his arguments and evidence (Brown, 2017). He argued that the huge growth in income inequality in most Western economies over the past 30 years or so was linked to the growth in higher education. He supported this by considering the development of global markets or neoliberalism in higher education and separately the notion of institutional developments and the ways in which higher education institutions had responded to the growth in global markets. Gender was not once mentioned and nor were ethnicity or race, although his book is about the implications for socioeconomic equalities.

Global expansion has led to increasing inequalities, including, but not only, for women (David, 2016a, p. 51). While women have secured a foothold in universities, not only as students but also as academics, they remain belittled and subject to forms of sexual harassment, rather than being treated as equals. This is what some have called the feminization crisis (Morley, 2011). With the expansion of universities, and the growing presence of women at both undergraduate and postgraduate levels, as well as among academics, we have also witnessed the rise of feminism, as a form of critique of traditional academic knowledge and activism to transform women's oppression in society. Feminism has taken diverse forms in the various countries of the global north with strong critiques of the differences between white and black feminisms, for instance. Heidi Mirza (2018a, 2018b) recently argued about the contestations between these diverse forms of feminism, drawing on her work over a 20-year period (Mirza, 1997).

There are also contestations about how to typify forms of feminism within higher education. What is often called second wave feminism arose out of the women's liberation movements (WLM) of the 1960s and 1970s (David, 2014, 2016a, 2016b). First wave feminism, by contrast, largely arose in the nineteenth and early twentieth century, focusing upon political, economic, and social changes for women's emancipation. This first wave was largely through the suffrage movements, as Banks (1986) has argued. The various arguments about how feminism has influenced both the sociopolitical and economic changes into the twenty-first century and the forms of academic knowledge developed to underpin these movements are also heavily contested stories (David, 2016a, 2016b). Nevertheless, the thread is one of the two forms of feminism: liberal or socialist.

In 2014, I undertook a study of over 100 feminist activists in the arts, humanities, and social sciences in international academia, to capture the views and values of these intergenerational and emerging feminists (David, 2014). The journeys of these 110 international educators were presented, grouped into three different generational groups, using the methodology developed by the feminist sociologist of education, Olive Banks (Banks, 1986). The three groups were those born between 1935 and 1950; 1950 to 1965; and 1965 to 1980. While these three groups are now senior and not younger generations, they do illustrate both the expansion and impact of higher education in women's lives and their limitations on involvement. All subscribed to the notion of being a feminist activist or educator and discussed how they engaged with feminism within higher education or outside. The older generations were relatively more politically engaged whereas the younger were more theoretically inclined.

In a subsequent study, I focused on just the feminist educators within the study of over 100 international academics: these were over a third (David, 2016b, pp. 89–125). I looked at how these women negotiated higher education, given that it "is typified by a misogynist or sexist approach within higher education management and leadership" (David, 2016b, p. 89). There were international networks of the participants in the study, although they were mainly resident in the United Kingdom at the time but had come from a large range of disparate countries. This makes it clear that there is a diversity of countries of residence, which is not at all continuous with countries of origin. The study was made up of a diversity of women academics, across the generations and ages, and also extremely varied in terms of their social and geographic locations: illustrative of the mobile, transnational academics who are characteristic of the overall academic profession in the twenty-first century (David, 2014, p. 17, 2016b, p. 100; Kim & Brooks, 2013).

Neither particular individuals nor institutions were targeted, but given research interests and predilections, it is not surprising that the study had many participants who saw themselves as feminist activist educators or academics. "Education feminists" was the term coined in the United States for the group who are committed to and publishing in feminist studies of education and gender (Stone, 1994). Over half the women from the first cohort, with three-quarters from the second, and the vast majority of the youngest were identified as part of this group

(David, 2016b, p. 101). There remain clear social class differences in origins and approaches to feminism, gender, and education.

The notion of social class used was drawn from the participants' own accounts, in replies to online questions or through interviews, given that they were all social scientists and were involved in using such notions. Family backgrounds were defined not only by parents' social class as being about income or means but also by occupation, with many women having parents who were either schoolteachers or university professors. This turned out to be significantly more usual than expected, especially in relation to "education feminists."

Indeed, one of the major transformations of higher education over the last 50 years, responsible for the increasing numbers of women as students in higher education, has been the incorporation of teacher education as an undergraduate study, with different patterns of types of teacher education across different countries in separate colleges or linked with other types of professional work (Acker & Wagner, 2019). Many of the participants in my study also had parents, mothers especially, who had participated in teacher education, not then named as higher education, and so were not (technically) "first-in-the-family" or "first generation" to go to university, although they felt it to be so. All evidence was through self-identification.

In a subsequent study, with Pam Alldred and others, funded by the European Union (EU) through its Daphne program attending to violence against women and girls (VAWG), we considered how to challenge gendered violence, bullying, and sexual harassment through higher education. Questions about gender and sexual relations, VAWG, sexual harassment, and sexual abuse are now more overtly in the public eye, globally, nationally, and locally. The question of why these issues are now more in the public eye is not clear, although it may have to do with both feminist activism and the transformations in culture, social media, and communications, contributing to new forms of capitalism and the commercialization of gender and sexuality as new forms of sexualization. Such violence against women and sexual harassment is no longer seen as just a problem for the global south but also the global north. But the roots of such gender-related violence are not adequately tackled and remain side-lined in political discourse.

In *A Feminist Manifesto for Education* (David, 2016b), I address the ways in which feminists in the academy have developed analyses of gender and education and, separately, gender-related violence. I also considered the above research study with Pam Alldred on how to challenge gender-related violence for children and young people. This education and training project was based in four universities across Europe, namely in Ireland, Italy, Spain, and the United Kingdom.

> Improved knowledge and understanding were essential for "youth practitioners" to better identify and challenge sexist, sexualizing, homophobic or controlling language and behavior, and know when and how to refer children and young people to the most appropriate support services.
>
> (David, 2016b, p. 40)

There has been increasing levels of attention to issues of sexual violence in higher education over recent years, as its prevalence has become increasingly visible. There are clearly few political solutions that tackle the roots of this VAWG as forms of abuse of male power or patriarchy and misogyny.

On the contrary, gender mainstreaming as a policy notion became more commonplace in the early twenty-first century, in response to growing economic and social demands for women's involvement in employment and politics. The institutionalization of some feminisms and the mainstreaming of their demands (Walby, 2002) affected changes in political rhetoric. Among other things, they led to greater attention to the use of sexist and homophobic language (Millns & Skeet, 2013) and they were useful when it came to certain gender politics. However, the institutionalization also brought about a cooptation of many feminist claims (Montoya, 2009). This is well illustrated by the mainstreaming of the term "gender." On the one hand, the use of the concept made it possible to recognize the sociocultural norms and values, pressures and incentives involved in constructing gendered subjects, and binary, heterosexual order. On the other hand, the term is frequently used to dismiss the necessity of feminist analysis. In fact, it is mostly employed in mainstreaming policies that tend not to be sensitive to central feminist issues in regard to power, hierarchies, and difference (Biglia, Olivella-Quintana, & Cagliero, 2015). Furthermore, the frequent use of gender-neutral language in laws produces inattention to gendered power relations (David, 2016b, pp. 65–66).

In recent times, there have been feminist contestations on university campus particularly over sexual harassment among students and training students to challenge sexual violence and between feminists as academics and students. Some of these contestations are very unfortunate and have become public media debates between waves of feminists on campus, showing how feminism per se has been brought into public disrepute (David, 2016a, p. 174). Yet feminist campaigning has successfully exposed sexual assault or harassment, rape culture, or lad culture on campus, although policies remain woefully inadequate, not only for students but also for women and feminist academics (David, 2016a). The old liberal-humanist arguments about how universities are spaces for creative thinking and allow for academic freedom and/or freedom of expression are being eroded in the neoliberal university. Even more importantly, new quasi-legal notions of radicalization are also having an impact on campus cultures and constricting and confining sociocultural debates.

There is an increasingly overt sexualized and laddish culture on campus, particularly, but clearly from above, not only among students. This has been the subject of increasing amounts of feminist research to try to make the campus safe for students and for others, including in developing policies dealing with sexual assaults, harassment, and a rape culture. Issues of campus safety are, however, only just beginning to be part of more inclusive gender policies internationally. British policies remain muted, although there have been some recent institutional responses to developing lessons in *sexual consent* for incoming undergraduate students. This is in contrast to the policies on rape and sexual assault on campus that the then US President Obama tried to initiate in 2014. Nevertheless, although in the public eye and with official sanction, these remained highly contested questions and few campuses in either the United States or United Kingdom have developed clear and comprehensive guidelines for dealing with these issues either for students or for academics (David, 2016b, pp. 184–185).

A Feminist Critique of Leadership in Higher Education

It seems clear that there is a toxic mix of globalization and changing gender and sexual relations, especially in higher education. Louise Morley (2012, p. 29) argued that part of the problem in higher education was "the cycle of domination of top roles by men in universities." She continued that it was important to transform that vicious cycle in higher education to make education, and higher education especially, less misogynistic.

Morley has been a particularly strong critic of developments in the neoliberal university. In particular she has argued passionately about the moves toward creating new metrics (a term that is itself a twenty-first century neologism) and the numbers game is a form of misogyny posing as measurement. She also suggests that it is important for feminist academics to consider how to change the rules of the (patriarchal) game (Morley, 2013) so as to have a more gender appropriate future for universities. The contested nature of global changes especially around gender equality in education, including in higher education, means that the ideas have become emasculated rather than feminized by incorporation into neoliberal global universities.

Yet, as Morley (2011) has shown, most countries of the global north have developed policies for gender equity in the public sphere and education; and many countries of the global south also have developed frameworks for gender equity in public life and higher education. Based in Centre for Higher Education and Equity Research (CHEER) at the University of Sussex, she has conducted many innovative studies of global higher education. For example, one study of gender equity looked at examples from the global south, namely two African countries—Ghana and Tanzania—in terms both of widening participation and of how gender is done, undone, and redone in higher education via policies, practices, and the micro-political relays of power.

In another study, Morley (2013) argued trenchantly about how new managerialism and the so-called "leaderist turn in higher education" are subverting and reinforcing the rules of the game in patriarchal ways. She provided

> ...an international review of feminist knowledge on how gender and power interact with leadership in higher education... to unmask the "rules of the game" that lurk beneath the surface rationality of academic meritocracy.

She further argued (Morley, 2013, pp. 116–131) that:

> ...curiously, in a culture of measurement and audit in higher education, women's representation in different roles and grades is not always perceived as sufficiently important to measure, monitor or map comparatively...The data that do exist suggest that women disappear in the higher grades...This under-representation reflects not only continued inequalities between men and women, but missed opportunities for women to influence, and contribute to universities of the future.

Blackmore and Sachs (2007), two critical feminist researchers, based in Australia also undertook a major international study of how neoliberal changes were impacting upon forms of leadership and management in different forms of education and higher education. Entitling their study *Performing and Reforming Leaders: Gender, educational restructuring and change*, they clearly demonstrated that the concept of gender institutionalizes forms of change and does not necessarily lead to reverses in patriarchal power in educational institutions. What they focused on were the ways in which emotions were handled in education and how this linked with collective feminist work. In a subsequent critical piece, Blackmore (2013) developed her feminist perspective on educational leadership, particularly here with respect to universities. Again, she illustrated the diverse notions of leadership in higher education.

Conclusions about Women, Gendered Involvement, and Participation in Higher Education

Drawing on feminist critiques to shed light on complex and diverse inequalities in higher education, I have shown how gendered inequalities continue to intersect with other forms of difference despite decades of higher education policy focused on equity and widening participation. I have discussed and analyzed the emergence of widening participation and equity policies in many countries of both the global north and the global south, often for both social and economic reasons. Yet this is in a context where intersecting forces of globalization, neoliberalism, and marketization have repositioned students as consumers of the market of global higher education, leading to an individualizing focus on student access and participation, without attention to the contextual and structural inequalities that profoundly undermine institutional commitment to equity and widening participation. The individualist discourses have implications for students' experiences of higher education in relation to the different social location and in relation to the gendering of education, work, and family, reinforcing patriarchal assumptions that universities should be "careless" (Lynch, 2010; Moreau, 2016) and privileging the productive over reproductive dimensions of social life (Burke & Jackson, 2007). I have tried to show the power of feminist analyses of questions of equity, excellence, and WP to bring to light the ways that gendered, classed, racialized, and sexualized or intersectional inequalities are reproduced and exacerbated rather than eroded through the neoliberal, patriarchal university.

The array of research papers included in this volume edited by Paivandi, Fontanini, and Joshi will contribute greatly to furthering knowledge about the diverse impacts of the varied changes in global higher education have on *female students* in a range of countries from both the global south and the global north. Given that the countries range across Africa, Asia, the Americas, and Europe, there is much nuance about the specificities, recent developments, and impact of the marketization about *the presence of girls* in higher education. This project includes countries that are not traditionally covered by this higher education research and will reveal fascinating insights into the workings of patriarchy and misogyny in relation to regimes of higher education. It takes as a central emphasis the colonial developments from France and other European countries. It focuses on a French colony in Africa (Cote D'Ivoire), and in Asia, Iran, and two countries of the Indian subcontinent (Bangladesh and India), two countries of Latin America (Brazil and Colombia), both linked to the two countries of the Iberian peninsula (Portugal and Spain), with the other European countries being Flanders, Greece, and Hungary, and only two other countries of the global north, namely Canada and Japan. The tendency is therefore for a balance toward cultures and ethnicities not central to previous research on gender and higher education. Nevertheless, this is limited to studies of women students, although conducted by researchers in higher education.

Through feminist perspectives, I have shown that neoliberalism, corporatization, and managerialism or academic capitalism work together with patriarchy to perpetuate and generate new forms of inequality and power relations. New managerialism and the so-called leaderist turn in higher education aimed at gender equity are subverting and reinforcing the "rules of the game" in patriarchal ways. Indeed, the effects of neoliberalism and managerialism have been to confine women to relatively junior academic positions and rarely the most senior leadership positions. Furthermore, tenacious feminist campaigning has successfully exposed sexual assault or harassment on campus and cast a light on how policies have not adequately protected female students and academics (David, 2016a).

References

Acker, S., & Wagner, A. (2019). Feminist scholars working around the neoliberal university. *Gender and Education*, *31*(1), 62–81.

Archer, L., Hutchings, M., Leathwood, C., & Ross, A. (2003). Widening participation in higher education: Implications for policy and practice. In L. Archer, M. Hutchings, & A. Ross (Eds.), *Higher education and social class: Issues of exclusion and inclusion*. London: Routledge Falmer.

Ball, S., & Vincent, C. (1998). I heard it on the grapevine: Hot knowledge and school choice. *British Journal of Sociology of Education*, *19*(3), 377–400.

Banks, O. (1986). *Becoming a feminist: The social origins of first wave feminism*. Brighton: Wheatsheaf Books.

Biglia, B., Olivella-Quintana, M., & Cagliero, S. (Eds.). (2015). *Gender related violence legislation in Europe*. Tarragona: Universitat Rovira I Virgili.
Blackmore, J. (2013). A feminist critical perspective on educational leadership. *International Journal of Leadership in Education*, *16*, 139–154.
Blackmore, J., & Sachs, J. (2007). *Performing and reforming leaders: Gender, educational restructuring and change*. Albany, NY: State University of New York Press.
Brown, R. (2017). *The inequality crisis: The facts and what we can do about it*. Bristol: Policy Press.
Burke, P. J. (2012). *The right to higher education: Beyond widening participation*. London; New York, NY: Routledge.
Burke, P. J. (2015). Re/imagining higher education pedagogies: Gender, emotion and difference. *Teaching in Higher Education*, *20*(4), 388–401.
Burke, P. J. (2017). Difference in higher education pedagogies: Gender, emotion and shame. *Gender and Education*, *29*(4), 430–444.
Burke, P. J., Crozier, G., & Misiaszek, L. (2017). *Changing pedagogical spaces in higher education. Diversity, inequalities and misrecognition*. London; New York, NY: Routledge.
Burke, P. J., David, M. E., & Moreau, M. P. (2019). Policy implications for equity, gender and widening participation in higher education. In G. Redding, A. Drew, & S. Crump (Eds.), *The Oxford handbook of higher education systems and university management* (pp. 432–453, chapter 26). Oxford: Oxford University Press.
Burke, P. J., & Jackson, S. (2007). *Reconceptualising lifelong learning: Feminist interventions*. London; New York, NY: Routledge.
Connell, R. (2007). *Southern theory: The global dynamics of knowledge in social science*. Cambridge: Polity Press.
Crenshaw, K. (1989). Demarginalizing the intersection of race and sex: A black feminist critique of antidiscrimination doctrine, feminist theory and antiracist politics. University of Chicago Legal Forum, University of Chicago Law School 1989 (pp. 139–208).
David, M. E. (2014). *Feminism, gender & universities: Politics, passion and pedagogies*. London: Ashgate and Informa.
David, M. E. (2016a). *Reclaiming feminism: Challenging everyday misogyny*. Bristol: Policy Press.
David, M. E. (2016b). *A feminist manifesto for education*. Cambridge: Polity Press.
David, M. E. (2018). Challenging inequalities in education: A feminist approach. In G. Craig (Ed.), *Handbook on global social justice*. Cheltenham: Edward Elgar.
David, M. E., & Amey, M. J. (Eds.). (2020). *The SAGE encyclopedia of higher education*. Thousand Oaks, CA: SAGE Publications.
David, M. E. with Bathmaker, A. M., Crozier, G., Davis, P., Ertl, H., Fuller, A., … Williams, J. (Eds.). (2010). *Improving learning by widening participation in higher education*. London: Routledge.
David, M. E., Burke, P. J., & Moreau, M. P. (2019). Macro changes and implications for equality, social and gender justice in HE. In G. Redding, A. Drew, & S. Crump (Eds.), *The Oxford handbook of higher education systems and university management* (pp. 236–255, chapter 14). Oxford: Oxford University Press.
Kim, T., & Brooks, R. (2013). *Internationalisation, mobile academics and knowledge creation in universities: A comparative analysis*. Final report. London: Society for Research in Higher Education.

Langa Rosado, D., & David, M. E. (2006). A massive university or a university for the masses? Continuity and change in higher education in Spain and England. *Journal of Education Policy*, *21*(3), 343–365.

Lynch, K. (2010). Carelessness: A hidden doxa of higher education. *Arts and Humanities in Higher Education*, *9*(1), 54–67.

Millns, S., & Skeet, C. (2013). Gendered equality and legal mobilization in the United Kingdom: Using rights for lobbying, litigation, defence and attack. *Canadian Journal of Law and Society*, *28*(2), 169–188.

Mirza, H. (Ed.). (1997). *Black British feminism*. London: Routledge.

Mirza, H. S. (2018a). Racism in higher education: 'What then, can be done?'. In J. Arday & H. S. Mirza (Eds.), *Dismantling race in higher education: Racism, whiteness and decolonising the academy* (pp. 3–23). London: Palgrave Macmillan.

Mirza, H. S. (2018b). Black bodies 'out of place' in academic spaces: Gender, race, faith and culture in post-race times. In J. Arday & H. S. Mirza (Eds.), *Dismantling race in higher education: Racism, whiteness and decolonising the academy* (pp. 175–193). London: Palgrave Macmillan.

Montoya, C. (2009). International initiative and domestic reforms: European union efforts to combat violence against women. *Politics and Gender*, *5*, 325–348.

Moreau, M. P. (2016). Regulating the student body/ies: University policies and student parents. *British Educational Research Journal*, *42*(5), 906–925.

Moreau, M. P., & Kerner, C. (2015). Care in academia: An exploration of student parents' experiences. *British Journal of Sociology of Education*, *36*(2), 215–233.

Morley, L. (2011). Misogyny posing as measurement: Disrupting the feminisation crisis discourse. *Contemporary Social Science: Special Issue: Challenge, Change or Crisis in Global Higher Education*, *6*(2), 223–237.

Morley, L. (2012). Cycles of domination of top roles by men must be broken. *Times Higher Education*, December 6, p. 29.

Morley, L. (2013). The rules of the game: Women and the leaderist turn in higher education. *Gender and Education*, *25*(1), 116–131.

OECD. (2011). *An overview of growing income inequalities in OECD countries: An overview*. Paris: OECD.

Reay, D., Davies, J., David, M., & Ball, S. J. (2001). Choices of degree or degrees of choice? Class, "race" and the higher education choice process. *Sociology*, *35*(4), 855–974.

Redding, G., Drew, A., & Crump, S. (2019). Preface and acknowledgements. In G. Redding, A. Drew, & S. Crump (Eds.), *The Oxford handbook of higher education systems and university management*. Oxford: Oxford University Press.

ShavitY., ArumR., & GamoranA. (Eds.). (2007). *Stratification in higher education: A comparative study*. Palo Alto, CA: Stanford University Press.

Slaughter, S., & Leslie, L. (1997). *Academic capitalism: Politics, policies and the entrepreneurial university*. Baltimore, MD: John Hopkins University Press.

Slaughter, S., & Rhoades, G. (2004). *Academic capitalism and the new economy: Markets, state and higher education*. Baltimore, MD: John Hopkins University Press.

Stambach, A., & David, M. E. (2005). Feminist theory and educational policy: How gender has been involved in home school debates about school choice. *Signs: Journal of Women in Culture and Society*, *30*(2), 1633–1659.

Stone, L. (Ed.). (1994). *The education feminism reader*. London; New York, NY: Routledge.

UNESCO. (2012). *World atlas of gender equality in education*. Paris: UNESCO Publishing. Retrieved from www.uis.unesco.org/Education/Documents/unesco-world-atlas-gender-education-2012.pdf

Walby, S. (2002). Feminism in a global era. *Economy and Society*, *31*(4), 533–557.

International Perspectives on Gender and Higher Education: Student Access and Success

The proportion of girls in tertiary education has grown steadily in different continents for several decades. Since the 1990s, more women than men have completed higher education in most countries. According to the most recent available data,[1] there are more women than men graduating from tertiary education in four out of five countries (80%).[2] Despite improved access to higher education, the distribution of women and men varies considerably across the different fields of study. It's the same for the higher education level attained by women and men.

Women are less likely than men to pursue PhD programs and fields of research. Women outnumber men to obtain a bachelor's degree (undergraduate level 6 of ISCED), men making up 47% of graduates and women 53% in countries for which data are available. Women are also more likely (55%) to hold a master's degree (ISCED level 7). On the other hand, men represent 54% of graduates of PhD programs (ISCED level 8) and 71% of all researchers. Women are more likely than men to graduate in five major fields of higher education: education; letters and arts; social sciences, commerce, and law; natural sciences, mathematics, and statistics; and health and social protection. Men make up the majority of tertiary education graduates in three broad areas: ICTs; engineering, manufacturing, and construction; and agriculture. In these fields, there is a significant imbalance between the sexes in engineering, manufacturing, and construction.

Historically, women's access to higher education has been a phenomenon of the twentieth century. Women were excluded from higher education prior to nineteenth century. The few women who were able to enter university during the seventeenth, eighteenth, and nineteenth centuries (Juliana Morell in Spain, Anna Maria van Schurman in the Netherlands, Ursula Agricola, Maria Jonae Palmgren, and Aurora Liljenroth in Sweden, Elena Cornaro Piscopia, Laura Bassi, and Cristina Roccati in Italy, Elizabeth Blackwell in the USA, Natalia Korsini in Russia, Mary Putman and Julie-Victoire Daubié in France) were pioneers

[1]See UNESCO. (2016). *The Global Education Monitoring Report 2016: Gender review*. Paris: UNESCO. Retrieved from https://unesdoc.unesco.org/ark:/48223/pf0000246045

[2]https://www.tellmaps.com/uis/gender/?lang=fr#!/tellmap/79054752?lang=fr%20eAtlas%20Unesco.

belonging to privileged social groups. All started with the entry of a few women into certain sectors of higher education in Europe and in North America and the creation of establishments reserved for women like Bedford College in London (UK), Georgia Female College of Macon (USA), Oberlin College in Ohio (USA), Women's College Hospital (Canada), and Bethune College (India). It was from the middle of the nineteenth century that European universities began to allow women to enroll in different fields, a situation which is explained by the transformations observed in the European education system, in particular in secondary school, became accessible to a large number of young girls. However, it was from the 1930s and especially after the Second World War that girls massively crossed educational and social barriers to pursue studies and moved into leadership positions in higher education.

Progress in access to higher education seems to be the result of socioeconomic, cultural, and sociological developments observed in different parts of our planet, although their extent varies from one country to another and from one region to another. High school is often democratized in most countries and the labor market often observes permanent feminization. Some countries have put in place a set of egalitarian policies to improve the presence of women in secondary and higher education. Even if the concrete effects of these policies are not measured, the willingness of public policies to promote parity between girls and boys seem to influence the general social context and changing attitudes. In a significant number of countries, it is the social dynamics and the mobilization of women that explain some of the progress made.

Recent evolutions show that the social relations of sex, marked by the balance of power that organizes society, are not fixed once and for all in their forms, their scale, and their effects. There is a space of change within societies opening the way for a gradual transformation. However, the different dynamics of improving the presence of women in the different sectors of higher education seem to vary considerably from country to country. One of the frequently mentioned issues concerns gender inequalities in terms of social origin and regional and ethnic disparities (ethnic and religious minorities, immigrant populations).

A very large number of researches have attempted to gain a better understanding of the meaning and reasons for gendered orientations in higher education, particularly the low presence of girls in certain scientific and technical disciplines in North America and Western Europe. Curiously, in some developing countries where there is recent feminization, the presence of women in technical and scientific disciplines is less unequal. This sociological analysis focuses on the social construction of gender differences and on the weight of the economy, culture, religion, legal setting, and the internal dynamics of societies. Sociological studies on gender generally dismiss the idea of a fact of nature that would lead to a division and complementarity of gender roles both at school and in society. Several hypotheses are advanced by the research work: the weight of sexist stereotypes, the representations of gendered social roles, the gendered socialization of young people within family context, the sexual division of fields of knowledge and skills, the structure of the labor market, the role of the school with differentiated expectations on the part of the teachers according to the disciplines and gender of the pupils, the non-neutrality of the curricula and the textbooks, and the hidden curriculum. But, beyond cultural, social, and economic barriers, access to higher education can be for many young girls a path to more power and more emancipation. Knowledge has become more than ever a power in society and the economy based on science and education. The individual and collective mobilization of women and a new awareness of gender issues seem to contribute to changing the social context and encourage girls to go further in access to education and the labor market.

The book focuses mainly on the situation of the females without considering the debates and research concerning the academic staff (except in direct relation with the students). An international comparison makes this volume interesting in view of the specificities of each country, and the imbalance in access for women to the different fields that show the convergences and divergences at the international level. The book presents a critical and objective analysis of this question while referring to research carried out in different countries on issue of the feminization of higher education.

In total, scholars from 15 countries representing four continents participated in the production of this work. The foreword is written by Miriam E. David.

Miriam E. David (University College London (UCL), Institute of Education, UK) in her foreword of the book reaffirms the phenomenon of massification of higher education. She notes that globally there has been a phenomenal improvement in enrollment in higher education in general and that for women in particular, from among the nontraditional socially diverse groups. The author assesses in an intriguing manner whether this rise in enrollment of socially diverse groups was an outcome of the need for equality and social justice or just a form of academic capitalism enabled by expanded market access. She emphasizes on how structural inequalities and patriarchal discourses are often disguised behind the assertion of gender neutrality. Drawing from her comprehensive empirical research evidence across various studies, the author further elaborates on the evolution of various forms of feminism within higher education until the recent time. She also laments the fact that women are largely missing in the leadership roles in higher education given the gendered inequalities with consequences on academics and students alike. In conclusion, she justifies the need for the book and the gap that it is expected to fill in the existing body of literature on feminism in higher education. In particular, she emphasizes the relevance of the inclusion of chapters from countries belonging to geographically widespread continents and with diverse socioeconomic and patriarchal scenarios.

Kurt De Wit and Tom Bekers (KU Leuven, Belgium) explore gender inequalities in higher education in Flanders (the Dutch-speaking Community of Belgium), thereby distinguishing between type of institutions, fields of study, and level of educational attainment. They turn their attention to the public policy on gender issues, the measures the government has taken to reduce gender inequalities in the student population, and the effects they have had. According to the authors, the question of gender-imbalanced student influx has seldom been addressed in Flanders. Most attention is given to raising awareness about and challenging traditional gender roles and stereotypes. Policy in Flanders with regard to gender imbalances in the student population in higher education to date seems to have difficulty in finding the right balance between a labor market perspective and a student-centered perspective, between short-term labor shortages and long-term societal changes, between initiatives focusing on awareness, culture, and initiatives aiming to bring structural changes. For the authors, what is needed is a more inclusive approach, encompassing all gender imbalances on both sides of the equations.

Georgios Stamelos and Georgia Eleni Lempesi (University of Patras, Greece) note that Greece never had an active policy for women's participation in higher education and the labor market. This political absence was changed after the abolition of dictatorship (1974) and more actively after the integration of European Union (1981). The authors point out the significant quantitative advances in the presence of girls in higher education that have been accomplished, but the disparities remain inside the higher education. This means that social, cultural, and economic stereotypes persist and are present. Particular attention was paid to the structure of the labor market because women's participation has increased over the time but simultaneously it is less than men's participation, less dynamic, and limited to selected sectors. The elements of analysis converge to affirm that women's participation in the economy appears to be more difficult to succeed in equal terms than the participation in education in general and more particular in higher education.

Christine Fontanini and Saeed Paivandi (University of Lorraine, France) show in their chapter on France that a lot of progress has been made in the feminization of higher education. However, girls have limited access to certain prestigious fields and institutions, which play an important role in the distribution of powers within society. The authors wonder about an important observation: how, despite the existence of social relations of sex, girls have been able to improve, for more than half a century, their presence in higher education and higher professions which they rarely attended or not earlier? The most recent studies have explored new themes which are interested at the same time in the contextual, personal and subjective characteristics. For example, the feminization of higher education can be analyzed by taking into account the specific dynamics of women and their individual and collective awareness of the challenges of education and knowledge in order to assert their place in society. In the learning trajectory, there is always a subject, therefore a form of consciousness which participates in giving sense to learning. Choosing a field of study, developing an intellectual or professional project, and learning constitute an experience lived by a learner who has a subjectivity. Learning sometimes involves going beyond of inherited representations and mobilizing to learn otherwise. The text of the chapter proposes to reflect on the reciprocal interactions between the feminization of society as a global process and the feminization of higher education.

Istvan Polonyi and Tamas Kozma (Institute of Educational Studies, University of Debrecen, Hungary) in their chapter on Hungary attempt to analyze the transition of a post-socialist country and the fact that the feminism of the state-socialist period was replaced by familism after the change of regime. The higher education policies of the past decade have led to a decline in the proportion of female students. The chapter reveals that support for female students in higher education is also fundamentally "familial," and very little is done to increase the proportion of women in higher education or to promote Roma girls' access to higher education. The authors severely criticize the government policy, characterized by the elimination of gender majors in public higher education, and the position of Hungarian women in terms of education, health, employment, and wages, besides extremely poor in terms of political and economic leadership.

Chiara Biasin (University of Padua, Italy) and Gina Chianese (University of Trieste, Italy) try to contextualize women's access to higher education in Italian society and in Europe and assert that their road has been long and not without ambiguity. The authors propose a holistic approach to understand the gender (in) equality question and the impact of different elements and variables in this process. They insist on the role of parents and teachers, curricula and guidance, stereotypes about male and female roles and functions. In other words, gender (in) equality is not simply a question to be solved in a restricted area (such as wages, education, etc.) but it requires the cooperation of institutions and stakeholders at the European and national, civil society, and community levels. Supporting the empowerment of girls and women does not mean taking power from men and giving it to women. Gender equality means empowering everyone, guaranteeing a win-win approach to improve society and the broader community.

Elisa Chaleta (University of Évora, Portugal), João Pissarra, and Jorge Correia Jesuíno (University of Lisbon, Portugal) stress that despite social advances, the rights conquered, the increased presence in higher education, and the higher qualification of women in Portugal still reflect a set of stereotypes that are manifested, more or less consciously, in job market. According to the authors, a lower number of young women drop out of school at early stages and a higher number complete higher education, being clear the major role that females have in the education field today. There are no constraints to women's access to higher education and are more qualified than men today. When we look inside the institutions, we observe that there has been a move toward greater numerical parity but there is still a discrepancy when we look at the place of women in management and at strategic levels.

Alejandra Montané Lópezm (University of Barcelona, Spain), José Beltrán Llavador, and Daniel Gabaldón-Estevan (Universty of Valencia, Spain) emphasize outstanding growth gender equality in Spain since the beginning of democracy, with developments in the civil, political, and social rights of women. The authors show how the instruments of equality policies have diversified, from plans to laws and gender units, generating advances in public policies against gender inequality. Two types of segregation are highlighted in the text of the chapter: a horizontal or quantitative segregation, which occurs to the extent that some areas of knowledge are very feminized while others are very masculinized; a vertical segregation that occurs in all fields, regardless of the degree of feminization of university students because there are very few women in the highest positions of science, even in the fields in which women have already made up the majority among graduates. According to the authors, the various obstacles that

Spanish public universities face even today in terms of equality, as well as the difficulties in incorporating specific programmes to benefit the development of women in their professional careers, slow down the achievement of substantive equality between men and women.

Rumana Ahmed (Monash University, Australia) and Nelia Hyndman-Rizk (University of New South Wales, Australia) assess the women empowerment through anomaly between higher education attainment of women and their labor force participation in Bangladesh. An empirical assessment is explored through a case study of a women's college in Northern Bangladesh. Authors attempt to examine the instrumental and intrinsic women empowerment in view of higher education attainment. In particular, five factors have been examined in detail viz, the quality of education, existing social norms, household dynamics, limited legal awareness, and job market aspirations. However, the lack of preparedness for the job market resulted in the prevalence of an "instrumental deficiency" in the higher education attainment of women in Bangladesh. The authors recommend that men should be facilitator and not act as barriers in higher education attainment of women and thereby their empowerment and agency development.

Saeed Paivandi (University of Lorraine, France) and Yasmin Nadir (CNRS, France) describe the feminization of higher education in Iran in the context of paradoxes and complexities. The authors appreciate that access to higher education for women has increased and is at par or greater than that of men in most of the disciplines except engineering and at various levels of education. However, a gendered quota in higher education linked with job market access for women exists in Iran. It is noted that the access and attainment of specific subjects in higher education are strongly linked with the prospects in the job market. While in the skilled job market women are giving greater competition to men, but the rate of unemployment is greater for women below the age of 30 as compared to men even though they possess higher education credentials. The chapter reflects upon various factors that have influenced the aspirations and motivation for women to pursue higher education including the tradition of *Mehrieh*. The chapter also reflects how Islamization of higher education has affected its various avenues like curriculum, daily processes, and making Hijab mandatory. To be specific, it has worked against the "democratization and gender justice" for women. The chapter concludes with a belief that women's access to higher education can enhance women's agency by influencing various sociocultural nuances of more inclusive and just societies.

Yukari Matsuzuka (Hitotsubashi University, Japan) highlights that amidst an increase in women enrollment in higher education in Japan, the enrollment of women in fields like sciences and engineering and at masters' and doctoral levels are in favor of men, biased against women. The author further describes the government incentives to motivate women participation both in the labor market and in higher education. The labor market in Japan is characterized by income disparities biased in favor of men and against women largely due to shorter tenures. "Interruptions" in the career path in the form of childbirth and child-rearing result in high turnover for women or for a compromise in the form of temporary or part-time job preference. Considering the rewards in the labor markets and discrepancies between male and female incomes thereby, the author argues that women can opt for a more rewarding career. Consecutively, the author identifies those career that allow women to return to their career after interruptions easily and with higher salaries. It has been envisaged that portable and occupation-specific skills provided by higher education would be more favorable for women to pursue a career after interruption. It would give greater mobility to women with lesser dependence on a particular firm or employer. Strategic choices at higher education level considering specific skills acquisition can convert the challenge in the form of interruption for women into an opportunity in the form of improved mobility and higher returns for aspiring women.

K. M. Joshi (Maharaja Krishnakumarsinhji Bhavnagar University, India) and Kinjal Ahir (Sardar Patel University, India) begin the chapter on India by providing a historical perspective of the status of women in Indian society. It gives a brief overview of the status of women during contemporary times with regard to health, political participation, legal provisions for the protection of women's rights, and educational status at school level. Although India has achieved complete parity in terms of access between men and women in higher education, a lesser number of women are enrolled in professional courses like engineering, polytechnic, and business administration. Marriage, social traditions, patriarchal norms, and the associated responsibilities remain the prime reasons for dropouts in higher education across various age groups. In contrast, motivation from parents and in-laws, a strong aspiration to pursue an economically rewarding career, desire for economically and intellectually independent life, and subsidized education were some of the reasons narrated by the respondents for pursuing higher education. India needs more apposite and effective policies to make the women participation in higher education socially inclusive and to achieve the equity in both participation and outcome of higher education.

Nobah Céline Sidonie Koco Epse Kacou-Wodjé (CAMES' Universities and Ecole Normale Supérieure in Abidjan) shows that despite better results of girls of the scientific baccalaureate in high school than boys, they continue less in STEMs in higher education especially in mathematic-technology and mathematic-computer science. According to the author, there is an effective students' self-censorship that is due to multiple factors: cultural, educational, psychological, and economic despite numerous efforts made by national institutions and especially the Association of Women Researchers of Côte d'Ivoire (AFEMCCI) to encourage young girls to choose scientific fields. Moreover, the author stresses that girls that choose both scientific studies and professional studies take risks in order to find a job and succeed in it unlike boys, who benefit from a high and respectful social position. Thus, it is obvious that these studies and positions are not opened yet for women in the Ivorian society.

Silvana Rodrigues de Souza Sato, Mariele Martins Torquato (Campeche College, Brazil), and Ione Ribeiro Valle (Federal University of Santa Catarina-UFSC) analyze access to higher education at the national level and in the case of the Federal University of Santa Catarina (UFSC) according to gender factor. They observe a greater access of women to higher education in the country, in contrast to UFSC, but it is the men who have achieved greater success. The authors attempt to also show that democratizing access to higher education is an important but not a defining part of social justice in education. Gender struggles in the fields of professions are very directly associated with class struggles, because for women, the highest admission courses are those with low social and economic value, such as the Pedagogy course. According to the authors, despite advances in the democratization of women's access to Brazilian higher education in recent years, there are many social barriers that the country has to fight against, mainly through public policies.

Lina Uribe-Correa and Aldo Hernández-Barrios (Konrad Lorenz University Foundation, Colombia) highlight that since the early 1990s, in Colombia, as well as Chili and Mexico, the number of women accessing higher education has been bigger than men. Nevertheless, the imbalance of women's presence exists within specific fields of study such as ICT programs, Engineering, Manufacturing, and Construction, and in general, in STEM fields despite efforts of Professional and Science Associations to promote gender balance in higher education. Concerning education level, the percentage of girls enrolling in bachelor's degree is higher than boys, but equivalent in master's degree and lower in PhD program. Furthermore, only half the individuals who enroll complete their programs and obtain educational degrees. As a consequence of this dynamic, only about 25% of the number of aspirants graduate from higher education in Colombia in time. The chapter highlights that men are most widely affected with the attrition phenomenon, as they have higher overall dropout rates, in general, by modality of teaching and education levels, with the exception of technical professional education. The abandonment of STEM programs is similar between men and women and is of a great magnitude. According to the author, Colombian women have occupied a larger number of places in the labor market but they still earn less than men in general, with all levels of education. This pattern is repeated within diverse fields of knowledge and specific disciplines, showing that there is an imbalance that has been hard to overcome.

Shirin Abdmolaei and Goli M. Rezai-Rashti (Western University, Canada) analyze the feminization of higher education in Canada with paradoxes. Since the early 1990s, women in Canada have accounted for a majority of full-time students' enrolled in undergraduate and graduate programs. But their entrance into traditional male disciplines, such as science, technology, engineering, and mathematics (STEM), is still greatly lagging behind men. Moreover, the female students who pursue a STEM degree do not always complete their degrees, which speaks of the social and structural barriers that often impede upon women's educational success and opportunities. The authors point out that when racial, ethnic, and socioeconomic differences are considered, not only differences with regards to which disciplines women pursue are observed, but also are noticed disparities in terms of access to, and success in, higher education as well as educational outcomes with respect to employment, income, and holding senior leadership positions.

Chapter 1

A Difficult Balance: Policies on Gender Imbalances in the Higher Education Student Population in Flanders

Kurt De Wit and Tom Bekers

1. Introduction

Gender gaps in higher education have over the years been documented extensively. With regard to the entrance of students to higher education, in general, women have reversed the gap in OECD countries and their share of first-time new entrants is now larger than that of men (OECD, 2019). This does however not mean that gender differences are no longer important in higher education. The share of women is unevenly distributed in different fields of study, with an underrepresentation in STEM and an overrepresentation in health and welfare, and tends to decline with the education level (highest share in short cycle programs below bachelor level, lowest share in programs at master level, and underrepresentation at the doctoral level; OECD, 2019). Conversely, when it comes to completion rates, it is the men who are doing worse, and this is true across all OECD countries (OECD, 2019).

The situation in Flanders, i.e., the Dutch-speaking community of Belgium, on the whole follows the same patterns. Women make up 55% of the total enrollments in higher education, with their share declining according to the education level, and with a clear underrepresentation in STEM fields of study (Ministerie van Onderwijs en Vorming, 2018a). When in higher education, women do better than men, attaining 58% of bachelor and master degrees (Ministerie van Onderwijs en Vorming, 2018b).

In this chapter, we explore gender inequalities in higher education in Flanders. We focus on the contemporary situation of students in higher education. We first describe the current situation in Flemish higher education, thereby distinguishing between type of institution, field of study, and level of educational attainment. Then we go into the public policy on gender issues and the measures the government has taken to reduce gender inequalities in the student population. Third, we turn our attention to the level of the higher education institutions and the gender policies they have put in place. We take stock of some of the initiatives

International Perspectives on Gender and Higher Education, 1–16

doi:10.1108/978-1-83909-886-420201001

taken and the effects they have (or have not) had. We give some specific examples from KU Leuven, in order to provide a detailed account of the issues that are at stake when tackling gender inequality with regard to students in higher education. To round up the chapter, a critical conclusion is drawn on the persistence of gender inequality in higher education and the different ways it keeps on challenging higher education policy in Flanders.

2. The Current Situation in Flanders

The higher education system in Flanders is in essence a binary system consisting of universities and universities of applied sciences. In recent years, a number of changes took place within this structure: some study programs were transferred from the universities of applied sciences to the universities, teacher training programs in adult education institutions were replaced by master programs at universities and universities of applied sciences, and study programs on ISCED level 5 were introduced in universities of applied sciences. These changes have however not changed the overall gender balance in higher education with women currently making up 55% of total enrollments and earning 58% of degrees (Ministerie van Onderwijs en Vorming, 2018a, 2018b) as stated in the introduction. In that sense, the democratization in HE might seem completed in terms of gender. But these overall figures hide many imbalances between types of institutions (universities vs universities of applied sciences), fields of study (STEM vs others), and levels of educational attainment (ISCED levels 5, 6, 7, and 8).

Female students are in the majority in both universities and universities of applied sciences in the academic year 2019–2020 (overall figures for ISCED levels 5, 6, and 7 combined). In universities, their share is 54%, in universities of applied sciences it amounts to 56% (AHOVOKS, 2020). In universities, the share of female students was larger than that of men for the first time in the academic year 1996–1997, whereas it was always larger at universities of applied sciences (Ministerie van Onderwijs en Vorming, 2019). This difference is related to the educational offering of both types of institutions, i.e., the different fields of study in which they offer study programs and also the different levels at which they offer these programs (ISCED levels 5 and 6 at universities of applied sciences, ISCED levels 6, 7, and 8 at universities).

Regarding fields of study, most attention has recently been directed at STEM, in Flanders as well as internationally. STEM stands for “science, technology, engineering, mathematics.” Note that the definition of what constitutes a STEM study program can differ between different sources. In the so-called STEM Monitor (Departement Onderwijs en Vorming, 2019), it is explained that differences between OECD figures and Flemish figures stem from the fact that in Flanders not only STEM “in the strict sense” is considered but also “study programs with a STEM component,” for example, biomedical sciences (classified internationally in “health”), traffic engineering (“transport”), or medical imaging (“health”). But all figures point in the same direction: in the STEM fields of study, girls are clearly underrepresented with regard to enrollments as well as the number of graduates – while labor market demand for graduates in these fields is high (Vlaamse Regering, 2012). In recent years, the share of females in STEM study programs has increased to around 24% in professional bachelor programs (at universities of applied sciences) and 39% in academic bachelor programs (at universities; Departement Onderwijs en Vorming, 2019). The share in professional bachelor programs has however not been a steady increase. Moreover, the study efficiency in these programs has declined (Departement Onderwijs en Vorming, 2019). The number of female graduates in all STEM bachelor and master programs is slowly increasing and now amounts to one-third of STEM graduates in Flanders (Departement Onderwijs en Vorming, 2019).

Above it was already hinted at that the issue of gender balance plays out differently at different ISCED levels. At ISCED level 5, 45% of enrollments are by female students (AHOVOKS, 2020). At ISCED level 6, Flanders differentiates between professional bachelor programs (with a vocational purpose) at universities of applied sciences and academic bachelor programs (as preparation for entering a master program) at universities. The student population in professional bachelor programs is 58% female, while this is 53% in academic bachelor programs. In master programs, the share of female students is 55% (AHOVOKS, 2020). When looking at the level of the doctorate, however, the ratio is turned the other way round, with 45% of doctorates awarded to women (in 2017–2018) and 55% to men (ECOOM, 2019).

This sudden change from a majority of women in master programs to a majority of men in doctoral programs is a first "leak" in what is known as the "leaky pipeline": the share of women decreases in each further phase of the academic career. In 2019, 39% of the postdoc positions in Flanders were held by women, as were 37% of the (tenure track) assistant professor positions, 31% of the associate professor positions, 26% of the professorships, and 17% of full professors (in FTE; VLIR, 2019). Although the share of women in all these positions is increasing steadily, the change is very slow. It should be borne in mind that for some faculties and disciplines, it is not self-evident to remedy the "leaky pipeline" with regard to academic positions because their influx of graduated master students is already imbalanced: on average more women than man graduate, but this average hides big differences according to study field.

In sum, despite overall figures showing that women have closed the gender gap in higher education with regard to enrollments and degrees, in several ways, gender gaps are still apparent in Flemish higher education. This is not to say that higher education is entirely to blame. It is a societal problem and gender differences in education manifest themselves already from secondary education onwards, although at that level the boys are the group that deserves attention because girls are more present in tracks preparing for higher education and also have a higher study success (Vlaamse Overheid, 2017). In any case, given the situation of persistent gender imbalances, it is useful to look at the policies that have been proposed and implemented in Flanders to tackle this problem.

3. Policies and Initiatives in Flanders

The participation of women in higher education grew exponentially in the 1960s and 1970s. In this first wave of democratization of higher education, social class, economic status, and gender became less important as reasons why people did not participate in higher education. Moreover, the education level acquired became one of the key determinants of labor market participation (Pelleriaux, 1998). Nevertheless, this evolution did not signify the end of inequality in higher education. The social and economic background of students remained a factor determining participation in higher education (Tan, 1998). And as we have seen above, gender imbalances have remained persistent as well.

It begs the question, therefore, what the Flemish government's stance has been on gender inequalities in higher education. Is there currently a public policy on gender issues and has the government taken the measures to reduce gender inequalities in the student population? In responding to these questions, it is important to keep in mind that the policy process in Flanders involves participation of the stakeholders in education, through their representative organizations. There is a Flemish interuniversity council (*Vlaamse Interuniversitaire Raad*, VLIR) and a Flemish council representing the universities of applied sciences (*Vlaamse Hogescholenraad*, VLHORA). More to the point in this case, the Flemish Education Council (*Vlaamse Onderwijsraad*, VLOR) played an important part in putting gender issues on the agenda. The Flemish Education Council is the body representing the educational providers, the staff, the students, the socioeconomic organizations, and the sociocultural organizations. In many cases, its advice is an obligatory step in drawing up new legislation, but it can also address policy issues on its own initiative.

In a broad sense, the gender issue is well acknowledged within education policy. For instance, breaking down tables according to gender is a standard practice in publications of the government and of other actors. The yearly publication of educational statistics by the government (Flemish Ministry of Education and Training, 2020; or for an overview in English see Flemish Ministry of Education and Training, 2019) is a case in point.

But on the other hand gender imbalances in the student population in higher education are seldom taken as an issue on itself. There are, for instance, few specific reports, or position papers, or policy texts – some reports on gender in a STEM context notwithstanding, see below. And when the issue is taken up separately, mostly the perspective taken is that of labor market needs. For example, in 2012, the then Minister for Equal Opportunities proposed to develop an action plan to address the career gap between women and men. Although this action plan was never actually realized (Vrouwenraad, 2019), some preparatory steps were taken (see Sels, 2012; SERV, 2012; VLOR, 2012). The preparatory documents started from the observation that there was a (too) large vertical and horizontal segregation on the labor market and pointed out the close relation between career gap and education gap: to really address the career gap, it would be necessary to tackle gender segregation in education too. In a similar vein, the shortage of graduates in STEM fields of study was addressed from a labor market perspective. The Flemish Government drafted an action plan with regard to STEM (Vlaamse Regering, 2012) that defined the "STEM problem" on the basis of two questions: Is there a sufficient number of employees with a STEM training on the labor market to meet the demand? And are the competences of STEM graduates sufficiently aligned with the demand from the labor market?

The labor market perspective is however not necessarily the right way to look at gender issues in the higher education student population. The Flemish Education Council posed the question to the minister "to what extent the labor market driven measures in national and international goal frameworks are in line with the key purposes of education" (VLOR, 2012, p. 6, our translation). The Flemish Education Council's starting point was the pedagogical mission of education, that is, personal development and critical-creative integration in society. And it referred to other complimentary goal frameworks rather than economic frameworks such as the Lisbon goals of the European Union: to guarantee equal opportunities, to prepare students for economic autonomy, to foster social cohesion, and to stimulate lifelong learning (VLOR, 2012). From this pedagogical perspective, the Flemish Education Council implied that the room for maneuver is rather limited. It contended that a more equal participation of men and women in different fields of study should never be a goal in itself, but could be an effect of study choice guidance. It further clarified that the curriculum and the pedagogical and didactical methods used by schools should lead to the defined minimal goals, including awareness of perceived gender roles and stereotypes, regardless of gender ratios in study programs (VLOR, 2012). In other words, it ruled out the number of enrolled women and men in study programs as a valid indicator of a good choice of study.

Moreover, the Flemish Education Council defined the link with the labor market as problematic in itself. It did not deny that preparation for the labor market should be a goal, among other goals, for education. But it contended, first, that there is a lack of information about the relation between a specific study program and one or more professions, and second, that it cannot be expected that a choice for a particular study program automatically implies a choice for a profession to which that study program prepares (VLOR, 2012).

A final point the Flemish Education Council made was that gender is not an issue that stands on its own, but intersects with other factors influencing the educational career as well, such as the education level of the parents, the socio-economic situation, the language spoken at home, and cultural capital (VLOR, 2012). These background characteristics and the interplay between them define to a certain extent the study choice process and study success or failure.

The Flemish Education Council concluded that not sex or gender or gender stereotypes should lead study choice or study choice guidance, but talent. There will always be different opinions about gender and its relation with certain professions, but being aware of gender stereotypes and their intersection with other background characteristics could prevent these stereotypes of being the basis for study choices.

In about the same time period, the issue of gender imbalances in academic staff and university boards and councils was once more brought to the attention of policymakers in Flanders. Since equal numbers of male and female professorships and equal representation of men and women in the decision-making boards and councils remained a distant dream – with a rate of progress toward gender balance in professorships somewhere around 2050 – the government proposed to install quota for some advisory and decision-making bodies by law. Having serious concerns about the feasibility and efficiency of such a radical measure, the Flemish Interuniversity Council countered this call for quota by launching a "gender action plan" (VLIR, 2013). This action plan focused on structural change in organizational culture and structure, therefore relying on the engagement of the universities themselves. This action plan did not, remarkably, refer to gender imbalances in higher education study programs and the effect this can have on the influx in faculties and disciplines. Its successor in 2019, the "gender in academia" charter of the Flemish Interuniversity Council and *Jonge Academie* (an organization of young academics within the Royal Flemish Academy of Belgium for Science and the Arts), does acknowledge the differences in gender imbalances between scientific disciplines, albeit in an implicit way, as something to keep in mind when monitoring the current situation and progress (VLIR-JA, 2019).

As mentioned above, in Flanders gender segregation in the student population in higher education is rarely named as a theme in itself. One of the reasons is because of the intersection with other themes, like national origin, and the focus on "diversity" and "inclusion" in general, which are more dominant themes in Flanders today (SERV, 2018). UNIA, for instance, an independent public institution which aims to combat discrimination and promote equal opportunities, advises in its diversity barometer (Unia, 2018) to work toward an inclusive culture by challenging segregation in education but does not mention gender as a segregating theme. Segregation is defined on the basis of socioeconomic status, national origin, health, or handicap of students. With regard to gender, the diversity barometer only mentions that gender stereotypes that lead to certain study choices should be addressed.

Another reason is the lack of explicit visibility, general awareness, and sense of urgency on this particular matter. An interesting exception is the "gender monitor" published by the Flemish Government in 2017 as part of its equal opportunities policy (Vlaamse Overheid, 2017). In that document, the societal position and participation of men and women is charted in areas such as health, income, labor market, and poverty. The monitor explicitly highlights gender inequalities and all the forms it takes in Flemish higher education, in a separate chapter on education. The chapter works its way to higher education by first describing gender differences in secondary education: in the choice for an area of study and a particular study, in reading and mathematical literacy, in problematic absences, and in unqualified dropout of secondary education. Most of the gender issues higher education faces can already be perceived in secondary education. In regard to higher education, first the gender segregation in the student population is discussed in detail on the level of the biggest study fields (in terms of student influx) of bachelor and master programs combined, thereby also distinguishing between universities and universities of applied sciences. Second, it is shown that women outperform men in all of these study fields. Next, the monitor establishes that the percentage of female teaching staff diminishes as the education level rises. The last parafigures of the chapter discuss the education level, reading literacy, mathematical literacy, and "aspirations" of the general Flemish population, establishing among others that Flemish women in general have attained a higher level of education and more often participate in posteducation training programs than Flemish men. The monitor even explicitly mentions targets, but does so only with regard to STEM study programs in secondary and higher education.

The explicit attention for STEM is not a unique feature for Flanders. At the European level, there seems to have been a momentum for the broader theme of gender inequality in higher education about ten years ago, when, for instance, a report issued by Eurydice (2010) concluded that gender inequality was a concern in many countries. But the same report came to the conclusion that overall policies were often missing, as a result of (1) the differences in comprehensiveness of legislative and policy frameworks, (2) the main focus on challenging traditional gender roles and stereotypes, and (3) the variety of policy instruments different countries developed, while lacking more general strategies.

In Flanders too, an overall policy seems to be missing. As stated above, a labor market perspective seems to be dominant. The European Union's so-called Lisbon strategy to make Europe the most competitive economy in the world also supported a focus on economic growth and jobs (European Commission, 2000). From this, a focus ensued on the overall number of STEM graduates, and on the gender imbalance among STEM graduates. In line with the Lisbon strategy, Flanders launched a STEM action plan in 2012 introducing long-, mid- and short-term goals for STEM programs in both secondary and higher education (Vlaamse Regering, 2012). For the latter, it means that by 2020, the number of female students in professional and academic STEM bachelor programs should be 25.2% and 33.5% respectively, and the market share of academic STEM bachelor programs should be 33.02%. In regard to these goals, a "STEM monitor" was developed and published yearly (for the latest edition, see Departement Onderwijs en Vorming, 2019).

Now that the end date of the action plan is near and the goals are very likely to be met (Departement Onderwijs en Vorming, 2019), plans are being developed for a second, more ambitious action plan for the period 2020–2030 (Vlaamse Regering – STEM-platform, 2019). The Flemish Education Council has already provided an advice on its own initiative (VLOR, 2019). The goal of the proposal is to broaden the scope with a view on increasing STEM knowledge overall, that is, to provide an essential STEM literacy to all students, scholars, and civilians in general. A multifaceted training offer is envisaged, to provide for "STEM for specialists" as well as "STEM for all" (Vlaamse Regering – STEM-platform, 2019, p. 9).

Note, however, that the proposal is not to broaden the scope to non-STEM study programs. Of course, the proposal was drafted by a STEM steering group and was focused on an action plan for STEM. But it seems a missed opportunity that the gender issue in non-STEM study programs was not taken into scope by, for instance, the Flemish Education Council, which could have led to a more inclusive approach addressing all gender issues in the student population in higher education.

To sum up, a general awareness of the gender issue in higher education is certainly present in Flanders. The government and the stakeholders regularly address gender aspects in policy proposals. However, with regard to gender imbalances in the student population in higher education, there is no encompassing policy and the initiatives taken clearly start from a labor market perspective. The latter has led to actions focused on STEM, with relative success on a general level.

4. Policies of Higher Education Institutions: The Case of KU Leuven

The relative absence of gender policy measures on the Flemish level with regard to students in higher education means that higher education institutions in Flanders are not particularly incentivized, but neither discouraged to take action themselves concerning this issue. It is therefore interesting to look at that level to see whether policies and measures with regard to gender imbalances in the student population have been taken and if yes, which effects these initiatives have yielded.

In order to provide a detailed account of the issues that are at stake, we focus on one university in Flanders, namely KU Leuven. This university is the biggest in Flanders with about 60,000 registered students. It is a comprehensive university offering academic bachelor and master programs in almost all fields of study, on nine campuses spread around Flanders. Figures provided below are our own calculations, unless otherwise stated.

In the academic year 2018–2019, KU Leuven on the whole had a balanced influx of students in bachelor programs, with 48% male students and 52% female students. Nevertheless, these figures vary considerably between study programs. The gender composition of the bachelor programs ranges on average from 3% to 97% female students (and vice versa). Moreover, these ratios are persistent. In the bachelor program in informatics at the campus in Kortrijk, for instance, only two women enrolled in the last ten years, while 63 men started in the program. An example in the other direction is the bachelor program in speech therapy and audiological sciences at the campus in Leuven, which enrolled 21 men compared to 779 women in that same period.

More in general the figures show that in the academic year 2018–2019 of the 72 Dutch-language bachelor programs offered at KU Leuven at the different campuses, no less than 19 have a student influx composed of more than two-thirds of men, and in 22 programs new enrollments comprise more than two-thirds of women. If two-thirds is taken as a maximum to speak of a "gender balance" (because you need at least a representation of one third of a minority group to be able to actually instigate a change in culture or structure, see, e.g., Dahlerup, 1988; Kanter, 1977), this means that only 31% or 43% bachelor programs have a gender balance. This has not always been the case at KU Leuven. In the academic year 1992–1993, for instance, the share of ISCED 6-level programs with a gender balance amounted to 63%. The share of unbalanced programs, and particularly the number of programs with an overrepresentation of women, gradually grew. Since the academic year 2012–2013, balanced programs are a minority.

The monitoring of such imbalances and more in general a social concern for students has a long tradition at KU Leuven. For almost 60 years now, KU Leuven has been monitoring student background characteristics that can have an impact on their study career. These data are being used to align education and services with the different needs of students. In the last decade, policies and structures have been put in place to address gender (and other) imbalances. Since 2010, KU Leuven has worked out a specific diversity policy and structure, aimed at networking and cooperation between faculties and departments on both general and specific diversity issues. A central policy advisory Diversity Council guides the universities decisions, in close coordination with staff members of university departments and the members of faculty diversity teams. These diversity teams consist of staff members in faculties who voluntarily take on a diversity role as a promotor, contact point, or person responsible for diversity. The diversity teams report on a yearly basis to the central Diversity Policy Office on their priorities, actions, and questions. Next to socioeconomic diversity, disability, inclusion, religious diversity, and sexual diversity, the theme of gender has often been a topic of discussion in this policy cycle, both with regard to staff and to student matters.

In 2011, an ad hoc working group was established to explore the question whether it was necessary for the university to take an active, steering role in addressing gender imbalances, which best practices existed, and what actions would be advisable for the university to take. In its final report (KU Leuven 2013), the ad hoc working group concluded that it was indeed up to KU Leuven to analyze gender imbalances, to indicate bottlenecks, and to initiate and coordinate actions within the university – while respecting the final individual choices of students. The ad hoc working group based this standpoint on the mission statement of KU Leuven (KU Leuven, 2012) on the one hand and the then general diversity policy of the university on the other. The mission statement refers to the societal responsibility of the university in that its ties with the labor market, the economy, and society urge the university to strive for a representation of societal ratios and dynamics in its student population. The then diversity policy (KU Leuven, 2014) stated that any minority in the study programs deserves policy attention. Based on this, the ad hoc working group's stance was that any student should find its "right" place in a study program that closely relates to her or his individual interests and capacities.

The ad hoc working group arrived at five important conclusions, based on its analysis of available figures, relevant literature, and existing initiatives both in Flanders and abroad. First, quantitative data too often are analyzed and shown on an aggregated level, but many imbalances show up only on a more specific level, for example, on the level of separate study programs on specific campuses. Second, attention was mostly drawn to the underrepresentation of women in STEM study programs. Third, gender imbalances seemed to increase rather than decrease in the last decades. Fourth, existing initiatives were often taken in a fragmented way, parallel to each other, and without a real impact study. Fifth, starting from a Social Cognitive Career Theory (Lent, Brown, & Hackett, 1994) and considering the study choice as part of a more general career decision process, the students' choice of study must be seen as a complex process in which many actors play a role, and the university can only strive to raise awareness of the gender issue with these actors.

From these conclusions, four operational goals were defined, and for each goal a timing, actions, and actors: (1) to analyze the situation in detail both quantitatively and qualitatively, in order to arrive at a thorough, detailed, and more truthful picture of the situation in faculties and study programs; (2) to cooperate and coordinate in order to avoid fragmentation and to create a global overview and increase effectiveness; (3) to communicate in a better and broader way to counter gender bias and to present a truthful picture of study programs and the professions they lead up to; and (4) to train students and teachers to make them aware of gender bias so that they can avoid it with regard to the creation of interest and the study choice process. The execution of these operational goals was included explicitly as a theme in the diversity policy plan for the period 2014–2017 (KU Leuven, 2014) and is also touched upon in the inclusivity-focused diversity policy plan for the period 2018–2022 (KU Leuven, 2018). At the central level of the university, a round table was organized in 2016 with all stakeholders, policy actors from KU Leuven, and Flemish experts, to keep the subject on the agenda.

In the period that followed after the final report of the ad hoc working group, many initiatives were taken, albeit not always in a coordinated way (notwithstanding the second operational goal). The first goal, analyzing the situation, was consistently followed up and integrated in the diversity monitoring cycle, comprising of yearly reports on diversity characteristics in the student population to faculty diversity team members, yearly updates of policy reports focusing on a specific diversity topic, and yearly updates of a public web page containing general numbers, figures, and themes on diversity (KU Leuven, 2020).

Regarding operational goals 3 and 4 (communication and training), examples of initiatives taken are the introduction of a diversity internship for 3 ECTS in the teacher training program, the organization of an interdisciplinary elective course on gender studies, the establishment of gender seminars, and the awarding of prizes for final papers or theses (Zonta prize, Marguerite Lefèvre prize). In addition, the five Flemish universities coorganize a master program on gender and diversity (www.mastergenderendiversiteit.be).

Next to these university-wide and interfaculty initiatives, on a decentral level, the faculty diversity teams were encouraged to take up the gender theme and to put the available quantitative information on the student population on the agenda of the Faculty Board. In 2018, in their yearly action plans, almost all faculty diversity teams at least at some point stated to have reflected upon the theme and most indicated to have taken some sort of action, for instance, concerning pictures in brochures and on web pages. Nevertheless, it is clear that in particular STEM faculties have taken initiatives to tackle gender issues, albeit mostly from a staff point of view. In a cooperative effort, three STEM faculties (engineering, bioengineering, and sciences) have, for instance, funded a policy researcher in 2018 to map gender issues in these faculties and to advise (new) policy measures.

This should not come as a surprise, since the ad hoc working group mentioned above already identified six reasons in its final report why more attention was being paid to the underrepresentation of women in STEM study programs than to men in non-STEM study programs (KU Leuven, 2013). These six reasons were

(1) Economic: In a number of scientific disciplines, the demand for graduates is much higher than the supply, which means that the demand for underrepresented groups is automatically higher, and therefore for women as well.
(2) Substantive: Companies sometimes look for specific profiles and/or skills, which increases the demand for a more diverse workforce and therefore also for women, all the more so if there is already a labor market shortage.
(3) Organizational: A number of study programs, mostly non-STEM, have a rather unclear and differentiated professional field, which means that there is little or no systematic contact between the course and (particular sectors of) the labor market. Although there may be a demand for certain profiles, there sometimes simply is no forum to raise this question.
(4) Historical: The shortage of women in certain STEM courses is due to the persistence of women having been historically always in a minority in these courses. Study programs with a traditional underrepresentation of men appear to have done a better job since they have evolved from an exclusively male to a predominantly female student population.
(5) Politics: Unlike women, men do not, or to a much lesser extent, dispose of movements and organizations that systematically collect information about and demand attention for gender imbalances and other gender-related problems.
(6) Financial: A number of initiatives in STEM programs are coorganized by the professional field and professional organizations. In non-STEM fields (e.g., public services), such organizations are rare and have limited financial scope.

In sum, a lot of the conclusions of the working group still seem to apply seven years after its publication. There has been an increasing awareness of and engagement toward gender disparities at KU Leuven, but most of the attention and actions kept focusing on STEM programs and the lack of female students they attract. As the working group argued, this is not surprising. Moreover, despite the efforts of the Diversity Policy Office, many actions still happened in a fragmented way, parallel to each other, and without a real impact study. To nevertheless get a view on the general impact of the initiatives on the student population, in Fig. 1.1, we visualize the evolution in gender ratio for first-time entrants in the university's bachelor programs.

The figure shows the percentage of female new entrants for all of the 72 bachelor programs at the campuses of KU Leuven as an average for two time periods: (1) for the five academic years prior to the release of the final report of the ad hoc working group on gender and students (KU Leuven, 2013), i.e., 2009–2010 to 2013–2014, and (2) for the five academic years after the release of that report, i.e., 2014–2015 to 2018–2019. The first period can be considered as a reference period and the second

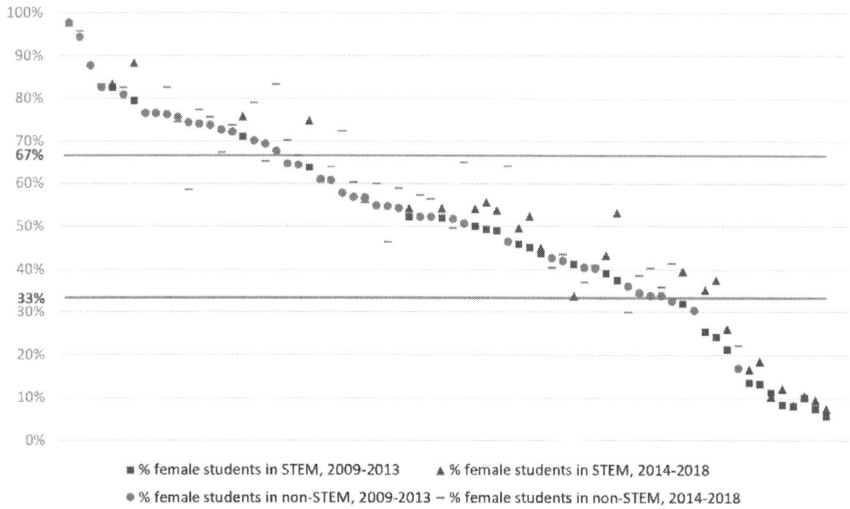

Fig. 1.1. Percentages of Female New Entrants in Academic STEM and Non-STEM Bachelor Programs at KU Leuven, between 2009–2010 and 2013–2014 and between 2014–2015 and 2018–2019.

allows us to see – in general – if the sum of all the actions that were taken made any difference. The figure makes a distinction between two types of study programs: STEM and non-STEM, with STEM defined "in the strict sense" (see above). The programs are sorted in descending order according to the percentage of women that started the program in the reference period, i.e., between 2009–2010 and 2012–2013. This means that study programs with an underrepresentation of men in the reference period, as, for example, psychology and speech therapy and audiological sciences, can be found on the left side of the figure. Study programs with an underrepresentation of women, as, for example, informatics, mathematics, and physics, can be found on the right side of the figure.

Although KU Leuven in general had a perfect gender balance in the influx of new entrants in bachelor programs, with a slight underrepresentation of women in the reference period (49.8%) and a slight overrepresentation in the second period (50.5%), the figure shows that separate study programs rarely mirror this general gender balance. The figure also shows that between these two periods there were a lot of (smaller and bigger) changes. Most study programs show an increase in female participation: the programs on the left side of the figure which already had an overrepresentation of women as well as the programs on the right side of the figure in which women were underrepresented. In almost all STEM study programs, the share of women has increased between the two periods. But given the general trend, it is unclear whether this is a direct result of initiatives concerning STEM. Overall the conclusion should probably be that little progress has been made in terms of gender imbalances in the student population, since the number of gender-balanced study programs has not increased.

This is not to say that the policies and initiatives have had no effect at all, on the contrary. The theme of gender did receive attention and that actions were taken. But when we look specifically at the gender composition of the student population broken down by bachelor program, which is the focus of this chapter, it is clear that the situation has hardly improved. It is illustrative that neither the "gender action plan" of KU Leuven (2014) nor the mid-term gender report (2016) mentions gender segregation in the student population.

5. Conclusions and Discussion

This chapter first examined the current situation regarding gender inequality in the student population in higher education in Flanders. Then it turned attention to the way this issue received policy attention at the level of Flanders. Next the case of KU Leuven was presented to identify policy perspectives from an institutional point of view.

It was established that in Flanders, as in many other OECD countries, the gender issue is well acknowledged within (higher) education policy. Many statistics are made available and breaking down tables according to gender is a standard practice in official publications (note that when a nonbinary gender conception would become more common, this standard practice would need to be reconsidered). In general, today, female students in Flanders make up a majority in both universities and in universities of applied sciences. Nevertheless, if we take a closer look, study programs rarely mirror the general gender balance: at KU Leuven, not even half of the academic bachelor programs can be considered gender balanced in terms of student influx.

This question of gender-imbalanced student influx has seldom been addressed in Flanders. Most attention is given to raising awareness about, and challenging traditional gender roles and stereotypes. The actual composition of the student population received much less attention. We know however from secondary education that class composition does matter (e.g., Van Houtte & Vantieghem, 2020). There seems no reason to assume that this would be different in higher education.

In the instances that the issue was raised in Flanders, it mostly happened from a labor market perspective, influenced by the European Union's Lisbon goals and leading to a focus on (gender imbalances in) the number of students and graduates in STEM, both at the Flemish level and at the institutional level This is of course a legitimate concern, but nevertheless leads to two question. First, should not all gender imbalances in all fields of study be addressed? Due to specific problems, or because of needs or preferences of clients, it seems necessary to have a more balanced presence, for instance, in mental healthcare, youth services, or the teaching profession. As we saw, the Flemish Education Council contends that gender roles and stereotypes should be tackled regardless of gender ratios (VLOR, 2012), but the question is whether this will be feasible if substantial structural measures are not taken as well?

Second, should not the perspective be broadened to a more pedagogical and/or student-centered perspective? The need to do so is acknowledged by the Flemish Education Council and at the level of KU Leuven. The main goal should be to have the right student in the right study program, regardless of gender imbalances. This presupposes taking a broad perspective, avoiding fragmentation, and coordinating efforts. A sense of urgency to go into that direction does however seem to be missing when it comes to looking at non-STEM as well as STEM initiatives, in other words to establish an overall policy or general strategies. This is somewhat surprising since the STEM initiatives, which are more frequent and better coordinated, might be successful in general terms but are perhaps less so when looked at in closer detail. The female influx in STEM study programs has increased, but so has the female influx in general. The effect of STEM initiatives is thus unclear, highlighting the need for proper impact studies. An interesting development in this regard is the current attention being paid to orientation tests in Flanders. In the context of open access to higher education, these nonbinding tests are being developed to provide prospective students with a more objective view on their skills and competencies. This might lead women and men to choose for "atypical" fields of study. However, a lot of issues remain to be tackled. For instance, so far these tests have been mainly focused on STEM study programs and relevant skills. Moreover, the effects on study choice are as yet not fully known. Some first indications show that disabled students and female students are more prone to let their study choice depend on their test results (Fonteyne, Schepers, Melis, & De Laet, 2018).

In conclusion, policy in Flanders with regard to gender imbalances in the student population in higher education to date seems to have difficulty in finding the right balance between a labor market perspective and a student-centered perspective, between short-term labor shortages and long-term societal changes, between STEM and non-STEM fields of study, and between initiatives focusing on awareness and culture and initiatives aiming to bring structural changes. What is needed is a more inclusive approach, encompassing all gender imbalances on both sides of the equations. If such an inclusive approach would not be feasible, for example, because of divergent (political) views, at least a more coordinated effort should be made, thereby taking into account every aspect of gender imbalances and, for instance, paying attention as well to the still ongoing feminization of many non-STEM study programs. It is important in this respect to pay sufficient attention to the figures on a detailed level: (balanced) averages can disguise (imbalanced) particularities.

References

AHOVOKS. (2020). Hoger onderwijs in cijfers. Academiejaar 2019–2020. [Higher education in figures. Academic year 2019–2020.] Agentschap voor Hoger Onderwijs, Volwassenenonderwijs, Kwalificaties en Studietoelagen, Brussel.

Dahlerup, D. (1988). From a small to a large minority: Women in Scandinavian politics. *Scandinavian Political Studies*, *11*(4), 275–298.

Departement Onderwijs en Vorming. (2019). STEM-monitor July 2019. Departement Onderwijs en Vorming, Brussel.

ECOOM. (2019). Vlaams indicatorenboek. [Flemish book of indicators.] Departement Economie, Wetenschap en Innovatie (EWI) & Expertisecentrum O&O Monitoring (ECOOM), Brussel.

European Commission. (2000). *Presidency conclusions Lisbon European council, 23 and 24 March 2000*. Brussels: European Commission.

Eurydice. (2010). *Gender differences in educational outcomes: Study on the measures taken and the current situation in Europe*. Brussels: Eurydice - Education, Audiovisual and Culture Executive Agency.

Flemish Ministry of Education and Training. (2019). *Flemish education in figures. School year 2018–2019*. Brussels: Department of Education and Training.

Flemish Ministry of Education and Training. (2020). Onderwijsstatistieken. [Statistics on education.] Retreived from onderwijs.vlaanderen.be/onderwijsstatistieken. Accessed on February 21, 2020.

Fonteyne, L., Schepers, W., Melis, L., & De Laet, T. (2018). *Rapport verplichte ijkingstoetsen burgerlijk ingenieur (architect)*. [Report on oblibatory calibration tests for civil engineer (architect).] VLIR, Brussel.

Kanter, R. M. (1977). *Men and women of the corporation*. New York, NY: Basic Books.

KU Leuven. (2012). Identiteit en opdracht van de KU Leuven. [Identity and mission of KU Leuven.] Retrieved from https://www.kuleuven.be/over-kuleuven/opdrachtverklaring. Accessed on February 21, 2020.

KU Leuven. (2013). Nota Werkgroep Gender en Studenten. [Report working group gender and students.] KU Leuven, Leuven.

KU Leuven. (2014). Visie en beleidskader diversiteit. [Vision and policy framework on diversity.] KU Leuven, Leuven.

KU Leuven. (2016). How does one find her? KU Leuven gender action plan. Interim report. KU Leuven, Leuven.

KU Leuven. (2018). Beleids- en actieplan diversiteit 2018. Op weg naar een meer inclusieve universiteit. [Policy and action plan diversity 2018. On the road to a more inclusive university.] KU Leuven, Leuven.

KU Leuven. (2020). Diversity policy figures and actions. Retrieved from www.kuleuven.be/diversiteit/diversity/figures_and_actions. Accessed on February 21, 2020.

Lent, R. W., Brown, S. D., & Hackett, G. (1994). Toward a unifying social cognitive theory of career and academic interest, choice, and performance. *Journal of Vocational Behavior*, *45*, 79–122.

Ministerie van Onderwijs en Vorming. (2018a). *Hoger Onderwijs in cijfers. Academiejaar 2018–2019. [Higher education in figures. Academic year 2018–2019.]* Brussel: Ministerie van Onderwijs en Vorming.

Ministerie van Onderwijs en Vorming. (2018b). *Statistisch jaarboek van het Vlaams onderwijs 2017–2018*. [*Statistical year book of Flemish education 2017–2018*.] Brussel: Ministerie van Onderwijs en Vorming.

Ministerie van Onderwijs en Vorming. (2019). *Statistisch jaarboek van het Vlaams onderwijs schooljaar 2017–2018. [Statistical year book of Flemish education. School year 2017–2018.]* Brussel: Ministerie van Onderwijs en Vorming.

OECD. (2019). *Education at a glance 2019: OECD indicators*. Paris: OECD.

Pelleriaux, K. (1998). De keerzijde van de onderwijsdemocratisering. [*The downside of the democratisation of education.*] Vrije Universiteit Brussel, Vakgroep Sociologie, Brussel.

Sels, L. (2012). *De genderloopbaankloof.* [*The gender career gap.*] Leuven: Steunpunt Werk & Sociale Economie.

SERV. (2012). *Advies De genderloopbaankloof. Voorbereiding Vlaams actieplan ter bestrijding van de loopbaankloof mannen-vrouwen.* [*Advice the gender career gap. Preparation for a Flemish action plan to combat the career gap men - women.*] Brussel: Sociaal-Economische Raad van Vlaanderen.

SERV. (2018). *Advies Laaggeschoolde vrouwen met een migratie-achtergrond.* [*Advice low-educated women with a migrant background.*] Brussel: Sociaal-Economische Raad van Vlaanderen.

Tan, B. (1998). Blijvende sociale ongelijkheid in het Vlaamse onderwijs. [Continuing social inequality in Flemish education.] *Tijdschrift voor Sociologie*, *19*(2), 169–197.

Unia. (2018). *Diversiteitsbarometer onderwijs.* [*Diversity barometer education.*] Brussel: Unia, Interfederaal Gelijkekansencentrum.

Van Houtte, M., & Vantieghem, W. (2020). Do girls make boys study? Gender composition, gender role culture, and sense of futility in Flemish secondary schools, *Youth & Society*, *5*(2), 229–250.

Vlaamse Overheid. (2017). *Vlaamse Gendermonitor 2016.* [*Flemish gender monitor 2016.*] Brussel: Studiedienst Vlaamse Regering/Agentschap Binnenlands Bestuur, Afdeling Gelijke Kansen, Integratie en Inburgering.

Vlaamse Regering. (2012). *Actieplan voor het stimuleren van loopbanen in wiskunde, exacte wetenschap en techniek 2012–2020.* [*Action plan for stimulating careers in maths, sciences, and technology 2012–2020.*] Brussel: Vlaamse Regering.

Vlaamse Regering, STEM-platform. (2019). *Aanbevelingen van het STEM-platform voor een STEM-actieplan 2020–2030.* [*Recommendations of the STEM platform for a STEM action plan 2020–2030.*] Brussel: Vlaamse Regering.

VLIR. (2013). *Actieplan gender. Vrouwen in de academische loopbaan en het universitair beleid.* [*Action plan gender. Women in academic careers and university policy.*] Brussel: Vlaamse Interuniversitaire Raad.

VLIR. (2019). *Statistische gegevens betreffende het personeel aan de Vlaamse universiteiten (telling 1 february 2019).* [*Statistical data regarding staff at Flemish universities (counted on 1 February 2019).*] Brussel: Vlaamse Interuniversitaire Raad.

VLIR-JA. (2019). *VLIR-JA charter gender in academia 2019.* [*Charter of VLIR-JA gender in academia 2019.*] Brussel: Vlaamse Interuniversitaire Raad / Jonge Academie.

VLOR. (2012). *Advies over de nota 'De genderloopbaankloof'.* [*Advice on the report the gender career gap.*] Brussel: Vlaamse Onderwijsraad.

VLOR. (2019). *Krijtlijnen voor een STEM-actieplan 2020–2030.* [*The contours for a STEM action plan 2020–2030.*] Brussel: Vlaamse Onderwijsraad.

Vrouwenraad. (2019). *Gelijke Kansen V/M in Vlaanderen. Memorandum. Aanbevelingen voor de Vlaamse Regering.* [*Equal opportunities F/M in Flanders. Memorandum. Recommendations for the Flemish government.*] Brussel: Vrouwenraad.

Chapter 2

Gender in Higher Education: Portuguese Landscape*

Elisa Chaleta, João Pissarra and Jorge Correia Jesuíno

1. Introduction

From the eighteenth century onwards, the movement to claim women's rights was internationally triggered by the ideals of freedom, equality, and fraternity of the French Revolution. The movement, driven in the nineteenth century by the emerging European liberal society, growing in the twentieth century, had no significant impact on Portuguese society due to the autocratic regime (*Estado Novo*) that prevailed in Portugal between the 30s and the 70s.

During the twentieth century, the dictatorship of the *Estado Novo* in Portugal established different educational models for men and women to be implemented from the age of 7, leading in 1936 to the creation (for boys) of the *Mocidade Portuguesa* (Decree-Law no. 26611, of May 19, 1936) whose purpose was to encourage the development of physical capacity, character, and devotion to the Fatherland, in the taste for discipline and order, in the cult of the moral, civic, and military duties and intended to cover all youth, in school or not (Vieira, 2008). All the youths between the ages of 7 and 14 should belong to it, although it intended to cover young people up to 25 years old organized in four age groups (Lusitos, from 7 to 10 years old; Infants, from 10 to 14 years old; Vanguardists, from 14 to 17 years old; and Cadets, from 17 to 25 years old). In the following year, Decree-Law No. 28262, of December 8, 1937, concerning the regulation of the *Mocidade Portuguesa Feminina* was published, with very different objectives, given that for girls it was intended to cultivate the taste for domestic life, social security, collective work, and the various forms of social spirit inherent to the female gender. The idea was that the woman fulfilled her mission in the family, in the environment to which she belonged and in the life of the State (Pimentel, 2007).

*This chapter is supported by the Project "Learning and Teaching at the University" (PTDC/CED-EDG/29252/2017) financed by FCT—Ministry of Science, Technology and Higher Education, Portugal Government.

International Perspectives on Gender and Higher Education, 17–32

doi:10.1108/978-1-83909-886-420201002

In Portugal, since the 1930s and for nearly 4 decades, the *Estado Novo* invested in a youth policy by adopting methods of political socialization to perpetuate its structures and culture, aiming to politically and socially shape the behavior of youth in order to control, as much as possible, their involvement in political and social life and inducing a behavior of political passivity (Formosinho, 1987). The mission of socializing the youth, which was traditionally a family prerogative, would pass to the control of the State. The totalitarian tendency of framing all the Portuguese youth (including those that did not attend school) was hampered by the church that offered resistance to the dissolution of the scout organizations, by the employers who did not show willingness to collaborate in the integration of the non-school youth in such mandatory youth program, and by difficulties in the attempt to militarize the *Mocidade Portuguesa*, which generated tensions due to competences' overlap with the Ministry of War (Kuin, 1993). However, the educational system was more vulnerable to the political control of *Estado Novo*, undergoing profound reforms in the sense of transforming itself into a centralized system characterized by strong state instrumentalization that inverted the republican education policy (which saw the school as an institution that generated social mobility), converting it into an instrument for preserving the social structure of Portuguese society.

In the early 60s, Portugal's economic development was marked by a major backwardness in terms of industrial development, with little need for female labor (70% of women between 20 and 54 years old were housewives), which reinforced the conception of Estado Novo about the role of women in society (for example, they could not work or travel without male consent and some professions were forbidden to them, such as the judicial magistracy, the public ministry, diplomacy, and security forces). The regime's authoritarianism, the colonial war, and the consequent financial crisis provoked a significant emigration outbreak (particularly among men) and led to the progressive need to increase the female labor force (although with lower salaries than men). During this period, a visible movement of female resistance emerges (Canço, 2004).

The fall of the Estado Novo allowed, according to international reflections already carried out in this field, a new approach to the notion of "feminine" as primarily social and only secondarily natural (Beauvoir, 1952; Greer, 1970; Mead, 1949). In Western society, in general, the female socialization process was a result of the internalization by women of a set of passive and submissive values that would later lead them to conform to the occupation of a subordinate position in society and, in the perspective of some authors, this female subjugation essentially derived from the capitalist order. Women were relegated to the private domain and the change required their entry into the public sphere (Mitchel, 1971).

The democratization resulting from regime change has radically changed the role and participation of women in society in terms of social, political, and economic rights (Tavares, 2000). During this period, there is a great articulation between women in various areas, the creation of women's associations in various fields, and the enshrining of equal rights between men and women in the Portuguese Constitution of 1976, which finally translates into the recognition of a new status and new roles in society, at work and in the family. From the Civil Code of 1966, which stated that

> The husband is the head of the family, and it is up to him in this capacity to represent her (his wife) and decide in all the acts of common conjugal life (…).

the Constitution of 1976 in which it is enshrined that "*All citizens have the same social dignity and are equal before the law.*"

The reference to the historical process of transition to a democratic society and the struggle for rights in Portugal are essential to understand the current situation in terms of equal opportunities between men and women, whether in terms of education, work, or social participation. The change that took place in the mid-1970s has a history behind it, reflecting a reality in which the illiteracy of women was much higher than men and in which, in the various degrees of education, the percentage of men enrolled was considerably higher.

Inequality and asymmetry were thus built based on a hierarchy that valued the productive dimension over the reproductive one, relegating the role of women in the sphere of production, reproduction, and sexuality to a second-rank status. The symbolic devaluation of care and of the feminine, instilled early, would necessarily influence the development of socialization processes, construction of identity, organization of daily life, and view of the world (Torres, 2001). This trend, as we will see later, only began to change in the mid-1980s. So, the history of gender equality is relatively recent in a context where much remains to be done. It should be noted that in 2015 Portugal was still the third most unequal country in the European Union (European Commission, 2017) despite European gender policies and its strategic objectives of equality between men and women in terms of equal opportunities and combating gender-based discrimination (CIG, 2017).

Nowadays and in general, we can consider inequalities as

> …differences in access and distribution of not only valued resources such as, for example, the economic ones, but also of other types of goods and resources such as education, culture, power, recognition, and prestige. (Almeida, 2013, p. 25)

Regarding gender equality, it is expected to be translated into symmetry between men and women, but this symmetry enshrined in Portuguese and European legislation, as can be seen in the data we present that it is still far from being achieved. Gender inequality has material and symbolic disadvantages that women experience in relation to men (Connell, 1987) and may also, in certain circumstances, according to Torres et al. (2018), create disadvantages for men when they are remitted to professions that tend to be more dangerous, when they are incited to adopt violent behaviors or that involve greater risk for health or are kept out from the affective sphere of care.

Gender equality is now considered as a human rights issue and enshrined in the legislative framework of countries, but traditional ways of functioning, even if covered by the discourse of equality, often tend toward inertia and resistance, making change difficult.

Along with greater visibility and the growing affirmation of female protagonism in different fields, there is a process that has been considered as "agency" or individualization in women (Torres, 2001), but which faces less visible barriers that show the limits of this progression and that, indisputably, is present in Western societies. As we will see later, still exist more or less subtle or conscious mechanisms that continue to feed inequalities such as the preference that is given to men in situations of professional recruitment (Moss-Racusin, Dovidiob, Brescollc, Grahama, & Handelsmana, 2012). In any case, contemporary societies have undergone profound changes in social, legal, and political terms, accentuating and making more visible the egalitarian tendencies that feminist movements initiated.

2. The Female Presence in Higher Education in Portugal

We can consider that the democratization of education, with a history of just over 4 decades, marked significantly the path and living conditions of men and women in Portugal. The path followed was designed by policies which reflected different State models and different conceptions of economic development and social well-being, although, during a decade, it has been affected by the economic and financial crisis that hit Portugal.

Despite the economic turmoil, in the last 2 decades, there was a sharp decrease in young people with low education levels in Portugal (basic education) and a significant increase regarding those who completed secondary or higher education, the results being even more evident in the case of young women. In this context, we observed better results at the level of secondary education, which subsequently translated into a significant increase in female presence in higher education, bringing Portugal closer to the European Union average. It also contributed to the increase of the female presence in more advanced levels of education, a lower early dropout of school that remains still masculine (PORDATA, 2019a, 2019b, 2019c, 2019d).

The masculinization of school dropout has been explained in a perspective that crosses gender, social class, and other factors of social vulnerability. Regarding social class, early school dropout affects particularly the poorly educated social classes (Kimmel, 2010). The lack of identification of these young people with the school organization at a stage of life (adolescence) in which they tend to adopt challenging and risky behaviors as a way of affirming their masculinity (with a very traditional ideological mark that affirms masculinity as "never showing weakness, never crying, never being vulnerable, and, above all, not being gay," according to Kimmel (2010, p. 29) often collides with the expectations of the education system in relation to what a good student should be. In the perspective of these young people, leaving school is often seen as masculinity reinforcement. Girls tend to meet these expectations more easily, as they adopt a more stereotyped female behavior, associated with greater obedience and conformity, accepted and encouraged behaviors in the school environment (Borgna & Struffolino, 2017; Byrne & Smyth, 2010).

It should be noted, however, that school dropout has decreased considerably since 2000, when there was a rate of 50.7% for boys and 36.4% for girls to values of 14.7% and 8.7%, respectively (PORDATA, 2019a, 2019b, 2019c, 2019d). Despite the significant drop, we can consider that, in this case, the gender disadvantage is more penalizing for young men due to the future implications that it may have at the level of labor market integration. The 2010 PISA (Program for International Student Assessment) report underlined at the time that social origin, despite being an important factor in explaining global inequalities in academic success, had more weight in some countries than in others (OECD, 2010).

The Portuguese educational system was characterized by a still traditional social structure, when compared with other European countries, and by an emerging small middle class where low rates of higher education attendance and low results in international tests, which according to (Abrantes & Abrantes, 2014), were a result of the low and still recent public investment in education, low private investment, a model of selective but undifferentiated secondary education, high levels of failure, and a centralized structure at the national level. The Portuguese educational system, although today a relatively open system, reflected, at that time, the weight of social origin, determining inequality in the access to higher education. OECD (2012) data for Portugal related the probability of pursuing higher education studies with being born in an academically more qualified family (young people from households with higher education were three times more likely to enter higher education), although in the following decade (from 2000 to 2010) there was a considerable increase in the student population, in which about half came from households with qualifications under the ninth grade (Costa, Lopes, & Caetano, 2014).

When analyzing the probability of entering higher education in Portugal, from a gender perspective, young women always have a higher probability than in the young men, regardless of the household's educational level. These differences between boys and girls in educational pathways can also be explained by a multiplicity of variables such as boys' higher school failure, dedication to study, and leisure/sports practices, and there also seems to exist better practices associated with girls' good school performance (Chaleta, 2011, 2013; Sobrinho, Ennafaa, & Chaleta, 2016).

Gender inequality in education thus takes many forms and is a consequence of wider forms of inequalities present in society. The democratization of Portuguese society and the universality of education for all have allowed the number of women to increase considerably over the years, while systematically remaining at the highest number since 1986. We can consider 1985 as the turning year, when Portugal signs the Portugal's accession treaty to the so-called Economic and European Community (EEC) and the country starts to experience a new phase in its history. In that year, of the 102,145 young people who took their first steps in higher education, almost half (51,043) of those students enrolled in colleges and polytechnics were girls (a difference of 59 places still with an advantage for boys). It happened 35 years ago, and it was the last time that male advantage existed. In addition to becoming the majority, they stand out for the good results achieved and, according to Guinote (2014), they are generally more educationally successful because they are better to adapt to a mass organization based on discipline and conformism.

The arrival of women to the college benches in the mid-1980s is a consequence of previous political decisions, initiated in the 1950s, from the greater participation of women in the basic education system, although only 2 decades later, with the democratization of public school, the first steps were taken at the level of secondary education. In the 1980s, political decisions lead students to higher education as a result of the privatization process when the State was no longer able to respond to the growing demand for degrees, and also due to the emergence of polytechnic institutes in more inland areas of the country that allowed girls to study close to their cities especially in families that maintained strong parental control over girls (Alves, 2004). One of the reasons that determined the predominance of women in higher education institutions was the fact that men had given up higher education because they had previously prepared less and because they continued to maintain a privileged position in companies (the labor market had a clear preference by men). To obtain equal wages, women needed higher levels of qualification (Guinote, 2014).

The private higher education network, for various reasons, has lost expression and currently 82% of students attend public education. The number of female students is currently higher both in the public (56%) and in the private (58%) sector. Regarding the type of education (university/polytechnic), we note that polytechnic education is less chosen by students in general (36%) and there is also a greater predominance of females (58%) in this type of education (DGEEC/MCTES, 2019; PORDATA, 2019a, 2019b, 2019c, 2019d). If we consider the students' attendance in the various study cycles, as we can analyze in Fig. 2.1, only Professional Technical Courses are predominantly male, being the percentage of male students completing these courses naturally higher (58%).

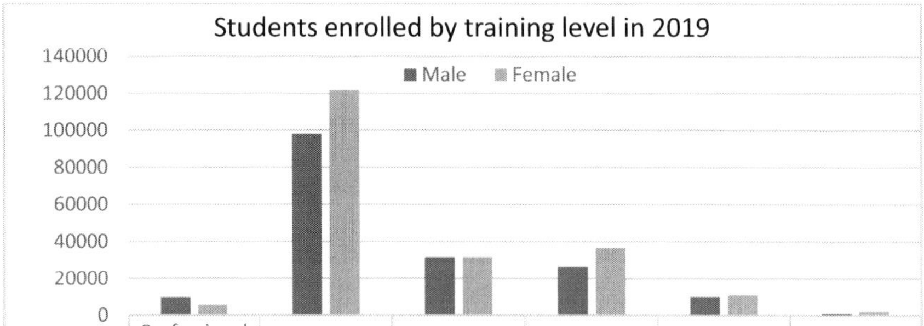

	Professional Technical Course	Graduation - 1st cycle	Integrated Master	Master	Doctorate	Specialization
Male	9629	97924	31502	26389	10100	1118
Female	5796	121691	31552	36587	10990	2171

Fig. 2.1. Students Enrolled by Training Level in 2019. *Source:* DGEEC/MCTES (2019) and PORDATA (2019a, 2019b, 2019c, 2019d).

Considering the conclusion of the courses at the various levels, according to data from 2018, we found that at the level of degrees (59%), Integrated Masters (53%), Masters (62%), PhDs (53%), and Specializations (69%) are more the women who complete them (DGEEC/MCTES, 2018).

Despite the increasing feminization of higher education, certain stereotypes have marked some areas of study as being male or female. In 2019, the male population was considerably higher (the majority) in the areas of Engineering, Manufacturing, and Construction, with a greater balance in Sciences, Mathematics, and Informatics despite some male predominance. Also, in the Services area, we find values close to male predominance. In areas such as Education, Social Sciences, Commerce and Law, and Health and Social Care, the female population almost doubles compared to the male, being also predominant in Arts and Humanities and in Agriculture as we can see in Fig. 2.2.

The latest data published by the Ministry of Science, Technology and Higher Education (DGEEC/MCTES, 2018) show that there is a relationship between the high attendance of courses and their completion, existing more graduates in Education (80%), Health and Social Care (79%), Social Sciences, Commerce and Law (64%), Agriculture (62%), and Arts and Humanities (61%). In Sciences, Mathematics, and Informatics, the completion rate is identical (50%), being only lower in Engineering, Manufacturing, and Construction (32%) and Services (45%). As we will see later, these results will have an influence on the insertion in the labor market. Although the presence of women in higher education has become progressively more striking, some difficulties remained in achieving the expected equality.

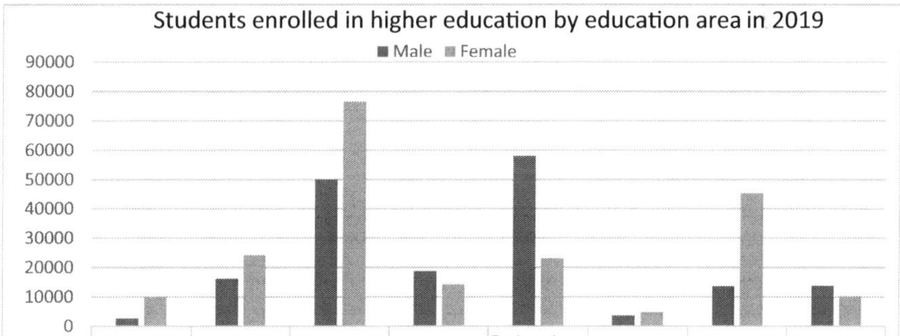

	Education	Arts and Humanities	Social Sc., Commerce and Law	Sciences, Mathematics and Inf.	Engineering, Industry and Construction	Agriculture	Health and Social Care	Services
Male	2734	16149	49964	18692	58058	3635	13589	13747
Female	9951	24197	76573	14174	23079	4787	45397	10254

Fig. 2.2. Student's Enrolled in Higher Education by Area of Education in 2019. *Source:* DGEEC/MCTES (2019) and PORDATA (2019a, 2019b, 2019c, 2019d).

In Portugal, the data show an expressive presence of women in the areas of natural sciences, technology, and engineering, which are traditionally considered as male strongholds (Hadjar, Krolak-Schwerdt, Priem, & Glock, 2014). Studies show that in 2012 Portugal was the European country with the highest proportion of women graduates in the areas of Sciences, Mathematics, and Informatics (57.9%) with values well above the average that was, at the time, of 41.8%. In the areas of Engineering, Manufacturing, and Construction, Portugal ranked second with 38% when the European average stood at 28.3%. However, that did not mean a decrease in the presence of women in traditionally more feminized areas: education, health, and well-being. Portugal also registered a higher average than the European in the areas of Education (76.8% compared to 64.1%), Health and Social Care (70.1% compared to 58.8%), and Social Sciences, Commerce, and Law (55.5% compared to 50.9%).

In relation to men, they tend to maintain their educational choices. This fact can be explained by the symbolic hierarchy, according to which the existing models in society of what it is to be male or female do not have the same weight or social value as men and the male domains are already socially recognized and valued (Amâncio, 1994).

Women and the feminine domains that are often invisible and socially diminished tend to participate in the traditionally recognized and prestigious male areas, a trend that is not followed by men in relation to integration in educational and professional areas traditionally associated with women, emotions, and care because that would imply subordination of men in the field of masculinity (Kimmel, 2000).

A more detailed analysis of the training areas called STEM shows that in Portugal Mathematics and Statistics are predominantly female (60.9%) (while in the European average only about 35% are women); in the Manufacturing area, despite the predominance of men in the European Union (64.7%), there is a balance between men (49.3%) and women (50.7%). The areas of "Computing" (69.6%), "Mechanical and Industrial Engineering" (64.1%), "Architecture and Construction" (61.9%), and "Physical Sciences" (52.0%) remain essentially masculine in Portugal (as in the European Union), although in all of them, Portugal presents higher values for women in these areas than the European average. This trend toward feminization of traditionally male areas began in the 1990s, progressively increasing over time, given that the job market offered to this small group of student's compatible employment opportunities in the civil service (particularly as teachers) and companies.

Another analysis can be made considering the participation of women within higher education institutions. In 2001, the data indicated that teaching in higher education was mostly assured by men (60%). Until 2018, although the difference was gradually reduced, women remained in the minority (45%). This lower presence of women is found in public institutions, in private institutions, and in the two subsystems of education, university and polytechnic (PORDATA, 2019a, 2019b, 2019c, 2019d).

If we consider leadership positions in universities and polytechnics, it is possible to verify that only 29.8% are occupied by women, a result that places the country in seventh at the European level, but only in 13% of institutions (15 universities and 15 Higher Polytechnic Institutes), women occupy the highest leadership position. In the presidencies of colleges or schools, women have a slightly higher expression (36.9%) but, still, considerably lower than the position held by their male counterparts (European Commission, 2019).

The rise of women in the academic career has encountered obstacles with the "glass ceiling syndrome" prevailing, which is characterized by the fact that women have, in demanding professions, difficulties in reaching the last levels of their careers. For women who are in the teaching career, progression in the first stages is made through criteria that privilege merit, which is why they have almost an equal presence. However, when it comes to the top position, only one in four Full Professors and one in three Associate Professors is a female. When access to positions is determined by election (collegiate bodies), in a context where there is still a very marked patriarchal concept of leadership, male individuals are usually favored (often by the vote of women), a situation that is similar to that found in public administration positions or in companies (SAGE, 2018; Santos & Amâncio, 2016).

Female underrepresentation in the top academic career category, at the head of higher education institutions and in the research profession, exists all over Europe. Influenced by a European project on gender inequalities, ISCTE developed a "Charter of Principles for Equality in Higher Education," which covers aspects related to equality policies in access to decision-making positions, progression opportunities, and wage values, as well as the lack of knowledge of gender inequalities that higher education tends to reproduce (SAGE, 2018).

Another concern began to emerge considering the importance of scientific research in the university context. According to UNESCO (2015), only 28% of worldwide researchers are women. Although an almost identical number of men and women conclude degrees and master's degrees, it is in the doctoral stage that the scientific research system loses a significant number of women, which is later reflected in the highest organizational levels, resulting in the somewhat controversial phenomenon described as a "leaky pipeline."

In general, at the international level, women's representation is higher in health and life sciences and lower in engineering and computer science. In addition to the gender imbalance in the number of researchers, studies (Larivière, Ni, Gingras, Cronin, & Sugimoto, 2013) show a great disparity in terms of academic publication, revealing that men produce a higher number of articles (70%) and have more first authorships (66%) than women, even in the most productive countries. Regarding the national scientific system, according to the Diagnostic report of the National Research and Innovation System (FCT, 2013), in Portugal, 46% of researchers are women, and in terms of the gender distribution of research staff, the female presence (0.88%) is above the community average (0.76%). According to data from PORDATA, in 2017, women corresponded to 43.1% of researchers in I&D, registering a small decrease compared to 2013. If we compare the situation in the various countries, it is possible to understand that is common the concern of the lower participation of women in the so-called STEM areas being more significant its representation in the field of Social and Human Sciences and Natural Sciences.

3. Female Insertion in the Labor Market

Portugal was governed for almost 50 years by a conservative, reactionary, and antiliberal ideology, in which the social division of labor was well defined. The family was the basic unit of society, with the wife and husband having separate and independent spheres of activity, that is, the woman should stay between the walls of the house and take care of the children (good domestic, good wife, and good mother) while the husband should leave and earn the family's livelihood. It was a model like the woman of the three KKK: Kinder, Kuche, Kirche (children, kitchen, church) of Nazi and fascist inspiration (Lucena, 1976). This conception of the women role in society was strongly supported by the Catholic Church, with the 1940 Concordat being an important example of the alliance between the State and the Church, in which it was agreed that Catholic marriages could not be dissolved by civil courts or required civil ceremony.

According to Santos, Lima, and Ferreira (1975), between 1959 and 1966, the average percentage of Catholic marriages carried out was 89.2%, regardless of the degree of religiosity and the regular attendance of the Church, which became for the Portuguese population surreptitiously mandatory the principle of the indissolubility of marriage professed by Catholics. The protection that Church received from the State was also manifested in the proliferation of traditional Catholic symbols throughout the country, including schools. The Sanctuary of Fátima and the relevance it acquired during the Estado Novo attested well the relevance of the symbolism of Virgin Mary, which provided women with a feminine ideal of motherhood in the context of an ideal that refused sexual intercourse (the Virgin Mary was a mother without ceasing to be a virgin).

The housewife position was a privileged position for Portuguese women, so it was not surprising that at the time of the 25th of April they were in an inferior position regarding the workforce. Portuguese women who worked outside the home constituted a minority group. In the first period of the Estado Novo, women were confined to the home. In the 1950s, 18.2% of women were part of the workforce, increasing considerably in the 1960s to 26.2% (Miranda, 1975), which was a result of the rapid expansion of industry and services, and as mentioned earlier, from the wave of emigration in which about a million people left the country (mostly men) and colonial wars that occupied thousands of men (Ferreira, 1976). The lack of male workforce determines the entry of a considerable number of women into the labor world, and in 1960, 28.4% of women were employed in industry and 44.3% were employed in services (Agria, 1968). In these same sectors, a decade later, the number increases to 30.8% in industry and 47.2% in services, with the passage of women from the private sphere to the production sphere notorious (Romão, 1976).

Although the entry of women into wage labor has gained some relevance in the course of the industrialization process, it emerged as an extension of domestic work, so that women would work mainly in the textile industry. Female work obeyed certain typical functions of female "nature," seen as less productive which was translated cheaper labor. It was common the absence of legal protection, low remuneration, and attitudes of competition and aggression on the part of their colleagues at work and, often, housemates (Alambert, 1986).

The 25th of April brought a turnaround in the situation, as it provided, in general, the entry of women into the public sphere. Women joined the first workers' organizations and the associative movements that created centers of direct democracy in the workplace. An era of "double power" was introduced, giving women the opportunity to move beyond the family sphere (private) and the mere participation in the workforce, to participate in decision-making in the public sphere. At this stage, different situations coexist in the female universe. We find women of a generation that grew up and was educated in a political system that valued their private role in the home, a new generation of women who had started to participate in urban productive activities during the 1960s, and also, from 1974, a generation that experienced a revolutionary process that allowed them to have public roles in the centers of direct democracy in the workplace. The increasing levels of female education (possible from the 1970s onwards) and the later age for marriage are two other phenomena that contribute to women's access to higher levels of professional qualification.

From 1986 onwards, the number of more qualified women increased, gradually surpassing the male qualification rate. Despite this, when the labor market is analyzed, what is seen is an inversion of these values because in this context women continue to be seen as something "unnatural," especially with regard to leading positions that is, even having the necessary qualifications, they are generally overlooked when it comes to occupying managerial positions. Thus, women occupy mainly positions socially linked to care, assuming roles related to education, health, and social action, and even in these spaces, leadership functions are predominantly male (Macedo & Santos, 2009).

An increasing number of OECD countries already have initiatives to bridge these disparities, and the significant progress in the qualification of women is already beginning to translate into gains in the labor market. In 2018, in the universe of the active population, 5.5% of the female population with higher education was employed, being the value of 5.1% for the male population with the same level of education (INE, 2018; PORDATA, 2019a, 2019b, 2019c, 2019d).

One of the biggest problems with which Portugal has been struggling in terms of employment is the lack of employment of young graduates, about 40,000, thousand today. In 2019, about 14% of Portuguese young people aged between 20 and 34 years old were unemployed 3 years after completing their academic degree. In this field, Portugal is in line with the European Union average, where the value reaches 14.5% (EUROSTAT, 2019).

The economic independence of women has long been identified as a European priority and it is, therefore, necessary to integrate women into the labor market, increasing their participation in economic activity and in the sustainability of social security systems (Rubery, 2011). Some difficulties exist at this level because the labor market in Portugal is characterized by a conservative organizational culture that reproduces and reinforces gender inequality (Casaca, 2012) and because socially women continue to be seen as primarily natural caregivers and only afterward workers and professionals (Rubery, 2014).

Thus, it becomes difficult to break the normative expectations and stereotypes that are culturally attributed to women and men and to change the pattern that persists in the labor and social relations in the workplace, which generate unequal status because they are based on the conventional pattern of masculinity (Wall et al., 2016).

The Portuguese financial crisis of the last decade had a disruptive effect on the labor market, particularly affecting young people, causing them to emigrate massively after completing their university courses (Ferreira, 2014). The upward trend in youth unemployment continued until 2015 as a result of international rescue and austerity policies (Karamessini, 2014). This issue is still unresolved because although Portugal needs its most qualified young people in the labor market, in reality it deals with difficulties in their insertion, with the country presenting employment rates for both women and men below the European average. This contradiction results from difficulties in the transition from school to the labor market or, otherwise, from the lack of active school work articulation policies (Kovács & Lopes, 2012).

Considering the period of economic crisis to be atypical, because it led to a sudden increase in unemployment for all, it was found that men and women were affected differently. Before the crisis, female unemployment was higher; however, in the first years of the crisis, this pattern was reversed, affecting men more (Rubery, 2014), because the greatest impact was felt in industry and construction (Bergman & Lechner, 2012).

In a subsequent phase, with the advance of the adjustment program, women were again the most affected by significant budget cuts in the public sector (Addabbo, Bastos, Casaca, Duvvury, & Léime, 2015). The unemployment had a lower impact among young people (boys and girls) with higher education levels, although situations of greater precariousness and marked by a reduction in wages became common. The logics of labor market flexibility and precarious hiring essentially affected young people and, in particular, young women, becoming a form of standardized hiring (ILO, 2016), with an impact on the consolidation of gender equality. In fact, women's investment in longer education paths does not represent an advantage in the integration in the labor market, with "glass ceilings" and wage differences persisting. This maintenance of "glass ceilings," that is, the tacit or explicit imposition of limits on the progression of women in their professional careers, continues to determine greater difficulty in accessing positions of responsibility, supervision, or leadership and, consequently, to limit their salary levels. There is a great disparity in Portugal, as the best paid places are less occupied by young women and, in almost all professional categories, women earn less than men, reaching a salary gap of 28.8%.

4. Final Considerations

The Portuguese context was very influenced by fifty years of dictatorship which forced greater efforts in the last 4 decades. Despite social advances, the rights conquered, the increased presence in higher education and the higher qualification of women, still exists a set of stereotypes that are manifested, more or less consciously, in labor contexts.

Women have high educational levels, but they continue to face a whole range of barriers to their professional growth or access to leadership positions. Gender remains a social representation of difference that penalizes women. In the labor market, characteristics considered to be masculine continue to be valued, such as competitiveness and leadership, so the argument of feminine "nature" still prevails to distance women from certain functions (mainly leadership roles), in particular, to distance them from power and decision-making positions.

Although there are no constraints to women's access to higher education, being today more qualified than men, when we look inside institutions, it is clear that there still exist obstacles at various levels. When we focus on teaching work in higher education, we observe that there has been a move toward greater numerical parity but that there is still a discrepancy when we look at the top, whether in careers or management of institutions. The data related to the study areas showed that some are more feminine and others that are more masculine, which, of course, ends up influencing the social value given to professions according to gender. In conclusion, the country has experienced a significant increase in the education of its young population, being more expressive in the case of women. In Portugal, as in many countries of the European Union, a lower number of young women drop out of school at early stages and a higher number complete higher education, being clear the major role that females have in the education field today. Higher education thus constitutes a privileged space for discussing these issues and finding solutions for greater gender equality.

References

Abrantes, P., & Abrantes, M. (2014). Gendering social mobility: A comparative perspective on the nexus of education and class across Europe. *Gender and Education, 26*(4), 377–396.

Addabbo, T., Bastos, A., Casaca, S. F., Duvvury, N., & Léime, Á. N. (2015). Gender and labour in times of austerity: Ireland, Italy and Portugal in comparative perspective. *International Labour Review, 154*(4), 449–473.

Agria, F. (1968). A mulher e o trabalho: características do trabalho feminino na época actual/Women and work: characteristics of women's work in the current era. *Estudos Sociais e Corporativos, 28*, 90–113.

Alambert, Z. (1986). *Feminismo: o ponto de vista marxista/Feminism: the marxist point of view*. São Paulo: Nobel.

Almeida, J. (2013). *Desigualdades e perspetivas dos cidadãos: Portugal e a Europa/Inequalities and perspectives of citizens: Portugal and Europe*. Lisboa: Mundos Sociais.

Alves, N. (2004). Les femmes et la politique au Portugal/Women and politics in Portugal. *Femmes Méditerranéennes*, 31–38.

Amâncio, L. (1994). *Masculino e Feminino. A Construção Social da Diferença/Male and female. The social construction of difference*. Porto: Afrontamento.

Beauvoir, S. (1952). *The second sex*. New York, NY: Random House.

Bergmann, N., & Lechner, F. (2012). *The role of men in gender equality – European strategies & insights* (Org.). Luxenbourg: Publications Office of the European Union.

Borgna, C., & Struffolino, E. (2017). Pushed or pulled? Girls and boys facing early school leaving risk in Italy. *Social Science Research, 61*, 298–313.

Byrne, D., & Smyth, E. (2010). *No way back? The dynamics of early school leaving*. Dublin: Liffey Press.

Canço, D. (2004). *Women and men in Portugal*. Lisbon: CIDM.

Casaca, S. F. (2012). Mercado de trabalho, flexibilidade e relações de género: tendências recentes/Labor market, flexibility and gender relations: recent trends. In S. F. Casaca (Ed.), *Mudanças Laborais e Relações de Género: Novos Vectores de (Des)Igualdade/Labor Changes and Gender Relations: New Vectors of (In) Equality*. Coimbra: Almedina.
Chaleta, E. (2011). Aprender no Ensino Superior – Contributos para a Qualidade da Aprendizagem e do sucesso Académico (Org)/Learning in Higher Education – Contributions to Quality of Learning and Academic Success (Org). *Educação Temas e Problemas, 9* ISSN:1646-2831.
Chaleta, E. (2013). *Orquestração da Aprendizagem no Ensino Superior* (Org)/*Learning Orchestration in Higher Education* (Org). Mangualde: Pedago. ISBN:978-989-8339-19-5.
CIG. (2017). *Igualdade de género em Portugal: indicadores-chave 2017/Gender equality in Portugal: key indicators 2017*. Lisboa: Comissão para a Cidadania e a Igualdade de Género.
Connell, R. W. (1987). Gender and power: Society, the person, and sexual politics. *Bulletin of Science, Technology & Society*, *8*(4), 445.
Costa, A. F., Lopes, J. T., & Caetano, A. (2014). *Percursos de estudantes no ensino superior (Coord)/Student paths in higher education* (Coord). Lisboa: Editora Mundos Sociais.
DGEEC/MCTES. (2018). *Estatísticas da Educação 2018–2019/Education Statistics 2018–2019*. Retrieved from http://www.dgeec.mec.pt
DGEEC/MCTES. (2019). *Principais resultados do RAIDES 19 – Diplomados 2018–2019/Main results of RAIDES 19 – Graduates 2018–2019*. Retrieved from https://www.dgeec.mec.pt/np4/1131.html
European Commission. (2017). Report on equality between women and men in the EU. Brussels. Retrieved from https://www.csee.etuce.org
European Commission. (2019). *She figures 2018*. Luxembourg: Publications Office of the European Union.
EUROSTAT. (2019). Labour market. Retrieved from https://ec.europa.eu/eurostat/371
FCT. (2013). Diagnóstico do Sistema de Investigação e Inovação: desafios, forças e fraquezas rumo e 2020/*Diagnosis of the research and innovation system: challenges, strengths and weaknesses towards 2020*. Retrieved from https://www.fct.pt/esp_inteligente/docs/SWOT_FCT_2013_Pt.pdf
Ferreira, E. (1976). *Origens e Formas de Emigração: o Impacto da Emigração sobre o Desenvolvimento Português/Origins and Forms of Emigration: The Impact of Emigration on Portuguese Development*. Lisboa: Iniciativas Editoriais.
Ferreira, V. (2014). Employment and austerity: Changing welfare and gender regimes in Portugal. In M. Karamessini & J. Rubery (Eds.), *Women and austerity: The economic crisis and the future for gender equality* (pp. 207–227). London: Routledge.
Formosinho, J. (1987). *Educating for passivity – A study of Portuguese education (1926–1968)*. Ph.D. thesis, University of London: Institute of Education, London.
Greer, G. (1970). *The female eunuch*. London: MacGibbon and Kee.
Guinote, P. (2014). *Educação e liberdade de escolha/Education and freedom of choice*. Lisboa: Fundação Francisco Manuel dos Santos.
Hadjar, A., Krolak-Schwerdt, S., Priem, K., & Glock, S. (2014). Gender and education achievement. *Educational Research*, *56*(2), 117–125.

ILO. (2016). Women at Work Trends 2016 – Report. Retrieved from https://www.ilo.org/wcmsp5/groups/public/—dgreports/—dcomm/—publ/documents/publication/wcms_457317.pdf

INE. (2018). Estatísticas do Emprego – 4.º trimestre de 2018/*Employment Statistics – 4th quarter 2018*. Retrieved from///C:/Users/mec/AppData/Local/Temp/06IE_4T2018.pdf

Karamessini, M. (2014). Introduction – Women's vulnerability to recession and austerity: A different crisis, a different context. In M. Karamessini & J. Rubery (Eds.), *Women and austerity: The economic crisis and the future for gender equality* (pp. 3–16). London: Routledge.

Kimmel, M. (2000). *The gendered society*. New York, NY: Oxford University Press.

Kimmel, M. (2010). *Misframing men: The politics of contemporary masculinities*. New Brunswick, NJ: Rutgers University Press.

Kovács, I., & Lopes, M. (2012). A juventude e o emprego entre a flexibilidade e a precariedade/Youth and employment between flexibility and precariousness. In S. F. Casaca (Ed.), *Mudanças Laborais e Relações de Género: Novos Vectores de (Des)Igualdade/Labor Changes and Gender Relations: New Vectors of (In) Equality*. Coimbra: Almedina.

Kuin, S. (1993). A Mocidade Portuguesa nos anos 30: anteprojectos e instauração de uma organização paramilitar da juventude/The Portuguese Youth in the 1930s: preliminary projects and the establishment of a paramilitary youth organization. *Análise Social*, *28*(122), 555–588.

Larivière, V., Ni, C., Gingras, Y., Cronin, B., & Sugimoto, C. R. (2013). Global gender disparities in science. *Nature*, *504*(7479), 211–213.

Lucena, M. (1976). *A Evolução do Sistema Corporativo Português/The Evolution of the Portuguese Corporate System. I. O Salazarismo*. Lisboa: Perspectivas e Realidades.

Macedo, E., & Santos, S. (2009). Apenas mulheres? Situação das mulheres no mercado de trabalho em quatro países europeus. [Just women? The women situations in labour market among four European countries.] *Ex Aequo*, *19*, 129–155.

Mead, M. (1949). *Male and female: A study of the sexes in a changing world*. New York, NY: William Marrow and Company.

Miranda, D. (1975). *Estimativa da População Activa Portuguesa por Sexos 1890–1970/Estimate of the Portuguese Active Population by Sex 1890–1970*. Lisboa: Policopiado.

Mitchel, J. (1971). *Woman's estate*. New York, NY: Vintage Books.

Moss-Racusin, C. A., Dovidiob, J. F., Brescollc, V. L., Grahama, M. J., & Handelsmana, J. (2012). Science faculty's subtle gender biases favor male students. *PNAS*, *109*(41), 16474–16479.

OECD. (2010). *PISA 2009 results: Executive summary*. Paris: OECD Publishing.

OECD. (2012). *Education at a glance*. Paris: OECD Publishing.

Pimentel, I. (2007). *Mocidade Portuguesa feminina/Portuguese Female Youth*. Lisboa: Esfera dos Livros.

PORDATA. (2019a). Alunos matriculados no ensino superior: total e por sexo-Portugal/*Students enrolled in higher education: total and by sex-Portugal*. Retrieved from http://www.pordata.pt/Portugal/Alunos+matriculados+no+ensino+superior+total+e+por+sexo-1048

PORDATA. (2019b). Taxa de abandono precoce de educação e formação: total e por sexo/*Rate of early dropout from education and training: total and by sex*. Retrieved from https://www.pordata.pt/Portugal/Taxa+de+abandono+precoce+de+educa%C3%A7%C3%A3o+e+forma%C3%A7%C3%A3o+total+e+por+sexo-433

PORDATA. (2019c). População empregada do sexo masculino e do sexo feminino: total e a tempo completo e parcial/*Employed male and female population: full and full-time and part-time*. Retrieved from https://www.pordata.pt/Europa/Popula%C3%A7%C3%A3o+empregada+a+tempo+parcial+por+sexo+(percentagem)-1765

PORDATA. (2019d). População desempregada à procura de novo emprego: total e por sexo/*Unemployed population looking for a new job: total and by sex*. Retrieved from https://www.pordata.pt/Portugal/Popula%C3%A7%C3%A3o+desempregada+%C3%A0+procura+de+novo+emprego+total+e+por+sexo-438

Romão, I. (1976). *Participação das Mulheres na Vida Sindical, Cívica e Política*. Cadernos Condição Feminina/Participation of Women in Union, Civic and Political Life. Lisboa: Comissão da Condição Feminina.

Rubery, J. (2011). Towards a gendering of the labour market regulation debate. *Cambridge Journal of Economics*, *35*(6), 1103–1126.

Rubery, J. (2014). From women and recession to women and austerity. In M. Karamessini & J. Rubery (Eds.), *Women and austerity: The economic crisis and the future for gender equality* (pp. 17–36). London: Routledge.

SAGE. (2018). Carta de Princípios do SAGE para Igualdade de Género/*SAGE Charter of Principles for Gender Equality*. Retrieved from https://www.iscteiul.pt/assets/files/2019/09/04/1567591162042_Charter_of_Principles_vTCD5_August_vers_o_portuguesa.pdf

Santos, M., Lima, M., & Ferreira, V. (1975). As lutas sociais nas empresas e a revolução do 25 de Abril/Social struggles in companies and the April 25 revolution. *Análise Social*, (42/43), 266–335.

Santos, M. H., & Amâncio, L. (2016). Gender inequalities in highly qualified professions: A social psychological analysis. *Journal of Social and Political Psychology*, *4*(1), 427–443.

Sobrinho, M., Ennafaa, R., & Chaleta, E. (2016). *La educación superior, el estudiantado y la cultura universitaria* (Orgs)/*Higher education, the student's and university culture* (Orgs). Valência: Editorial NEOPATRIA.

Tavares, M. (2000). *Movimentos de mulheres em Portugal: décadas de 70 e 80/Movements of women in Portugal: the 70s and 80s*. Lisboa: Livros Horizonte.

Torres, A. (2001). *Sociologia do casamento: A família e a questão feminina/Sociology of marriage: The family and the female issue*. Oeiras: Celta Editora.

Torres, A., Pinto, P., Costa, D., Coelho, B., Maciel, D., Reigadinha, D., & Theodoro, E. (2018). *Igualdade de género ao longo da vida: Portugal no contexto europeu/Gender equality throughout life: Portugal in the European context*. Lisboa: Fundação Francisco Manuel dos Santos.

UNESCO. (2015). UNESCO science report: Towards 2030. Retrieved from https://unesdoc.unesco.org/ark:/48223/pf0000235406

Vieira, J. (2008). *Mocidade Portuguesa/Portuguese Youth*. Lisboa: A Esfera dos Livros.

Wall, K., Cunha, V., Atalaia, S., Rodrigues, L., Correia, R., Correia, S. V., & Rosa, R. (2016). *Livro Branco – Homens e Igualdade de Género em Portugal/Men and Gender Equality in Portugal – White Book*. Lisboa: CITE.

Chapter 3

Girls in French Higher Education: Real Progress despite Persistent Inequalities in Scientific and Technological Fields

Christine Fontanini and Saeed Paivandi

1. Introduction

Feminization of higher education in France has been accelerating since the 1970s and girls have been in a majority since 1981, accounting for 55% of students enrolled in 2019 (DEPP-RERS, 2019). However, although all fields of study in higher education are open to girls and boys alike, very few are followed by equal numbers of girls and boys. Research on education and gender continues to highlight a "paradox": girls and boys have grown much closer in physical terms and follow identical educational pathways, but educational and professional orientation is still marked by gender segregation in secondary and higher education (Ayral & Raibaud, 2014; Baudelot & Establet, 1992; Duru-Bellat, 2014; Fontanini, 2015; Gaussel, 2016; Kieffer and Marry, 2011; Mosconi, 1989; Rosenwald, 2006) even though study and career possibilities have developed significantly for women. This reality shows that laws and institutional injunctions are not enough to do away with the processes of social construction of gendered identities, which themselves lead to inequalities.

2. Higher Education in France: An Atypical Model

France has seen unprecedented opening up of higher education since the 1960s. Currently, almost 57% of a generation accesses its various branches. The proportion varies depending on social origin, however: over 90% for privileged groups (teachers and intellectual professions) as against 32% for ordinary workers (DEPP, 2019).

In order to understand the major disparities between girls and boys in the various branches of higher education, it is above all necessary to take a look at France's atypical education system.

French higher education is characterized by its historical fragmentation between the university sector and the elite institutions, as well as by the existence

International Perspectives on Gender and Higher Education, 33–56

doi:10.1108/978-1-83909-886-420201003

of a vocational short training sector. The higher education system's fragmentation makes the French model quite atypical if we compare it with other countries (Attali, 1998; Hazelkorn, 2009; Husén, 1991; Paivandi, 2018; Salmi, 2009). The university sector only includes public universities that host nearly 61% of students in France. The nonuniversity sector, which shares almost a third of the student population, is composed of elite institutions (preparatory classes and *Grandes Ecoles*) and Vocational Training Institutions (2 or 3 years).

The presence of an elite sector outside the university epitomized a State-directed meritocratic society, where professionals with a particular education are viewed as exquisite elites. These institutions, which are focused solely on excellence teaching and do not carry out research activities, are intellectually and socially highly selective (Husén, 1991). The symbolic and real effects of the duality of the Public University and non-University sectors is affecting the image and effective functioning of higher institutions in France. According to Merrien and Musselin (1999), a striking feature of the fragmented French system is that public Universities have never been institutions that were recognized by the upper class.

3. Women's Long Road to Majorityhood

In the nineteenth century, the Camille Sée law (1880) introduced secondary education for girls, based on "*the idea of radical separation of the positions and functions of bourgeois men and women and female subordination*" (Mosconi, 1994, p. 194). It was a question of a social order based on a division of men's and women's roles in society: men in economic, social, political, and cultural life and women in family life. What was more, nineteenth -century physicians considered women to be the weaker sex by nature (and men strong), as well as being frivolous, fickle, credulous, and altogether incapable of reflection (Mosconi, 1994). Various scientific pseudotheories supported by this naturalist ideology legitimized the male monopoly of the sciences. According to the neurologist Gall, "the gift for mathematics" was not to be found in women. In 1808, Philippe de Maistre put forward the basic argument upheld by the enemies of "science in petticoats":

> As for science, it is a very dangerous thing for women. We know of almost no learned women who have not been made unfortunate or ridiculous by science. Women who wish to be like men are no more than apes, yet wanting to be like a man is wanting to be learned. (Mosconi, 1994)

Such theories legitimized girls' preparation to become

> ...good wives and good mothers, good housewives who know how to please their husbands, instruct their children, govern their houses economically and spread good feeling and wellbeing all around them. (Lelièvre & Lelièvre, 1991, p. 108)

Boys were subjected to comprehensive instruction "*as it is the man whose mission it was to lead the political fight, earn his living and deal with ideas*" (Camille Sée, quoted in Lelièvre & Lelièvre, 1991).

Girls therefore had to wait 104 years to access the secondary and higher education that had been boy's preserve since 1820 (Mosconi, 1994). Confronted with ever-increasing social demand, public institutions were finally authorized to prepare girls for the baccalaureate in 1908, but it was not until 1925 that they had access to the same secondary school programs, timetables, and sections as boys. Girls were then able to study all the subjects that had previously been forbidden to them or which they had only been taught in rudimentary manner, such as Latin, Greek, philosophy, mathematics, and natural sciences. Nonetheless, there were very few female holders of science baccalaureates up until the Second World War: 12% in 1933 and 13% in 1938 (Baudelot & Establet, 1992).

Until the end of the nineteenth century, there were very few girls at French Universities, "*never more than 3% of the total student body*" (Thikhonov Sigrist, 2009, p. 53); their numbers then increased, slowly but steadily, throughout the twentieth century: 10% in 1914; 25% in 1930; 34% in 1950; 44% in 1968; and 50% in 1981 (Lelièvre & Lelièvre, 1991). However, the proportion of girls in the various branches did not increase homogeneously: the percentage of girls in arts faculties increased the most rapidly (33% in 1914; 50% in 1939); as far as law was concerned, it started to increase in the interwar period (19% in 1939; 26% in 1946; and 50% in 1970), as was the case with medicine (11% in 1914; 21% in 1939; 31% in 1968). As regards to the sciences, the percentage of girls increased quite steadily, only to stagnate in the 1970s and after: 3% in 1900, 9% in 1914, 24% in 1939, and 31% in 1960 (Lelièvre & Lelièvre, 1991).

Engineering schools, which were created in the mid-eighteenth century, did not start accepting female students until the end of the First World War. Initially, however, they were only to be seen in a few schools, mostly studying chemistry. Women's attraction to chemistry may be explained by the fact that the work carried out by chemists in analysis and control laboratories requires qualities of order, method and care, which were developed in the traditional education given to girls (Cachelou, 1984). The National Agronomic Institute in Paris opened its doors in 1917 and was mixed from the outset, although women were to remain the exception up until the 1970s (9%). In the aftermath of the Second World War, industry needed engineers and schools sprang up in consequence, open to men and women alike, and little by little, all schools, once reserved for boys only, began to accept girls. Nonetheless, there were very few female students at engineering schools up until the 1960s and 1970s (4% in 1964; 7% in 1975) (Fontanini, 1999).

4. Progress and Inequalities

In France, the second half of the twentieth century was marked by two major socioeducational changes: an unprecedented increase in numbers of pupils and students and the spectacular evolution of girls' education, in particular with regard to higher education. Starting in the 1960s, a series of reforms was carried out in the French education system, universalizing secondary education and improving access to higher education. In the mid-1980s, the goal of getting 80% of an age group through the baccalaureate, and then, in the mid-2000s, that of ensuring that 50% of an age group obtained a higher education qualification, resulted in what can only be termed an explosion in numbers in secondary education and then in higher education. In 50 years, the number of baccalaureate holders in a generation increased more than sixfold (Chevaillier, Landrier, & Nakhili, 2009; Le Laidier & Thomas, 2014) and student numbers tenfold (DEPP-RERS, 2012).

The presence of girls has been a major factor in the democratization of secondary and higher education in France. Since 1971, the proportion of girls in a single generation who complete their secondary has always been higher than for boys, reaching 86% for girls and 76% for boys in 2018 (DEPP-RERS, 2019). Since 1981, girls have been in the majority in higher education, accounting for 55% of students enrolled in 2019 (DEPP-RERS, 2019).

For almost 30 years now, despite the fact that all higher education programs are open to girls and boys alike, there have been very few branches other than business, management, and accounting schools where there are as many girls (51%) as there are boys (49%) (DEPP-RERS, 2019). These fields are of particular interest to girls and boys alike due to the employment opportunities they provide, ensuring that their graduates enjoy upscale professional and social positions without necessarily having studied at the most prestigious institutions such as HEC and ESSEC in Paris (Blanchard, 2009).

Whatever the sector in question (university or not, short or long, elitist or otherwise), there are always significantly more girls in the subject areas that have been their traditional favorites, such as languages, literature, and human and social sciences (69.5%) and paramedical and social courses (86%), and, since the first half of the twentieth century, their numbers have continued to increase in such branches as law (66%) and the medical sciences (64%) (Table 3.1). They are still in a minority in traditionally male preserves such as engineering (28%) (DEPP-RERS, 2019). In these, as in short vocational training courses, there are major disparities between fields of study: there is a low proportion of girls in such specialties as mechanics, electricity, electronics (less than 10%), and computer science (less than 20%) but a very high one in flexible materials (91%), agronomy/agrifood (59%), and chemistry, process engineering and life sciences (58.5%) (Lièvre, 2016). The same contrast between the various scientific specialties is to be found in universities, with a 26% feminization rate for basic and applied sciences and a 61% rate for life, earth, and universe sciences (DEPP-RERS, 2019, Table 3.2).

For over 30 years now, girls have been enrolling en masse in various higher education programs that they had previously shown less or little interest in, such as veterinary science (76%), training for the Bar (70%), notarial studies (63%), schools of architecture (55%), and senior police officer training schools (53%) (Fontanini, 2015; DEPP-RERS, 2019).

Elitist institutions, the so-called "G*randes Ecoles,*" which are highly selective and prestigious, training young people to fill top political, administrative, and

Table 3.1. Students Enrolled in the Different Sectors of the French Higher Education in 2018–2019 (DEPP, 2019).

Institutions	% of Total	Major Characteristics	% Women
Public universities	*61*	Public institutions (an average of 19,000 students enrolled)	57,4
Short Vocational Training			
IUT (University Institutes of Technology)	*4*	Part of the university, but independent management, small sizes, public (an average of 1,100 students)	40
Sections of technicians	*10*	Organized in secondary education, selective admission, small sizes, public and private (an average of 110 students)	49
Paramedical and social Work	*4.50*	Selective admission, small sizes, public and private (an average of 350 students)	63
High selective and elitist sector			
CPGE (Preparatory Classes for *Grandes Ecoles*)	*3*	Preparatory courses with the main goal of training undergraduate students for enrollment in the *Grandes Ecoles*, competitive and selective admission, small sizes, public and private (an average of 200 students)	42.5
Engineering schools (*Grandes écoles*)	*6*	Competitive and selective admission, public and private, small sizes, public and private (an average of 540 students)	28
Business Schools (*Grandes écoles*)	*7*	Competitive and selective admission, public and private, small sizes, (an average of 700 students)	51
Schools of art/ architecture, Vet schools (*Grandes écoles*)	*3*	Selective admission, public and private, small sizes (an average of 250 students)	66
Other institutions	*2*		53
Total	***100 (2,680,400 students)***		**55**

Table 3.2: The Evolution of Proportions of Women in the Various Sectors of Higher Education in France.

	1998 (%)	2018 (%)
University		
Law	61	67
Literature	73	75
Humanities	66	67
Medical sciences	58	64
Sciences and technology university	28	30
Natural sciences	57	62
Languages	65	67
Economics	47	49
Short Vocational Training		
IUT: production/industry	22.50	25
IUT service	55	51
STS production/industry	21	24
STS service	58	60
Paramedical sector	80	86
Highly selective and elitist sector		
Business schools	46	51
Engineering schools	28	28
CPGE sciences	27	31
CPGE others	59	63
Total higher education	*53*	*55*

Source: DEPP, 2003, 2019.

scientific positions, are feminized to varying degrees: although the National School of the Magistracy is very much feminized (74%), male dominance continues at the ENA (an average of 33%) and Polytechnique (an average of 20%) (Fontanini, 2015).[1,2]

For Marry (2004), gendered segregation of studies exists, both horizontally (by field of study) and vertically (by level); i.e., boys enroll in academically and

[1]Examples include Ecole Polytechnique, Ecole des Mines de Paris, Ecole Nationale des Ponts et Chaussées, Ecole Centrale Paris, l'Ecole Normale Supérieure, and Ecole Nationale de l'Administration.

[2]https://www.enm.justice.fr/actu-29012019-Promotion-2019-de-l-ENM-qui-sont-les-juges-et-procureurs-de-demain, consulted on 19 August 2019.

professionally advantageous sectors, while girls are more interested in long, largely undervalued studies with few professional opportunities at the end of them.

5. Lack of Significant Impact on the Part of Official Texts

The rapid feminization of higher education raises the question of the existence of public policies in favor of girls. In France, the education system has an "explicit project of individual emancipation and equality for all" (Collet, 2012), and there is certainly no lack of circulars and interministerial agreements; in addition, actions promoted by public institutions and associations have been developed with a view to reducing the gendered character of postsecondary orientations.[3] From the 1980s onwards, policies were above all designed to encourage girls to enroll in scientific and technical fields of study (Dauphin, 2010; Epiphane, 2016; Fontanini, 2015; Gaussel, 2016; Lemarchant, 2017). Such texts and initiatives seem to have had limited effects on practices, however, as they provided few concrete plans (Blanchard, Orange, & Pierrel, 2016; Bouchareu, 2012; Gemego & Wacheux, 2017). According to the authors, public policies tend to reproduce gendered representations if only implicitly, basing themselves on a homogenizing vision of the sexes and largely leaving the question of boys' orientation to one side.

It was not until the first interministerial convention on "*promotion of equal opportunities for girls and boys, men and women, in the education system,*" signed in 2000, that there was any plan to improve "*the widening of girls' and boys' professional choices*" by systematically training all categories of educational staff, in initial and continuing training programs alike. Various other texts have also been drawn up to the same end since then. However, a report by the Economic, Social and Environmental Council highlights the fact that

> …thirty years after universalisation of coeducation, it has not yet succeeded in overcoming gendered segregation of studies. (…) Up until the present, it would seem that, apart from the announcement effect, the various actors involved have done little to give substance to these goals and put them into practice in concrete manner. (Crosemarie, 2009, p. 45)

6. Gendered Disparities: Research Tries to Understand

The development of girls' access to higher education, the disparities observed between girls and boys depending on field of study, and the feminization of the

[3]The *Femmes Ingénieurs* (Women Engineers) association, created in 1982, promotes engineering as a profession among girls and female engineers and scientists in the world of work. The *Femmes et Mathématiques* (Women and Mathematics) and *Femmes et Sciences* (Women and Science) associations were created in 1987 and 2000, respectively, to stimulate girls' interest in scientific careers.

higher professions are all social transformations that have become subject to a significant amount of research work in France. Research on girls' postsecondary orientations in France over the last 40 years has attempted to explore the various factors that have probably contributed to the differentiated feminization of higher educational branches. The resulting publications make it clear that the process of orientation of higher educational study choices is multidimensional and complex. Despite thematic and paradigmatic divergences, research work is in agreement in asserting the socially constructed character of gaps between the two sexes. A great deal of research on acquisition of gender roles and construction of sexual identity stresses the importance of socialization from the very beginning of schooling (Chiland, 2003; Gausset, 2016; Rouyer, Mieyaa, & Blanc, 2015). In other words, in order to understand girls' and boys' differentiated orientations in secondary and higher education, we need to examine the process of differentiated socialization or gender socialization which is underpinned by the gender roles assigned to men and women, as well as by the unequal system that connects masculinity and femininity in the French context.

Socialization of gender is largely based on sexual stereotypes, defined as shared beliefs regarding individual characteristics, generally personality traits along with behaviors typical of boys and girls, men, and women (Leyens, Yserbyt, & Schradon, 1996). Masculine and feminine are not natural categories but social norms (Gaussel, 2016). Girls and boys alike learn their gender roles and those of the opposite sex. Generally, sexual stereotypes naturalize differentiated gender roles that denote the psychological traits, behaviors, social roles, and activities assigned mostly to men or mostly to women in a given culture (Bem, 1974). Such gender roles require them to be and behave in accordance with the norms of femininity and masculinity that prevail in a given society.

To choose a branch of study is to project oneself into a professional and personal future, and each individual's perception of the gendered character of a social role or profession is likely to influence their postsecondary orientation. This is why research on women's presence in higher education often focuses on the socializing processes and experiences that may influence young people's culture prior to entering higher education.

7. Family Socialization

Some research works see the family as a key source of gendered socialization, as parents tend to provide physical and cultural environments supposedly best suited to girls or boys (Chapon, 2014; Dafflon, 2006, 2010; Gaussel, 2016; Gresy & George, 2012). In addition, the ways in which parents interact with their very young child differ depending on its sex: more verbal, prosocial solicitations for girls and more stimulation of boys' self-sufficiency in resolution of problems and physical game-playing. Such differentiated attitudes on the part of parents and the social environment as a whole lead to girls and boys developing specific skills and aptitudes (Rouyer, 2007). Family socialization

> ...appears of key importance as the 'primary' place where interiorisation of models of gendered behaviour is the most 'silent' and therefore has the most chance of imposing itself with the obviousness of the natural and the naturalness of what is obvious. (Blöss, 2001, p. 2)

Researches show that parental monitoring of and involvement in their children's schooling varies depending on their sex. Gouyon and Guérin (2006) suggest that parents help girls and boys alike in their schoolwork, but that they invest less time on their daughters' schooling than on their sons'. Parents monitor their daughters' schoolwork less as they are regarded as being more self-sufficient than boys. They are also freer to choose educational alternatives and pathways than boys are. As the authors emphasize, this greater self-sufficiency may lead them to make mistakes in their choices as they benefit less from their parents' experience and knowledge of the labor market (Gouyon & Guérin, 2006). The greater freedom left to girls in making their choices enables (at least partial) better understanding of why they make choices that turn out to be less advantageous as far as the labor market is concerned than those made by boys, as they lack information and underestimation of their capacities is not questioned or at least discussed by their parents (Caille, Lemaire, & Vrolant, 2002).

Parents' academic ambitions for their children differ: scientific branches are favored more highly for boys and literary branches for girls (Duru Bellat, 2010; Dubet, 2010; Fuma, 2010; Mosconi, 1994). Parents probably have doubts about their daughters' abilities in scientific subjects, mathematics in particular; even when they are very good at the subject, in which boys and girls are equally successful, parents stress how much work their daughters had to do, as if it was more difficult "in spite of everything" as well as being less useful to them, or more "natural" for boys (Duru Bellat, 2010, 2014). Hence, parents are less ready to pressure their daughters into the most prestigious upper-secondary branch enabling access to prestigious scientific fields.

Like most people, parents have a gendered image of professional sectors. However, parental ambitions are higher for girls when parents are higher education graduates, although they still do not equal those for boys (Gouyon & Guérin, 2006). The authors point out that there is less social and family pressure on them than there is on boys. According to Marry, "*Girls are under less pressure than boys to succeed in accordance with the canonical model of excellence based on competition, the diktat of mathematics and exclusive investment in careers*" (2004, p. 61). This being so, they may have a less instrumental relationship with their studies and prioritize their "tastes." For example, girls are more likely than boys to choose agronomic engineering as they are more interested in biology (Alaluf et al., 2003; Veleine, 2004).

Parents' professions and a family's academic tradition may also influence boys' and girls' choices. Two studies carried out among women engineers (Marry, 2004; Stevanovic, 2006) highlight the mother's role in transmission of a taste for school and occasionally for science. Such women often have fathers who are engineers, mothers in a scientific profession of some sort and/or who are teachers, or women scientists in their family circle, so familiarizing them with a scientific or engineering profession (Marry, 2004; Sutour & Pozzi, 1997). Another study on ENS students also reports the importance of maternal transmissions, but goes on to cite paternal influences, which enable *"an opening up of possibilities, an authorisation [for girls] to join this male world"* (Ferrand, Imbert, & Marry, 1997, p. 185).

Researchers have also examined the possible relations between inequalities in postsecondary orientation and social inequalities (Tanguy, 1986). A number of pioneering studies had stressed their partial independence of each other (Girod, 1977) as well as their mutual reinforcement (Bourdieu & Passeron, 1964).[4] Such research had also suggested the existence of a "dual handicap" (Bisseret, 1974; Girod, 1977) for girls from working-class backgrounds, who would have less chance of academic success and be less likely to make an atypical educational choice (Ferrand, Imbert and Marry).

8. Socialization at School

Another area of research on the effects of gendered socialization focuses on the two sexes' experiences at school. Most such work shows that girls and boys are confronted with a socioeducational construction of the differences between the sexes (Ayral, 2011; Ayral & Raibaud, 2014; Courteau, 2014; Depoilly, 2014; Dubet, 2010; Duru-Bellat, 2016, 2014; Gaussel, 2016). According to De Boissieu (2009), educational gender is a construction specific to school culture, which results in determination of girl-pupil and boy-pupil identities, with which ways of "being in class" and preferred choices are associated. In general, interactions in the classroom between teachers and pupils and between pupils and the curriculum are favorable to boys, generating less self-confidence in girls and different attitudes between the two sexes in the face of various areas of knowledge (Courteau, 2014; Duru-Bellat, 2014). A study on interactions in mathematics showed that boys receive more individualized interactions, information, open questions, and feedback and girls fewer remarks of a cognitive nature (Jarlégan, 1999). In general, and not only in mathematics, it seems that teachers interact more with boys (Mosconi, 2004). Consequently, girls and boys develop different relationships with knowledge and a gendered perception of their own skills and attitudes.

As regards to school results (performance), boys are often regarded as what Duru-Bellat (2014) refers to as underachievers, i.e., intelligent, with undeniable abilities that they do not fully exploit due to lack of sufficient "effort." In contrast, girls are more often seen as "doing what they can," i.e., succeeding because of hard work. Such opinions on the part of teachers come very close to being

[4]A number of studies carried out in France in the 1960s and 1970s tended to perceive inequalities depending on gender as being secondary to inequalities in class (Prost, 1986) or to treat them as a "difference in the difference" (Passeron & De Singly, 1984; Ferrand et al., 1996).

stereotypes: the intelligent boy who doesn't do any work and the girl who is only of average intelligence but who works hard.

These general observations show themselves to be all the more true in science, mathematics in particular. Here again, we observe fewer interactions with girls on the part of teachers, less encouragement and fewer remarks of a cognitive nature. The majority of teachers think that most boys are capable of succeeding, while girls' capacities are rather more questionable; those who succeed are the exception. In addition, success in mathematics is undoubtedly considered more important for boys than for girls. It may be assumed that such expectations by teachers have significant effects, at least partly bringing about what those expectations predict (Duru Bellat, 1990, 2014).

9. The Place of Mathematics

In the French context, mathematics, as well as often being associated with such terms as "rigor" and "logic," which are generally ascribed to the masculine register, also constitutes the spearhead of academic competition. Consequently, the subject does not seem to be in compliance with "*the cultural identity of women, who value relationships with others, imagination and affectivity"* (Duru Bellat, 1995), which results in girls being readier to assert that they "don't like maths" as it is commonly held that girls are not interested in the subject and even that they do not always have a talent for it (Mosconi, 1994, 2014). Conversely, boys state that they like maths, even when they are not very good at it, as the subject is associated with such "masculine" traits as logic...an exclusion of sensitivity (Duru Bellat, 1995). What is more, girls know that they will be able to "chuck it" more easily than boys in their future higher studies; girls are less subject to pressure to take up prestigious scientific studies, on the part of their parents and teachers alike (Fontanini, 1999).

Comparative examination of study programs according to gender shows that mathematics and physics are two elitist fields marked by sustained imbalance between girls and boys. The place assigned to mathematics and physics, and the programs in which they occupy a preponderant position in production of elites, sheds light on the social construction mechanisms that naturalize the exclusion of women. It is not a natural taste for the sciences that explains why boys are so attracted to them, but rather the prospects of the dominant positions that they will finally enable (Collet, 2011; Gaussel, 2016; Detrez & Piluso, 2014). As a dominated group, women cannot legitimately claim access to such positions (Ferrand, Imbert, & Marry, 1996). Girls' supposed lack of talent for mathematics, a notion that has held sway for almost two centuries, seems to still have had a hold on French minds at the beginning of the twenty-first century. Hence, after being excluded from scientific and technical knowledge, women themselves tend sometimes to turn their backs on knowledge that they had been told was not suited to their capacities. In this context, girls tend to underestimate their performances in scientific subjects and lack self-confidence in comparison with boys, even though their upper-secondary academic results are very similar, in particular in their final year in science sections (Breda, Grenet, Monnet, Van Effenterre, 2018; Caille & O'Pey, 2005; OCDE, 2012).[5] Hence, girls' "self-censorship" in their orientation is socially constructed: "girls censor themselves because they are censored" (Blanchard et al., 2016, p. 23).

10. The Orientation Process

The orientation process implemented at the beginning and end of pupils' upper-secondary education has become the subject of numerous questions with a view to understanding the role of institutional actors and pupils' family circles play in their decisions. Landrier and Nakhili (2010) and Reay, David, and Ball (2005) show that school staff, with little training in matters of gender, endorse and reinforce families' gendered choices by encouraging girls and boys to select different pathways.

Gendered orientation choices persist. The proportion of girls in *terminale scientifique* has increased by 12 points in 34 years: from 35% in 1985 to 47% in 2019 (Collet, 2011; Stevanovic, 2006; UNESCO, 2016).[6,7] The continuing limited choice of scientific studies on the part of girls is paradoxical as their best academic results compared with boys in all subjects over previous years should lead many more of them to opt for such studies (Fontanini, 2015).

Girls' continuing attraction to life and earth sciences compared with other scientific disciplines undoubtedly has much to do with the idea that has persisted since the nineteenth century, with regard to the natural sciences: "*it is the feminine science par excellence, the only one that gives no cause for holding women up to ridicule*" (Bricard, 1985). Biology and chemistry are seen as requiring meticulousness, a taste for substance and a good ability to learn by heart (Marry, 2004), qualities that are generally still associated with women. What is more, girls' attraction to life and earth sciences enables them to indulge their subject preferences compared with those preferred by boys, and stand out in their own right (the same in reverse goes for boys). And in their teenage years, girls and boys "*have to [...] mutually prove themselves to be proper masculine boys and feminine girls*" (Vouillot, 2007, p. 95). Boys with science baccalaureates are pushed more toward courses focusing on mathematics or computer science, which are regarded as more prestigious and remunerative (Ferrand et al., 1996). We may also make

---

[5]Gender stereotypes (like other stereotypes) are generally interiorized and may have an impact on individual performances. In social psychology, the term "stereotype threat" is employed. For example, Spencer & al (1999) highlighted the fact that girls' performance in mathematics tests is better when the exercise is presented as being equally well completed by women and men alike than when it is explicitly set in order to measure their performances in mathematics. Gender stereotypes therefore generate performances of lesser quality (in this case, by girls in mathematics) and decisions that lead to underoptimization of individual skills (girls who are good at maths but who self-censor and study literature instead, for example; Weinberger, 1998).

[6]Final year of upper-secondary education.

[7]Section enabling continuation to postbaccalaureate scientific studies.

the hypothesis that, in higher education, girls prefer programs that are not dominated by men, such as life and earth sciences (Ecklund, Lincoln, Tansey, 2012).

According to some authors, when girls opt for science in secondary education, their goals are not the same as boys' goals (Fontanini, 1999). They do so in order to keep all doors to higher education open, whereas boys tend to choose this pathway specifically in order to take up scientific studies after their baccalaureate. As school-leavers with science baccalaureates have a very wide range of possibilities to choose from, and as they have not necessarily chosen this particular pathway because of their attraction to the sciences (Duru-Bellat, 2014; Lemaire & Leseur, 2005), they may end up studying in one or other of the many non–science-orientated fields that higher education has to offer, girls in particular. There are only half as many girls in preparatory classes for scientific *Grandes Ecoles* as there are boys, and girls are also less likely than boys to opt for undergraduate courses at engineering schools. It is only at universities, in Bachelor of Science, that there are almost as many girls as there are boys. Conversely, twice as many girls than boys choose courses in the field of healthcare and at paramedical schools (Lemaire, 2012).

11. Gendered Division of the Labor Market and Domestic Work

The labor market's structure into "prototypes" is often perceived as a factor that influences girls' and boys' postsecondary choices (Gaussel, 2016; Huteau, 1982; Kergoat, 2014). Such prototypes seem to possess specific attributes that play a major part in their definitions ("being good at maths" for engineers, for example). As Kergoat sees it, people tend to look for congruence or a matching process between "*self-representations*" and "*prototypes*" (Kergoat, 2014). Likewise, upper-secondary and university students tend to see professions in terms of typical practitioners, assigning them personality traits, skills, professional values, interests, and even lifestyles and physical characteristics (Marro & Vouillot, 1991). According to Vouillot,

> …in order for a training programme or profession to be initially considered and then adopted as a possible project, there must be a measure of congruence, of resemblance between these two images. (Vouillot, 2007, p. 94)

Although women currently account for almost half (48%) of France's working population, most of the jobs they occupy are still concentrated in a limited number of long-since feminized professions and activity sectors associated with their supposed natural qualities: taking care of others, children's education, and listening to and paying attention to others.

> Half the women who work are involved in 28 professions under the current nomenclature (out of the 486 listed), while it would need 75 professions on the list in order to reach half the number of men in employment. (Maruani & Méron, 2012, p. 168)

In addition and despite their major presence on the labor market, women still do most of the domestic work (Roy, 2012). The time women devote to it increases with the presence and number of children, very young children in particular, so increasing the imbalance in division of domestic tasks between couples (Régnier-Loilier, 2009). According to Zarca, before confronting the other, each partner in the couple must first of all do battle… with him/herself (…). Before she even takes a stand, a woman has to convince herself that she can give up part of the role that contributes to the definition of her identity (1990, p. 36). Even though consequences may differ according to their educational levels, we nonetheless observe that 49% of BA-level women with several children work fulltime, 35% work part-time, and 11% are inactive, whereas 94% of men in the same situation work fulltime (Couppié & Epiphane, 2007).

Girls are quick to understand that they will be responsible for most domestic tasks when they reach adulthood and have families of their own, and adapt their educational and professional ambitions accordingly. Hence, girls' orientation choices are realistic and rational as they take account of the objective factors of the labor market and division of work within the family (Duru Bellat, 1990, 2004). According to the author, girls tend to plan their educational and professional choices in line with the conditions under which they will be able to use their qualifications when they become adults, and often wives and mothers. For Dubet (2010), it may also be supposed that girls anticipate a domestic and maternal role that leads them "rationally" to make educational and professional choices that differ from those made by boys.

Nonetheless, such anticipated choices of compromise are not necessarily made by all girls in the same way, and are influenced in particular by social origin. Working-class girls are undoubtedly less likely to focus on their futures given their living conditions (Duru-Bellat, 2014; Détrez, 2015). Middle- and upper-class girls, well endowed with cultural capital, probably spend little time anticipating their future family roles as they often have parental models in which division of domestic and family tasks is relatively egalitarian (Court, Bertrand, Bois, Henri-Panabière, & Vanhée, 2013). The authors also hypothesize that educationally and socially advantaged girls do not make their higher educational choices in anticipation of their future family and domestic responsibilities.

Because of their academic success, girls have turned to professions little exercised by the female sex 30 years ago, including medicine, the law, and journalism. Nonetheless, women do not occupy the same positions, have the same specialties, or even have the same status as men (Maruani, 2011). In addition, young women's employment conditions are not as good as those enjoyed by men with equivalent qualifications. Qualified women entering the labor market are less well paid than their male counterparts, are less often recruited under permanent or fulltime contracts than men, and are less likely to hold positions in management or intermediate professions (Mainguené & Martinelli, 2010).[8]

12. Discussions and Conclusion

Research on the feminization of higher education often tends to focus on the social relations of sex based on male domination in the family, school, the job market, etc. (Blöss, 2001; Gaussel, 2016; Maruani & Méron, 2012; Mosconi, 2004; Olivier, 2018; Rouyer et al., 2015; Mosconi & Stevanovic, 2007; Vouillot, 2011). However, these analyses do not often show how, despite the existence of social relations of sex, girls have been able to improve, for more than half a century, their presence in higher education and higher professions which they rarely attended or not before. The most recent studies have explored new themes which are interested at the same time in the contextual, personal, and subjective characteristics by approaching the diversity of the situations concerning as well the individuals as the social and educational structures. For example, the feminization of higher education can be analyzed by taking into account the specific dynamics of women and their individual and collective awareness of the challenges of education and knowledge in order to assert their place in society. Similarly, we can question the reciprocal interactions between the feminization of society as a global process and the feminization of higher education.

A girl in school or university, even if she is dominated, mobilizes, acts on and in the world, according to the meaning she attributes to going to school and learning. Learning at school or university thus refers to the learning trajectory and the history of an active, temporal learner, to his/her desires and projects. In the learning trajectory, there is always a subject, therefore a form of consciousness which participates in giving sense to the act of learning (Charlot, 1997; Paivandi, 2015). Choosing a field of study, developing an intellectual or professional project, living the moment of university and learning constitute an experience lived by a learner who has a subjectivity. Learning sometimes involves going beyond of inherited representations and mobilizing to learn otherwise (Paivandi, 2015). Women and girls seem to have understood the power of emancipation that higher education has represented since the 1960s. Social structures have not changed without the active participation and awareness of girls at school or university. There is a dialectical relationship between social structures, social processes, and individuals. The question then arises as to how young girls have taken over the education system in order to improve their presence in different fields.

---

[8]It is certainly true that women have gradually been taking over positions of responsibility. They currently account for 48% of companies' senior administrators and 44% of civil service executives (Nahapétian & Pech, 2011), but according to Maruani (2011, p. 39), "*the likelihood of their being assigned such positions is still undoubtedly lower than it is for men.*" In addition, women are always limited by the glass ceiling: in the private sector, 20% of company directors are women, and only 16% of senior civil service executives are female (Nahapétian & Pech, 2011). Finally, jobs occupied by women, even the most qualified among them, are still less diversified than is the case for men.

A historical interpretation of women's place in higher education in France is necessary if we are to understand how a division of functions between men and women developed from the nineteenth century onward, leading to women's marginalization in various branches of higher education, science and technology. Over the last three or four decades, a new dynamic has emerged resulting in reduction of inequalities between the two sexes in numerous fields of study. Statistical data and the results of much research work on gender and education tend to show that the differences between the two sexes are not set in stone. Over the course of the last century, there were spectacular developments in girls' education, characterized in particular by their increasingly wide access to higher education and eventually to professions from which they were previously excluded, such as medicine, engineering, and the law (Buscatto & Marry, 2009; Hardy-Dubernet, 2005; Marry, 2004; Schweitzer, 2009). These feminization processes are reducing the tendency to associate this or that sector permanently with one or the other sex, leading rather to the adoption of a dynamic perspective in the study of changes in what is on offer and in girls' and boys' orientation choices and/or disaffection in each field of study (Blanchard et al., 2016), as well as the ways in which the differences between the sexes are being reworked in fields that were previously more mixed – via specialization choices, for example (Jaisson, 2002; Lapeyre & Le Feuvre, 2009).

The research work carried out tends to confirm how the family, the media, the social environment as a whole, and consequently school and the labor market contribute to the construction and reproduction or evolution of gender norms and roles, as they are themselves permeated and shaped by a separation of roles and skills according to biological gender. Taking the question of gender into account has led to a re-examination of the data resulting from various studies on young people's education. Such data show that just because girls and boys sit next to each other in class, this does not mean that they are expected to behave in the same way or achieve the same results. Coeducation does not systematically mean equality of treatment. Classroom reality is nothing more or less than a reflection of what happens in the great majority of families: an education, whether knowingly gendered or not, centered on the social roles of gender (Fumat, 2010). It was the emergence of coeducation that began to make people aware of the influence of the gender stereotypes that are initially developed in families and then reinforced or even accentuated at school and in society as a whole (Duru Bellat, 2010).

Girls' inroads into various branches of higher education seem to be explained by numerous factors connected with the social and family environment. A feminine dynamic in a given branch of studies does not systematically originate in girls' having better results but is sometimes due to lower male enrollments. Boys are turning away from some branches and choosing others in their stead, leading to "*a 'new' form of sexual division of professions, a reflection of a division of work that has been revamped in the higher social categories*" (Hardy-Dubernet, 2005, p. 36). Lemaire's research (2005) sheds a different light on gendered perceptions of the advantageousness of given study pathways: "comparison of the 'profitability' of medical studies in relation to that of other branches in higher education and the *grandes écoles*, which correspond more to a 'canonical' model of success, tends to lessen boys' attraction to the medical branch" (Lemaire, 2005, p. 145).

Quantitative changes in the labor market clearly show that representations of what qualities are required to become a judge, lawyer, doctor or vet, etc., have evolved to some extent. One might be led to think that as girls are still socialized to become experts in relations with others, benevolence and provision of care, they tend to choose higher education pathways and professions that require such qualities. In addition, reconciliation of family and professional life seems easier in certain professions: for example, among judges and lawyers who choose specific activity sectors, or doctors and vets who manage to adapt their professional practices to the different facets of their lives without affecting their careers. Finally, girls' strong desire to engage in work that is useful to society (Fontanini, 2015; Lemaire, 2005) is satisfied in many recently feminized professions, such as dispensing justice or provision of healthcare.

Sociological interpretation of the evolutions observed in the feminization of higher education in France has enabled identification of several dynamics and movements, in universities, families, society, and the economy as well as in women's and men's mentalities. The relationship between the labor market and girls' higher education choices has operated in dialectical fashion: the dynamic of feminization of student numbers in branches previously regarded as male has led to increased female presence in specialized fields and reduction of disparities between the two sexes on the labor market. This evolution has itself contributed to a change in professional projections through reconfiguration of professional images and perception and the gendered character of certain sectors and society's mindset. This is a recursive phenomenon characterized by the confluence of several movements and dynamics that have contributed reciprocally to the acceleration of higher education's feminization. It is very difficult to make an artificial separation of the role and influence of social, individual, family, and economic factors that interact and produce unprecedented effects.

The progress that girls have made so far does not mean the end of psychological and cultural inhibitions and obstacles for all girls and all sectors. The existence of glass ceilings that hinder women's careers (Dubet, 2010) shows that school, family, the professional world, and the media, whether consciously or thoughtlessly, help keep certain sexist stereotypes alive. The idea that choices of educational and professional orientation are simply a matter of taste or of natural aptitudes for such and such a subject or skill is still firmly anchored in public opinion. It is reinforced by the media, which regularly disseminates discourse "biologizing" human behaviors. This is why girls' and boys' educational and professional orientations are seldom seen as inequalities and even less as discrimination on the part of pupils, actors in education, and families (Vouillot, 2011). What are the consequences of girls' and boys' educational and professional orientations? Is it really possible to say that the progress made by girls over the last three or four decades has made any significant difference in the nature of inequalities between the sexes? French research provides a nuanced and critical analysis. Without denying the major progress made and the consequent transformation in the relations between gender and knowledge, a number of authors have tried to identify less visible forms of inequalities between women and men that have developed within the education system. Mosconi (1994, 2010) tried to identify the connection between knowledge and power and its evolution in the light of female progress into various sectors. For the author, there is greater feminization in fields where there has been a loss of power or which lead to midrange positions in the hierarchy of functions, while men maintain their dominance in the scientific and technological sphere. According to Mosconi (1994), gendered division has not been done away with but simply modernized. Gendered division of postsecondary orientation is evolving and changing, but remains a societal challenge that cannot be put down to the education system alone.

References

Alaluf, M., Imatouchan, N., Marage, P., Pahaut, S., Sanvura, R., Valkeneers, A., & Vanheerswynghels, A. (2003). *Les filles face aux études scientifiques. Réussite scolaire et inégalités d'orientation* [*Girls face scientific studies. Academic success and inequalities in orientation*]. Bruxelles: Université de Bruxelles.

Attali, J. (1998). Pour un modèle européen d'enseignement supérieur [For a European model of higher education]. Rapport au ministre de l'Education nationale, de la recherche et de la technologie. Paris: Stock.

Ayral, S. (2011). La fabrique des garçons. Sanctions et genre au collège [Make boys. Sanctions and gender in college]. Paris: PUF.

Ayral, S. & Raibaud, Y. (Ed.). (2014). *Pour en finir avec la fabrique des garçons. Tome 1: À l'école* [To put an end to the boys' make. *Volume 1*: At school]. Pessac: Maison des sciences de l'Homme d'Aquitaine.

Baudelot, C. & Establet, R. (1992). *Allez les filles!* [*Go Grils*]. Paris: Seuil.

Bem, L. S. (1974). The measurement of psychological androgyny. *Journal of Consulting and Clinical Psychology*, *42*, 155–162.

Bisseret, (1974). *Les inégaux ou la sélection universitaire* [*Les inégaux ou la sélection universitaire*]. Paris: PUF.

Blanchard, M. (2009). S'orienter en écoles de commerce: goût de l'utile ou choix du raisonnable ? [Orientation to business schools: taste for the useful or choice of the reasonable]. *SociologieS, Premiers textes*, https://journals.openedition.org/sociologies/4077, consulté le 20/8/19.

Blanchard, M., Orange, S., & Pierrel, A. (2016). *Filles + sciences = une équation insoluble ? Enquête sur les classes préparatoires scientifiques.* [*Girls + science = an unsolvable equation? Survey on scientific preparatory classes*]. Paris: Éditions Rue d'Ulm.

Blöss, T. (2001). Introduction. Une égalité entre les sexes toujours incertaine [Introduction. Gender equality still uncertain]. In T. Blöss (Ed.), *La dialectique des rapports hommes – femmes*. Paris: PUF.

Bouchareu, M. (2012). Interpellations à l'égalité et voix du care. De l'objectivation de la situation scolaire des filles vers des propositions alternatives [Calls for equality and the voice of care. From the objectification of the school situation of girls to alternative proposals]. *Mémoire de master 2 en sociologie*, Paris 8 Vincennes Saint Denis.

Bourdieu, P., & Passeron, J.-C. (1964). *Les héritiers. Les étudiants et la culture* [*The Inheritors. Students and culture*]. Paris: Les Éditions de Minuit.

Breda, T., Grenet, J., Monnet, M., & Van Effenterre, C. (2018). Do Female Role Models Reduce the Gender Gap inScience? Evidence from French High Schools. Ecole d'Economie de Paris (Working Paper), halshs-01713068. Retrieved from https://halshs.archives-ouvertes.fr/halshs-01713068v3

Bricard I. (1985). *Saintes ou pouliches. L'éducation des jeunes filles au XIXe siècle* [*Saintes or fillies. The education of young girls in the 19th century*]. Paris: Albin Michel.

Buscatto, M., & Marry, C. (2009). Le plafond de verre dans tous ses éclats. La féminisation des professions supérieures au XXe siècle The glass ceiling in all its shards. The feminization of higher professions in the 20th century]. *Sociologie du travail*, *2*(51), 170–182.

Cachelou, J. (1984). De Marie Curie aux ingénieurs de l'an 2000 [From Marie Curie to the engineers of 2000]. *Culture technique*, *12*, 264–271.

Caille, J. P., Lemaire, S., & Vrolant, M. C. (2002). *Filles et garçons face à l'orientation* [*Girls and boys and the challenge of orientation*]. Note d'information 02–12. Paris: MEN.

Caille, J. P. & O'Prey, S. (2005, September). Estime de soi et réussite scolaire sept ans après l'entrée en sixième [Self-esteem and academic success seven years after entering in High School]. *Education & formations*, *72*, 25–52.

Chapon V. (2014). La sanction comme outil de construction des stéréotypes socio-sexués dans les établissements secondaires des classes dominantes [The sanction as a tool for constructing socio-gender stereotypes in secondary schools of the dominant classes]. In S. Ayral & Y. Raibaud (Eds.), *Pour en finir avec la fabrique des garçons*. Pessac: Maison des sciences de l'Homme d'Aquitaine.

Charlot, B. (1997). *Du rapport au savoir. Eléments pour une théorie* [*From the relationship to knowledge. Elements for a theory*]. Paris: Anthropos.

Chevaillier, T., Landrier, S., & Nakhili, N. (2009). *Du secondaire au supérieur: continuités et ruptures dans les conditions de vie des jeunes* [*From secondary to higher education: continuities and breaks in the living conditions of young people*]. Paris: La documentation française, collection « Panorama des savoirs ».

Chiland, C. (2003). *Le transsexualisme* [*Transsexualism*]. Paris: PUF.

Collet, I. (2011). Effet de genre: le paradoxe des études d'informatique [Gender effect: the paradox of computer science studies]. *TIC & société*, *5*(1), 11–34.

Collet, I. (2012). Faux-semblants et débats autour du genre et de l'égalité en éducation et formation [Pretenses and debates around gender and equality in education]. *Recherche et formation*, *70*, 121–134.

Couppié, T., & Epiphane, D. (2007). Vivre en couple et être parent: impact sur les débuts de carrière [Living as a couple and being a parent: impact on early career]. *Bref CEREQ*, *n° 241*, 1–4.

Court, M., Bertrand, J., Bois, G., Henri-Panabière, G., & Vanhée, O. (2013). L'orientation scolaire et professionnelle des filles: « des choix de compromis » ? Une enquête auprès de jeunes femmes issues de familles nombreuses [Educational and vocational orientation for girls: "compromise choices"? A survey of young women from large families]. *Revue française de pédagogie*, *184*, 29–40.

Courtheau, R. (2014). *Rapport d'information sur les stéréotypes masculins et féminins dans les manuels scolaires* [*Information report on male and female stereotypes in textbooks*], 645, Retrieved from https://www.senat.fr/rap/r13-645/r13-6451.pdf

Crosemarie, P. (2009). *1968–2008: évolution et prospective de la situation des femmes dans la société française [evolution and prospective of the situation of women in French society]. Conseil économique, social et environnemental.* Paris: Journaux officiels, mars.

Dafflon Novelle, A. (2006). D'avant à maintenant, du bébé à l'adulte: synthèse et implications de la socialisation différenciée des filles et des garçons [From before to now, from infants to adults: synthesis and implications of the differentiated socialization of girls and boys]. In A. Dafflon Novelle, *Filles-garçons: socialisation différenciée?* (pp. 361–391). Grenoble: PUG.

Dafflon Novelle, A. (2010). Pourquoi les garçons n'aiment pas le rose? Pourquoi les filles préfèrent Barbie à Batman ? [Why don't boys like pink? Why do girls prefer Barbie to Batman?] In V. Rouyer, S. Croity-Belz, & Y. Prêteur (Eds.), *Genre et socialisation de l'enfance à l'adulte* (pp. 25–40). Toulouse: Eres.

Dauphin, S. (2010). *L'Etat et les droits des femmes. Des institutions au service de l'égalité?* [*The state and women's rights. Institutions at the service of equality?*]. Rennes: PUR.

De Boissieu, C. (2009). Sexes et genres à l'école maternelle. Un essai de modélisation du concept de « genre scolaire » [Sex and gender in preschool. An attempt to model the concept of "school gender"]. *Recherches & Educations, n° 2*, 23–43.

Depoilly, S. (2014). *Filles et garçons au lycée pro. Rapport à l'école et rapport de genre* [*Girls and boys in vocational high school. Relationship to school and gender relationship*]. Rennes: Presses universitaires de Rennes.

DEPP-RERS. (2012, 2019). *Repères et références statistiques sur les enseignements, la formation et la recherche* [Benchmarks and statistical references on education and research]. *Ministère de l'Education nationale, de l'Enseignement supérieur et de la Recherche, Direction de l'évaluation, de la prospective et de la performance.*

Détrez, C. (2015). *Quel genre?* [*What gender?*]. Paris: Éditions Thierry Magnier.

Détrez, C., & Piluso, C. (2014). La culture scientifique, une culture au masculin? [Scientific culture, a male culture?] In S. Octobre (Ed.), *Questions de genre, questions de culture* (pp. 27–51). Paris: Ministère de la Culture-DEPS.

Dubet, F. (2010). *Les places et les chances. Repenser la justice sociale. Places and chances* [*Rethinking social justice. Places and chances*]. Paris: Seuil.

Duru Bellat, M. (1990 & 2004 rééd.). *L'école des filles – Quelle formation pour quels rôles sociaux ?* Paris: L'Harmattan.

Duru Bellat, M. (1995). Filles et garçons à l'école, approches sociologiques et psychosociales [Girls and boys at school, sociological and psychosocial approaches]. *Revue Française de Pédagogie, 110*, 75–109.

Duru Bellat, M. (2010). Ce que la mixité fait aux élèves [What gender mix education does to students]. *Revue de l'OFCE, 3*(114), 197–212.

Duru-Bellat, M. (2014). *Garçons et filles à l'école de la différence [Boys and girls at the school of difference]*. Paris: La Découverte.

Duru-Bellat, M. (2016). À l'école du genre [At gender school]. *Enfances & Psy, 69*, 90–100.

Ecklund, H. E., Lincoln, A. E., Tansey, C. (2012). Gender segregation in elite academic science [Gender segregation in elite academic science]. *Gender and Society, 26*(5), 693–717.

Epiphane, D. (2016). Les femmes dans les filières et les métiers "masculins": des paroles et des actes [Women in "male" sectors and professions: words and deeds]. *Travail, genre et sociétés, 36*, 161–166.

Ferrand, M., Imbert, F., & Marry, C. (1996). Femmes et sciences: une équation improbable ? L'exemple des normaliennes scientifiques et des polytechniciennes [Women and science: an improbable equation? The example of normaliennes scientists and polytechnicians]. *Formation Emploi*, *55*, 3–18.

Ferrand, M., Imbert F., & Marry C. (1997). L'excellence scolaire: une affaire de famille [Excellence at school: a family affair]. *CSU-LASMAS, IRESCO/CNRS.*

Fontanini, C. (1999). Les filles face aux classes de mathématiques supérieures et spéciales: Analyse des déterminants des choix d'une filière considérée comme atypique à leur sexe [Girls facing higher and special mathematics classes: Analysis of the choices of a field seen as atypical to their gender]. Thèse de doctorat Sciences de l'Education, Université de Bourgogne.

Fontanini, C. (2015). Les représentations peu sexuées des professions chez des élèves de terminales scientifiques: un pas en avant vers plus de mixité professionnelle ? [Low-gender representations of professions among high school students in the science section: a step towards more professional diversity?] In M. Estripeaut-Bourjac & D. Gay-Sylvestre (Eds.), *Mixité et éducation: pratiques sociales et dimensions culturelles* (pp. 127–137). Limoges: Presses Universitaires de Limoges.

Fumat, Y. (2010). Mixité et égalité dans la famille et à l'école [Gender diversity and equality in the family and at school]. *Tréma*, *32*, 7–20.

Gaussel, M. (2016). L'éducation des filles et des garçons, paradoxes et inégalités [The education of girls and boys, paradoxes and inequalities]. *Dossier de veille de l'IFÉ*, *n° 112*, octobre. Lyon: ENS de Lyon. Retrieved from http://ife.ens-lyon.fr/vst/DA/detailsDossier.php?parent=accueil

Gemego, P., & Wacheux, F. (2017). *Evaluation des actions publiques en faveur de la mixité des métiers* [*Assessment of public actions in favor of the gender diversity of professions*]. Paris: Rapport IGAS & IGAENR.

Girod, R. (1977). *Inégalité, inégalités* [*Inequality, inequalities*]. Paris: PUF.

Gouyon, M. & Guérin, S. (2006). L'implication des parents dans la scolarité des filles et des garçons: des intentions à la pratique [Parents' involvement in the education of girls and boys: from intentions to practice]. *Economie et Statistiques*, 398–399, 59–64.

Grésy, B. & Georges, P. (2012). *Rapport sur l'égalité entre les filles et les garçons dans les modes d'accueil de la petite enfance* [Report on equality between girls and boys in early childhood care arrangements]. Rapport n° RM2012–151P. IGAS.

Hardy-Dubernet, A. C. (2005). Femmes en médecine: vers un nouveau partage des professions ? [Women in medicine: towards a new division of professions?]. *Revue française des Affaires Sociales*, *59*(1), 35–58.

Hazelkorn, E. (2009). Rankings and the battle for world-class excellence: Institutional strategies and policy choicesJanuary. *Journal of Higher Education Policy and Management*, *21*(1), 2–21.

Husén, T. (1991). The idea of the university: Current crisis and future challenges. *Prospects (UNESCO)*, *78*, 169–181.

Huteau, M. (1982). Les mécanismes psychologiques de l'évolution des attitudes et des préférences vis-à-vis des activités professionnelles [The psychological mechanisms of changes in attitudes and preferences vis-à-vis professional activities]. *L'Orientation scolaire et professionnelle*, *2*, 95–111.

Jaisson, M. (2002). La mort aurait-elle mauvais genre? [Does death have the wrong gender?]. *Actes de la recherche en sciences sociales*, *143*, 44–52.

Jarlégan, A. (1999). Les interactions verbales maîtres-élèves en cours de mathématiques [Teacher-student verbal interactions in math class]. In F. Vouillot (Ed.), *Filles et garçons à l'école: une égalité à construire. Autrement Dit, Ministère de l'éducation nationale, de la recherche et de la technologie*, CNDP, *1999*, 75–81.
Kergoat, P. (2014). Le travail, l'école et la production des normes de genre. Filles et garçons en apprentissage (en France) [Work, school and the production of gender norms (in France)]. *Nouvelles Questions Féministes*, *33*(1), 16–34.
Kieffer, A., & Marry, C. (2011). Filles et garçons minoritaires dans leurs filières d'études. Variations et fugues sur les étudiant-e-s transfuges [Minority girls and boys in their studies. Variations and fugues on defector students]. In Galland, O., Verley, E., Vourc'h, R. (Ed.). *Les mondes étudiants. Enquête Conditions de vie 2010* (pp. 27–36). Paris: La Documentation Française.
Landrier, S., & Nakhili, N. (2010). Comment l'orientation contribue aux inégalités de parcours scolaires en France [How orientation contributes to inequalities in educational pathways in France.]. *Formation Emploi*, *109*, 23–36.
Lapeyre, N., & Le Feuvre, N. (2009). Avocats et médecins: féminisation et différenciation sexuée des carrières [Lawyers and doctors: feminization and gender differentiation of careers]. In Demazière, D. & Gadéa, C. (Ed.), *Sociologie des groupes professionnels. Acquis récents et nouveaux défis* (pp. 424–434). Paris: Armand Colin.
Le Laidier, S., & Thomas, F. (2014). Le baccalauréat 2014, session de juin [The 2014 baccalaureate, June session]. *Note d'information*, 29–14, juillet, MENESR.
Lelièvre, C., & Lelièvre, F. (1991). *Histoire de la scolarisation des filles* [*History of girls' education*]. Paris: Nathan.
Lemaire, S. (2005, September). Les premiers bacheliers du panel: aspirations, image de soi et choix d'orientation [The first baccalaureate graduates of the panel: aspirations, self-image and choice of orientation]. *Education et formations*, *72*, 137–153.
Lemaire, S. (2012). Les bacheliers S: des poursuites d'études de plus en plus dispersées [Les bacheliers S: des poursuites d'études de plus en plus dispersées]. *Note d'information*, 12–10, août, MEN.
Lemaire, S. & Leseur, B. (2005). Les bacheliers S: motivations et choix d'orientation après le baccalauréat [The graduates of the scientific section: motivations and choice of orientation after the baccalaureate]. *Note d'information*, 05–15, avril, MEN.
Lemarchant, C. (2017). *Unique en son genre. Filles et garçons atypiques dans les formations techniques et professionnelles* [*Unique in it's genre. Atypical girls and boys in technical and vocational training*]. Paris: Presses universitaires de France.
Leyens, J-P., Yserbyt, V., & Schradon, G. (1996). Stereotypes and social judgeability. In W. Stroebe & M. Hewstone (Eds.), *European Review of Social Psychology* (*Vol. 3*, 91–120). Chichester: Wiley.
Lièvre, A. (2016). Les étudiants en formation d'ingénieur [Engineering students]. *Note d'information*, 16–04, MEN - MENSR.
Mainguené, A., & Martinelli, D. (2010). Femmes et hommes en début de carrière. Les femmes commencent à tirer profit de leur réussite scolaire [Women and men at the start of their career. Women are starting to profit from their academic success]. *INSEE Première*, 1284, février.

Marro, C., & Vouillot, F. (1991). Représentation de soi, représentations du scientifique type et choix d'une orientation scientifique chez des filles et des garçons de 2nde [Self-representation, representations of the typical scientist and choice of a scientific orientation in girls and boys in high school]. *L'Orientation Scolaire et Professionnelle*, *20*(3), 303–323.

Marry C. (2004), *Les femmes ingénieurs, une révolution respectueuse* [Women engineers, a respectful revolution]. Paris: Belin.

Maruani, M. (2011). *Travail et emploi des femmes* [*Women's work and employment*]. Paris: La Découverte, Repères.

Maruani, M. & Méron, M. (2012). *Un siècle de travail des femmes en France 1901–2011* [*A century of women's work in France 1901–2011*]. Paris: La Découverte.

MENESR-DEPP, (2019). *Filles et garçons sur le chemin de l'égalité de l'école à l'enseignement supérieur* [*Filles et garçons sur le chemin de l'égalité de l'école à l'enseignement supérieur*]. Paris: Ministère de l'éducation nationale.

Merrien, F.-X. & Musselin, C. (1999). Are French universities finally emerging? Path dependency phenomena and innovative reforms in France. In D. Braun & F.-X., Merrien (Ed.), *Towards a new model of governance for universities? A comparative view in higher education* (pp. 220–238). London/Philadephia: Jessica Kingsley Publishers.

Mosconi, N. (1989). *La mixité dans l'enseignement secondaire: un faux semblant ?* [*Gender mix education in secondary education: a false pretense?*]. Paris: PUF.

Mosconi, N. (1994). *Femmes et savoir* [*Women and knowledge*]. Paris: L'Harmattan.

Mosconi, N. (2004). Effets et limites de la mixité scolaire [Effects and limits of mixed education]. *Travail, genre et sociétés*, *1*(11), 165–174.

Mosconi, N. (2010). Rapport au savoir et pratiques du travail social [Relation to knowledge and social work practices]. In Olivier A. (Ed.), *Sexe, genre et travail social* (pp. 17–34). Paris: L'Harmattan.

Mosconi, N., & Stevanovic, B. (2007). *Genre et avenir: les représentations des métiers chez les adolescentes et les adolescents* [*Gender and the future: representations of jobs among adolescents*]. Paris: L'Harmattan.

Nahapétian, N., & Pech, T. (2011). Le temps des femmes [Women's time]. *Alternatives économiques, Hors série Poche*, 51.

OCDE. (2012). *Inégalités hommes-femmes* [*Gender inequalities*]. Paris: OCDE.

Olivier, A. (2018). *Étudiants singuliers, hommes pluriels. Orientations et socialisations masculines dans des formations « féminines » de l'enseignement supérieur* [Singular students, plural men. *Male orientation and socialization in "female" fields in higher education]*. Thèse de doctorat (doctoral thesis), Institut d'études politiques de Paris.

Paivandi, S. (2015). *Apprendre à l'université* [*Learning at University*]. Bruxelles: De Boeck.

Paivandi, S. (2018). Where does France stand in world university rankings? In M. Mabossi, K.M. Joshi and S. Paivandi (Eds.), *In Pursuit of World-Class Universities: A Global Experience*. New Delhi: Studera Press.

Passeron, J. C., & De Singly, F. (1984). Différences dans la différence: socialisation de classe et socialisation sexuelle [Differences in the difference: class socialization and gender socialization]. *Revue Française de Science Politique*, *34*(1), 48–78.

Prost, A. (1986). *L'enseignement s'est-il démocratisé ?* [*Has education democratized?*]. Paris: PUF.

Reay, D., David, M. E., & Ball, S. J. (2005). *Degrees of choice, social class, race and gender in higher education*. Sterling, VA: Trentham Books.

Régnier-Loilier, A. (2009). L'arrivée d'un enfant modifie-t-elle la répartition des tâches domestiques au sein du couple ? [Does the arrival of a child change the distribution of domestic tasks within the couple?]. *Population & Société*, *461*, 1–4.

Rosenwald, F. (2006). Filles et garçons dans le système éducatif depuis vingt ans [Filles et garçons dans le système éducatif depuis vingt ans]. *Données sociales – La société française*, 87–94.

Rouyer, V. (2007). *La construction de l'identité sexuée* [*The construction of gender identity*]. Paris: Armand Colin.

Rouyer, V., Mieyaa, Y., & Blanc A. (2015). Socialisation de genre et construction des identités sexuées [Gender socialization and construction of gender identities.]. *Revue française de pédagogie*, *187*, 97–137.

Roy, D. (2012). Le travail domestique: 60 milliards d'heures en 2010 [Domestic work: 60 billion hours in 2010]. *INSEE Première*, *1423*, 1–4.

Salmi, J. (2009). *The challenge of establishing world-class universities*. Washington, DC: The World Bank.

Schweitzer, S. (2009). Du vent dans le ciel de plomb ? L'accès des femmes aux professions supérieures, XIXème–XXème siècles [Wind in the leaden sky? Access of women to higher professions, 19th – 20th centuries]. *Sociologie du travail*, *51*(2), 183–198.

Stevanovic, B. (2006). *La mixité dans les écoles d'ingénieurs* [*Gender diversity in engineering schools*]. Paris: l'Harmattan.

Sutour, N., & Pozzi, R. (1997). Les filles élèves-ingénieurs à l'Ecole Nationale des Ponts et Chaussées: les déterminants d'une orientation sexuellement atypique [Girl engineering students at the Ecole Nationale des Ponts et Chaussées: the determinants of a sexually atypical orientation]. Mémoire de DECOP.

Tanguy, L. (1986). *L'introuvable relation formation emploi: un état des recherches en France* [*The untraceable relationship between education and employment*: research in France]. Paris: la Documentation française.

Thikhonov Sicrist, N. (2009). Les femmes et l'université en France [Women and universities in France]. *Histoire de l'éducation*, *122*, 53–70.

UNESCO. (2016). *Out in the open: education sector responses to violence based on sexual orientation or gender identity/expression: summary report*. Paris: UNESCO.

Veleine, C. (2004). *L'égalité des chances entre les filles et les garçons: la première insertion professionnelle des ingénieurs agronomes* [*Equal opportunities between girls and boys: the first professional integration of agricultural engineers*]. Rapport à la DGER, Ministère de l'agriculture, de l'alimentation, de la pêche et de la ruralité, décembre.

Vouillot, F. (2007). L'orientation aux prises avec le genre [Orientation grappling with gender]. *Travail, genre et sociétés*, *18*, 87–108.

Vouillot, F. (2011). *Orientation scolaire et discrimination. Quand les différences de sexe masquent les inégalités*. Paris: La Documentation Française.

Weinberger, C. J. (1998). Race and Gender Wage Gaps in the Market for Recent College Graduates. *Industrial Relations*, *37*, 67–84.

Chapter 4

Gender and Higher Education: The Greek Case

Georgios Stamelos and Georgia Eleni Lempesi

1. Introduction

The objective of this text is to present and analyze the Greek case concerning women's participation in the higher education and in the labor market. First, it will attempt a brief historical presentation of women participation in the education system and specifically in higher education. We will insist on the latest data to analyze the actual situation in Greece. After that, we will focus on disparities that exist inside scientific fields and sectors at higher education. In the third part, we will try to link higher education to the labor market and specifically analyze women's participation in the labor market in order to find out imbalances and limitations. In the fourth part of the text, we will present a selection of works that analyze women's participation in higher education and labor market. Furthermore, we will consider the developed relative policies as an interesting point due to the European influences. Subsequently, we will insist more persistently on the European policies transferred to the Greek context. Finally, we have to pinpoint that Greece is one of the most ethnic homogeneous states, so this issue is less important than in other states concerning the question of women's participation. However, someone should keep in mind that migration and refugee flows are intense recently and this dimension is going to be important in the future. In any case, the refugee and migration issue is already here. So, we will give some first data on this issue

1.1 The Feminization of Greek Higher Education: Evolution and the Actual Situation

In general, during the first 100 years of the Greek state, women's education was not excluded but no policies were adopted to enhance it (Lambraki-Paganou, 1995). The first Greek woman was admitted to the university in 1890. According to Champidis and Taratori (2008), despite the increasing number of women entering higher education during the period 1890–1920, the significantly less number of women is considered something normal. The access of women to higher education

International Perspectives on Gender and Higher Education, 57–74

doi:10.1108/978-1-83909-886-420201004

varies by sector. The women's choices back then were Medicine and Philosophy and their second choice were Pharmaceutical School, School of Dentistry, School of Science and Mathematics, Law and Theology. In the twentieth century, with the contribution of the feminist movement, changes begin and women's demand for access to the labor market increases, with the result that women's position at the university is being claimed (Ziogou - Karastergiou, S. & Kelesidou, E., 1997).

The number of women in higher education continued to grow during the 1960s, and in the 1980s, the numerical superiority of male students was overthrown. After the dictatorship (the military regime 1967–1974), the main social demand was "democratization" (of the political system, of society, of the education system, of the labor market, etc). This demand creates a convenient context for highlighting the issue of woman participation. In the case of education, the changing method for access to higher education (national exam) seems to have facilitated the increased access of women to higher education. In the early 1980s, the rise to power of the socialist party for the first time had as a result, on one hand, the development and/or the creation of policies and structures for a more equal treatment of the two genders and, on the other hand, the broadening of the access to higher education. Indeed, in the late 1980s, women exceeded men in the student population (Dalakoura & Ziogou-Karastergiou, 2015; Frosi, Kouimtzi, & Papadimou, 2001). Concerning the attendance of women in the Technological Educational Institutes (TEIs), a balance in the numbers of men and women studying in TEI appears during 1990 (IOBE, 2019).

According to Frantzis (2005), despite the increase in the number of women in higher education, there was a gender shortage in science. The author cites as an example that from 1962 to 1997, women graduates of Polytechnic Schools registered in the Technical Chamber accounted for 20% of the total and mainly worked in public services.

In the years to come, women's education in higher education shows a balance with slight fluctuations, as shown in the Table 4.1 from a survey conducted by the Foundation for Economic and Industrial Research (IOBE, 2019; Fig. 4.1).

The latest data provided by the Hellenic Statistical Authority (ELSTAT) concerning the access to University Institutions refer to the years 2015–2017. There are no particular changes observed in numerical difference between women and men. There is still a predominance of women in the total number of students.

Table 4.1. Students by Gender (2015–2017).

The Two Genders at Greek Higher Education: 2015–2017				
	2015/2016	%	2016/2017	%
Men	192.936	49	198.617	48.5
Women	203.878	51	210.796	51.5
Total	396.814	100	409.413	100

Source: (Hellenic Statistical Authority, https://www.statistics.gr/en/home/).

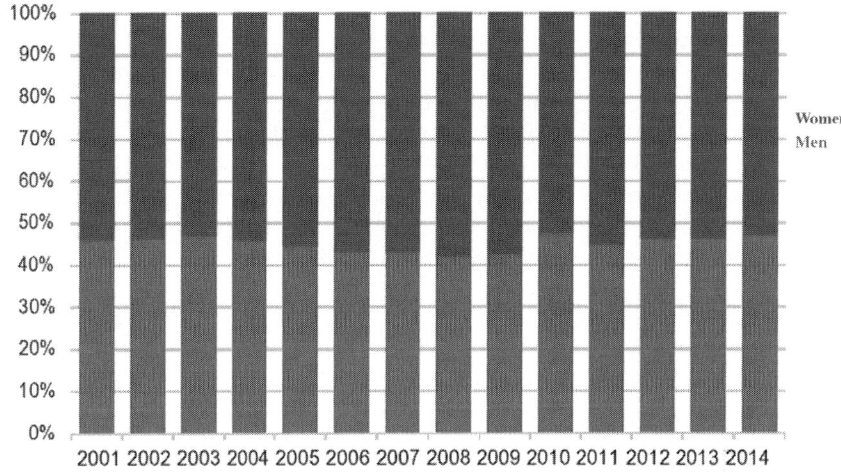

Fig. 4.1. Students by Gender. *Source:* (IOBE, 2019, p. 60).

However, bear in mind that Greek higher education system was binary till late 2018 (University/TEIs). University's Schools were, in the most cases, the first choice for the candidates. This preference constituted as a first internal hierarchical division. A second internal hierarchy was set up with the creation of new regional institutions in different cities of Greek countryside during 1980s, 1990s, and early 2000 or the tertiarization of existing institutions. The oldest institutions that were located to central cities were more attractive than the new ones. Moreover, students' choice was made after the results of the national exams.

1.2 Disparities by Gender and Fields of Study

In the context of the Greek higher education, women seem to obtain, as a general overview, better results than men during the national exams. However, women's choice for programs of studies is different than men's. So, as Monioukas (2011) and Tsikalaki and Kladi-Kokkinou (2016) argue, women are represented at higher rates in universities so in quantitative terms, gender equality in access to and participation in higher education has been achieved or even an imbalance exists against males. However, there are disparities between gender concerning institutions and programs of studies. It seems that men prefer more prestigious studies, or studies which lead to professional fields with social prestige or more dynamic career perspectives, or studies which lead to more promising future salaries. On the other hand, women are choosing fields of study that lead to obtaining a job at the public sector, mainly at social policy domains, such as education and/or health. These are activities that seem to be less intense and competitive, and with this choice, women are able to balance their career with the traditional social role of woman. Furthermore, economic crisis seems to influence gender participation at higher education. Indeed, before the financial crisis (2008), women were 58% of the total student population. Their percentage has degreased to 53% in 2014.

Men's proportion was 42.9% at universities in 2014 (40% in 2008, 39.3% in 2001), 53.6% at TEI (54.6% in 2010 and 52% in 2001), and 80.4% in "other institutions" (82% in 2010 and 85.8% in 2001). A regional dimension seems also to occur. Men are 42.5% at the central universities and 43.3% at the regional ones. At TEI, men were 56.3% at the regional institutions and 47.2% at the central ones (IOBE, 2019).

Specifically, at universities (2014), men are 77.8% at Schools of Informatics and Communication and 63.5% at Schools of Engineering. At TEI (2014), men are 78.1% at Schools of Technological Applications and 73.6% at Schools of Informatics and Communication Applications (73.1%). On the contrary, men are 20.3% at Professions of Health and Welfare (Paramedical Studies) and 30% at Graphic and Artistic Studies (IOBE, 2019).

Gender disparities could also be seen between institutions. For example, men are 66.1% at the Polytechnic of Crete but only 22.6% at School of Fine Arts of Athens. In the TEI's case, the disparities are also considerable. Men are 73.1% at ASPAITE and 72.3% at TEI of Piraeus but only 36.1% at TEI of Athens and 40% at TEI of Epirus (IOBE, 2019).

For a deeper and detailed analysis, we will give interesting example. In the case of health education, gender's participation to Medicine Schools is equitable, but at Athens and Thessaloniki, males are more than females. On the contrary, at the Departments of Nursery, women are the 85% of student population, and at the Departments of Midwifery, they are more than 95% (Stamatopoulou, 2020). Furthermore, Women's participation is similar at the Departments of Preprimary and Primary Education (85%). On the other hand, males are more than 80% at the departments of Mechanical Engineering. At the other hand, in the Departments of University Engineering Schools, males are usually more than females, between 51% and 75% (63.5% as mean).

Two more issues are relevant concerning woman participation at Greek higher education. First, at doctoral level, the new doctors are equal 50%–50% by gender. However, women are 57.8% at Humanities and 35.4% at Engineering and technology (EKT, 2019). Second, as an overall, Greek higher education suffers from students dropping out or prolonging their studies. This problem contains a gender dimension insofar as it concerns men more than women. Indeed, according to a KANEP survey (data of 2012), the distribution of students who delay their studies was 57.7% for men and 42.3% for women. However, it is to be noted that during the period 2002–2012, that percentage for women was increased by 88.1% and for men by 102.5% (KANEP, 2014, p. 217).

1.3 The Links between the Structure of the Labor Market and the Disparities in Access and Persistence in Higher Education According to Gender/Access to Labor Market by Gender and Level of Education

Nowadays, despite the women's progression in the labor market, there are always disparities that persist. For the second trimester of 2018, the Greek labor active population was 1,615,800 women and 2,244,600 men. The economic crisis has greatly affected the participation of young people to the labor market. For example, for ages 30–34, young graduates (ISCED levels 5–8) who find a job (1–3 years after graduation) were 60.8% in 2008 and 59% in 2018. This rate is very low considering that the European average was 85.5% in 2018 (European Commission, 2019). Women were more influenced by the crisis. In addition, woman work more often at a part-time jobs. In many cases, part-time jobs are considered to be the only way for a woman to combine professional and family obligations and duties. Women's work is concentrated in certain areas of professional activities: education, welfare services, and health, as office and service employees, and in tourism and agriculture/forestry/fisheries (Sailer, 2018, p. 15). On the other hand, there are more women graduates than men from higher education in the fields of (a) Education (6.3%–0.9%), Health and Welfare (8.6%–3.3%), Business, Administration, and Law (11%–7.7%), Social Sciences, Journalism and Information (8.3%–4.5%), Humanities, Language, Arts (10.4%–3.3%), and Science, Mathematics, and Computing (4.2%–3.6%) (KANEP, 2019).[1]

As an overview, at the public sector, there are not formal gender inequalities or discriminations during public calls for job offers. However, internal professional development and access to power positions clearly differentiates by gender. This is also obvious even in the field of education, a field propitious for woman's participation. Indeed, women's participation is 95% at preprimary education, 70% at primary, 66% at gymnasium, 55% at lyceum, and 44% at professional lyceum (Elstat, 2014). However, at positions of responsibility situation is pretty different. For example, in a case study from Peloponnese Region, the percentage of principals was 41% women and 59% men (primary education 43%–57%, secondary education 40%–60%). Furthermore, at a higher level, at regional Educational Administration, for 10 positions of responsibility, there was no woman presence (Ntoulas, 2018). Concerning higher education, despite the progression, only 31% of the total professor's population was women (2014). Indeed, this percentage could be interpreted in two opposite ways. Positively, the progression of woman participation to university teacher staff positions is considerable from 1980s to nowadays. For example, at the oldest Greek university, University of Athens, women were the 3% of the teacher staff population in 1963/1964, 5% in 1973/1974, 29.5% in 1983/1984, 35% in 2003/2004, and 38% in 2018 (Lakasas, 2018; Vosniadou & Vaiou, xx). Negatively, significant disparities exist between scientific fields and when considering the hierarchical ranks of faculty members. For example, at Polytechnics and Schools of Science and Technology, the disparity is 82% men and 18% women. Concerning the hierarchical ranks of faculty members, at the position of full professor, women are only 21% (45% at Humanities). Analyzing in depth, in positions of responsibility, the numbers are disappointing, women are at 32% Chairman at a Department, 16% Deans, and 15% Rectors (Moutsidou, 2018).

Concerning the private sector, the situation appears to be different. But in many cases, the situation is not easy to be reflected in the data because of informal

[1]In majority, these graduates are directed at the secondary education, as teachers.

practices undertaken in the private sector. The indicator of the salary difference between genders seems to be a good reference point. According to Eurostat's survey (2015), the salary difference between the two genders was 15%. The main discriminations that women face are (1) lower earnings per hour, (2) fewer hours in paid jobs, and (3) lower employment rates. To be noted, pay gap in Greece is under the European mean (Greece 12.6% and EE-28 countries 16%; 2017, https://ec.europa.eu/info/policies/justice-and-fundamental-rights/gender-equality/equal-pay/gender-pay-gap-situation-eu_en). However, there are considerable differences between sectors. For example, the average equivalent income for managers was 43,811 euros for men and 32,772 for women, in 2014. On the contrary in Clerical support workers, the difference was not so significant (21,134 for women and 21,911 for men; KANEP, 2019).

The analysis shows that women are charged with duties that remain unpaid. An estimate calculates that for a man the unpaid duties are 9 hours per week. On the contrary, for a woman, these duties are 26 hours per week (Ball & Lagemann, 2014).

Another dimension that influences woman participation and gender disparities is the landscape of Greek labor market at the private sector. Indeed, in Greece, small and very small enterprises constitute the 99.7% of Greek entrepreneurship (2019). These enterprises employ the 78.2% of the total private employees. In many cases, these enterprises are families and their needs are specific (less specialization and more general and multifaced skills). In parallel, many times woman participation is informal and shady but crucial (KANEP, 2019).

1.4 A State of Work Knowledge

Gender is an important issue in the specific bibliography. The distance between quantitative and qualitative dimension of woman participation in higher education is a first point to be noticed. Sianou-Kyrgiou (2007) highlights the impact of gender stereotypes on the professional choices of women who maintain the differences between boys and girls when moving to the labor market.

The choice of sector of studies in the third grade of high school contains gender characteristics. For example, girls tend to choose the Theoretical-oriented sector that leads to corresponding university schools, while boys choose the Science-oriented sector. This is also supported by the fact that the majority of girls do not choose to go to TEI (Monioukas, 2011, p. 181).

The evidence presented by Tsikalaki and Kladi-Kokkinou (2016) in their research on students' educational choices for higher education is helpful. Specifically, they report that

> …half of the girls (51.1%) choose the theoretical sector, 26.2% the technological sector and 22.7% the positive sector (science-oriented). Of the boys two thirds 63.6% choose the technological, 24.5% the theoretical and 11.8% the positive sector. That is to say gender stereotypes are still being reproduced.

Similar are their observations of student performance where it appears to be influenced by the gender factor, with girls performing better in their direction lessons.

Sianou-Kyrgiou (2007, p. 123–124) in her study on Higher Education Studies Choices states that differences in Department or School choices

> …show that boys have clearer career aspirations and decide, more often than girls, for the choice of studies with financial criteria, that is to say, to get a good job and earn more money and they have reported higher prospects as more important reasons [...] Girls, by contrast, stated, more often from the boys, that the criterion was their desire to stay in the place of permanent residence or their interest in acquiring knowledge of a particular scientific subject or their desire to pursue a profession of social standing.

Her study concludes that the effect of gender stereotypes is crucial to the choice of studies.

A good educational course for women is not connected to their work and career choices after high school and/or university; therefore the perspective that gender equality issues – especially in education – have been resolved cannot be supported as the gendered profession and career choices are continuing. There is a complex interaction among various factors that may all contribute to gender differences with regard to academic achievement, motivation, and future planning (Clark, Thompson, & Vialle, 2008). The view that gender equality issues – particularly in education – are overcomed cannot be supported as gender and career options continue. According to Spinthourakis, Lempesi, and Papadimitriou (2009),

> …this can be seen in gender segregation in the educational system and the under-representation of women in specific studies such as those related to science and technical subjects as well as the underachievement of boys. The choice of course of study to be followed is reinforced by traditions and stereotypes which influence employment patterns.

Nonetheless, the advantage of better performance in school is lost by girls when they find themselves entering the labor market. Two are the explanations offered. One factor is that girls choose different courses than boys while still in school, which leads to different skills. The second is that even though some women make study choices that are traditionally considered male, their choices when entering the labor market are differentiated mostly in accordance to their role as mothers and spouses.

Another area worth mentioning relates to women in academia and in positions of responsibility. The General Secretariat for Gender Equality (GSGE) has issued a relevant Information Note in 2018, which lists data on the percentage of female faculty members and on women in positions of responsibility in education in

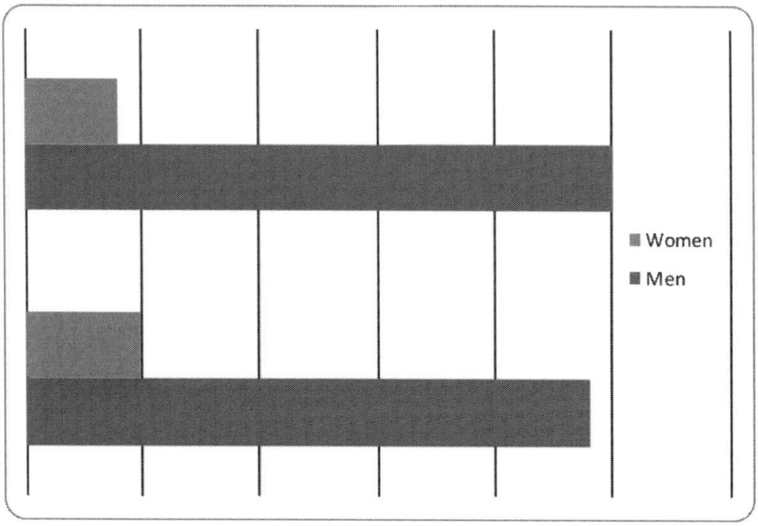

Fig. 4.2. Number of Principals of Offices of Educational Administration (School Year 2017–2018).

general and in the administration of the Ministry of Education. According to that Note, there are still scientific fields and professions that are considered to be predominantly male or female.

Indicatively, according to data for the year 2014–2015, women make up about 2/3 of the teaching staff in public junior high schools. In an area where women make up two-thirds of the teaching staff, their head teacher positions are below 50%. In this percentage, the positions of subprincipals are also calculated. The percentage of women in senior management positions, i.e., in the Offices of Educational Administration, is much lower (18 women in 116 positions). Similarly, underrepresentation of women is also observed in teachers unions (General Secretariat for Gender Equality (GSGE), 2018; Fig. 4.2).

The rates are not particularly different when looking for data concerning higher education. Women are pursuing postgraduate studies, but the situation is changing when we look at the gender of teaching and research staff in higher education and related scientific fields. According to Anagnostou and Avlova (2019, p. 5), the situation of women in research and academia in Greece it is within the EU average or below.

> Data generated in an important study by Nancy Papalexandris shows that in 2016, women were 31% of all faculty members in Greek universities, up from 27% in 2003, and their presence is significantly higher in the humanities and in the arts (40%–45%), moderate in social and economic sciences (28%), and small in computers and engineering (18%). The "glass ceiling" is well

> entrenched here too. While women make up 43% of lecturers (this rank was abolished in 2013?) and 37% of assistant professors, their presence sharply diminishes as they advance in the rank of full professors, only 21% of whom are women. Limited is the presence of women in decision-making positions in Greek universities, where they make up only 15% of university rectors, and 23% of heads of departments (with large variation across disciplines, 34% in Department Heads in Humanities, but only 7% of Department Heads in Engineering and Computer Science).

When looking for the reason behind these percentages, the explanation offered has to do with the lack of awareness concerning gender inequality issues and gender mainstreaming in public research institutes in Greece and also with factors such as "*family responsibilities, and the prevalence of networks of male scientists especially in decision-making and institutional structures, constrain women researchers from reaching high-rank positions.*" (Anagnostou & Avlova, 2019, p. 5).

The Muslim Minority of Western Thrace is the only minority which is officially recognized by the Greek state. It is estimated that their population is from 80,000 to 100,000. The Muslim Minority consists of three distinct groups of population. Half are of Turkish origin or Turkish-speaking, 35 percent are Pomacs, speaking Pomac, while the remaining 15% are Roma, speaking Romani. According to Spithourakis et al. (2008), the Muslim minority in Thrace has generally been isolated and economically depressed for decades. Teaching in minority schools is carried out in the Greek and Turkish language. These schools function on the basis of the Lausanne Convention (1823) and according to the Greek–Turkish Protocols. The educational needs of the Muslim population are covered by Minority general schools. The overall schooling of the Muslim Minority was problematic. Since 1997, an educational project called "Education of Muslim children" has been implemented in the territory of Thrace since 1997, aiming to improve the educational status of the Muslim minority. The implementation of this specialized program has produced significant results. Now, more than 70% of children of the Muslim Minority complete the compulsory education and more of its representatives participate in the national exams in order to get accepted in the university (Askouni & Stamelos, 2004). Indeed, there is a legal provision, since 1996, of a positive action for the minority students who finish their secondary education. A percentage of 0.5% the total students can be students from the Muslim minority, who are accepted in higher education following a special ranking (Askouni, 2006; Karafyllis, xx). As far as the female presence is concerned, traditionally there has been a problem even with the completion of primary education to the extent that girls withdraw from the social life at the age of 11–12. However, since the late 2000s, the girls from the minority that complete the compulsory education are more than boys and are usually better students (Askouni & Stamelos, 2004). That characteristic results to more girls being accepted into the university. This is a significant development as far as the core cultural stereotypes of the minority are concerned.

On the other hand, on the issue of immigration, the latest data show that migrant students (who were born abroad and live in Greece) drop out of school 4.5 times more than students born in Greece. According to data from 2018, students born in Greece who drop out of education (18–24 years old) were 3.9%, while those born abroad 17.9%. Of course, a major improvement has been made in the period 2009–2018 to 43.8%. But much remains to be done. Concerning the completion of higher education of the ages of "30–34," again a large difference seems to be formed against young people who were not born in Greece. For those born in Greece, the graduation rate is 48.1%, while for those not born in Greece only 15.1%. The percentages 10 years ago were 29.7% and 10.3%, respectively (European Commission, 2019).

2. Public Policies in Favor of Gender Balance in Higher Education and the Possible Effects of Measures in Favor of Greater Parity

For Greece, and in particular for the Greek state, dealing with these issues has not been an easy task insofar as Greece was not a segregate state but in the same time it did not support actively women's participation. So, tradition remained strong. It was rather the integration of European Union (1981) that has pushed Greece to start to get involved into this issue. Indeed, European policies on gender equality have their origin in 1957 under Article 119 of the Treaty of Rome. Since then, different approaches to the design and implementation have been followed. There are three key approaches: "equal treatment of men and women" (equal treatment perspective), the consideration of women as a "disadvantaged group" (women's perspective/specific action), and "gender perspective/gender mainstreaming in all policies" (gender perspective/gender mainstreaming; Booth & Bennet, 2002). These specific perspectives are complementary (Daly, 2005) and use different tools for the implementation of policy, such as legislation, positive actions, and gender mainstreaming strategy.

EU and the national governments of Member States have adopted gender mainstreaming policies since middle 1990's. According to the Council of Europe (1998), the term gender mainstreaming is defined as follows:

> Gender mainstreaming is the (re)organisation, improvement, development and evaluation of policy processes, so that a gender equality perspective is incorporated in all policies at all levels and at all stages, by the actors normally involved in policy making.

As the beginning of gender policies in Greece, we can consider 1975 constitution, in which for the first time equality between men and women was established. In article 4 par. 2 of the Constitution, it is stated that "Greek man and Greek women have the same rights and obligations". Developments that have emerged since 1980 in the field of gender policies are due both to women's organizations, which have been strongly politicized and have acted as important pressure-makers, as well as to Greece's entrance to the European Union (Papadiamadaki & Riga, 2003). Another example of the European Union's role in promoting gender policies, whether successful or not, is the setting up of bodies such as the GSGE and KETHI (Research Center for Equality Issues) in 1985 and 1989, respectively.

Since 1996 onward, the European Union adopted the so-called Dual Approach, namely that the gender mainstreaming into all policies and the parallel implementation of specific actions for women, recognizing the gender policy as a field of horizontal action. Member States were invited, following guidelines, to develop policies to achieve the objectives of the Union (Lempesi, 2012).

Within the framework of the third CSF, gender mainstreaming has been a horizontal principle and obligation of the Member States in the design and implementation of Operational Programs, for the period (2000–2006) (EYSEKT, 2003; Papayannopoulou et al., 2008; GSGE, 2004). Specifically for Greece, it is mentioned as a strategic objective, in addition to reducing long-term unemployment for women, to increase the female employment rate to 50%, to reach the corresponding European average (EYSEKT, 2003; Papayannopoulou et al., 2008). In this context, the country is committed to designing and implementing integrated programs for women in all policy areas (education, employment, welfare, entrepreneurship, research, technology), which, as Stratigaki (2006, p. 290) comments, are directly linked or indirectly with the labor market. Greek Governments following EU Guidelines designed action plans on gender equality. Specifically two, the "National Action Plan for Equality (2001–2006)" implemented until the change of government in 2004 and the "National Policy Priorities and Gender Equality Actions (2004–2008)."

This shift toward actions related to improving the position of women in the labor market is considered to be the result of the impact of the European Social Fund objectives on the whole of the third CSF (EYSEKT, 2003). To this end, a rate of 11.8% of the total funding of the European Social Fund has been set aside to be invested exclusively in programs aimed at equality policies for men and women (EYSEKT, 2003; Papayannopoulou et al., 2008).

The area of education, in the context of European and Greek gender policy, is related to training women to be integrated into the labor market, to combat stereotypes and girls' professional orientation in order to combat gender segregation at work. To this end, specific programs on stereotyped concepts with particular emphasis on primary and secondary education, textbooks, and school career guidance were organized. The Ministry of Education was motivated by this adjustment in order to include in EPEAEK II (Operational Programme for Education and Initial Vocational Training) the Priority Axis 4 "Improving the Access of Women in Labour Market", which included program for training teachers on issues related to gender, vocational training for women, and education in general (Deligianni-Kouimtzi & Ziogou-Karastergiou, 2007). The actions for women and the whole EPEAEK were transpired by the direct link between education and labor market (Lempesi, 2012). Axis 4 consists of two distinct measures (EPEAEK, 2007), specifically:

Measure 4.1: Support programs for women initial vocational training and education.

Action 4.1.1: Initial vocational training and support programs for women.

Measure 4.2: Support programs for women in pregraduate and postgraduate studies. Curricula and research programs for women.

Action 4.2.1: Undergraduate, Postgraduate, and Research programs targeted at women. Support for women's research action.

Some of the actions that were indirectly related to higher education and were incorporated in Measure 4.1 were

- Programs related to teacher awareness. One of the objectives was to promote the perspective of gender equality in education, as part of its connection with the labor market, by exploring the content of male and female identities in adolescence and applying intervention methods throughout the education system.
- Actions related to Counseling and Vocational Orientation Programs aiming at changing study and career choices as boys and girls move from school to university and into the labor market.

In addition to the above actions, there have been several actions concerning the enrichment of the libraries of educational units such as IEK and EPAL with books on gender equality. In general, the purpose of this Measure (4.1) was to make the benefits multiply over time so they impact higher education.

As for Measure 4.2 (Support programs for women in pregraduate and postgraduate studies. Curricula and research programs for women.), it was in direct relation to higher education. Among others measure 4.2 includes the following:

- Establishment of undergraduate and postgraduate programs in gender and equality. The main objective of the measure was to promote Women's Studies and thereby promote the principle of equality in higher education.
- Scholarships for research on gender equality issues. Support to research teams of AEI and TEI which focus their research on gender issues.

The actions described above were assessed through the European research program EQUAPOL, "Public gender equality policies." The EQUAPOL European research program aimed at exploring gender equality policies in eight European countries. Between these countries, Greece also took part in the program. Within the framework of the program, the results of gender mainstreaming were evaluated in the design and implementation of all public policies in the country, including education. The research covered the period from 2000 to 2006 (Stratigaki, 2008).

Stratigaki (2008, pp. 340–346), who undertook the EQUAPOL study on the design and implementation of EPEAEK II, cites a number of factors that have negatively affected the successful implementation of Measure 4.1, which related to secondary education: organizational disadvantages, lack of know-how, lack of willingness from the Ministry to acquire the expertise needed, corporative and client-side demands of teachers, bureaucratic problems due to the collaboration of different institutions, for example, between the Ministry of Education, GSGE, and the Research Center for Gender Equality (KETHI), etc.

She also states that the implementation of the measure varied depending on the teachers who undertook it. This is also supported by the qualitative study of Lempesi (2017) conducted in three prefectures of the country. Moreover, the teachers who participated in this research and had implemented EPEAEK II programs had not used the curriculum material in any subsequent program or action at school afterward. So their engagement to activities connected to gender equality ended with the end of the EPEAEK II program in 2008.

Similar bureaucratic and organizational problems and obstacles are described in the EQUAPOL research in relation to the implementation of Measure 4.2 for the development of gender studies in AEIs and TEIs. The most important problem was the inability to create new faculty positions on gender related subjects. This inability resulted in the new courses being taken up by part-time teachers whose contracts were not renewed after the program ended and therefore the subjects were not repeated (Stratigaki, 2008).

Stratigaki (2008, pp. 340–342) states that, the policies were largely designed by people who "perceived the policies for women as highly feminist measures and treated them with caution." In general, gender mainstreaming remained only in announcements and did not have meaningful content. Stratigaki characterizes EPEAEK II as a "missed opportunity" for gender policies at all levels of education.

The next gender equality policy programming text is the "National Program for Gender Equality 2010–2013," which lists proposals and programs on equality from the GSGE for three years. This program was followed until 2015. It is worth noting that after the multitude of gender equality educational programs funded through the CSF and joined EPEAEK II, the lack of references in the field of education is noticeable (Lempesi, 2019).

The most recent policy text is the National Action Plan on Gender Equality 2016–2020, in which actions are revived in a way that can be beneficial to both men and women. An important reference in relation to education is the recognition that

> …the interconnection of Gender Equality and Education remains an open question, in spite of the fact that gender inequalities are mitigated, gendered discrimination and stereotyped choices are produced, reproduced and socially assimilated in public and private life. The current gendered dichotomous recruitment and the resulting divisions and inequalities are identified, reflected and reflected in the field of education throughout the entire educational process. (GSGE, 2017, p. 71)

In order to search for information on gender education policies that have been implemented in recent years, texts and press releases of the General Secretariat for Gender Equality have been explored. Three reports were identified for the period 2016 to 2018:

- The 44 actions of the GSGE for Education in the 2016–2017 school year (GSGE, 2018a)

- The 67 actions of the GSGE for Education in the 2017–2018 school year (GSGE, 2018b)
- The 87 actions of the GSGE in Education in 2018 (GSGE, 2018c).

These texts are more references to many actions that can be described as isolated and fragmentary. For example, public awareness campaigns, workshops, student competitions related to gender equality themes in kindergarten, primary, and secondary schools, activities undertaken by the Library of Gender Equality, school visits to the General Secretariat, actions for enhancing the cooperation of GSGE with other bodies and actors, and the update of those actors in gender equality issues. There is no description of any national action plan that has the characteristics of a program such as those of previous years designed and implemented in the context of EPEAEK II. Nonetheless, these actions belong and derive from the National Action Plan on Gender Equality 2016–2020. Taking into consideration the abovementioned documents and the press releases, we can distinguish two actions:

- "Gender mainstreaming in administrative documents", which includes the publishing of a Guide for the use of nonsexist language in administrative documents.
- "Establishing Gender Equality Committees in Universities."

This last action has to do with women in academia and research. Academia is a sector in which little has been done to promote gender equality and to implement gender mainstreaming actions. Gender mainstreaming in higher education has not been on the agenda of Greek governments. Also it can be characterized as a low-priority policy target and in the national plans for equality designed and undertaken by the GSGE. In recent years, in an effort to align with European policies, national organizations, like the National Documentation Center, seek to promote EU policy developments in gender equality in academia. Gender mainstreaming is also mentioned in the *Greek Strategy for the European Research Area (ERA) – National Roadmap, 2016–2020* as a policy priority together with relevant EU tools and principles. It has to be noted that the National Roadmap is mostly a list of intention and not of actually implemented policies.

Anagnostou and Avlova (2019) comment on the Law 4386/2016 on "Regulations on research and other provisions." This law recognizes the need to achieve greater gender balance in the composition of evaluation and selection committees and of various advisory bodies in the field of research, technology, and innovation. It also establishes a quota, according to which at least one-third of the members of these advisory bodies and of the scientific councils of research institutes must be from one sex, "as long as the candidates have the necessary qualifications as required by each position" (Law 4386/2016, Art. 25 in Anagnostou and Avlova (2019). There are no data available that can provide us with information of whether these provisions have been incorporated in research organizations or in higher education institutions until now.

3. Conclusion

Greece never had an active policy for women's participation to higher education and to the labor market. However, it was not a segregate state. This situation was changed after the abolition of dictatorship (1974) and more actively after the integration of European Union (1981). Nevertheless, as Greece did not have a previous experience on the issue, as a Member State, just followed the European policies. The fact that these policies were supported by funded programs had as a result for Greece to take part actively. Nonetheless, someone could observe problems of understanding, meaning, and interpretation or even of instability.

On the other hand, in the field, women's participation to education has constantly increased from the end of nineteenth century to nowadays. Actually, the picture of woman's issue is ambiguous. Somebody could argue that women are more than men in higher education. This is true on a quantitative approach. Nevertheless, inside of higher education, the disparities remain existent. This means that social, cultural, and economical stereotypes persist and are present.

In this way, it seems that women's participation to the labor market increased during time, but simultaneously, it is less than men's, less dynamic and limited in some sectors. Thus, someone could argue that women's participation to the labor market seems to be more difficult to be succeeded in equal terms than the participation to education in general and more particular to higher education.

As conclusion, in Greek case, women's participation was increased from 1980 to nowadays, but the issue rests open and it merits for consideration in the future.

References

Anagnostou, D., & Avlova, N. (2019). Policy text: The European union and gender equality in research and higher education: A view from Greece. ELIAMEP, Athens.

Askouni, N. (2006). The education of the Muslim minority of Thrace. Kritiki, Athens. (in Greek).

Askouni, N., & Stamelos, G. (2004).*Report: Analysis of Muslim minority student attendance at the Gymnasium*. Athens: Muslim-schooling program. (in Greek).

Ball, C., & Lagemann, A. (2014). *Gender pay gap in EU countries based on SES*. Luxembourg: European Commission.

Booth, C., & Bennett, C. (2002). Gender mainstreaming in the European Union: Towards a new conception and practice of equal opportunities? *European Journal of Women's Studies*, 9(4), 430–460.

Clark, M. A., Thompson, P., & Vialle, W. (2008). Examining the gender gap in educational outcomes in public education: Involving pre-service school counsellors and teachers in cross-cultural and interdisciplinary research. *International Journal for the Advancement of Counselling*, 30, 52–66.

Council of Europe. (1998). *Gender mainstreaming: Conceptual framework, methodology and presentation of good practices, final report of activities of the group of specialists on mainstreaming*. Strasbourg: Council of Europe.

Dalakoura, A., & Ziogou Karastergiou, S. (2015). *Women's education - women in education. [Appl. Book]*. Athens: Association of Greek academic libraries. (in Greek). Retrieved from http://hdl.handle.net/11419/2585

Daly, M. (2005). *Gender mainstreaming in theory and practice* (pp. 433–450). Oxford: Oxford University Press.

Deligianni-Kouimtzi, V., & Ziogou-Karastergiou, S. (2007). *Educational interventions to promote gender equality in school: Book - handbook for teachers*. University of Ioannina, EPEAEK II-2000-2006. (in Greek).

EKT. (2019). *Statistics for PhDs graduating from Greek universities in 2018*. Athens: National Documentation Centre and Electronic Content. (in Greek).

ELSTAT. (2014). University Department - Students - Individual Statistical Bulletin (Start)/2014. Retrieved from https://www.statistics.gr/el/statistics/-/publication/SED34/2014

EPEAEK II. (2007). Retrieved from http://www.epeaek.gr/epeaek/sitecontent/Kef_2_Anath.pdf. (in Greek).

European Commission (2019). Monitoring education and training: Greece (2019). European Commission, Brussels.

EYSEKT. (2003). Guide for the implementation of gender equality policies in the planning and evaluation of OP actions of the GFCM. Ministry of Employment and Social Security. Athens. (in Greek).

Frantzis, K. (2005). Female science graduates in Greece and the case of teachers. In E. Close, M. Tsianikas, & G. Frazis (Eds.), *Greek Research in Australia: Proceedings of the international biennial Conference of Greek studies, Flinders University April 2003* (pp. 513–530). Adelaide: Flinders University Department of Languages - Modern Greek. (in Greek).

Frosi, L., Kouimtzi, E., & Papadimou, Ch. (2001). *The gender factor and school reality in primary and secondary education*. (Review Study). Thessaloniki: Equality Research Center. (in Greek).

General Secretariat for Gender Equality (GSGE). (2004). Framework for proposals of GGI with a view to drawing up the national strategic development plan 2007–2013. (in Greek).

General Secretariat for Gender Equality (GSGE). (2017). National action plan on gender equality 2016–2020. National Printing House, Athens. (in Greek).

General Secretariat for Gender Equality (GSGE). (2018). 16th fact sheet: Women in Education in positions of responsibility. (in Greek). Retrieved from http://www.isotita.gr/wp-content/uploads/2019/04

General Secretariat for Gender Equality (GSGE). (2018a).The 44 actions of the general Secretariat for gender equality for education in the 2016–2017 school year. Ministry of Internal Affairs and G.S.G.E, Athens. (in Greek).

General Secretariat for Gender Equality (GSGE). (2018b). The 67 actions of the general Secretariat for gender equality for education in the 2017–2018 school year. Ministry of Internal Affairs and G.S.G.E, Athens. (in Greek).

General Secretariat for Gender Equality (GSGE). (2018c).The 87 actions of the general Secretariat for gender equality in education in 2018. Ministry of Internal Affairs and G.S.G.E, Athens. (in Greek).

Hambidis, T., & Taratori, E. (2008). The course of inclusive education in Greece. Report at the 5th scientific conference on history of education on Education and Social Justice (in Greek). Retrieved from http://eriande.elemedu.upatras.gr/?section=985&language=en&page706=3&print=1&itemid706=1038.

IOBE. (2019). Educational inequalities in Greece, Access to higher education and the impact of the crisis. Foundation for Economic and Industrial Research, Athens. (in Greek).

KANEP. (2014). 2014 the basic numbers in education, Part 2: National Reference Framework (2002–2012). Thessaloniki. (in Greek).

KANEP. (2019). The basic numbers in education 2019-2020 Education & Employment in Greece - The European Reference Framework (2001-2018) Special research report - Indicator update, Thessaloniki. (in Greek).

Karafillis, A. (xx). The profile of a Greek Muslim student of the department of primary education of the Democritus university of Thrace. (in Greek). Retrieved from http://www.eriande.elemedu.upatras.gr/eriande/synedria/synedrio4/praktika1/karafyllis.htm. Accessed on January 24, 2020.

Lakasas, A. (2018). Women professors, a minority in Greek universities. *Kathimerini*. (in Greek). Retrieved from https://www.kathimerini.gr/952415/article/epikairothta/ellada/meioyhfia-oi-ka8hghtries-sta-aei

Lambraki-Paganou, A. (1995). Women's education and legislation in Greece (1878–1985). In *Education and equality of Opportunities (conference proceedings)*. Athens: Ministry of the presidency of the government - general Secretariat for equality. (in Greek).

Lempesi, G. E. (2012). Teacher perspectives concerning project implementation in the school community: A part of a case study, creating communities: Local, national and global. Fourteenth annual CiCe network conference, University of York, York , pp. 24–26.

Lempesi, G. E. (2017). Educational and social policy transfer in Europe: The case of projects about gender issues in Greek schools. unpublished PHD, Department of Primary Education, University of Patras, Patras. (in Greek).

Lempesi, G. E. (2019). European policies on gender equality and their connection to gender mainstreaming in Greek educational policies: An overview of policy texts. *International Journal of Humanities and Social Science*, 9(7), 39–48.

Moniukas, F. (2011). Educational preferences of secondary school graduates. *The case of the University of Patras. Academia*, 1 (1), 176–196. (in Greek).

Moutsidou, F. (2018). *Evolution of woman present at Greek higher education institutions*. Athens: Athens University of Economics and Business. (in Greek).

Ntoulas, P. (2018). *Equality is delaying in education*, alfavita (on line journal, in Greek). Retrieved from https://www.alfavita.gr/ekpaideysi/248463_i-isotita-argei-akomi-stin-ekpaideysi.

Papadiamadaki, Y., & Riga, V. (2003). *Country Greece State of the art report for the project EQUAPOL. Gender-sensitive and women friendly public policies: A comparative analysis and assessment of their progress and impact*. Athens: KEKMOKOP.

Papagiannopoulou, M., Katsamagou, M., Kalyveza, M., Paparounis, P., & Tabossi, S. (2008). *Series of monitoring and evaluation of the effects on the nature of actions of EPEAEK. II*, Athens: KETHI. (in Greek).

Sailer, X. (2018). Women and academic career: Obstacles and Difficulties in their career path. unpublished master thesis, Department of educational and Social Policy, University of Macedonia, Macedonia. (In Greek).

Sianou-Kyrgiou, E.. (2007). Study choices for higher education and gender inequality. In E. Maragoudakis (Ed.), *Essays: Introduction to gender issues in the educational process* (pp. 115–126). Thessaloniki: Lithography. (in Greek).

Spinthourakis, J., Karatzia-Stavlioti, E., Lempesi, G.-E., & Papadimitriou, I. (2008). Country report: Greece, educational Policies that address social inequality (EACEA action 6.6.2). IPSE, London.

Spinthourakis, J., Lempesi, G.-E., & Papadimitriou, I. (2009). Gender thematic report. Educational Policies that address social inequality (EACEA action 6.6.2). IPSE, London.

Stamatopoulou, A. (2020). The impact of gender, social origin, place of residence and financial crisis on higher education and choice of studies. The case of the Departments of Health Sciences. unpublished master thesis, Postgraduate Interdepartmental Postgraduate Program Higher Education Policy: Theory and Practice (MaHep), Patras. (in Greek).

Stratigaki, M. (2006). Policies for gender equality in Greece: European directions or national practices. In N. Maraveia & T. Sakellaropoulos (Eds.), *European Integration and Greece: Economy, society, policies*. Athens, Dionikos Publications. (in Greek).

Stratigaki, M. (2008). *Gender equality policies. European guidelines and national practices*. Athens: Gutenberg. (in Greek).

Tsikalaki, I., & Kladi-Kokkinou, M. (2016). Economic crisis and social inequalities in education: The educational choices of candidates for higher education. *Academia - Boletín de la Real Academia de Bellas Artes de San Fernando*, 6(7), 34–82. (in Greek).

Vosniadou, S., & Vaiou, L., (xx), The position of women in the scientific staff of the University of Athens. (in Greek). Retrieved from https://ec.europa.eu/info/policies/justice-and-fundamental-rights/gender-equality/equal-pay/gender-pay-gap-situation-eu_en

Ziogou-Karastergiou, S., & Kelesidou, E. (1997). Legislation foreducating girls in Greece during the 20th century: Gaps and antagonisms. In B., Deligiannis & S., Ziogou (Eds.), *Gender and School Act*. Thessaloniki: Vania. (in Greek).

Chapter 5

Italy: Gender Segregation and Higher Education

Chiara Biasin and Gina Chianese

In recent years, Italy has changed profoundly with regard to areas like the organization of work, the structure of the family, and the idea of motherhood. Although lifestyles and the working world have changed, the country holds a very low position internationally in terms of equity, ranking 70th out of 149 countries according to the Global Gender Gap Report (WEF, 2018), and last among EU countries.

OECD (2017b), ISTAT (2018), and Almalaurea (2019a) data show a worrisome situation: women rarely choose to study STEAM subjects and are poorly represented in technical and scientific professions. The percentage of employed women in Italy is still much lower than that of men. Other critical areas of concern are wages, levels of participation in, and access to, highly qualified professions.

The main elements contributing to this *educational segregation of gender* are often "invisible constraints," prejudices and stereotypes, socially and historically assigned roles and models, and traditional patterns of study choices influence access to specific professional paths. As a result, educational and professional *self-segregation* is often added to an *imposed segregation.* This chapter analyses the current situation in Italy and critically discusses recent data and research on the presence of women in higher education (HE) and in the job market.

1. Gender (In)equality: The Current Situation and Its Evolution

The fight against inequalities represents one of the priority objectives of the UN's 2030 Agenda, which delineates a close link between women's empowerment and sustainable development, and supports an approach based on gender being transversal to all objectives for orienting future policies and strategies.

Among the "17 Sustainable Development Goals" established in the 2030 Agenda, Goal number 5 "Equality", states: "Gender equality is not only a fundamental human right, but a necessary foundation for a peaceful, prosperous and sustainable world" (UNESCO, 2015).[1]

[1]https://www.un.org/sustainabledevelopment/gender-equality/.

International Perspectives on Gender and Higher Education, 75–92

doi:10.1108/978-1-83909-886-420201005

In addition, during the open session of the 70th General Assembly, United Nations Secretary-General Ban Ki-Moon emphasized the key role of gender equality as a stimulus for development progress, underscoring that the potential of women is not being fully realized because of enduring social, economic, and political inequalities.

Framed in this scenario, providing women with balanced access to education, adequate work, equal wages, and equal representation in decision-making activities and processes could be a starting point to support sustainable economies, societies, and the community as a whole.

According Hausmann, Tyson, & Zahidi (2013), "empowering women means a more efficient use of a nation's human capital endowment and [...] reducing gender inequality enhances productivity and economic growth" (p. 31). In this sense, gender inequality could be considered a waste of women's human capital due to several factor in societies that prevent them from expressing their full potential.

Until the 1990s, there were more male than female students in HE in OECD countries. Since then, the latest increase in female participation has reversed that trend due to several factors: first, the so-called "fecundity management" allowing women the choice to postpone maternity to a later age. The result is a reduction in women dropout rates, support for female participation in the job market, and better career plans (Vincent-Lancrin, 2008).

> Even though higher education leads to individual returns in the form of higher income, women often need to have more education than men to get some jobs [...] women continue to confront discrimination in jobs, disparities in power, voice and political representation and laws that are prejudicial on the basis of their gender. As a result, well-educated women often end up in jobs where they do not use their full potential and skills. (UNESCO, 2012, p. 84).

Gender inequality could be considered an "umbrella term" encompassing various concepts and ideas: segregation, inequality, and discrimination. In this essay, we will focus on gender inequity in Italian HE.

A distinction can be made between horizontal and vertical segregation in gender equality.

Horizontal segregation describes the concentration of females in specific study paths (specifically in the fields of teaching, social studies, and care) and their underrepresentation in technical and scientific studies (Science, Technology, Engineering, and Mathematics – STEAM). This means that women tend to be overrepresented in employment sectors that often guarantee lower wages (University Report – Observatory JobPricing, 2018).[2] These sectors generally

---

[2]https://www.jobpricing.it/wp-content/uploads/2018/06/University_Report_2018.pdf.

require skill levels considered lower than those required by the occupations in which men are overrepresented (OECD, 2018). This is considered a major factor contributing to the gender pay gap in the European Union (EC, 2011a; 2011b).

The basis of this form of segregation is that it is often composed of "invisible bonds": women almost automatically introject representations, stereotypes, different attitudes attributed to the sexes, and different social roles and models of behavior assigned to women and men.

These representations often coexist with an "illusion of equality" and with the conviction that discrimination and the disparity of power and opportunities have been overcome (Biemmi & Leonelli, 2017).

Based on these data, study paths – from high school to university – are chosen on the basis of *self-segregation* according to which certain fields of study and work contexts are more suitable for men and women.

When choosing studies and/or a career, a significant role is played by the conditioning and attitudes of parents, teachers, friends, and the job market. All these elements propose a symbolic and imaginary world of the feminine and masculine with different professional realizations.

Vertical segregation describes the situation whereby opportunities for career advancement within a company or working sector are limited based on gender. This situation usually contributes to increased gender inequality such as the gender wage gap. This phenomenon is defined as the "glass ceiling" describing an invisible ceiling preventing women from accessing the highest levels of career.

Gender inequality in the workplace can affect women's health and safety in the workplace, and there are considerable links between discrimination issues and health (EU-OSHA, 2013; 2016).

Moreover, according to European data (GEC, 2016), the underrepresentation of women in decision-making processes is closely related to traditional roles and stereotypes, the imbalance between men and women in caring responsibilities (children, family), and the political and corporate culture.

How can the evolution of gender inequality in Italian HE be explained? There is no simple answer because several factors contribute to these data. Research suggests that gender and socioeconomic status could be risk factors in relation with attitudes toward learning and school in addition to parental expectations. They often have stereotypical notions about what is the best career and/or job and studies for women and men to pursue.

Another influencing factor is represented by classmates and friends who can influence the academic choices, achievement, and behavior of an individual student. Boys appear to succumb to peer pressure to conform to gender identities more than girls. In this sense, teachers using specific teaching strategies could play a strategic role in supporting the development of students' attitudes and inspiring them to work at their best (Andrus, Jacobs, & Kuriloff, 2018; Geven, Jonsson, & Tubergen, 2017; Warrington, Younger, & Williams, 2000).

2. Gender Inequality: Italy on the National and International Landscape

2.1 The National Landscape

The Italian Constitution states that "all citizens are equal, without differences of sex, religion and social status" (Art. 3). This declaration constitutes the base guaranteeing that there are no barriers for women in the educational system and in jobs and careers.

In addition to this constitutional statement, antidiscrimination laws and documents assure equal treatment and opportunities for men and women:

- Law 183/2010 launched the Unique Guarantee Committee for Equal Opportunities in Public Administrations for workers' well-being and against discrimination;
- The National Code of Equal Opportunities between Women and Men (2006) establishes the responsibility for Public Administrations to approve a Positive Action Plan[3];
- Law 240/2010 on the General Reform of University Education defines two key aims in terms of equal opportunities: (1) it calls for a gender balance on the boards of trustees of research institutions; and (2) it extends maternity leave to postdoc researchers;
- The Memorandum of Understanding between the Ministry of Education, University and Research and the Department for Equal Opportunities of the Italian Presidency of the Council of Ministers (DPO) (2011) creates a pioneering tool promoting equal opportunities in science. Due to government instability, the Memorandum has yet to be applied;
- The introduction of the so-called "pink quotas" (2011) to ensure measures for female participation in decision-making processes in companies and administrations;
- the Guidelines for the University Gender Budget (2017). This document involves not only the collection of data but also the definition of policies for equal opportunities and the enhancement of diversity and organizational well-being, as well as the promotion and dissemination of good practices.

In Italy, the road to women's access to HE has been long and not without ambiguity. Yet, the country is home to the world's first female university graduate, Elena Cornaro Piscopia, who wanted to study theology but, due to the opposition of Cardinal Barbarigo, graduated with a degree in Philosophy from the University of Padua in 1678.

A first important push toward the process of feminization of Italian culture was given by the Casati Law (1859), which introduced the "normal school" for the training of elementary teachers (men and women). However, it also reproposed more traditional stereotypes relating to the predestination of women to the

[3]See Legislative Decree 198 of April 11, 2006.

care of family life. The feminization of teaching caused a massive influx of women into the educational sector, given the apparent natural contiguity with the maternal role of the teacher. Although the idea that women should remain ignorant had been overcome, prejudices regarding the education of women persisted in Italian culture.

At the time of the proclamation of Italian unification, the 1861 census revealed a 78% illiteracy rate in the general population, with women representing 84% of that percentage. At the start of the century (1911), the percentage of illiterate women fell to 50% and the law establishing women's inferiority and dependence on men was repealed (1911).

The process of revising gender roles and stereotypes was suddenly interrupted during the Fascist period. Convinced of the importance of having a populous nation for colonial purposes, Mussolini launched a campaign supporting births and calling on women to be exemplary wives and mothers as well as prolific. The "Rocco law" reduced the penalty for honor killings of women and permitted violent punishment of females within the family group. Women were forbidden access to higher studies (except for teachers' college), and their role of bearing children for the family and homeland was exalted.

During World War II, the role of women changed as, on the one hand, the Fascist government needed them in manufacturing, while, on the other, they played a crucial role in the partisan movement during the Resistance, fighting fascism through the collection of funds, communication, and propaganda and in transporting provisions and resources. Despite their important role in Italian society, only five women – symbolically called the "Founding Mothers" -participated in the commission responsible for drafting the Italian Constitution following the proclamation of the Republic. On June 2, 1946, women were granted the right to vote in national elections for the first time, but only 21 women were elected in 1948, representing just 4% of all deputies.

2.2 Gender Segregation in Italian Academia

University studies for women were introduced by the University General Regulation in 1875. Despite this, cultural prejudices and the opposition of the Catholic Church prevented women from accessing university studies, so that by 1890, only about 20 women had graduated from university in Italy.

In 1877, the first woman graduated in medicine after the birth of the Italian State. The year 1881 saw the first two Italian female graduates in the natural sciences. In 1894, the first woman graduated in law, 1908 saw the first female engineer, and 1932 the first female architect. In 1926, females represented just over 14% of all graduates, and very few women actually completed their university studies. They were limited to certain faculties (Letters and Philosophy) and had very few employment prospects. Examples of this situation are Maria Montessori, who graduated in medicine in 1896 but worked as a pedagogue and educator, and Lidia Poet, who graduated in law in 1881 and became a member of the bar, but was not permitted to practice law following cancellation of her registration by the Court of Cassation because she was a woman. Progress in reducing gender segregation has been very slow in all sectors. As recently as 1996, the Accademia della Crusca, one of the world's most prestigious language societies, was called on to rule on the feminine form of professions having only a masculine form. This is doubtlessly a linguistic rearrangement of the Italian language that not only reflects changes in society but also highlights the persistence of sexist use of language reflecting occupations still linked to the gender of the person exercising them. In fact, Italy had its first woman police officer only in 1952, the first female judge in 1964, the first female Minister of State in 1976, the first female Prefect in 1997, the first female Union President in 2010, the first female President of the Senate in 2018, and the first female President of the Supreme Court in 2019.

The situation was no different in academia because Italian universities were not and still are not gender-neutral institutions (Eddy & Ward, 2017). In the past, academic careers were considered prestigious and too demanding to permit a family–work balance. And so, the few female university professors gave up a life as wife and mother, remaining unmarried academics being preferred. Admission to university studies diverted women from an interest in marital and family life and challenged the wisdom of the principles of social ascent usually based on family affluence work and her husband's income. In order to "have a career," especially an academic one, women were required to adopt a working style mimicking that of men forcing her to "sacrifice" both motherhood and marriage to her work. For this reason, it was not until in 1911 that the first woman was named full professor at the University of Pavia, and only four Italian universities had appointed female professors in the early decades of the twentieth century (in Bologna, Pavia, Naples, and Rome).

During the twentieth century, a number of factors contributed to a general renewal in Italian culture and to the weakening of gender-related stereotypes: the economic boom, processes of societal modernization, feminist movements and demands for women's rights, and democratic governments. This process certainly cannot be considered concluded but in constant development (Covato, 2003, 2012).

During that century, female university students participated actively in labor movements, protests, and political militancy, attacking universities and their professors' privileges (Ulivieri, 2007). Gender demands went hand in hand with demands for political democracy, the need for social participation, and awareness of the condition of women (Ulivieri, 2015) that sought to move beyond the stereotypes and the system of social expectations. In "*La donna contro sé stessa*" (*The Woman against herself*) (1969), Carla Ravaglioli explained the dichotomy of the condition of contemporary women stuck between following traditional models and stereotyped roles and the quest for independence and emancipation. In her book, "*Dalla parte delle bambine*" (*What Are Little Girls Made of?*) (1973), Elena Gianini Belotti denounces the exclusion of women from the world of culture, academia, and employment, governed by asymmetrical roles and by an educational adaptation of models of dependence with respect to males, that lock women in a "gender cage."

Reflection on the relationship between gender and HE developed in Italy a few decades late with respect to the European debate and international research (Dillabough, 2001). This can be seen in the unavailability of certain books on the national publishing market: for example, Simon de Beauvoir's *Le Deuxième Sexe* (1949) was not translated into Italian until 1961, and Betty Friedan's *The Feminine Mystique* (1963) only in 1976. Certain fundamental books of the 1970s, like *The Psychology of Sex Differences* (1974) by Eleanor Maccoby and *The Traffic in Women* (1975) by Gayle Rubin, have never been translated into Italian.

The 1970s saw numerous legislative and social steps taken to oppose segregation: the law prohibited dismissing pregnant women in 1971, family law decreed legal equality between spouses in 1975, and a 1979 law established equality between men and women in the labor world. Still, discrimination against women persisted until the mid-1990s, with sexual violence still regarded as a "crime" against public morality and not as a crime against women. Only toward the end of the century was the first female Faculty Dean hired at the University of Palermo (1981), and a woman was appointed Rector of the University of Udine (2008) for the first time at the start of the new millennium.

Just a few decades ago, under strong pressure from the European Union (EC 2010; 2011a), HE policies began to understand fully the need to close the gender gap. At the same time, laws were enacted to oppose gender-based violence and feminicide (Law 113/2013), violence against women, and the introduction of the offenses of revenge porn and permanent injury to the face (Legislative Decree 1200/2019). Gender research centers and interdisciplinary women's studies centers have been established in many Italian universities (Padua, Trieste, Naples, Catania, Milan, Turin, Bologna, Pavia, and Bari) examining the issue of feminine identity and permanent postgraduate gender studies. These centers are often paired with Unique Guarantee Committees (Comitati Unici di Garanzia – CUG) and supported by initiatives undertaken by female professors delegated by rectors to oversee the issue of equality in HE, prepare gender reports, conferences, publications, research projects, annual reports, and codes of conduct, and create observatories and networks in order to promote equality in HE. However, interest in the initiatives and research conducted by university centers on gender studies often remains limited to certain cultural distribution circuits because the thematisation of the gender–university relationship is still not systematically present and is often too weak to direct the public debate and to have an effective impact on changing cultural mentalities and social stereotypes. A 2013 research study conducted by the University of Rome shows that, out of some 60 public universities in Italy, barely a dozen provides a gender studies program, mostly in the north and with most of these programs at the University of Bologna. Students are offered about 50 courses – graduate and undergraduate – almost all of which are available in humanist and social degree programs; only six master's programs and four doctorates are proposed in the entire country. In recent years, a line of research devoted to gender pedagogy has been reflecting on the educational importance of gender and how it is established and reinforced by educational institutions (Leonelli, 2011). While gender education more or less intentionally and formally influences choices and women's agency capacity has an impact on the pressure of tradition shaping representations and expectations of women, gender pedagogy, on the other hand, problematises the role of the gender divide in schools and in HE.

Three major chronological phases can be identified in Italian pedagogical reflection on the topic (Leonelli, 2011):

(1) 1970–1990: Studies on *sexual equality* criticize the idea of feminine knowledge being inferior to dominant male knowledge and discuss the sense of social and cultural inferiority transmitted to girls in order to emancipate them from the male world and aim for equal rights and access to education and training;
(2) 1990–2000: studies on *gender differences* theorize the specificity of the feminine, stressing the conflict between the genders in HE as well. Luisa Muraro's book *Diotima: Il pensiero della differenza sessuale* (1987) clearly highlights the attempt to address sexual, educational, biological, and social issues, associating them with the emblem of Diotima: priestess-seeress and teacher of Socrates. Still, the idea of feminine excellence tends to identify the difference with the paradigm of maternity and care, generating a broad debate on the "place of the feminine" in schools, society, and in the media (especially on television), which has led to a backlash against the awareness of feminism in previous decades;
(3) 2000–2020: *postgender* studies complexified the gender category no longer according to the male–female binary opposition through a critical and demanding decentralization of the female point of view on reality, with multiple interpretations of sexual, individual, and social identities. Studies on storytelling and on women's life stories, on the role of women in society, of female students in HE and on diversity go hand in hand with research on the construction of female professionalism (in school) in order to deconstruct stereotypes.

However, in Italian HE, gender studies, teaching and learning continue to be of little value despite being cultural, scientific, and educational issues crucial for the country. HE continues to resist changes to a sexist vision and forms of segregation and self-segregation of teachers and students.

2.3 International Data

ISTAT (2018) data reveal an increase in women's participation in HE: currently, 59% of all university graduates are women.

A number of factors help explain the constant rise in female participation in the labor market: cultural changes, the image of foreign occupations in services to families, etc. However, despite the general improvement in the female employment rate, profound differences remain with respect to their participation in the labor market.

Almalaurea data on Graduate Profile (2019a) reveal that 53.1% of women graduated on time (compared with 48.2% of men) with an average final grade of 103.5 out of 110 (101.6 for men). Additionally, female graduates come largely from less supportive family contexts both from a cultural and socioeconomic point of view.

According to Almalaurea data (2018), women appear to have strong cultural motivations for enrolling at university (33.3%, compared to 28.7% of men), and many of them participate in internships (61.4%, compared to 52.6% of men).

The survey highlights the different gender composition of STEAM graduates, with more males (59.0%) than females (41%), particularly in engineering and scientific subjects.

Despite their superior university performance, the Almalaurea survey on the employment status of graduates (2019b) highlights that women continue to be penalized in the job market. Five years after graduation, the overall employment rate is 89.3% (92.5% for men and 85.0% for women). The wage gap between men and women remains high: after five years, male STEAM graduates reported a salary of 1,699 euros per month compared to 1,375 euros for women.

The Global Gender Gap Report (WEF, 2018) confirms the gender gap for graduates by degree type: women are overrepresented in Humanities and Education and underrepresented in Engineering and Technologies (Table 5.1).

The European Gender Equality Index (2019) ranks Italy among the countries in the European Union with the lowest gender equality, assigning it a score of 63

Table 5.1. Graduated b Degree Type.

Graduates by Degree Type	Female	Male	Value
Agri., Forestry, Fisheries and Veterinary	1.7	2.6	0.65
Arts and Humanities	19.2	10.9	1.75
Business, Admin and Law	17.2	21.5	0.80
Education	10.3	1.7	6.02
Engineering Manuf and Construction	9.5	26.5	0.36
Health and Welfare	18.5	12.8	1.45
Information and Comm Technologies	0.3	1.9	0.13
Natural Sci., Mathematics and Statistics	6.4	6.8	0.94
Services	1.7	3.0	0.58
Social Sci., Journalism and Information	14.4	11.4	1.26

Source: Global Gender Gap Report (WEF, 2018).

out of 100, which puts it in 14th place.[4] Despite having improved its ranking, Italy's ranking remains below the EU-28 average (67.4).

Italy's scores are lower than the EU's scores in all domains except "health." At the same time, it is important to highlight that the number of years women and men can expect to live in good health has decreased.

The most critical items concern "money," "power," "time," and "work." Italy's "money" score has improved since 2005 but reveals increased poverty and inequality in income distribution, with women earning 18% less than men. In couples with children, women earn 30% less than men.

As regard the comparison with other European countries, EUROSTAT (2017) ranks Italy 17th out of 24 European nations for differences in pay for men and women in the private sector, while the gap is just 4.1% in the public sector and is one of the lowest in Europe.[5]

In terms of "power," Italy's score is the lowest of all domains, but has improved the most over time.

Challenges continue in the "time" domain, where Italy's score has stagnated since 2005, underscoring persisting inequalities in the household division of tasks between women and men.

Italy has the lowest score of all EU Member States in the domain of "work," not reaching its national EU 2020 employment target of 67–69% (the overall employment rate is 63%).

The gender gap decreases as education levels increase, but the percentage of women in part-time work is more than three times that of men (around 33% of women work part-time, compared to 9% of men).

Key critical issues remain the inequal distribution of men and women in the workforce and in different study fields in tertiary education: around 26% of women work in education, health, and social work (compared to 7% of men). Approximately 6% of women work in STEAM (compared to 31% of men); 44% of women study education, health and welfare, or humanities and art (compared to 27% of men).

---

[4]"The Gender Equality Index is a tool to measure the progress of gender equality in the EU, developed by EIGE. It gives more visibility to areas that need improvement and ultimately supports policy makers to design more effective gender equality measures. Measuring gender equality is integral to effective policymaking in the EU. Since the first edition in 2013, the Gender Equality Index has tracked and reported progress by providing a comprehensive measure of gender equality, tailored to fit the EU's policy goals. It reveals both progress and setbacks and explores what can be done better to seize opportunities for change. Building on previous editions and EIGE's approach to intersecting inequalities, the Gender Equality Index 2019 continues to show the diverse realities that different groups of women and men face. It examines how elements such as disability, age, level of education, country of birth and family type intersect with gender to create different pathways in people's lives. For the first time, the Index highlights the situation of LGBTQI* people and Roma and Muslim women in areas where statistics are available" (see https://eige.europa.eu/gender-equality-index/about).

[5]See https://ec.europa.eu/eurostat/web/products-datasets/-/tesem180.

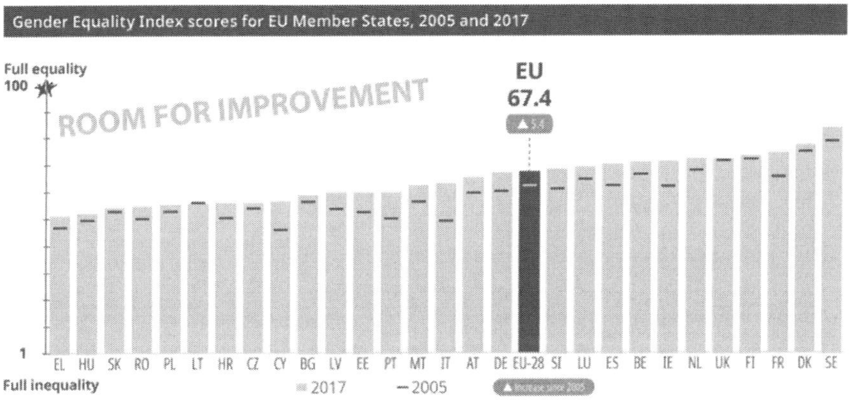

Fig. 5.1. Gender Equality Index Scores for EU Member States, 2005 and 2017. *Source:* Global Gender Gap Report (WEF, 2018).

These results reveal that Italy's Gender Equality Index score is slightly below the EU-28 average, with considerable room for improvement. A more holistic approach is needed to reach fuller gender equality (Fig. 5.1).

3. Gender Trends in Italian HE

The ANVUR report (2018) on the Evaluation of Italian Universities and Research shows a strong contradiction in the Italian HE system; while most Bachelor and Master graduates (58%), half of PhD graduates (52%), and post-doctorate (51%) are women, these percentages are inverted when it comes to an academic career. Men continue to prevail as researchers (58%), associate professors (63%), and, especially as full professors (78%). These data show that universities remain predominantly masculine institutions, where women represent the majority of students but the minority of instructors. And so, HE is a conservative system of gender inequality (Eddy & Ward, 2017), reproducing sexual discrimination (Stake, 2006), subordinate to the dominant male narrative with little interest in gender recognition (Francis, Burke, & Read, 2014), oriented to perpetuate the gender gap that consolidates stereotyped construction and socialization (Bank, 2011). HE plays an important role in the "doing gender" process because it conditions the concept of femininity and masculinity, as well the expectations, objectives, and projects closely linked to the roles (Burke, 2015).

In Italy, the prevalence of women in the areas of education, humanist studies, and social work is more pronounced than in other European countries. Subsequently, the choice of the area of university study sustains the high occupational segregation between women and men in the working world. Comparing eight European countries (including Italy) with different educational systems, labor markets, and social and welfare systems, Barone (2011) shows how the contradiction between the feminization of the HE system and inequalities in the labor market in Italy can be explained by two different and coexisting forms of gender divide. On the one hand, gender differences in HE are stabilized around the humanist–scientific divide opposition: women tend to choose humanist–social fields of study, rather than scientific ones, and therefore prepare for careers in these areas. On the other hand, gender differences solidify within a second opposition: the care–technical divide. Women prefer areas of study related to professional roles that can more easily be reconciled with family and social responsibilities and that are more in agreement with traditional stereotypes of the female gender.

In Italy, the predominance of female students in three-year Bachelor's programs in education (95%), languages (83%), and psychology (82%) reinforces the conviction that university preparation is functional to work related to teaching (nursery school, kindergarten, primary, and secondary school teachers) or care (nurses, midwives, dietitians, and social workers) that have a lower employment status in the national labor market and are penalized in terms of economic, social, and professional recognition with respect to predominantly male professions.

This dual divide (humanist–scientific; care–technical) is rooted in the different contents of university curricula and is found in teaching-learning styles, in representations of educational roles, in the type and value of the knowledge produced, and in the function and application of academic knowledge. Two parallel and opposing curricula coexist in Italian HE: an explicit curriculum, identical for males and females, is that of the school understood as an institution guaranteeing equal opportunity for growth and learning to all, regardless of specific conditions like gender. The second, hidden, curriculum presupposes a symbolic gender order, with different representations, expectations, and behaviors that distinguish between the possibilities and capacities of males and females (Biemmi, 2015a), which may or may not lead to real opportunities.

The level, duration, and pervasiveness of gender inequality have remained almost unchanged for many decades despite the transformations of society, the structure of the family, the Italian labor market, and numerous educational and university reforms (Barone, 2011). Recent studies confirm that there have been no significant changes in university program choices in the past 20 years. Males remain predominantly career-oriented with respect to females, who continue to prioritize a family-centered career. Even the impact of the recent financial crisis has not changed this attitude: gender differences in HE persist both in the period before (2003–2008) and after (2009–2012) the major production and economic crises in Italy (Cattaneo, Horta, Malighetti, Meoli, & Paleari, 2016), continuing to separate the different expectations of graduates with respect to their future and selecting gender-based careers in an increasingly competitive, performance-based, and global world of work (Stake, 2006).

The gender socialization and conditioning process perpetuated in HE begins in earliest childhood. One of the reasons is the "complicity" of female teachers, who represent four-fifths of Italian teachers and implicitly accept a difference that is considered innate. Italian teachers generally consider boys to be more intelligent, more capable, and with better performance though with greater behavior problems. On the other hand, girls' scholastic success is considered to be due more to hard work than to true ability (Biemmi, 2015c). Paradoxically, female teachers represent the main barrier to gender parity in Italy. Instead of promoting educational activities aiming to develop male and female students or create a critical gender awareness, they continue to perpetuate restrictive educational practices and feed discriminatory representations. Although Italian schools (and their teachers) do not bear sole responsibility for the persistence of gender stereotypes, they continue to strengthen the "hegemony of a symbolic neutral-universal-male order" (Musi, 2015, p. 122) and waste the opportunity to create a more equitable school and society. Research on a representative sample of Italian primary school textbooks shows that females are still represented mostly in the role of loving mothers, naturally capable of caring for their children, home, and husband. Women are shown in primarily family contexts or in the private sphere, while they are associated with a limited number of jobs (one-third) in the working world with respect to professions attributed to males (Biemmi, 2015b). Although girls who do not reflect the traditional model (such as Pippi Longstocking or Malala Yousafzai) and women who are identified with the male pattern (working late, having no children, not cooking) are present, there are no examples of boys or men in nontraditional models. So, the Italian school system and HE remain elements of educational segregation due to the stereotypic gender message that they continue to transmit as a model for the development of female identity in Italy (Biemmi, 2015a).

4. Study Paths and the World of Work

Despite higher educational qualifications guaranteeing greater access to the labor market, the employment rates of women are still very low.

These inequalities between men and women cannot be attributed solely to different qualifications and to related professional choices but relate to a broader framework.

Various data and research reveal that one of the causes of this result is the poor division of work and care times between men and women. Women who participate in the working world are required to interrupt their careers more frequently, earn lower wages, and have less chance of being promoted to top positions. These disparities in turn lead to more difficult economic conditions and systematically lower levels of pension benefits.

Moreover, one of the first elements of analysis to understand the reason for gender wage differences is certainly that inherent in women's actual career opportunities (WEF, 2019).

Analyses – broken down by gender – on the levels of education reached and the subsequent school–work transition reveal scarce use of female capital in Italy; women have significantly higher levels of education than their male peers, but differences in employment rates are significant.

The report on the employment status of graduates (Almalaurea, 2019b) once again shows significant and persistent gender inequalities: among Master graduates, gender differences are confirmed to be significant five years after graduation at 6.4 percentage points in terms of employment, with women's employment rate at 84.6% and men's 91%. Furthermore, permanent employment contracts are a male prerogative (60.3% of men and 50.1% of women). Five years after graduation, 49.4% of women and 59.2% of men are highly skilled. The report shows that it is more difficult for women to find a suitable placement on the labor market based on their studies. Bachelor graduates employed four years after graduation are occupied in professions suited to their level of education in 67% of cases (79% of men). Distribution by profession is more balanced in the case of Master's graduates, with female graduates falling less than two percentage points behind their male counterparts.

The gender wage gap for graduates working three years after graduation is €233 for Bachelor graduates and €275 for Master graduates due to the different incidence of part-time work for men and women.

Men have an advantage over women even within the same area of study including in programs in great demand by the labor market, such as Engineering, Healthcare, and Economic Statistics (STEAM).

Wage differences in Italy do not appear to be linked to a greater presence of women in less remunerative sectors, but rather to a persistent discrimination: thus, gender itself causes the wage gaps.

Women are predominantly employed in nonindustrial sectors (services, financial services, trade), where pay differentials with respect to male colleagues are even more frequent: the fact that the wage level of female workers is lower than that of men is due not only to their choice of employment sectors that are less profitable (so-called horizontal segregation), but is the outcome of persistent wage discrimination *tout court*.

Data confirm that women are more highly penalized at work if they have children. In fact, the significant gap in terms of employment, contracts, and pay between men and women increases in the presence of children. Even in the comparison between graduates, those with children are penalized: five years after graduating, the employment rate of childless graduates is 84.1%, with a differential of 18.4 percentage points compared to women with children.

The She Figures Report (EC, 2019) confirms that women still suffer from more precarious working conditions than men; they are paid less (with the gender wage gap increasing with age), struggle to reach top positions in their career, struggle to be recognized as the creators of patentable inventions, and have difficulty raising funds for their research.

The OECD's The Pursuit of Gender Equality Report (2017a) emphasizes that Italy has the fewest women in the workforce with respect to other countries. This means that women who work have a greater opportunity to be better educated and have well-remunerated jobs or better professional career.

With respect to work satisfaction, Italian women are less satisfied with their work than their male counterparts, especially with regard to lesser opportunities for contacts with foreign countries, lower earnings, and poorer career prospects. The scope of the social utility of work and available free time are exceptions.

According to the data of the Salary Satisfaction Report (2018), in a general context of low satisfaction of Italian workers (3.7 on a scale of 1–10), women are less happy than their male colleagues and least happy about the perceived fairness of their salaries.[6]

---

[6]https://www.jobpricing.it/blog/salary-satisfaction-2018/.

While 63% of female workers would change jobs to improve their salary (compared to 68% of men), women emphasize other elements of satisfaction not directly linked to monetary remuneration such as flexibility of working hours, work–life balance, welfare services, and interpersonal relationships in the workplace.

From this perspective, it appears clear that the issue of the gender wage gap should be tackled more broadly, and not just limited to monetary remuneration.

5. Critical Points and Perspectives

The European Pact for Gender Equality for 2011–2020 aims to improve equality between men and women in the labor market.[7] In order to support this declaration, the European Council advised EU Member States in 2011 to take concrete action to fight gender segregation and promote gender equality at different levels and in different areas: education, training, and the labor market.

Nevertheless, according the Global Gender Gap Report (WEF, 2018), a very critical situation persists in the world, which is changing much too slowly: from 2006 to today, the gender gap has shrunk a mere 3.6% overall. Obviously, the gender gap is not the same everywhere: Western Europe and North America represent the "driving force" in a situation that is not encouraging.

In order to meet the ambitious aims posed at national and European levels, a "pedagogical perspective" must be adopted to view the gender (in)equality question and proposals (Agenda 2030; UNESCO,2010; 2012): a holistic approach is needed to consider the rule and the impact of different elements and variables in this process, such as dicussed below.

5.1 A Broad Question of Collaboration

A broad perspective must be adopted. Gender (in)equality is not simply a question to be solved in a restricted area (such as wages, education, etc.) but also requires the cooperation of institutions and stakeholders at the European and national, civil society, and community levels. This collaboration will be strategic to ensuring progress in that field.

5.2 Stereotypes about Male and Female Roles and Functions

For centuries, stereotypes have contributed to disseminating a culture of inequality between men and woman. While many States encourage girls to study STEM, to prove their skill in fields usually dominated by men, and to promote gender wage equality, too few push men to participate in fields and sectors traditionally dominated by women.

This is not only a question of fighting for woman rights but for men's rights as well. Differences in labor fields, education paths and fields of study, and wage

---

[7]See https://eur-lex.europa.eu/legal-content/EN/TXT/?uri=CELEX%3A52011XG0525%2801%29.

payment are typically rooted in social norms that feed on stereotypes. These stereotypes are usually used to justify – and/or tolerate – physical, psychological, and emotional violence against women (or men).

5.3 The Key Role of Parents and Teachers

Parents and/or teachers could help improve the gender (in)equality between men and woman by supporting their children in undertaking specific study paths or work. Their ideas and/or stereotypes reinforce – usually unconsciously – gender roles and reflect expectations regarding gender/sex (Kuriloff, Andrus, & Jacobs, 2017).

Fighting female inequality starts at home: parents have the first direct impact on children's social and cognitive development. Parents express their gender orientation by choosing "gendered toys" for their children or guiding them toward specific educational and working options and opportunities. They also promote and support gender inequality by expressing disapproval of specific female behaviors (such as ambition or competitiveness) or influence it through their parenting style and offering role models. These ideas and stereotypes rooted in society can contribute to expanding gender achievement gaps and the under-representation of women in leadership or in top work positions.

The second most influential channel is represented by teachers who represent an authority figure in the classroom and may push students to adopt their ideas. They also disseminate their beliefs through feedback on performance, answering and/or dismissing questions and evaluating performance and tests.

Parents and teachers generally lack awareness of these situations; teachers do not receive specific training regarding gender stereotypes during their formal education and are not provided tools, guidelines, etc., during their professional career development.

In this sense, it could be interesting to train teachers and distribute the recent UNESCO (2015) documents, practices, and guidelines among them.

5.4 Curricula and Guidance

Scholastic curricula generally do not take gender into consideration when defining subject contents or when adopting teaching methods to make science and technology more "girl friendly" and humanities more "boy friendly." In this sense, the proposal by the Female Historians Italian Association to adopt a gender-neutral perspective when teaching history or the national "DIVA project" initiative (Science in a different voice) which aims to improve awareness of gender equality in science is of interest.[8]

In short, gender equality is the responsibility of all in the society. Supporting the empowerment of girls and women does not mean taking power from men and giving it to women. Gender equality means empowering everyone, guaranteeing a win–win approach to improve society and the broader community.

---

[8]http://www.irpps.cnr.it/diva/progetto.php.

References

Agenzia Nazionale di Valutazione del Sistema Universitario e della Ricerca (ANVUR)/National Agency of Evaluation of the University System and Research. (2018). Rapporto biennale sullo stato del Sistema Universitario e della ricerca. Roma: MIUR/ANVUR.

Almalaurea. (2018). *Graduates' profile*. Bologna: Almalaurea.

Almalaurea. (2019a). *Graduates' profile*. Bologna: Almalaurea.

Almalaurea. (2019b). *Graduates' employment status*. Bologna: Almalaurea.

Andrus, S., Jacobs, C., & Kuriloff, P. (2018). Miles to go: The continuing quest for gender equity in the classroom. *Phi Delta Kappan, 100*(2), 46–50.

Bank, B. (Ed.). (2011). *Gender and higher education*. Baltimore: The Johns Hopkins University Press.

Barone, C. (2011). Some things never change: Gender segregation in higher education across eight nations and three decades. *Sociology of Education*, *84*(2), 157–176.

Biemmi, I. (2015a). Towards a gender-sensitive orientation. *Pedagogia Oggi*, *13*(1), 401–416.

Biemmi, I. (2015b). Gender in school and culture: Taking stock of education in Italy. *Gender and Education*, *27*(7), 812–827.

Biemmi, I. (2015c). Gender stereotypes in childhood: When is difference born? *Education Sciences & Society*, *6*(2), 127–133.

Biemmi, I., & Leonelli, S. (2017). *Gabbie di genere: Retaggi sessisti e scelte formative*. Torino: Rosenberg & Sellier.

Burke, P. (2015). Re/imaginig higher education pedagogies: Gender, emotion and difference. *Teaching in Higher Education*, *20*(4), 388–401.

Cattaneo, M., Horta, H., Malighetti, P., Meoli, M., & Paleari, S. (2016). Effects of the financial crisis on university choice by gender. *Higher Education*, *74*, 775–798.

Covato, C. (2003). Il genere come norma nella storia dell'educazione. *Studium Educationis*, *2*, 355–364.

Covato, C. (2012). Maestre d'Italia. Uno sguardo sull'Italia liberale. *Storia Delle Donne*, *8*, 165–184.

Dillabough, J.-A. (2001). Gender theory and research in education: Modernist traditions and emerging contemporary themes. In B. Francis & C. Skelton (Eds.), *Investigating gender: Contemporary perspectives in education* (pp.11–26). Buckingham/Philadelphia: Open University Press.

Eddy, P. L., & Ward, K. (2017). Problematizing gender in higher education: Why 'learning in' isn't enough. In P. L. Eddy, K. Ward, & T. Khwaja (Eds.), *Critical approaches to women and gender in higher education* (pp. 13–39). New York, NY: Palgrave Macmillan.

European Agency for Safety and Health at Work (EU-OSHA) (2013). *New risks and trends in the safety and health of women at work*. Luxembourg: Publications Office of the European Union.

European Agency for Safety and Health at Work (EU-OSHA). (2016). *Women and the ageing workforce: Implications for occupational safety and health*. Luxembourg: Publications Office of the European Union.

European Commission (EC). (2010). Communication from the commission to the European Parliament, the council, the European economic and social Committee and the committee of the regions Strategy for equality between women and men 2010-2015. Brussels, COM(2010) 491 final.

European Commission (EC). (2011a). *Strategy for equality between women and men 2010–2015*. Luxemburg: Publication Office of the European Union.

European Commission (EC). (2011b). *Tackling the gender pay gap in the European Union*. Luxemburg: Publication Office of the European Union.
European Commission (EC). (2019). *She figures 2018*. Brussels: European Commission.
Francis, B., Burke, P., & Read, B. (2014). The submergence and re-emergence of gender in undergraduate accounts of university experience. *Gender and Education*, *26*(1), 1–17.
Gender Equality Commission (GEC). (2016). *Balanced participation of women and men in decision-making*. Strasbourg: Council of Europe.
Geven, S., Jonsson, J., & Tubergen, F. (2017). Gender differences in resistance to schooling: The role of dynamic peer-influence and selection processes. *Journal of Youth and Adolescence*, *46*(12), 2421–2445.
Hausmann, T., & Zahidi, S. (2013). *Global gender gap*. Cologny/Geneva: World Economic Forum.
Istituto Nazionale di Statistica (ISTAT)/National Institute of Statistics. (2018). *Livelli di istruzione della popolazione e ritorni occupazionali: i principali indicatori*. Roma: Istat.
Kuriloff, P. K., Andrus, S. H., & Jacobs, C. E. (2017). *Teaching girls: How teachers and parents can reach their brains and hearts*. Lanham, MD: Rowman & Littlefield.
Leonelli, S. (2011). La pedagogia di genere in italia: dall'uguaglianza alla complessificazione. *Ricerche di Pedagogia e Didattica*, *6*(1), 1–15.
Musi, E. (2015). One learns equity in the classroom. *Pedagogia Oggi*, *13*(2), 117–133.
Organization for Economic Co-operation and Development (OECD). (2017a). *The pursuit of gender equality: An uphill battle*. Paris: OECD Publishing.
Organization for Economic Co-operation and Development (OECD). (2017b). *Education at glance: OECD indicators*. Paris: OECD Publishing.
Organization for Economic Co-operation and Development (OECD). (2018). *Good jobs for all in a changing world of work: The OECD jobs strategy*. Paris: OECD Publishing.
Stake, J. E. (2006). Pedagogy and student change in the women's and gender studies classroom. *Gender and Education*, *18*(2), 199–219.
Ulivieri, S., (a cura di). (2007). *Educazione al femminile: Una storia da scoprire*. Milano: Guerini.
Ulivieri, S. (2015). Gender, citizenship, education. Asymmetric identities. *Education, Sciences & Society*, *6*(2), 21–36.
UNESCO. (2010). *Gender issues in higher education: Advocacy brief*. Bangkok: UNESCO.
UNESCO. (2012). *World atlas of gender equality in education*. Paris: UNESCO.
UNESCO. (2015). *A guide for gender equality in teacher education policy and practices*. Paris: UNESCO.
University Report. Observatory Job Pricing. (2018). Retrieved from https://www.jobpricing.it/wp-content/uploads/2018/06/University_Report_2018.pdf
Vincent-Lancrin, S. (2008). *The Reversal of gender inequalities in higher education: An on-going trend. Higher education to 2030, Volume 1: Demography*. Paris: Organisation for Economic Co-operation and Development (OECD).
Warrington, M., Younger, M., & Williams, J. (2000). Student attitudes, image and the gender gap. *British Educational Research Journal*, *26*, 393–407.
World Economic Forum (WEF). (2018). *Insight report. The global gender gap report*. Cologny/Geneva: WEF.
World Economic Forum (WEF). (2019). *Insight report. The global gender gap report*. Cologny/Geneva: WEF.

Chapter 6

Gender and Higher Education: The Hungarian Case

István Polónyi and Tamas Kozma

1. A Brief History of Hungarian Women's Politics

The women's politics of the state-socialist period were characterized by "state feminism." As a pillar of emancipation, "full employment" appeared as an external, state-imposed constraint. At the same time, it did not result in economic equality (strong segregation in employment, few female managers, women's wages lagged behind men by about a quarter or a third). Furthermore, this full employment did not result in the extinction of the paternalistic family ideal – women spent three to four times more time doing domestic work than men. Women's political participation was high in a parliament without real political power, but this did not reflect the real social situation of women, nor did they increase their political influence. The task of a single, "official" women's movement was to involve women in productive work and to convey the ideology of the party to women. The introduction of measures that positively influenced the social situation of women was linked to the oppressive state, the rejection of which also resulted in the rejection of certain women's policy measures (e.g., rejection of women's quotas, official women's movements, etc.) (Kelemen, 2008).

After the change of regime, feminism is replaced by "familism," which is not only an ideology, a state policy, but also a social state (Dubcsik & Tóth, 2008). At the same time, the collapsing state industry and agriculture brought high unemployment in women's employment, which, in the face of emerging capitalist conditions, also led to the increased disadvantage of women with young children in the labor market. As a result of the changing economy and the rise of services, white, blue collar, and pink collar work – that is, poorly paid office, commercial and service jobs – are gaining more and more employment among women. While the proportion of women in parliament before the change of regime was also internationally comparable, it fell below the level of 1949 after the change (Kelemen, 2008). It should be added that this has not changed significantly until the middle of the second decade of the 2000s. "The proportion of female representatives in Hungary is low, not only in developed European countries. Nor does it keep pace with Eastern European and Third World countries" (Koncz, 2014).

International Perspectives on Gender and Higher Education, 93–114

doi:10.1108/978-1-83909-886-420201006

The gap with the requirements of equal opportunities and international norms is growing and becoming more permanent. Women's NGOs are small in number and weak in advocacy because of a lack of resources. Instead of cooperation, there is a lack of rivalry, division, and solidarity. They refuse to cooperate with one another because of their attachment to political parties, the "undoing of power" (Kelemen, 2008).

Hungary is characterized by conservative values regarding gender roles. In Europe, Hungarian respondents gave the highest priority to the family and the child in the field of women's work, while in Hungary they favored the traditional division of family work and opposed at the same time the switching of traditional roles (Pongrácz, 2005). In European comparison, Hungarian women do most of the domestic work and are most satisfied with the division of family responsibilities (Pongrácz & Murinkó, 2009).

According to a recent study, Hungarian women are primarily present in Hungarian public speech through their family roles.

> This has been intensified since 2010, with Hungarian government parties talking about women mainly as mothers. Within this framework, various employment and family policy measures were adopted to the benefit of certain groups of women. (…) This shift in the political scene poses a number of challenges for political and other social actors committed to improving the position of women and gender equality. (Gregor & Kováts, 2018, p. 4)

Another recent study concludes:

> Despite the fact that the Equal Treatment and Promotion of Equal Opportunities Act has been in force in Hungary for almost 15 years, there is a significant gender pay gap. With tertiary education, women's income rises by less than two-thirds that of men. (…) Nevertheless, in Hungary, the proportion of women graduating under the age of 30 is significantly higher than that of men. Although women's employment in the labor market is in the middle range compared to other countries, the gender pay gap is very significant. (Simonovits & Szeitl, 2018)

According to a recent analysis,

> …results based on different methods suggest that there is some degree of discrimination against women in the labor market in Hungary (…) Estimates based on wage surveys show an unexplained gender pay gap of around 0.09–0.13. Limited test results underline occupational segregation and employers' preferences for it. The low number of legal cases indicates that there is a lack of legal awareness and redress in society. And

> Hungarian perception surveys have clearly shown that various forms of discrimination against women are also present in the labor market and in other areas of social life, and this problem is most acute among older women. (Lovász & Simonovits, 2018)

The above is well reflected in the evolution of the Hungarian Gender Gap Index, which has stagnated since 2010, while the average of 49 developed countries in the OECD, EU28 and G20 countries, as well as the OECD average. As a result, Hungary's ranking in the index is gradually deteriorating. It dropped from 55th place in 2006 to 102th place in all countries surveyed.

There are several reasons for the stagnation of the Hungarian Gender Gap Index between 2000 and 2016 and the decline of its position:

- the health component has been stabilized at a high level since 2006, and the country's ranking has remained broadly stable at 34–38 around,
- the education subcomponent has been favorable since 2006, at a relatively high level, and may well rank from 48 to 71 between 2006 and 2018 as the educational situation of women has improved in several countries behind us,
- the economic participation subcomponent also moved at a relatively constant level, but here Hungary fell back from 48th place in 2006 to 68th place in 2018,
- the indicator of political participation has decreased by a third since 2006. As a result, between 2006 and 2018, we fell from 82nd to 145th place among all the countries studied (and so we are last place among both the 49 developed countries and the OECD countries also).

Overall, the situation of Hungarian women, as measured by the Gender Gap Index, has not deteriorated significantly, but that of several countries behind us has improved, which can be interpreted as meaning that the world has gone along with Hungary in this respect.

The other indicator that characterizes the situation of Hungarian women well is the Gender Equality Index, which the European Union publishes every year, and which characterizes how far they are from achieving gender equality in each member state. The index uses a scale from 1 to 100, where a value of 1 refers to total inequality and a value of 100, on the other hand, refers to total equality.

> The scores are based on the gaps between women and men and levels of achievement in six core domains: work, money, knowledge, time, power, and health. Two additional domains are integrated into the Index but do not have an impact on the final score. The domain of intersecting inequalities highlights how gender inequalities manifest in combination with age, dis/ability, country of birth, education, and family type. The domain of violence against women measures and analyzes women's experiences of violence. In addition to providing a snapshot into the Index scores, the Gender Equality Index 2019 includes a thematic focus on work–life balance. (Gender Equality Index, 2019)

Hungary was 25th in the ranking of the Gender Equality Index in 2005, but by 2015 it had slipped back to 27th, i.e., the penultimate position, and remained there in 2017 as well. Among the components of the index, Hungary is the last among all member states in terms of the "Power" sub-index (measuring political and economic leadership positions). In the "Work" sub-index, our country is ranked 23rd, and in the "Money" sub-index, it is ranked 22nd (Gender Equality Index, 2017).

Both international indices show the same. In Hungary, women's equality is a major problem, particularly in terms of political and economic participation. In addition, there are inequalities in employment and pay characteristics to the detriment of women.

2. General Tendencies of Hungarian Higher Education and the Proportion of Women

Hungarian higher education has undergone a very radical transformation in the last quarter of the century, which has also fundamentally shaped the position of women in higher education.

2.1 The Gross Enrollment Ratio

The overall turnout was less than 15% of the early 1990s, following its expansion after the change of the political system in 2007 (close to 70%). That is, in less than 20 years, it has increased more than 4.5 times. After that, however, it began to decline, falling from 68% in 2007 to 61% in the 5 years between 2007 and 2012, and then declined radically to 48% in 2016 as a result of the Conservative Government's educational policy.

As a result, Hungary fell to 33rd place in the 35 OECDreporting countries in 2016, behind only Slovakia and Lithuania, and 25th place out of the 28 EU Member States (only Slovakia, Romania, and Luxembourg behind us).[1,2]

In essence, the development of the domestic audience is similar, with 2017 being one-third smaller than the peak in 2005. Within the total number of full-time students, the number of full-time students dropped by 17% compared to the full-time peak in 2008, while the share of part-time students fell by more than 58.6% in 2017 compared to the peak in 2004. Thus, the proportion of part-time students has fallen to less than half over the last slightly more than 10 years.

2.2 Headcount and Female Ratio

If we also look at gender relations relevant to our topic, we can see an even more radical transformation in this regard. While the male gross enrollment ratio was

[1]The OECD had 35 member states in 2016 (there are 36 from 2018) – here we were treated as having had 35 members in 2016 since 1990.

[2]In the case of the EU member states, we considered that the 28 member states of 2016 had been members since 1990.

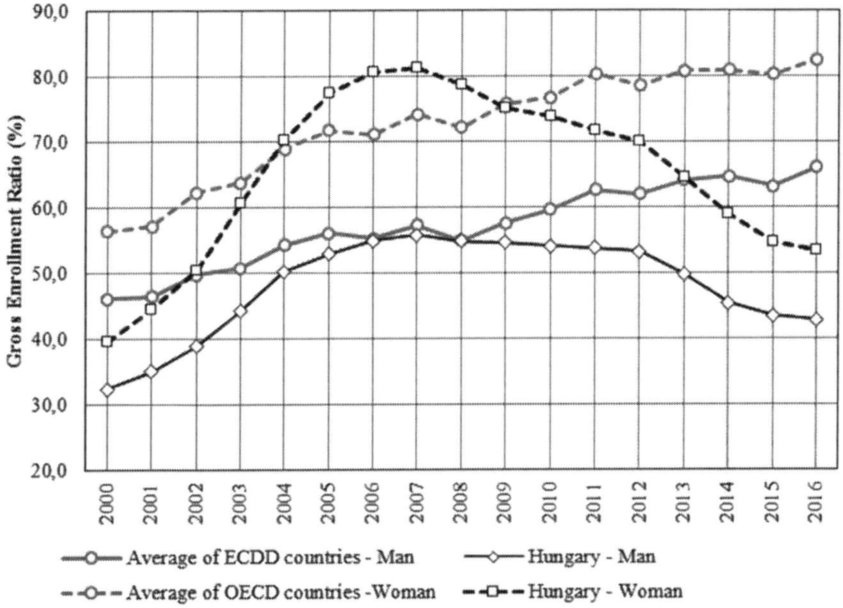

Fig. 6.1. Development of the Total Participation Rate of Higher Education by Gender in Hungary and OECD Average. *Source:* Own calculation and editing based on UNESCO database.

at its peak below the OECD average, the Hungarian female higher education gross enrollment ratio was nearly 10 percentage points higher in the mid-2000s than the female OECD average and about 25 percentage points higher than the Hungarian average men. Ten years later, in 2016, the gross enrollment ratio of Hungarian women in higher education was nearly 30 percentage points below the OECD average for women, and their advantage over Hungarian men was halved (Fig. 6.1).

In terms of gender distribution, the proportion of female students in tertiary education reached 50% in the early 1980s, but fell in the early 1990s, following the change of social regime, between 1990 and 1992. It was again above 50% in 2000, after which it reached its peak in the middle of the first decade of the 2000s (58.2%). Since then, with some volatility, but steadily declining, in 2017, it was slightly below 54%. The surplus for the first time among full-time students was in 1993, reaching its maximum in 2004 (54.3%), since then. In 2017, it was 51.7%, which means it dropped to the 1993 level. Thc proportion of female students in part-time education is still close to 60%, although here again it is declining.

2.3 Recruitment Trends and Female Ratio

The trend in the proportion of women is better understood by analyzing trends in recruitment.

Between 2000 and 2018, the number of students enrolled in each year shows considerable fluctuations. The volatility is basically due to changes in higher education policy. The decline in the number of applicants and enrollments in higher education in 2007 and 2013 is a consequence of the announced education policy. In 2007, the left-wing government announced a plan to introduce a development contribution, which was not implemented as a result of the 2008 referendum initiated by opposition parties. In 2013, the then-right-wing government announced a reform of higher education funding. The essence of this was the shift toward self-sustaining higher education, which would have led to the widespread introduction of tuition fees and also increased the cost reimbursement of nonpublicly funded students to (essentially double) their cost. The introduction of tuition fees in 2007 turned out to be nothing, and the idea of 2013 was only partially realized due to student movements, but their effect resulted in a very significant reduction in the number of applicants and enrollments. This is obviously due to the fact that the cost-bearing capacity of a large number of students in higher education is severely limited, and the reputation of tuition fees greatly discourages them. The lower enrollment rate after 2013 is the effect of the Conservative Government's higher education policy, which has been in operation since 2010, as a result of raising admission scores and linking entry to a number of majors to advanced maturity.[3] In essence, this is an elite higher education policy that significantly impedes social mobility. As a result of higher education policy, the female enrollment rate also declined, mainly due to the government raising the entry score for a number of liberal arts and social sciences, which are primarily sought by female students (Fig. 6.2).

It should also be added that the above-mentioned higher education policy measures particularly impaired the chances of obtaining a first degree for part-time students (since these are predominantly older, with lower admission scores, who are no longer able to achieve advanced maturity, etc.). As there were always more women in part-time training, this also led to a decline in the proportion of women.

3. Distribution of Women by Field of Study in Higher Education

We examine the distribution of Hungarian female students by field of higher education from two aspects. Partly compared to Hungarian men in 2 years in 2005 and 2016 (Table 6.1). And the distribution of female students by field of study in international comparison (Fig. 6.3).

The distribution of women and men by profession differs markedly – the areas of education, business, and health most preferred by women. They have the

---

[3]The Hungarian higher education admissions system is based on scores based on students' high school performance, maturity, and some other factors (such as foreign language exams, professional qualifications, placement at national study competitions, outstanding sports performance, etc.). Each higher education institution enrolls students with the highest scores up to the capacity of the institution.

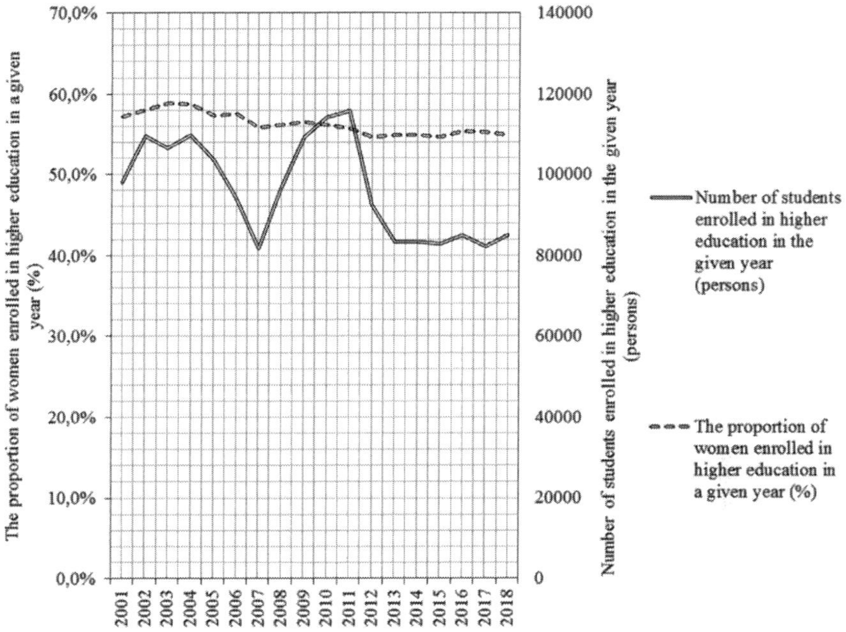

Fig. 6.2. Changes in the Proportion of Women Recruited in the Given Year and the Proportion of Women Recruited in Hungary 2001–2018. *Source:* Own construction based on higher education enrollment data.

highest rates in these areas. While in 2005, social sciences still were dominant, in 2016, humanities were also included. For men, business and engineering are the most dominant. Over the last 10 years, there has been relatively little change in the distribution of female students beyond the decline in the share of business specialization. However, the concentration of engineering specialties among men has increased significantly.

In international comparison, the distribution of Hungarian women by program is broadly similar to that of developed countries, with the difference that education is significantly more popular, while business, service, and engineering are slightly more popular than the OECD or 49 developed countries' average. However, they are lower in the humanities, social sciences, and natural sciences.

All in all, as a recent study states,

> Despite the large increase in women's participation in higher education, horizontal gender segregation in higher education remains high, with women they are selected less than men. This has a negative effect not only on women's labor market opportunities but also on the supply of graduates in STEM disciplines. (Declercq & Varga, 2018)

Table 6.1. Distribution of Hungarian Female and Male Students by Field of Higher Education in 2005 and 2016 (%).

	2005		2016	
	Male	**Female**	**Male**	**Female**
Education programmes	8.5	16.2	4.3	16.9
Arts and Humanities programmes	6.4	8.8	7.2	10.2
Social Sciences Journalism and Information programmes	8.9	11.8	6.4	9.4
Business Administration and Law programmes	26.9	35.8	20.9	26.0
Natural Sciences Mathematics and Statistics programmes	2.7	1.7	4.2	3.4
Information and Communication Technologies programmes	6.1	1.3	6.4	1.3
Engineering Manufacturing and Construction programmes	26.0	5.5	31.3	7.9
Agriculture Forestry Fisheries and Veterinary programmes	4.0	2.4	3.8	2.7
Health and Welfare programmes	4.3	10.0	7.2	13.3
Services programmes	6.1	6.5	5.8	6.4
Unspecified fields			2.5	2.3

Source: Based on own calculations http://data.uis.unesco.org/.

The material also states that Hungarian women are less likely to choose a technical or IT training area than men, but there is no difference between the sexes in the choice of a science training area, meaning that women are less likely to choose a STEM field.

> Estimates also show that women are much more likely than men to consider their incidence, which confirms the findings of international literature that women are much more risk-averse in their choices. (Declercq & Varga, 2018)

The final conclusion of the authors:

> Instead of the Conservative government's higher education policy since 2010, more students would apply for further education without restriction and more men and women would apply for STEM courses, but the impact would be less for women, as with men, however, the proportion of women choosing STEM majors would more than double. (Declercq & Varga, 2018)

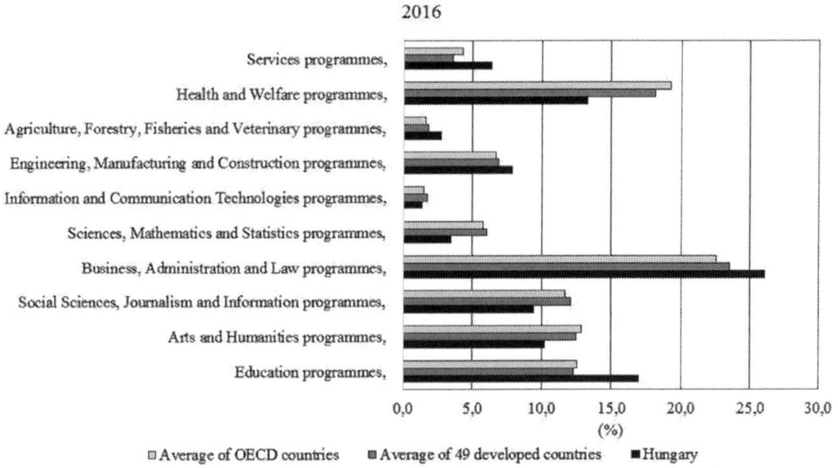

Fig. 6.3. Distribution of Female Students by Field of Higher Education in Hungary in 2016, as Well as the Average of OECD Countries and 49 Developed Countries. *Source:* http://data.uis.unesco.org/. Based on your own calculation and editing.

4. Women in Higher Education and the Labor Market

Varga's (2018) analysis, based on an extensive review of international literature, points out that

> …by the end of the 1990s, gender differences in educational attainment had been reversed in most developed countries (…) While men were always better educated than women in recent decades, women have already obtained a higher level of education or higher than men and have a lower proportion of those with low levels of education.

Literature has presented various reasons for explaining this increase in women's education. Among economic approaches, the fact that women's steady participation in the labor market has become generally accepted has encouraged women's investment in human capital. As Varga writes, "Increasing demand for jobs at tertiary level and extra women's earnings from tertiary education have also facilitated tertiary education for women." She adds that "they also obtain a degree (…), which further increases their advantage in the ratio of tertiary attainment" (Varga, 2018).

4.1 The Proportion of Women in Higher Education and Their Completion Rate

According to Fényes (2009), in Hungary, the majority of girls are in grammar schools and tertiary education. Girls have an advantage in school performance.

Reasons for this include greater success in girls' learning methods, better noncognitive abilities, greater self-discipline, greater girls' willingness to conform – external recognition is more important to them – girls' greater willingness to learn, and finally girls' cultural activity (read more, their cultural consumption was higher). The research found that despite their poorer (social) background performance, girls were more successful (more language exams, better averages, bolder continuing education plans, more study competitions). However, the situation is not so clear in higher education. At the time of admission, girls have an advantage (more students continue their studies, have better maturity scores, have more language exams), but according to some indicators (academic student activity, publications, college membership, doctoral plans), boys are already favored. These results are already predicting that boys will be more successful in the labor market, particularly in terms of scientific careers. Boys, if they are going to college (and not "lost" in apprenticeship training), may have a stronger emphasis on PhD and research careers.

According to Fényes's research results, the gender structure of the Hungarian higher education graduation rate is only partly consistent. Hungarian female students complete tertiary education at a rate of about 8 percentage points higher than male students. This gender gap is below the average in OECD countries (reporting data) – the Hungarian graduation rate may well be the lowest among women (and lowest among men) (Table 6.2).

Table 6.2. Completion Rates in Tertiary Education (2011).

	Men	**Women**
Sweden	53	53
United States	51	54
Hungary	**48**	**56**
New Zealand	56	61
Norway	52	64
Mexico	61	72
Portugal	59	73
Poland	48	74
Czech Republic	64	78
Netherlands	65	78
Turkey	72	78
Belgium (Fl.)	66	79
Finland	66	83
Denmark	78	84
Japan	87	92

Source: Education at a Glance (2013).

4.2 Status Consistency between Women's Educational and Labor Market Status

According to Fényes' research,

> While women's educational attainment is in many respects more favorable, other researches and our findings show that they are still at a disadvantage in the labor market. According to our studies, the post-graduate position of graduate women is also much less favorable than that of men, and in addition to income disadvantages, we have also been able to detect the underlying horizontal and vertical segregation in the labor market by gender. Three years after graduation, men had significantly higher monthly net income and women had a much higher share in education, health and social care, which are well known to be underpaid. In addition, the proportion of female graduates was lower in the private sector and higher in the public and non-profit sectors, which is also a source of lower earnings. Finally, three years after graduation, we have shown that boys hold a much higher proportion of managerial positions than women, and this is true for middle and non-senior executives.

Women pay less for investment in education than boys. It also states that boys' social mobility is greater and that they gain a more favorable position than their parents by examining not only their education but also their income and other status (Fényes, 2011).

According to Adamecz-Völgyi's research, since the early 1990s, the gender-adjusted wage gap has decreased in Hungary. However, if we look at the question by educational attainment, we see only a decrease in the low-skilled, and the gender pay gap among the high-skilled. This phenomenon may take the form of a so-called glass ceiling. As they write:

> We find that the gender-adjusted wage gap is nearly one and a half times higher in tertiary education than in the other educational attainment categories. A woman of the same age and tertiary education at the same company and occupation earned an average of 16 percent less in 2016 than a man, while the difference between those with lower qualifications was around 11 percent. This difference is due to the fact that the wage gap between men and women with low educational attainment has decreased over the past two decades, but has increased among those with higher education. (Adamecz-Völgyi, 2018)

Based on research, Keczer (2014) draws the following conclusions regarding the position of women in the specific labor market segment in the academic labor market:

- Although women are already in the majority in higher education, the proportion of women in university and research positions is lower. One reason for this may be prejudice against women, both male and female critics, which prevents them from gaining these jobs.
- There is clearly a so-called glass ceiling in the scientific career, that is, women get stuck in lower pay-grades.
- The main reason for this is the traditional role of women in the family; having children and caring for the family delays and slows down scientific progress. The interviewed interviewees consider this a natural, welcome and voluntary task.
- The role of the partner and the family is also crucial. It is common for women to overshadow their professional careers for the benefit of their husbands, and one reason for the breakup of young marriages is that the husband does not support his wife's professional pursuits.
- According to international literature and Hungarian research, women have to cope with serious discrimination and have to do more to advance than their male counterparts. However, if they succeed in breaking through the glass ceiling, there will be greater professional acceptance and support. Obstacles also depend on the field of science and the topic of research: it is more difficult to advance in "male" fields of science.
- Universities' masculine organizational culture also has an impact on leadership: international studies report a number of masculine, female-negative leadership practices, and lead interviewees show initial resistance from male leaders and malicious attitudes toward women.
- Women are rather underrepresented in scientific decision-making. In many countries, women's quotas have been introduced, but interviewees say this is not an option. Since most of the above-mentioned phenomena are caused by social traditions and attitudes, progress can only be achieved by changing them.

5. Public Policies to Promote Gender Balance in Higher Education

In 2015, the Hungarian Government issued a Higher Education policy paper (Shifting of Gears, 2015) and supplemented it with an Action Plan (Shifting of Gears, 2016).

The strategic material deals with female students in one place. According to the policy changes,

> The rigid institutional structure, which has in many cases become obsolete, is also hampering a more open training supply and research portfolio. Rethinking institutional-level capacities for specific disciplines requires exploring and activating the currently untapped infrastructure and human resource potential (one example of which is the low proportion of female students in technical and IT disciplines) and re-positioning institutional profiles. (Shifting of Gears, 2015, p. 21)

Higher education policy, accompanied by an action plan, is already paying more attention, albeit somewhat one-sided, to the issue. According to the material,

> Although there has been a significant surplus of female graduates for decades, women are lagging behind men at higher ranks in the scientific hierarchy. The employment hierarchy is gradually opening up in the university hierarchy, while the proportion of full-time students is female, with only one-third of associate professors and only one-fifth of university professors being female. In the event of significant disparities in training (and thus in the professions), early career guidance, already in grades 6–8, can provide appropriate intervention. They have very successful programs, but need to be expanded nationally. (Shifting of Gears, 2016, p. 12)

The material states in the strategy that as a result of measures in the field of higher education women's participation in STEM degree programs will increase (Shifting of Gears, 2016, p. 18).

Later, the material formulates as one of its objectives the "Development of education systems providing opportunities, social advancement, and wide access," one element of which is that Hungarian higher education, as one of the best functioning social mobility channels in modern society, promotes access to higher education. The objective is particularly focused on young people living in disadvantaged regions, the disabled, the Roma and women (Graduation, 2016, p. 20). In this context, it envisages niche investments in promoting distance learning opportunities for female students, as well as child-friendly solutions on-site (changing diapers and nursing facilities, children's corners, child care facilities) in the campus student service area (Graduation, 2016, pp. 21–22).

Another objective is to "increase the number of female educators and researchers in under-represented areas and in leadership positions." In support of this, the text states:

> Although there has been a significant surplus of women with higher education for decades, women are lagging behind men at higher levels of the scientific hierarchy. The employment hierarchy is gradually opening up in the university hierarchy, while the proportion of full-time students is female, with only one-third of associate professors and only one-fifth of university professors being female. Promoting part-time employment and childfriendly workplaces, as well as the necessary infrastructure and organizational improvements to achieve these goals, can be achieved through teaching and career development (Shifting of Gears, 2016, p. 31) to ensure gender mainstreaming in operations to ensure the recruitment of young people, in order

to reduce the disadvantages of a female research career from the postdoctoral phase.

Furthermore, the material states that the infrastructural and organizational improvements necessary for the spread of part-time employment must be initiated and the infrastructural and organizational improvements necessary for the creation and expansion of child-friendly workplaces must be implemented. In order to increase the supply of female educators and researchers, investments are needed that promote women's part-time and teleworking opportunities and implement child-friendly solutions at the sites (rooms where mothers can child diaper, where they can breastfeed their children, rooms where children can play, and childcare rooms) (Shifting of Gears, 2016, pp. 31–32).

A further objective of the police: "Provide sufficient STEM candidates for graduate graduates to meet the needs of business and science professionals." One element of this is the implementation of science education and awareness raising activities that facilitate the IT and technical education field. Here, women's participation is significantly lower than men's (only 14% and 24%, respectively) – higher involvement of talented women and support for women's participation (Graduation, 2016, p. 80).

As a result of the policy, child-friendly solutions (changing and nursing areas, children's corners, nurseries) have been developed at universities. At the same time, the impact of the measures is rather moderate, although there is no doubt that some time has passed since the policy was made public. The proportion of female students enrolled in the IT group was 14% in 2014, 15% in 2016, and 16% in 2018. Between 2014 and 2017, the proportion of women among all professors increased by 1%, including 16% of university professors in 2014, 17% of women in 2017, and 30%–32% of associate professors the female ratio.

The aims of the policy essentially reflect the "familist" approach: on many occasions, the promotion of child-friendly infrastructure appears in the material, while measures to eliminate barriers to women's participation, promotion, and earning opportunities are scarce.

6. Employment Characteristics of Graduate Women

6.1 Employment Rate, Unemployment Rate, Inactivity Rate

The employment rate of Hungarian women graduates fell as a result of the 2008 economic crisis and only started to return to the OECD average after 2010. Compared to the employment rate of graduate men, the gap of 10 percentage points in 2000 increased slightly by 2017. While the employment rate of higher-educated men has risen above the OECD average in recent years, female graduates have fallen short of the OECD average (while it was in 2000).

The unemployment rates of Hungarian graduate women and men are very close to each other and have been moving along much over time, and both are better (lower) than the OECD average.

Table 6.3. Employment, Unemployment, and Inactivity Rates for Men and Women with a Tertiary Education in the 25–64 Age Group in Hungary and OECD Average 2000–2017.

		2000	**2007**	**2010**	**2017**
			Employment rate		
Man	Hungary – Man	87.4	86.5	83.1	92.4
	Average of OECD countries	88.6	89.5	87.4	89.4
Woman	Hungary – Woman	78.0	75.6	75.2	79.6
	Average of OECD countries	78.0	80.4	79.1	81.0
			Unemployment rate		
Man	Hungary – Man	1.3	2.2	4.5	1.3
	Average of OECD countries	3.5	2.9	4.9	3.7
Woman	Hungary – Woman	1.2	2.9	3.8	1.6
	Average of OECD countries	4.3	3.6	5.0	4.4
			Inactivity rate		
Man	Hungary – Man	11.4	11.5	13.0	6.4
	Average of OECD countries	8.2	7.9	8.1	7.2
Woman	Hungary – Woman	21.0	22.2	21.8	19.1
	Average of OECD countries	18.6	16.6	16.8	15.3

Source: OECD.Stat Dataset: Educational attainment and labour-force status: Trends in employment, unemployment and inactivity rates, by educational attainment and age group. Retrieved from https://stats.oecd.org/Index.aspx?DataSetCode=EAG_NEAC#

The inactivity rate explains why the Hungarian female employment rate is lower than that of men. Inactivity for women is significantly higher than for men (essentially as much as the employment rate for men is higher). But it also appears that the inactivity of Hungarian graduate women is relatively significantly higher than the OECD average. One reason for this, supported by research, is that the division of labor between the sexes is very traditional in Hungary. Lower Hungarian female inactivity is obviously related to childbearing and childcare, and shorter or longer female inactivity after childbirth. It is also part of the picture – and this is another reason for high inactivity – that the legal paid childcare period for Hungarian women is one of the highest among developed countries, which, as research has shown, is leading to an increase in inactivity. At the same time, the decline in the inactivity rate of Hungarian women during the period under review is striking, which is in line with international trends (Table 6.3).

6.2 Graduate Wage Benefit and Individual Rate of Return on Higher Education

The Hungarian graduate wage advantage was the highest among OECD countries until 2010, and then slipped to second only because Chile became a member of the organization, where the wage of tertiary education to the upper secondary level was more than 40 percentage points higher compared to Hungary, and from 2015, Mexico will also be ahead of us by a few percentage.

When analyzing the individual costs of education, two costs are used to account for direct education costs and foregone earnings.[4] And, as an individual income from education, they sum up the growth in life earnings, reduced by taxes and duties, compared to the previous grade, taking into account labor market success.[5] Total individual higher education expenditure is among the lowest for both men and women (22 out of 25 reporting countries, 21 for women).

Based on all these, the individual rate of return on higher education can be calculated.[6]

In 2011, the individual rate of return on Hungarian higher education qualifications for men was the second highest among the 24 reporting countries (after Poland, before the Czech Republic, Slovakia, and Estonia) among OECD countries. In the case of women, the Hungarian rate was fourth after Poland, Portugal, and the Czech Republic before Slovenia and Slovakia. However, in 2015, out of 29 reporting countries, men had only a sixth ROI (after Chile, Turkey, Israel, Korea, and Ireland) and women only 17th.

In 2015, the rate of return on private expenditure on higher education was 20% for Hungarian men and 14% for women. (Among OECD countries, the highest returns for men were in Chile and Turkey with 31% -31. For women, the same countries were in the lead in Turkey with 41% and Chile with 35%). So higher education is a good investment for both sexes.

The lower rates of return for women are the result of lower earnings (which is partly due to discrimination against women in earnings and structural differences in employment, which also have discriminatory features).

Between 2011 and 2015, the rates of return for both genders decreased, by just over 5 percentage points for men and about 2 percentage points for women. Nevertheless, the position of women deteriorated significantly more than that of men. The reason for this is that the rate of return on women increased significantly in 2015 compared to 2011 in significantly more countries than men.

---

[4]For a detailed definition, see Education at a Glance (2013, pp. 138–141).

[5]For definition and methodology, see Education at a Glance (2015, pp. 138–141).

[6]Just as Education at a Glance OECD Indicators does so regularly.

It can be stated that the situation of Hungarian graduates in the labor market is characterized by the fact that Hungarian graduates, including female graduates, have a significant wage advantage over those with upper secondary education, and due to the relatively low costs of individual higher education rate of return among OECD countries. However, since the mid-2010s, rising tuition rates have led to a decline in the rate of return on individual costs, especially for women, due to a reduction in the number of publicly funded female – some of them pay tuition fees.[7]

7. Critical Points in the Scientific and Social Debate on Women and Their Perspectives in Higher Education

As has been said, the conservative government's policy on women since 2010 has been characterized by a very strong familiarization, that is, women are seen primarily as mothers (Gregor & Kováts, 2018, p. 4). The government policy on higher education presented earlier sees the expansion of female student facilities as the basis for child-friendly solutions (changing diapers and nursing facilities, children's corners, child care facilities). While it briefly addresses the issue of helping Roma young people to enter higher education, it does not mention, for example, promoting Roma girls' access to higher education (e.g., admission or tertiary education programs, etc.). It also identifies the child in the child-friendly design of the premises (diapers and nursing facilities, children's corner, baby sitting room). There are no options like the use of women's quotas for teacher training.

This also shows that government policy on women is one-sided in many ways. The UN Conclusions on Women in Hungary 2013 (United Nations, 2013) make recommendations to the Hungarian state in more than 40 points. Of these, we only cite educational recommendations.

While noting women's high level of education, the Committee remains concerned that women and girls continue to choose traditionally female-dominated fields of education, such as social sciences and humanities, and that they are underrepresented in technical and vocational training. The Committee also notes that women are overrepresented as teachers but it regrets that no data are provided on women holding decision-making positions in schools and faculties. While noting the Strategic Plan of the Roma Integration Decade Program, the Committee is concerned about the lack of information on the situation of Roma girls in the education system. The Committee is further concerned that

[7]Public funding of Hungarian higher education distinguishes between publicly funded (scholarship-free, tuition-free) and nonpublicly funded (self-financed, i.e., tuition fee) students. Each year, the state determines the number of publicly funded admitted staff per degree program. During admission to higher education, based on the scores outlined above, the category of admitted student is decided. Since the mid-2010s, the state has preferred STEM courses, also in terms of the score a student receives from government support. A significant proportion of the humanities and social sciences, with a high female participation rate, receive only state support above a high score.

educational programs aimed at strengthening family life skills reinforce traditional gender stereotypes.

The Committee recommends that the State party

- Intensify its efforts aimed at diversifying academic and vocational choices for women and men and take further measures to encourage women and men to choose nontraditional fields of education and careers;
- Adopt a system to collect disaggregated relevant statistical data regarding the situation of Roma girls in the education system that allows the State party to measure the results of its programs and resource allocation;
- Eliminate segregation of Roma girls in the educational system and provide them with equal access to quality education at all levels; and
- Ensure that educational programs on family life skills adequately address the principle of nondiscrimination and substantive equality of women and men as well as the prevailing stereotypes against women.

The Committee also recommends that the State Party apply temporary special measures to

- Promote the equal participation of women in public and political life and decision-making by means of concrete result-oriented measures, such as quotas and timetables; and
- Facilitate access to education and employment for women in rural areas, Roma women and women with disabilities.

In connection with stereotypes and discriminatory practices, the Committee calls on the State Party to adopt the necessary steps to adequately include nondiscrimination and gender equality in educational policies, in particular the National Core Curriculum and related documents, as well as in basic and continuing education for teachers and healthcare professionals and other service providers.

It can be seen from the above that Hungarian higher education policy is in many respects indebted to it by taking some more radical steps – e.g., the use of women's quotas, the special support for Roma women – formulated in the 2013 UN Recommendation. Hungarian higher education policy, and also government policy as a whole, lacks radical action against discrimination against women and the effect of the glass ceiling.

However, as one of the recommendations of a comprehensive analysis points out,

> There is no political risk for parties to open the gates of big politics to more women politicians. A negligible percentage of people think that this would have negative effects; the majority have positive expectations or expect no change in women's greater political participation. (Gregor & Kováts, 2018)

> The symbolic policy of the [regrettable] regime has clearly prioritized women's reproductive and household functions over other functions of social participation (negligible number of female politicians, degradation of "female affairs"), and a series of specific governmental measures to combat "gender ideology" associate (compulsory parental care, CSOK [Housing Allowance, dependent on number of children]). (Barna, Csányi, Gagyi, & Gerőcs, 2018)

8. For Closing

In our analysis, we presented some characteristics of the position of women in higher education and in the labor market in Hungary, with a somewhat broader social horizon. The Hungarian situation is special in many respects, though not unprecedented among postsocialist countries. The feminism of the state-socialist period was replaced by familism after the change of regime.

In the foreword of a study published by a women's advocacy organization on women's politics in the postcommunist period,

> Whether ignorance or awareness was in the background, gender equality was not important to any party or government. Hungarian women's politics are still maintained by the family and social policy systems developed in state socialism. (Juhász, 2014, p. 27)

The position of Hungarian women in terms of education, health, employment, and wages is above average and extremely poor in terms of political and economic leadership.

In 2010, women's politics changed in the direction of further strengthening of familism. The incumbent Conservative Government is advocating the protection of the traditional family, and, given the desperate demographic situation, would encourage women to have more children and therefore to slow down their pursuit of education (which fundamentally affects their willingness to have children). At the same time, girl students are an indispensable source of immersion in tertiary education institutions, which is why they are seeking to create a family- and child-friendly environment for women who have already entered tertiary education and have children.

Government policy is also characterized by the elimination of gender majors in public higher education, as well as the marginalization of various women's organizations by disabling NGOs (Ilonszki, 2014).

Ultimately, the higher education policies of the past decade have led to a decline in the proportion of female students. Support for female students in higher education is also fundamentally "familial," and very little is done to increase the proportion of women in higher education or to promote Roma girls' access to higher education.

Hungary, which has one of the highest masculinity indices among developed countries, does not seem to be able to move away from masculinity, which has its effect on women's politics and higher education's women's politics.[8]

References

Adamecz-Völgyi, A. (2018). Nemek közötti bérkülönbség az iskolai végzettség függvényében. (Gender pay gap as a function of education) In K. Fazekas & Á. Szabó-Morvai (Eds.). *Munkaerőpiaci tükör 2017* (Labor market mirror 2017.) (pp.152–156). Budapest: MTA Közgazdaság- és Regionális Tudományi Kutatóközpont Közgazdaság-tudományi Intézet.

Barna, E., Csányi, G., Gagyi, Á., & Gerőcs, T. (2018). A rendszerváltozás utáni magyar feminista mozgalom globális, történeti perspektívából. (The Hungarian feminist movement after the regime change, from a global, historical perspective). *Replika, 108–109*(3–4), 241–262. Retrieved from http://www.replika.hu/system/files/archivum/replika_108-109-14_barna_csanyi_gagyi_gerocs.pdf

Declercq, K., & Varga, J. (2018). Horizontális nemi szegregáció a felsőoktatásban – STEM-jelentkezések. (Horizontal gender segregation in higher education – higher education applicants for STEM courses.) In K. Fazekas & Á. Szabó-Morvai (Eds.). *Munkaerőpiaci tükőr 2017* (Labor market mirror 2017.) (pp. 114–121. Budapest: MTA Közgazdaság- és Regionális Tudományi Kutatóközpont Közgazdaság-tudományi Intézet.

Dubcsik, C., & Tóth, O. (2008). Feminizmus helyett familizmus. (Familism instead of feminism.) *Demográfia, 51*(4), 307–328.

Dumetz, J., & Cadil, J. (2018). Challenging the masculinity index: The end of across-cultural myth. *International Journal of Social Science, 7*(1), 49–68. Retrieved from https://pdfs.semanticscholar.org/76be/256c8809ef3e890bc5b5dc63b637280bfefb.pdf

Education at a Glance. (2013). *OECD Indicators*. Paris: OECD Publishing.

Fényes, H. (2009). Nemek szerinti iskolai eredményesség és a férfihátrány hipotézis. (Gender school achievement and the male disadvantage hypothesis.) *Magyar Pedagógia, 109*(1), 77–101.

Fényes, H. (2011). A felsőoktatásban tanuló férfiak és nők tényleges mobilitása, státuszinkonzisztencia a nők oktatásbeli és munkaerő-piaci helyzete között. (Actual mobility of men and women in higher education, status inconsistency between women's educational and labor market situation.) *Felsőoktatási Műhely, 4*(3), 79–95.

Gender Equality Index. (2017). *Gender Equality Index 2017 methodological report*. Luxemburg: Publications Office of the European Union. Retrieved from https://eige.europa.eu/sites/default/files/documents/ti_pubpdf_mh0417333enn_pdfweb_20171030101356.pdf

Gender Equality Index. (2019). *Gender Equality Index 2019 in brief: Still far from the finish line*. Vilnius: European Institute for Gender Equality. Retrieved from https://eige.europa.eu/sites/default/files/documents/20190390_mh0419039enn_pdf.pdf

Gregor, A., & Kováts, E. (2018). *Nőügyek 2018. Társadalmi problémák és megoldási stratégiák. A kutatási eredmények összefoglalója.* (Women's Affairs 2018. Social

[8]Hungary is ranked third behind Slovakia and Japan. See Dumetz and Cadi (2018).

Problems and Solution Strategies. Summary of research results.) Budapest: Friedrich-Ebert-Stiftung.

Ilonszki, G. (2014). Jó kormányzás és a nemek egyenlősége. Magyarországi helyzetjelentés. (Good governance and gender equality. Situation report in Hungary.) In B. Juhász (Ed.), *A nőtlen évek ára. A nők helyzetének közpolitikai elemzése 1989–2013* (The price of years without women. Public Policy Analysis of the Situation of Women 1989–2013) (pp. 29–58). Budapest: Magyar Női Érdekérvényesítő Szövetség. Retrieved from https://mek.oszk.hu/14900/14936/14936.pdf

Juhász, B. (2014). Előszó. (Foreword.) In B. Juhász (Ed.), A nőtlen évek ára A nők helyzetének közpolitikai elemzése 1989–2013 (The price of years without women. Public Policy Analysis of the Situation of Women 1989–2013) (pp. 29–58). Budapest: Magyar Női Érdekérvényesítő Szövetség. Retrieved from https://mek.oszk.hu/14900/14936/14936.pdf

Keczer, G. (2014). Üvegplafon III. Nák a kutatói pályán – fékek és akadályok. (Glass ceiling III. Women on the research field – brakes and obstacles.) *Taylor*, *6*(1–2), 392–402.

Kelemen, I. (2008). Nőpolitika Magyarországon a rendszerváltás előtt és után. (Women's policy in Hungary before and after the change of regime.) Retrieved from https://seed.hu/files/munchen_kelemen_ida.pdf

Koncz, K. (2014). Nők a parlamentben, 1990–2014. (Women in parliament, 1990–2014.) *Demográfia*, *92*(6), 514–540.

Lovász, A., & Simonovits, B. (2018). Klasszikus munkapiaci diszkrimináció. (Classical labor market discrimination.). In K. Fazekas & Á. Szabó-Morvai (Eds.). *Munkaerőpiaci tükür 2017* (Labor market mirror 2017.) (pp. 174–176). Budapest: MTA Közgazdaság- és Regionális Tudományi Kutatóközpont Közgazdaságtudományi Intézet.

Pongrácz, T. (2005). A nemi szerepek társadalmi megítélése. Egy nemzetközi összehasonlító vizsgálat tapasztalatai. (Social perception of gender roles. An experience from an international comparative study.). In I. Nagy, T. Pongrácz, & I. G. Tóth (Eds.), *Szerepváltozások. Jelentés a nők és férfiak helyzetéről 2005* (Role changes'. Report on the situation of women and men 2005.) (pp. 15–43). Budapest: Tárki – Ifjúsági, Családügyi, Szociális és Esélyegyenlőségi Minisztérium.

Pongrácz, T., & Murinkó, L. (2009). Háztartási munkamegosztás. Azonosságok és különbségek Európában. (Division of household work. Similarities and differences in Europe). In I. Nagy & T. Pongrácz (Eds.), *Szerepváltozások. Jelentés a nők és férfiak helyzetéről 2009* (Role changes'. Report on the situation of women and men 2009.) (pp. 27–51). Budapest: TÁRKI – Szociális és Munkaügyi Minisztérium.

Shifting of Gears. (2015). *Fokozatváltás a felsőoktatásban 2015. A teljesítményelvű felsőoktatás fejlesztésének irányvonalai.* (Shifting of Gears in Higher Education. Guidelines for the development of performance-based higher education.) Budapest: Emberi Erőforrások Minisztériuma. (Ministry of Human Resources.) Retrieved from https://www.kormany.hu/download/d/90/30000/fels%C5%91oktat%C3%A1si%20koncepci%C3%B3.pdf

Shifting of Gears. (2016). *Fokozatváltás a felsőoktatásban, középtvùé szakpolitikai stratégia 2016, Cselekvési Terv 2016–2020.* (Shifting of Gears in Higher Education. Mid-term Policy Strategy 2016. Action Plan 2016–2020.) Budapest: Emberi Eröforrások Minisztériuma. (Ministry of Human Resources.) Retrieved from https://www.kormany.hu/download/b/fa/11000/EMMI%20fokozatv%C3%A1lt%C3%A1s%20fels%C5%91oktat%C3%A1s%20cselekv%C3%A9si%20terv%20Sajt%C3%B3%20%C3%A9s%20Kommunik%C3%A1ci%C3%B3s%20F%C5%91oszt%C3%A1ly%2020170627.pdf

Simonovits, B., & Szeitl, B. (2018). Nők és férfiak helyzete – nemzetközi összehasonlításban. (The situation of women and men – in an international comparison.). In T. Kolosi & I. G. Tóth (Eds.), *Társadalmi Riport 2018* (Social Report 2018.) (pp. 166–183). Budapest: TÁRKI.

United Nations. (2013). *Concluding observations on the combined seventh and eighth periodic reports of Hungary adopted by the Committee at its fifty fourth session (11 February –1 March 2013)*. New York, NY: United Nations – CEDAW. Retrieved from https://www2.ohchr.org/english/bodies/cedaw/docs/co/CEDAW.C.HUN.CO.7-8.pdf

Varga, J. (2018). A női-férfi iskolázottsági különbségek átalakulása. (Transformation of female-male educational differences.). In K. Fazekas & Á. Szabó-Morvai (Eds.): *Munkaerőpiaci tükör 2017* (Labor market mirror 2017.) (pp. 97–102). Budapest: MTA Közgazdaság- és Regionális Tudományi Kutatóközpont Közgazdaságtudományi Intézet.

Chapter 7

Gender and Higher Education in Spain: A Changing and Hopeful Landscape

Alejandra Montané López, José Beltrán Llavador and Daniel Gabaldón-Estevan

1. A Brief History of Women's Access to Universities in Spain

The Royal Decree dated March 8, 1910, which was promoted by Emilia Pardo Bazán, gave women in Spain unrestricted access to university education. Before that, female presence in Spanish universities was an exception. In 1882, women were excluded by a Royal Order which put an end to a legal loophole which had allowed some women to undertake university studies. During the second half of the nineteenth century, there emerged the belief that although the main mission of women was to care for children and the family, they could undertake other tasks with the appropriate education and instruction and support the earnings of their husbands. In Spain, much discussion centered on the ability of women to acquire the knowledge needed to practice a profession, and how they should acquire it. In the meantime, in some other countries, women were obtaining high school certificates and being accepted to study at universities.

Consuelo Flecha (1989, 1996, 1997, 2013) describes the position of women in universities at that time. The legal loophole mentioned above allowed María Elena Masseras Ribera to be the first female student enrolled in Spain in 1872 in the Faculty of Medicine at the University of Barcelona, although there is anecdotal evidence that in 1849, Concepción Arenal disguised herself as a man in order to study law at the University of Madrid

International Perspectives on Gender and Higher Education, 115–133

doi:10.1108/978-1-83909-886-420201007

(Flecha, 1996).[1,2] The male cultural model was ingrained and denial of female capacity for study persisted. Sáez de Melgar (1871) (cited by Flecha, 1996, p. 70) pondered on the reasons for the denial of female intelligence and wondered what men feared about enlightened women. Flecha (1996, p. 71) cites an editorial from the magazine *La Ilustración de la Mujer* (*The Enlightenment of Women)*, which describes the reluctance of men to allow women to enroll at a university:

> The fact that some young people abroad and in our homeland have distinguished themselves in scientific professions frightens the other sex in such a way that they no longer see a reasonable average term, and the memory of the Sanchichas spinning a bast flake, give way to the vision of Mari-Sabidillas invading courts, congresses and academies. Nothing more common among us, when this point of higher education and equality of the beautiful sex is touched, than to see certain people climb on the stilts of their ignorance and ridicule the idea, exaggerating its applications.[3]

After that, up to 1910, a total of 77 women enrolled for university courses, of whom only 36 graduated. In 1935, the number went up to more than 2000. The subsequent war and the Franco regime did nothing to improve women's access to universities. The problem this time was not one of legal regulations, but rather the medieval ecclesiastical model that persisted in Spanish universities well into

---

[1]With the exception of Italy, universities in Europe were mostly exclusively male until the nineteenth century in some countries and the twentieth century in others. However, there are some notable exceptions. In 1678, the Venetian noblewoman Elena Lucrezia Cornaro Piscopia obtained a PhD in Philosophy, which was an unprecedented event. Also in 1678, Anna Maria von Shuurman died; she was the first woman to study at the University of Utrecht on condition that she was locked "in a wooden room placed inside the same university classroom, separated by a wooden wall in which holes had been made" (de Lauretis, 2000, p. 12, 13). Early universities adhered to the traditional misogynistic androcentrism of the patriarchal culture, as reflected in the Decree Resolution of 1377 issued by the faculty staff of the University of Bologna, which included in its first statutes: "And since women are the main cause of sin, the weapon of the devil, the cause of man's expulsion from paradise and the destruction of the old law, and since, consequently, it is necessary to carefully avoid all trade with her, we forbid and expressly prohibit anyone from allowing any woman to be brought in to the university, no matter who she may be, even the most honest of women. And if anyone does so in spite of everything, he will be severely punished by the rector."

[2]However, she needed a special permit and was not allowed to attend classes. Women's attendance in classes was allowed for the first time in 1875. María Elena Masseras obtained special permission from King Amadeo of Savoy to undertake secondary school studies and then to continue on to university. Dolores Aleu Riera was the first woman to obtain the Bachelor's degree in Medicine, awarded on April 20, 1882.

[3]*La Ilustración de la mujer* (Editorial. Barcelona), No. 14, 15 December 1883, p. 106.

the twentieth century. The influence of the church and consolidation of the Napoleonic model – subscribed to by Spanish universities until after the 1980s – was characterized by elitism, centralization, and the utilitarianism of higher education (Montané & Carvalho, 2012, 2013). An orientation to elitist professional utilitarianism allowed the emergence of highly centralized universities (Souvirón, 1989).

During the Franco regime, in the 1950s, the first transformation occurred, which increased the participation of women in higher and university education. Women's access to education – especially that of middle-class women – was enhanced by the exodus from rural life to industry and cities. Nevertheless, women's participation in higher education was generally considered inappropriate. The Spanish university was, until its reform in the early 1980s, anchored on a traditional model aimed at preparing men for a profession, rather than pursuing the mission of an open and scientific university (Montané, A., Beltrán, J., & Gabaldón-Estevan 2017). As a consequence, its function as a creator of science and transmitter of values and culture was delayed (Beltrán & Montané, 2016, 2018, 2019; Beltrán & Montané, 2015; Montané, Beltrán, Galleguillos, & Olivé, 2010; Montané & Carvalho, 2013).[4]

The establishment of democracy in Spain, together with its progressive integration in Europe, changed the position of women in society and education. The most profound changes were in the university system and allowed women full access to university education; this was enshrined in the Spanish Constitution of 1978 and specified in the 1983 University Reform Law (LRU in Spanish). It was clear that the university system needed restructuring, and its reform occurred sooner than reforms at other levels of education (the Organic Law of Secondary Education, or LOGSE, in 1990).

The 1982 elections resulted in a major Socialist victory, thanks in part to the transition, which up till then was still heavily influenced by the previous regime. The LRU was aimed at reform of the Spanish higher education system. However, this was controversial, since while moving toward a general university, it was anchored in the past with medieval-like didactics and no strong bourgeois participation (Sotelo, 2008). The combination of these heterogeneous elements was explosive. The LRU decreed an ideological transition and initiated a balanced transformation of higher education to reform the university system and higher education (Souvirón, 1989).

In this period, women's entry into universities was much lower than their participation in other types of education. Nevertheless, women's participation in higher education increased, although there was no equality of participation in Spanish universities. Spanish women born in the 1940s and 1950s experienced rapid social change over a very short period of time.

---

[4]These authors analyzed other aspects of the Spanish university system such as equity, governance, world-class university, and mergers (Beltrán & Montané, 2015; Beltrán, Montané & Gabaldón-Estevan, 2016, 2018, 2019).

Since the 1980s, as the result of international conventions and feminist movements, several organizations were established to promote gender equality. This was the beginning of the institutionalization of equality policies in Spain. The establishment of the women's Institute in 1983 was a significant milestone in this institutionalization and served to consolidate "state feminism" or institutional feminism (Bustelo, 2004).

2. Genesis of Gender Policies in Spain: Formal Equality, Real Equality?

The Organic University Law 6/2001 dated December 21, 2001 (LOU), established that Spanish universities should aim for a balanced representation of women and men in their collegiate bodies (art. 13). Law 7/2007, dated April 12, 2007, regulated the basic statute referring to public employees and required gender equality in the composition of tribunals that give access to public sector employment (art. 60.1).

Organic Law 3/2007, dated March 22, 2007, concerning gender equality (the LOIEMH in Spanish) was one of the most relevant events in the legal system to promote substantive change aimed at equality. The law transposes European Parliament and Council Directive 2002/73/EC, dated September 23, 2002, concerning equality, and obliges public authorities to ensure the inclusion of gender equality in public policies and recognition of the role of women in the fields of culture, history, and economics. This law was aimed at achieving equality between women and men and includes criteria that need to be fulfilled by public authorities. This, together with the goal of transversality, was responsible for the complexity and extent of this state legislative action whose development covers the various areas of the legal system where legislation to guarantee or promote equality is necessary.

Since the LOIEMH was approved for the effective equality of women and men in March 2007, a whole state, regional, and local mechanism of sensitization, awareness, and regulation of the situation of women to combat direct and indirect sexual discrimination was launched, with the purpose of making equality between women and men real and effective in all social spheres.

Thus, equality in the field of higher education is regulated via the following measures:

(1) In the field of higher education, public authorities, in the exercise of their respective competences, shall promote teaching and research on gender equality;
(2) To this end, public authorities shall promote

- The inclusion in curricula, where appropriate, of teaching about gender equality (in line with Royal Decree 1393, dated October 2007, concerning the teaching of curricula);
- The creation of specific postgraduate courses;
- Providing courses on gender equality.

In the public university, Title V of the Organic Law is applied, for the application of equality in public employment, while Article 51 establishes the criteria of action for public authorities to apply the principle of equality, according to which public authorities, within the scope of their respective competences and in application of the principle of gender equality, shall

- Remove obstacles that imply the persistence of any type of discrimination in order to provide conditions of effective equality between women and men in access to public employment and in their professional career.
- Facilitate the reconciliation of personal, family, and work life, without prejudice to professional promotion.
- Promote equal training, both in access to public employment and throughout their professional career.
- Promote the balanced presence of women and men in selection and evaluation bodies.
- Establish effective measures of action against sexual harassment and harassment based on gender.
- Periodically evaluate the effectiveness of the principle of equality in their respective fields of action.

The third additional provision of the law includes

(1) The composition of the bodies, councils, and committees regulated in this law, as well as the evaluation and selection bodies of the Spanish Science and Technology System, shall conform to the principles of composition and balanced presence between women and men, as established by the LOIEMH, mentioned above.
(2) The Spanish Science and Technology Strategy and the State Plan for Scientific and Technical Research shall promote the incorporation of gender perspective as a transversal category in research and technology so that its relevance is considered in all aspects of the process, from the definition of the priorities of scientific and technical research, research problems, theoretical and explanatory frameworks, methods, data collection and interpretation, conclusions, applications and technological developments, and proposals for future studies. It shall also promote gender and women's studies, as well as specific measures to promote and recognize the presence of women in research teams.
(3) The Information System on Science, Technology, and Innovation shall collect, process, and disseminate all data disaggregated by sex and shall include indicators of presence and productivity.
(4) The procedures for the selection and evaluation of research staff at the service of Public Universities and Public Research Organizations of the General State Administration and the procedures for awarding grants and subsidies by research funding agents shall establish mechanisms to eliminate gender biases that will include, whenever possible, confidential evaluation

mechanisms that prevent the evaluator from knowing the personal characteristics of the person being evaluated, in particular their sex and race.

(5) The State Innovation Strategy shall promote the incorporation of the gender perspective as a transversal category in all aspects of its development.

(6) The Public Research Organizations shall adopt Equality Plans within a maximum of two years after the publication of this law, which shall be subject to annual monitoring. These plans must include incentives for establishments that improve gender indicators in the corresponding annual monitoring.

Thus, Law 3/2007, dated March 22 (LOIEMH) and Organic Law 4/2007, concerning the Modification of the Organic Law of Universities (LOMLOU in Spanish), regulates the creation of structures and plans for equality, key, and mandatory elements for the institutionalization of equality at universities. In this regard, equality plans have become the main instrument through which gender equality policies are articulated at Spanish universities (Montané, 2013; Pastor & Acosta, 2016).

A study conducted by Pastor, Acosta, Torres, and Calvo (2020) summarizes the situation of universities with respect to the equality plan with data from 2016, highlighting that 38.5% of universities (both public and private) are in the I Equality Plan (compulsorily drawn up in the years after 2007). This is due, in part, to a late start of the Plan, as well as the existence of repeated extensions that delayed its implementation. However, reviewing the data from the latest Scientific Report in Figures (2018), it can be seen that there has been an improvement in the situation of Spanish universities in this regard, since, currently, according to the report, 96% of public universities and 83% of private universities have had at least one gender equality plan implemented. Likewise, the report also shows that the most widespread equality measures at universities are the internal protocols for prevention and protection against sexual and gender harassment and those that refer to the reconciliation of personal, work, and family life from an institutional coresponsibility standpoint.

Even so, as Pastor et al. (2020) showed the largest source of data for the diagnosis of equality plans is secondary data provided by universities. In this regard, they emphasize that the institutions themselves do not always collaborate by showing disaggregation by sex, so in many cases, there is insufficient information. Moreover, the timing or set of indicators can be inaccurate – or they simply do not exist – and sometimes do not show clear and measurable data, which can make it difficult to prioritize measures and actions. And, of course, the low number of universities that have a budget allocated to the plan can compromise compliance with the regulations that emerge from equality policies at universities.

On January 10, 2019, the "Women, Science, and Innovation Observatory" (OMCI in Spanish) was set up, for gender equality in the Spanish Science, Technology, and Innovation System, holding monitoring, reporting, and evaluation functions, as well as that of presenting proposals, in accordance with Royal

Decree 1401/2018, dated November 23, concerning the creation of the OMCI. This interministerial collegiate body is responsible for analyzing, monitoring, and measuring impacts on the situation of women in the field of research, development, and innovation, promoting the realization of public policies and actions for gender equality, and promoting the improvement of the situation of women in the Spanish System of Science, Technology, and Innovation, the participation of women at all levels and in all fields of science, technology, and innovation, as well as the appropriate integration of gender analysis in the content of R&D policies, programs, and projects.

3. Current Data on the Presence of Women at Spanish Universities

It becomes necessary, in this context, to present some data on the presence of women at universities in order to assess the strengths and weaknesses of the immense development of the Spanish university system and equality policies from the beginning of democracy to the present. According to the report by the Ministry of Science, Innovation and Universities *Datos y cifras del sistema universitario español, Publicación 2018–2019* (2019, p. 8), the number of students enrolled at Spanish universities on undergraduate and Master's degrees in the academic year 2017–2018 amounted to 1,575,579 (1,289,233 undergraduates, 205,049 completing a Master's degree and 79,386 a PhD). Regarding the gender of the students enrolled in the academic year 2017–2018, it can be seen that 54.8% of the total enrolled were women; 55.1% in undergraduate courses; and 49.8% in Master's degrees.

Distribution by sex in the different branches of education is not yet particularly homogeneous. The main differences, both in those enrolled in 2017–2018 and in students in 2016–2017 on undergraduate courses, are, on the one hand, in Engineering and Architecture where 75% of those enrolled and 71.8% of graduates are men and, on the other, in the branch of Health Sciences where only 30% are men and 29.6% among graduates. These figures are similar in Master's degrees, where the most pronounced variation of 4.7% in the population of graduates is in the branch of Social and Legal Sciences. With regard to students enrolled on a PhD, it should be noted that 50.2% are men, reversing the trend of lower university levels (Ministerio de Ciencia, Innovación y Universidades, 2019, p. 25).

In university entrance exams, women continue to account for a higher percentage than men; in 2017, the total number of women who sat the exams was 149,300, i.e., 56.3% were women, compared to 43.7% men. The percentage of passes does not vary very much according to the sex of the participants, 87% of men passed and 87.2% of women passed, out of those who sat the exams (Datos y cifras del sistema universitario español. Publicación 2018–2019, 2019).

If we restrict ourselves to generic university entrance exams, we can see that 57.2% of those enrolled are women, 4.8% are foreign, and 7% are over 20 years old. The number of doctoral theses examined in Spain in 2016, according to the same report, was 20,049, of which 35.4% were by women.

The teaching and research staff, in the academic year 2016–2017, stands at 120,383 people. Of these, 102,297 work at public universities and 18,086 in private ones. Full-time equivalent teaching staff stood at 82,469, 0.8% more than in the previous year. Although the division of teachers by gender and faculty maintains gender differences, it is necessary to mention the improvement that is taking place in terms of the presence of women in the body of university professors.

4. Spanish Universities in the European Framework for Equality Policies

The European Union provides Spanish gender equality policies with a frame of reference from a regulatory, political, and social point of view. If the European Union contributed politically to the democratization process in Spain, from the regulatory point of view, it provided a legal framework on which to introduce new legislation, by promoting the creation and development of women's organizations and ensuring the continuity of equality policies in Spain even during times of conservative governments.

Equality between women and men is a core value in the European Union, enshrined in the European Treaties. The European Union, through a large body of legislation, actively promotes gender equality in areas such as equal pay, working and personal life balance, health and safety at work, social security, access to goods and services, and protection from human trafficking, gender-based violence, and other forms of gender-based crime (European Parliament, 2002, 2018).

The European Commission's "Strategic Engagement for Gender Equality 2016–2019" (European Commission, 2016) is the current framework for the European Commission's work toward full gender equality. The strategy identifies five priority areas, which include the increasing economic independence and participation of women in the labor market, reducing gender pay, earnings, and pension gaps, and promoting gender equality in decision-making.

The Strategic Vision of the European Research Area (ERA) marks a clear goal for 2030, by which time half of all scientists, half of all those responsible for scientific policy, in all disciplines, and at all levels will be women (*Libro Blanco: situación de las mujeres en la ciencia española*, *White Paper: the situation of women in Spanish science*, 2011). In this way, the European institutions are developing in the scientific field the mandate to apply gender policies (gender mainstreaming) established by the Treaty of Amsterdam, a treaty that includes the principle of gender mainstreaming coined by the United Nations at the World Conference of Women in Beijing in 1995.

Despite the initiatives, the equality process is ongoing. In the European Union as a whole, women account for 23.7% of level A (European Commission, 2019); a fact that highlights that, despite the existence of regulations, both domestically and internationally, the urge to incorporate the gender perspective transversally and to adopt a nonandrocentric perspective in teaching materials and research projects, gender inequalities that limit the professional, scientific, and research development of women persist (Castaño, 2016). The context is one of "incomplete depatriarchization" (Nuño & Álvarez, 2017), in which various factors converge, such as a social organization strongly marked by the sexual division of labor, the persistence of traditional gender roles, and the existence of barriers such as the "glass ceiling" (Guil, 2006, 2016), which call for the need to develop greater measures that implement equal opportunities and promote the elimination of obstacles that impede the advancement of women in their scientific careers.

A good number of European scientific institutions point out the need to implement active measures to support women's careers (*Libro Blanco: situación de las mujeres en la ciencia española*, 2011). The goal is not to lose talent, and therefore, quality and excellence in European science. In its contribution, the European Research Area Board, for example, says:

> Europe needs excellent science and innovation to tackle the Grand Challenges. All resources are needed. Irrespective of age, race or gender, the European Research Area should exploit all available talents and to that end, specific instruments should be employed. The European Union should actively encourage Member States i) to develop their tertiary education so that science and technology too are attractive to all, ii) to put in place all measures to help the daily life of women in charge of young children when they have the ambition of a successful scientific career, iii) to require their research institutions to put in place a plan and strategy to raise the share of women amongst academic staff, and monitor their development. iv) When equally competent applicants compete for a post or resources, the one representing the minority gender should have priority. v) the European Commission should ensure adequate female representation on all Committees under its responsibility.

As Sánchez de Madariaga (2011) states, removing obstacles and barriers that hinder women's careers in European science today requires effective public policies. The European Commission set out on this path in 1999 with the creation of two bodies responsible for defining and implementing the lines of action: the Women's and Science Unit (UmyC in Spanish), part of the Directorate General for Research, and the Helsinki Group, an advisory group of the Commission in which the member states participate with two people each, one on behalf of the government and one on behalf of the scientific institutions. In 2001, the Commission published a first state document on the matter, the ETAN Report Promoting Excellence through Gender Equality, which, for the first time, provides a global overview of the situation of women in European science. The Women and Science Unit (UMyC)has changed its name on several occasions and, as we have detailed in the previous section, acts in the European context through H2020 in gender-related projects.[5]

5. The Spanish Case in the European Research Area Post-2020

Increasing the participation of women in the system is and will be a goal shared by numerous scientific institutions in Europe, as was promoted by the European Commission for the definition of the Horizon 2020 Research and Innovation Program, which has marked the way forward for research financed by the European Union in recent years and whose article 16 is specifically devoted to gender equality. It states that the program "will guarantee the effective promotion of equality between men and women and the gender dimension in the content of research and innovation" These goals, established on the Fact Sheet: Gender Equality in Horizon 2020, dated December 9, 2013, are as follows:

(1) Gender balance in decision-making
(2) Gender balance in research teams
(3) Inclusion of the gender dimension in research projects and training

In order to reinforce participants' commitment, gender balance is included in the research team as one of the factors that will give priority to proposals with the same score in the evaluation process.

2019 was the 20th anniversary of European activities promoting gender equality in research. Over the last two decades, Europe has taken great strides forward, and gender equality and gender mainstreaming have become one of ERA's priorities, together with the three goals of gender balance in research teams, gender balance in decision-making, and the gender dimension in research content. Actions have moved from "fixing women" to "fixing institutions" through comprehensive gender equality plans to achieve institutional change and to "fixing knowledge" with Horizon 2020 and several domestic research funders introducing measures to ensure that new research incorporates sex and gender analysis. The body of scientific knowledge on gender and other forms of inequality in research and innovation (R&I) has expanded greatly. The ERA Roadmap 2015–2020 is coming under review in 2020 with a view to developing a new Communication for the period beyond 2020, which should propose revised ERA priorities and ERA monitoring mechanisms at the domestic and EU level, to be followed by Council Conclusions on the new ERA advisory structure. The ERA Roadmap is a catalyst for gender equality policy and measures in many EU countries, especially those where such measures had not been in place previously (Standing Working Group on Gender in Research and Innovation 2018). *Genderaction* Deliverable report 3.1 shows that for 57% of the newer Member States and 25% of the older ones, the ERA Roadmap was the first

[5]See http://www.ciencia.gob.es/portal/site/MICINN/menuitem.26172fcf4eb029fa6ec7da690 1432ea0/?vgnextoid=25c55ef3677c4610VgnVCM1000001d04140aRCRD.

policy document devoted to gender equality in research. Europe must do more to build a fair, just and equal R&I environment that answers the needs of its population.

As an example, we could highlight some of the official initiatives in which Spain is taking part, and which are ongoing or have already paid off:

Project SUPERA (June 2018–June 2022): This is an H2020 support and coordination project (CSA), which began in June 2018 to develop equality plans in research centers and funding agencies.[6] The main goal is to implement six equality plans in four European universities and two funding agencies, including the State Research Agency (AEI). These equality plans, adapted to the situation and particular characteristics of each organization, will help articulate effective equality policies and the inclusion of a gender perspective in research.

SUPERA will address the three priorities of the European Commission on gender and science:

(1) Gender equality in research careers;
(2) Balanced presence in decision-making;
(3) Gender dimension in the content of the research.

Under the SUPERA project, the Secretary of State for Universities, Research, Development, and Innovation (SEUIDI in Spanish), through the UMyC, together with the AEI, has assumed responsibility for adapting the design of equality policies to the framework of funding agencies. Also, within the framework of this project, it is planned to share good practices with regional agencies.

GENDER-NET Plus (September 2017–September 2022) is an ERA-NET Cofund H2020 that began in September 2017 to strengthen transnational collaboration between research program management entities and funding agencies, support the promotion of gender equality (gender balance) through institutional change, and promote the integration of sex and/or gender analysis in research programs. Its specific goals are to[7]

- Implement a joint transnational call to cofinance international research projects in gender studies
- Design and implement joint transnational awareness and training actions on gender equality
- Update and expand mappings and analyzes developed in GENDER-NET
- Analyze gender differences and biases in access to research aids and define and develop appropriate conditions for equal opportunities
- Promote and disseminate the main results.

The Secretary of State for Universities, Research, Development, and Innovation (SEUIDI) is taking part in particular through the UMyC in goal 1, where it

---

[6]See https://www.superaproject.eu/.
[7]See http://gender-net-plus.eu/.

coordinates the follow-up of cofinanced projects. Also regarding goal 3, it will lead a mapping and analysis of the policies and strategies of agencies and governments regarding the integration of gender in research content.

GENERACTION is an H2020 CSA, for the promotion of equality policies in R&D&I in the ERA, and whose main lines of action are[8]

- Mapping, monitoring, and evaluating the implementation of priority four measures (gender equality) of the ERA roadmaps in participating countries. Comparison to the European roadmap.
- Exchange and mutual learning among representatives of national governments to coordinate policies aimed at said priority 4.
- Interactive training for relevant agents (national governments, funding agencies, research centers, National Contact Points, etc.) in order to provide them with competencies for said priority 4.
- Strategic advice on policies for relevant agents in gender equality in European R&D.
- Promotion of gender equality in international scientific cooperation.

The Secretary of State for Universities, Research, Development, and Innovation (SEUIDI), through the UMyC, is taking part in all of them, but is in particular coordinating the fourth line, where the most strategic task is to promote the appropriate integration of the gender perspective in the next European framework program for the financing of R&D&I: Horizon Europe.

6. The Influence of New Public Management and the Economic Crisis on Equality Policies at Spanish Universities

There are two elements to consider when analyzing gender equality policies, from both an international and domestic perspective: the so-called New Public Management and the austerity policies that emerged after the 2008 financial crisis.

On the one hand, European countries have carried out reforms in higher education institutions under the influence of New Public Management, which introduces business management strategies – with transparency mechanisms and productivity and quality assessment – in the relatively independent and self-governed areas of knowledge, departments, and chairs of universities and research institutions. The new mechanisms overlap the previous systems of academic excellence and meritocracy, which govern the operation of university and scientific institutions.

Although gender equality is more a matter of equity than of efficiency, one might expect that the principles of academic excellence and meritocracy reinforced by transparency mechanisms and linked to women's inclusion policies (what has been called *inclusive excellence*, Zippel, Ferree, & Zimmermann, 2016), favoring effective gender equality. However, the opacity of selection and promotion systems, gender bias in the evaluation of merits, and the undervaluation of

[8]See https://genderaction.eu/horizon-europe/.

teaching versus research persist in today's universities, which adds to the difficulties in reconciling work and private life. According to Castaño (2016), all these factors contribute to the persistence of an atmosphere of institutionalized sexism and a lack of awareness of gender inequality. Despite the reforms and restructuring with market criteria, the key cultural changes for the advancement of gender equality are the most difficult to establish because they call the current patriarchal system at universities into question.

Furthermore, even before 2010, both equality policies and their corresponding agencies directly suffered the effects of "austerity" policies. The two waves of "austerity" measures in 2010–2011 and 2011–2013 determined a loss of institutional rank and even dismantling in equality institutions in both the State and the Self-Governing Regions (González & Segales, 2014). The PSOE government itself, after a first term of substantive progress in policies of gender equality and democratic parity, abolished the Ministry of Equality in 2010 – it had been newly created in 2008 – as one of the first ministerial reorganization measures aimed at saving administrative expense. The institution became a lower-level body (Secretary of State) located within the Ministry of Health, Social Policy, and Equality. These changes imply a significant deterioration of equality institutions because it could negatively affect their capacity for political action. Although the social inclusion and gender equality programs adopted by the socialist government in 2004–2011 protected women in the early years of the economic crisis, according to Lahey and de Villota (2013), the spending containment policies implemented in the latter period of the PSOE government mandate negatively affected the programs already implemented.

Lombardo and León (2014) observe that while in the period 2002–2008, in 90% of the cases analyzed, the funds devoted to gender equality policies increased or remained constant, in the period of economic crisis, these funds increased or remained constant in only 25.6% of cases, and yet in 74.4% of cases, the funds for equality policies actually decreased.

Subsequently, with the conservative mandate of the Popular Party, the areas devoted to equality policies were dismantled or emptied of meaning and competencies. Even so, university equality plans are still in force, and their equality units or observatories survive with minimum budgets.

According to Castaño (2016), among the factors of the university context that impact the effectiveness of gender equality policies, he draws attention to the fact that in most countries these policies were implemented at the same time as the university reform processes oriented to the introduction of market logic in the management of higher education (New Public Management) and also to the process of matching the different European university systems (the Bologna Declaration of 1999 on the creation of the European Higher Education Area, Enders et al., 2011; Faber & Westerheijden, 2011) and coinciding with a period of austerity imposed as a result of the recession that led to a certain dismantling of the mechanisms proposed to ensure equality. In our country, the new government that was recently established (January 2020) has a program of measures to move toward greater gender equality on the agenda of its social priorities, through a new

Ministry of Equality. This Ministry and the new Ministry of Universities will necessarily have to work together to achieve common goals.

7. Final Remarks

Gender equality and social policies have enjoyed spectacular growth in Spain, and in the European context, since the beginning of democracy, with developments in the civil, political, and social rights of women. We have seen a progressive institutionalization of equality bodies at different levels of government and within Spanish universities. The instruments of equality policies have diversified, from plans to laws and gender units, generating advances in public policies against gender inequality that until the beginning of the economic crisis had shown a certain solidity and future perspective. In our country, a (Red de Unidades de Igualdad de Género para la Excelencia Universitaria, 2012) (RUIGEU in Spanish) was set up, with the participation of 50 universities, currently coordinated by the University of Valencia. Aware of its commitment to both academic reflection and social action, in late 2019, it prepared a Manifesto on November 25, the International Day for the Elimination of Violence against Women. This is an example of the relevance of universities – which assume gender equality as an inalienable goal for social emancipation – as a social player.

Currently, despite the fact that women make up a majority among students, there are branches of knowledge that still resist female participation and at the highest levels of the scientific career the number of women is very limited. Although important advances have been made, which are reflected in the increase in the number of university professors and researchers, there is a situation of stagnation that causes frustration among women because their presence is scarce at the highest levels and high at the lowest levels of higher education and gender balance has not been achieved in decision-making areas (European Commission, 2015). A certain disappointment for the fruits of gender equality policies may be due both to inadequate or unfinished design, as well as to the difficulties encountered in application in university institutions with gender-biased cultures and practices.

Even so, our science already boasts great women scientists, our universities have women – students, professors, researchers – but the stretch that remains to be traveled is at least as significant as everything already achieved. Thus, we can see that

(1) There is still an equality that formally forces institutions to adapt and incorporate gender policies, but resistance, slow development, lack of will and funds, and the patriarchal model have an excessive weight even in university structures.
(2) There is a horizontal, or quantitative, segregation, which occurs to the extent that some areas of knowledge are very feminized – especially those related to life sciences – while others are very masculinized – engineering and experimental sciences (Sánchez de Madariaga, 2011; Herráez, 1996).

(3) Vertical segregation occurs in all fields, regardless of the degree of feminization of university students: there are very few women in the highest positions of science, even in the fields in which women have already made up the majority among graduates for a long time, such as medicine (Sánchez de Madariaga, 2011). In the research career, the underrepresentation of women in the highest ranking category continues to be highlighted, showing a clear vertical segregation of gender (also known as a glass ceiling): Spanish public universities still have only 21% of women among their professors (Puy, 2018).
(4) Women have less access to academic networks (Doherty & Manfredi, 2005) and opt for the so-called "soft sciences," such as the humanities and social sciences. Meanwhile, men have more presence in the so-called "hard" areas, such as empirical and technological sciences.
(5) Women have a greater teaching load than men, while men are devoted to and stand out more for their research activity (Bagilhole & White, 2003) and management (Bagilhole, 2007).
(6) The reconciliation of family and working lives is also a distorting element. Given the same number of children, a man is four times more likely to be promoted to a professor.

Consequently, as Pastor, Pontón, Belzunegui, and Acosta (2015) already advanced, it becomes very important to implement actions which, beyond simple compliance with the regulations, place the priority on improving the situation of women in the academy and science, incorporating the daily work of universities, and more specifically, equality structures, key elements to achieving a transformation of the academy, and the functioning of scientific institutions. The various obstacles that Spanish public universities face even today in terms of equality, as well as the difficulties in incorporating specific programs to benefit the development of women in their professional careers, slow down the achievement of substantive equality between men and women.

Acknowledgments

This chapter is part of the research project entitled: "Las representaciones sociales de los contenidos escolares en el desarrollo de las competencias docents," reference PGC2018-094491-B-C32, approved by the Ministry of Science, Innovation and Universities (June 27, 2019).

The authors belong to the group of CLACSO Universities and Higher Education Policies and the International Research Universities Network.

References

Bagilhole, B. (2007). Challenging women in the male academy: Think about draining the swamp. In P. Cotterill, S. Jackson, & G. Letherby (Eds.), *Challenges and negotiations for women in higher education* (pp. 21–32). Dordrecht: Springer.

Bagilhole, B., & White, K. (2003). Created in their image: An analysis of male cultural hegemony in higher education in Australian and the United Kingdom. In B. Groombridge & V. Mackie (Eds.), *Re-searching research agendas: Women, research and publication in higher education. Proceedings of the Australian techology network-women's executive development (ATN-WEXDEV)* 2003 Research Conference (pp. 1–12). Perth: Curtin University of Technology Learning Support Network.

Beltrán, J., & Montané, A. (2015). Higher education in Spain: Framework for governance and autonomy in Spanish Universities. In K. M. Joshi & S. Paivandi (Eds.), *Global higher education: Issues in governance* (pp. 63–103). New Delhi: B.R. Publishing House.

Beltrán, J., Montané, A., & Gabaldón-Estevan, D. (2016). Higher education in Spain: Framework for equity. In S. Paivandi & K. M. Joshi (Eds.), *Equity in higher education. A global perspective* (pp. 149–185). New Delhi: Studera Press.

Beltrán, J., Montané, A., & Gabaldón-Estevan, D. (2018). Through the looking glass of world-class universities. In M. Rabossi, K. M. Joshi, & S. Paivandi (Eds.), *In pursuit of world-class universities. A gobal* (pp. 115–136). New Delhi: Studera Press.

Beltrán, J., Montané, A., & Gabaldón-Estevan, D. (2019). Mergers in Spanish higher education. Practices and policies. In P. Cremonini & K. M. Joshi (Eds.), *Mergers in higher education. Practices and policies* (pp. 79–99). New Delhi: Studera Press.

Bustelo, M. (2004). *Evaluación de las políticas de género en España* [*Evaluation of gender policies in Spain*]. Madrid: Los Libros de la Catarata.

Castaño, C. (2016). La nueva gestión pública y las políticas de igualdad de género en las universidades [The new public management and gender equality policies in universities]. *Investigaciones Feministas*, *7*(2), 225–245.

De Lauretis, T. (2000). Diferencias. Etapas de un camino a través del feminismo, Madrid, Horas y horas.

Doherty, L., & Manfredi, S. (2005). *Improving women's representation in senior positions in the higher education sector, stage findings*. Oxford: Centre for Diversity Policy Research, Oxford Brookes University.

Enders, J., De Boer, H. F. & Westerheijden (Eds.) (2011). Reform of Higher Education in Europe. Rotterdam, Sense Publishers.

European Commission. (2013). Fact sheet: Gender equality in horizon 2020. Retrieved from https://ec.europa.eu/programmes/horizon2020/sites/horizon2020/files/FactSheet_Gender_2.pdf

European Commission. (2016). Strategic engagement for gender equality 2016–2019. Retrieved from https://ec.europa.eu/anti-trafficking/eu-policy/strategic-engagement-gender-equality-2016-2019_en

European Commission. (2019). *She figures 2018*. Luxembourg: Publications office of the European Union. Retrieved from https://publications.europa.eu/en/publication-detail/-/publication/9540ffa1-4478-11e9-a8ed-01aa75ed71a1/language-en

European Parliament (2002). Directive 2002/73/ EC of the European Parliament and of the Council of 23 September 2002 amending Council Directive 76/207/EEC on the implementation of the principle of equal treatment for men and women as regards access to employment, vocational training and promotion, and working conditions (Text with EEA relevance). *Official Journal L* 269, 05/10/2002 P. 0015–0020.

European Parliament. (2018). Equality between men and women. Retrieved from https://www.europarl.europa.eu/factsheets/en/sheet/59/equality-between-men-and-women

European Union. (2011). *Innovation union competitiveness report 2011*. Retrieved from http://ec.europa.eu/research/innovation-union/pdf/competitiveness-report/2011/executive-summaries/es.pdf. Accessed on September 2013.

Faber, M., & Westerheijden, D. (2011). European degree structure and national reform. In J. Enders, H. J. de Boer & D. F. Westerheijden (Eds.), *Reform of higher education in Europe* (pp. 11–28). Rotterdam, The Netherlands: Sense Publishers.

Flecha, C. (1989). Algunos aspectos sobre la mujer en la política educativa durante el régimen de Franco [Some aspects of women in educational policy during the Franco regime]. *Historia de la Educación*, *8*, 87–88.

Flecha, C. (1996). *Las primeras universitarias en España* [The first university students in Spain]. Madrid: Nancea.

Flecha, C. (1997). *Las mujeres en la legislación educativa española. Enseñanza Primaria y Normal en los siglos XVIII y XIX* [Women in Spanish educational legislation. Primary and Normal Education in the 18th and 19th centuries]. Sevilla: GIHUS, Dep. de Teoría e Historia de la Educación.

Flecha, C. (2013). Políticas y espacios para mujeres en el origen y desarrollo del sistema educativo español [Policies and spaces for women in the origin and development of the Spanish educational system]. *Bordón. Revista de Pedagogía*, *65*(4), 75–89.

González, E., & Segales, M. (2014). Women, gender equality and the economic crisis in Spain. In M. Karamessini & J. Rubery (Eds.), *Women and austerity. The economic crisis and the future for gender equality* (pp. 228–247). London: Routledge.

Guil, A. (2006). Techos de Cristal Universitarios: Buscando, Visibilizando e Interpretando Datos [University glass ceilings: Searching, making visible and interpreting data]. In Various Authors, *Democracia, Feminismo y Universidad en el Siglo XXI* (pp. 167–198). Madrid: Editorial Universidad Autónoma de Madrid.

Guil, A. (2016). Techos universitarios de cristal blindado [Armored glass university roofs]. *Investigaciones Feministas*, *7*(2), 25–39. doi:10.5209/INFE.53964

Herráez, E. R. (1996). La posición de las mujeres en la ciencia española [The position of women in Spanish science]. In *La formación científica de las mujeres. ¿Por qué hay tan pocas científicas?* [The scientific training of women. Why are there so few women?] (pp. 15–26). Madrid: Editorial los Libros de la Catarata.

Lahey, K. A., & de Villota, P. (2013). Economic crisis, gender equality, and policy responses in Spain and Canada. *Feminist Economics*, *19*(3), 82–107.

de Lauretis, T. (2000). *Diferencias. Etapas de un camino a través del feminismo*. Madrid: Instituto de la Mujer/Ministerio de Trabajo y Asuntos Sociales.

Ministerio de Ciencia e Innovación [Ministry of Science and Innovation]. (2011). Libro Blanco: Situación de las Mujeres en la Ciencia Española [White book. Situation of women in Spanish science]. Retrieved from http://llet-131-198.uab.es/catedra/images/materials/libro_blanco_texto_completo_9%20de%20agosto.pdf

Ministerio de Ciencia, Innovación y Universidades [Ministry of Science, Innovation and Universities]. (2019). Datos y cifras del Sistema Universitario Español [Facts and figures of the Spanish university system]. Publicación 2018–2019. Retrieved from

http://www.ciencia.gob.es/stfls/MICINN/Universidades/Ficheros/Estadisticas/datos-y-cifras-SUE-2018-19.pdf
Montané, A. (2013). Mujeres, ciencia y universidad. In A. Montané, & M. E. Carvalho (Coord). Mujeres y educación superior (pp. 15–53). João Pessoa: UFPB.
Montané, A., & Carvalho, M. E. (2012). Diálogo sobre género: justicia, equidad y políticas de igualdad en educación superior (Brasil y España) [Dialogue on gender: justice, equity and equality policies in higher education (Brazil and Spain)]. *Revista Lusófona de Educação*, *21*(21), Lisbon, 97–120.
Montané, A., & Carvalho, M. E. (2013). *Mujeres y educación superior* [Women and higher education]. João Pessoa: UFPB.
Montané, A., Beltrán, J., Camus, P., & Olivé, C. (2010). Del elitismo a la internacionalización: Desafíos, recorridos y cambios en las políticas de educación superior en España [From elitism to internationalization: Challenges, paths and changes in higher education policies in Spain]. In A. Teodoro (Ed.), *Educación Superior en Iberoamérica* (pp. 69–92). Lisbon: Ediciones Universitarias Lusófonas.
Montané, A., Beltrán, J., & Gabaldón-Estevan, D. (2017). Higher education in Spain: Framework for quality assurance. In S. Georgios, K. M.. Joshi, & S. Paivandi (Eds.), *Quality assurance in higher education. A global perspective* (pp. 41–67). Delhi: Studera Press.
Nuño, L., & Álvarez, E. (2017). Androcentrismo académico: La ficción de un conocimiento neutral [Academic androcentrism. The fiction of a neutral knowledge], *Feminismos*, *29*, 279–297. doi:10.14198/fem.2017.29.11
Pastor, I., Acosta, A. (2016). La institucionalización de las políticas de igualdad en la Universidad española. Avances y retos [The institutionalization of equality policies in the Spanish University. Advances and challenges]. Investigaciones feministas, *7*(2), 247–271.
Pastor, I., Acosta, A., Torres, T., & Calvo, M. (2020). Los planes de igualdad en las universidades españolas. Situación actual y retos de futuro [Equality plans in Spanish universities. Current situation and future challenges]. *Educació XX1*, *23*(1), 147–172. doi:10.5944/educXX1.23873
Pastor, I., Pontón, P., Belzunegui, Á., & Acosta, A. (2015). Gender policies in Spanish Universities: From regulation to equality plans. In H. D. Syna & C. E. Costea (Eds.), *Women's voices in management* (pp. 34–51). London: Palgrave Macmillan.
Puy, A. (Ed.). (2018). *Científicas en cifras 2017. Estadísticas e indicadores de la (des) igualdad de género en la formación y profesión científica* [Scientists in figures 2017. Statistics and indicators of gender (in) equality in scientific training and profession]. Madrid: Ministerio de Ciencia e Innovación.
Red de Unidades de Igualdad de Género para la Excelencia Universitaria [Network of Gender Equality Units for University Excellence] (RUIGEU). (2012). Network of Gender Equality Units for University Excellence (RUIGEU). Retrieved from http://www.redunidadesdeigualdad.udl.cat/inicio/
Sáez de Melgar, Faustina (1871). La mujer: Revista de Instrucción General para el Bello Sexo [Women: Journal of General Instruction for the Fair Sex] [journal published from May to August 1871].
Sánchez de Madariaga, I. (2011). Políticas de género en la ciencia: prevenir sesgos y promover excelencia. In *Libro Blanco: Situación de las Mujeres en la Ciencia Española* [Gender policies in science: preventing risks and promoting excellence. In

White Paper. Situation of women in Spanish science]. Madrid: Ministerio de Ciencia e Innovación.

Sanchez de Madariaga, I., De la Rica, S., & Dolado, J. (Eds.). (2011). *Libro Blanco. Situación de las mujeres en la ciencia española* [White book. Situation of women in Spanish science]. Madrid: Ministerio de Ciencia e Innovación. Retrieved from http://www.ciencia.gob.es/stfls/MICINN/Ministerio/FICHEROS/UMYC/LibroBlanco_Interactivo.pdf

Sotelo, I. (2008). La Universidad en la encrucijada [The University at the crossroads]. *Claves de la razón práctica*, *181*, 66–73.

Souvirón, J. M. (1989). *La Universidad española: Claves de su definición y régimen jurídico institucional* [The Spanish University. Keys to its definition and institutional legal regime]. Valladolid: Publicaciones Universidad de Valladolid.

Tomas i Folch, M. (Ed.). (2011). *La universidad vista desde la perspectiva de género*. Barcelona: Octaedro.

Valiente, C. (2008). Las mujeres en España desde 1975: destacados avances en ausencia de ciertos debates. In V. Pérez Díaz (Ed.), *Modernidad, crisis y globalización: problemas de política y cultura*. Almería: Fundación Cajamar.

Zippel, K., Ferree, M. M., & Zimmermann, K. (2016). Gender equality in German universities: Vernacularising the battle for the best brains. *Gender and education*, *28*(7), 867–885. doi:10.1080/09540253.2015.1123229

Chapter 8

Girls, Orientation in Science-based Higher Education: The Case of Côte d'Ivoire

Céline Sidonie Koco Nobah

1. Introduction

Since its foundation, UNESCO has recognized the right of women and girls to education as a fundamental human right. In its Constitution, adopted in 1946, the Organization is committed to promoting "the ideal of equality of educational opportunity without regard to race, sex or any distinctions, economic or social." This concept is central to UNESCO's action and its approach to development, which takes the human being as a starting point, as the main subject and the ultimate goal. The Organization's programs aim at translating principles into concrete action, identifying and addressing the obstacles that, at all levels, prevent women from fully enjoying their rights, particularly in the field of education. In the 1960s, efforts focused on finding ways to promote increased school enrollment rates for girls. In the 1970s, it became clear that the question of quantity was only one aspect, and efforts were focused on the quality of education offered in schools and on society's attitudes toward education. Programs began to focus on the community, to sensitize parents to the need for school education for girls, and to set up literacy projects for illiterate women. Emphasis was then placed on technical and vocational education and on promoting women's access to higher education, particularly in the scientific and technical fields, as a means of preparing them for positions of responsibility. These actions were accompanied by reflection on the role models offered to girls and by measures aimed at bringing about a change in values through education. An important emphasis was placed on the revision of textbooks and teaching materials to rid them of gender stereotypes.

The Harare Declaration (MINEDAF V, 1982) called for

> …vigorous measures to promote the education of girls and women and to achieve for themselves the conditions for full and effective equality in education, particularly at the secondary and higher levels and in scientific and technical education, in order to improve their status and to promote their full participation in the various responsibilities of economic, social and political life.

International Perspectives on Gender and Higher Education, 135–145

doi:10.1108/978-1-83909-886-420201008

The Meeting of the African Consultative Group to Formulate Suggestions for the Development of Policies to Eliminate Inequalities in Education Affecting Girls and Women (Dakar, December 14–18, 1981), having reviewed the situation of inequalities concerning girls and women in education, made recommendations for regional and national action.

Despite the many actions that show an awareness of the situation of the young girl by national and international institutions, the number of girls in science, technology, engineering, and mathematics (STEM) remains low, especially in higher education.

The question arises as to what are the causes of the low representation of women in STEM and the challenges to be met in the particular Ivorian context.

Only a good understanding of these constraints and factors can lead to the implementation of ways and means likely to remedy a situation which, if not combated, would lead to the permanent exclusion of more than half of the Ivorian population and would constitute a major handicap for the development of Côte d'Ivoire.

The general objective of this chapter is to highlight the constraints and factors that contribute to limiting girls' access to science and technology education and to identify the challenges to be met.

At the specific level, it will be a question of (1) conducting an assessment of the university situation of girls in Côte d'Ivoire, (2) determining the causes of the low proportion of girls in STEM in higher education, (3) presenting historical and contemporary female scientific models of reference within Ivorian society, and (4) proposing strategies to enhance girls' motivation for science and technology education.

1.1 Overview of the University Situation of Girls in Côte d'Ivoire

Côte d'Ivoire, aware of the importance of science and technology in its development, formulated in the National Plan for the Development of the Education/ Training Sector (1998/2010), its willingness to reduce all disparities in education. This plan included, among other actions, the development of a national scientism and technological culture, and the promotion of an environment conducive to girls' access to general education, and technological and scientific training. Thus, its implementation has helped improve girls' access to school and especially to scientific fields. The number of girl students in the final year of secondary school, which stood at 208 in 1999, has improved significantly since then. Indeed, in 2006, the girls were 16% in the final year of secondary school, then 20.3% in 2007. Yet, girls remain a minority in the science streams of Higher Education in Côte d'Ivoire. Actually, unlike the figures observed at primary level, which reflect the achievement of parity, disparities in the number of girls in science streams are observed at secondary level and therefore in higher education. According to the latest statistical yearbook of the Ministry of Higher Education and Scientific Research (2007–2008), the statistics relating to the orientation of baccalaureate holders for the 2012 session indicate that 8.60% of girls are oriented to the

Mathematics and Computer Science (MI) department (UFR) and 12.67% to the Mathematical and Technological Structures Sciences (SSMT) department (UFR). Furthermore, the comparison of the performance of girls and boys in the C series indicates that girls achieve better results in the Baccalaureate C than boys. In 2006, 72.44% of girls compared to 69.41% of boys passed the Baccalaureate and in 2007, 66.29% of girls compared to 59.44% of boys passed the Baccalaureate C in Côte d'Ivoire.

In spite of this proven performance, 6.84% of the girls are attending the Mathematics and Computer Science department (UFR) and 6.87% the Mathematical and Technological Structures Sciences department (UFR).

As regards to the female teaching and research staff at the Félix Houphouet Boigny University in Cocody, in the science and technology teaching and research units, women represent only 6% at the Mathematics and Computer Science department, and 10% at the department of Sciences of Structures and Maters, and technology.

Ivorian female scientists, like most of their counterparts around the world, tend to specialize in biology, agriculture, chemistry, medicine, dentistry, pharmacy, and life sciences, all of which play a fundamental role in Africa's major problems. However, in these fields, there are women in insufficient number compared to men.

The distribution of the number of teacher-researchers in 2016–2017 shows 2,138 teacher-researchers of which 26% are women in all disciplines and grades.

The most feminized fields are Pharmacy, Medicine, and Odontostomatology, with 35% of women in the teaching staff.

1.2 The Causes of Girls' Low Representation in Science, Technology, Engineering, and Mathematics in Higher Education

Many causes may account for the low representation of women in STEM in higher education in Côte d'Ivoire.

1.2.1 Sociocultural Factors

In most African countries, like Cote d'Ivoire, prejudices against girls have been strongly established. Their rights to education, instruction, and freedom are violated (Cosnefroy, 2011; Pilon, 1996). The girl child is taken out of school either for early marriage or to teach her the rudiments of a good wife. Thus, girls' schooling can be hindered by early pregnancy (Goubo, 2013). In Côte d'Ivoire, this phenomenon occurs mainly in rural areas with more than three-quarters (78.7%) of the pregnancies. The unequal situation between girls and boys remains closely linked to the access and retention of girls in the school system. Thirty (30) girls out of 100 do not have access to school (Cosnefroy, 2011). A high dropout rate among girls is observed as they progress through the curriculum (Michaelowa, 2000). In Francophone Africa, until 1993, there were wide disparities in enrollment rates by gender, with more than 20 percentage point difference for some countries. In most African regions, girls' education is the responsibility of the family or social group. Sending one's daughter to school can even be felt as a "shame" (Michaelowa, 2000). On the other hand, it is sometimes stated that school life is necessary for boys for their future responsibilities as heads of households, which has the corollary of reserving for only one sex what is nevertheless recognized as important for both (Pilon, 1996). These obstacles hinder girls' access to higher education and to holding responsibilities equivalent to those of men. Hence, these inequalities persist in higher education institutions.

These sociocultural factors find their roots in the weight of tradition and the social role generally assigned to the girl child, who is oriented toward domestic work to prepare her for her tasks and responsibilities as a future mother. Family and social pressures are forcing the young girl to lower her ambitions in terms of scientific training. The gendered division of labor has classified occupations into girls and boys job, and opportunities for scientific training are preferentially kept for boys. As a result, rewarding scientific and technical occupations remain the preserve of men, whereas Biology and Medical Sciences (Medicine, Pharmacy, and Medical Analysis) are well accepted by girls. The interest in these disciplines lies in the fact that they enable an understanding of living beings and more particularly the human body and its functioning (Ouattara, 2010). This high interest of girls in biology emphasizes a deep need to confirm their woman identity, and their knowledge of their body, in order to eventually control it.

This choice ultimately brings us back to the roles and status of women in both traditional and modern societies. Bourdieu and Passeron (1970) argue that the difference between the fields chosen by girls and boys from the same socio-professional categories is based on the fact that "parents and girls themselves continue to adhere to the image dominated by the traditional model of the gender division of labor." The difference in the career plans of girls and boys through the choice of fields is related to family organization and social structures. Consequently, educational inequalities are based mainly on cultural capital and the weight of socialization.

The low representation of girls in STEM is therefore linked to the fact that there is a gendered representation that each group, girl or boy, has its scientific professions. More than 30% of girls think that women have difficulties than men to assert themselves in these occupations which you leave little free time. Consequently, the other occupations allow them to gain time to devote themselves to their future married life, which seem to attract them most. Thus, even the girls in the final year of secondary school take into account the social roles associated with the status of women before choosing a field in higher education.

For some people, girls' education in technology and science focuses on aspects related to health, nutrition, home economics, etc. Moreover, in nonformal girls education structures dealing with the vocational and "technical" training, the courses given revolve around sewing "techniques," dyeing, or secretarial work. But by limiting the domains in this way, aren't girls being enclosed in the traditional role of women, a vicious circle and difficult to break?

1.2.2 Factors Related to the Education System

Education in Africa continues to suffer from the discriminatory influence of our societies against women. In science education, reference is made, for example, to international (Bouya) rather than national scientists and inventors. Africa, therefore, in addition to its own discriminatory references, has inherited a colonial system of sexist and exclusivist education, which removes any reference to women's scientific and technological achievements. According to Jacobsen (1991), mathematics and science education has its main foundation in the belief that mathematics and science are useful subjects and that the methods and practices they inculcate will contribute to the well-being and prosperity of all. This conviction is, unfortunately, absent not only from the minds of African girls but also from the minds of curriculum developers and some teachers.

The school environment plays a significant role in guiding the girl child. Indeed, it would seem that girls perform better in science and technology when they find themselves in girls-only schools. In coeducational schools, lack of concentration due to the diversion of attention from girls to boys has been reported as well as the desire of girls themselves to attract both male classmates and teachers. The tendency to let boys "take care of" them and to give up in the face of difficulty and effort, as well as a lack of self-confidence, has been reported (Bouya, 1993).

The organization of the education system in Côte d'Ivoire and students' career plans also seem to be responsible for the situation. Indeed, technical and vocational education offers training that is resolutely female or male, i.e., discriminatory. These types of training are subordinate to the nature of the jobs reserved for men and women, which reproduce the traditional model of the division of labor between the sexes (BREDA).

Pedagogical factors are related to the fact that most educational literature presents stereotypes and reproduces social clichés by assigning low-valued roles and tasks to girls. It should also be noted that science and technology education is, for the most part, taught by male teachers. This situation can be a downstream blocking factor for girls' access to science and technology education. Indeed, by noting that very few women teach STEM, the conclusion can be drawn by female learners that these are areas reserved for the male. In addition, the negative attitude of some science teachers who tend to believe that science subjects are inaccessible to girls may act as a deterrent to the interest in science. Science and technology education must be oriented toward finding practical solutions to problems facing the community. It is therefore not clear that science and technology education, when taught by men, can take into account the specific problems and interests of girls and women.

1.2.3 Economic Factors

Economic factors point to a context of widespread poverty where parents, experiencing financial constraints, give preference to financing boys' education to the detriment of young girls. Moreover, the conflicts that occurred in 2002 aggravated impoverishment and were unfavorable to the enrollment of girls in primary education, which fell in comparison with previous years (Acka-Douabele & Bih, 2006).

It has been observed that the choices of streams differ according to the socioprofessional category of the parents. Indeed, those girls whose parents have a high social status are more ambitious in their choices. The girls from lower social backgrounds self-censor from studies such as civil engineering, petrochemicals. It should be noted, however, that a girl of executive parents has a less gendered representation of streams from higher education. As for boys, the group discussions revealed that their motivations focus on the financial cost-effectiveness of degrees. In their view, since men are the head of the family, they should be well paid to earn the respect of others.

1.2.4 Psychological Factors

Psychological factors take into account ignorance. This is the profile drawn by society, giving rise to fear of scientific disciplines and a negative representation of the scientist. Girls show a total lack of interest in physics and mathematics, in that they tend to consider themselves incapable of understanding the laws of physics and technology, which, for them, still refer to the idea of strength and the use of muscular force, despite the progress made in the field of technology. As for mathematics, they consider it too difficult, too complicated, too abstract, useless, and above all because it acts as a filter for selecting the best. Perceived, therefore, as an instrument of selection, mathematics seems to be a major obstacle to girls' orientation toward science and the choice of a future profession (Bouya, 1993). Bandura (1981) explains the gendered orientation by the theory of self-efficacy. According to this theory, an individual's perception of his or her ability to perform an activity influences and determines how he or she thinks, is motivated, and behaves. It claims that people avoid situations and activities that they perceive as threatening, but commit to doing the activities they feel capable of doing. For both girls and boys, a reduced development of these feelings of self-efficacy can limit their academic and career choices and development.

While science can sometimes, and for those who have chosen it, be seen as one of the routes to a well-paid profession and integration into working life, technology, especially when accompanied by the qualifier "appropriate," is perceived by girls as a step backward, a return to peasant life. This is simply because the term has been introduced in French-speaking Africa, and therefore in Côte d'Ivoire, in connection with so-called rural development projects.

The majority of boys have different professional projects from girls. Indeed, they want to study Aeronautics, Telecom engineering, Agronomy, etc., which girls do not mention. The justification of the choices of streams shows that girls and boys have different motivations. The motivations of girls relate to their good performance in mathematics or physics, to the feeling of loving the jobs to which the various studies lead, and to the time they could have to take care of their future family by working in such and such a job. Those who opt for medicine say they want to help and relieve those who are suffering. Those who wish to do math/physics plan to teach to have more time to take care of their future family. On the other hand, small proportions, especially those who want to study computer science, think that these are jobs with a future and that they are well paid. This inevitably leads to a certain gendered representation of the scientific professions. For boys, a scientific job is equivalent to a high social position and for girls; it is equivalent to a high-risk occupation where women have more than difficulties to integrate.

Studies by Post-Kammer and Smith (1985) and Blanchard and Virgnaud (1994) highlight the importance of adolescents' sense of competence influences their aspirations. According to Post-Kammer, girls express a higher sense of competence for women's occupations, while boys have a higher sense of competence for traditionally male occupations. In fact, if we consider trades such as civil engineering, aeronautics, and petrochemicals, only very few girls think of them. On the other hand, many of them (22.8%) opt for the medical profession and (24.58%) for the accounting profession. The important role of cultural stereotypes linked to gender with regard to professional practice must be taken into account. Generally speaking, women judge themselves less efficient for scientific professions than men (Bandura, 1981). The same is true of boys in professions considered particularly suitable for girls, such as esthetics, early childhood care, etc. Bandura's (1981) theory is one avenue for understanding these differences in career aspirations between girls and boys. According to this theory on the sense of competence, a person engages in a particular activity more or less easily depending on the system of expectations and self-images (especially the sense of competence) that the person has previously constructed. According to Bourdieu, the primary socializing agents of family and school play an important role in differences in orientation. The family, for its part, has a major role in the reproduction of male dominance and male vision. Consequently, girls in final year science studies in senior high school are oriented toward professions such as pharmacy, medicine, teaching, and rarely engineering because these professions and the conditions in which they work seem to be adapted to their status as women.

1.3 Ivorian Female Scientists of Reference

In Côte d'Ivoire, there are indeed contemporary female scientist role models. These models can be found among the first generations of Ivorian women who graduated from European universities and Colleges after the independence, as well as among the intermediate and current generations. Indeed, there are several pioneers of female scientist in Côte. Mrs Josephine Djidji Wandja is the first African and Ivorian woman, having obtained a PhD in pure mathematics, the first African woman university professor in mathematics at the Faculty of Science and Technology of the University of Abidjan, the current Félix Houphouët Boigny University, and the first African woman to receive an "agrégation" in mathematics. She is also a member of the board of the United Nations University in Tokyo, Japan, a member of the board of the United Nations Centre for Science and Technology for Development in New York, USA, and Regional President of African Women Mathematicians.

Professor Eholié Rose is the pioneer in Mineral Chemistry at the Faculty of Science and Technology of the University of Abidjan Cocody. Professor Anoma Gwladys is the first woman professor in plant biology in Côte d'Ivoire; in medical sciences, Professor Timité Marguerite and Professor Welfens Ekra are the pioneers, the first women to become Associate Medical Scientists. In Physical Sciences, they are Professor Chantale Kouassi Goffri, the first woman Lecturer in Physics and Dean of the UFR of Sciences of the structure of matter and technology. Professor Yao Kacou Rita Carolina, First woman Professor in Crystallography and Atomic and Molecular Physics, was the assistant director of the Laboratory of Crystallography and Molecular Physics, director of the CROU (Regional Center of University Works), and is the current president of the Association of Women Researchers of Côte d'Ivoire. The first woman Doctor in Computer Science is named Mrs Fadiga.

Within the middle generation that follows this first generation, Mrs Bakayoko Ly Ramata, University Professor in odontostomatology, paedodontist-prevention section, current Minister of Women, Family and Children, is the first woman Minister of Higher Education and Scientific Research in Côte d'Ivoire, the first Ivorian woman to be a member of the Academy of Overseas Sciences of Paris. She is the first Ivorian woman to lead research on oral pathologies in Africa, the first woman university president in Côte d'Ivoire, and the president of the scientific commission of the International Institute for Water and Environmental Engineering.

In Medical Sciences, Professor Dosso Mireille is the first female intern in Bacteriology and Virology, the first woman Full Professor of Microbiology at the UFR of Medical Sciences in Abidjan, and Director of the Pasteur Institute of Côte d'Ivoire. She is also the first woman scientist from Côte d'Ivoire to win the African Union's Kwamé N'Nruma Scientific Prize in 2011, the UNESCO-Institut Pasteur Health Science Research Prize in Hungary, and the exceptional prize awarded by the French Academy of Overseas Sciences in 2010. Professor Tidou Abiba Sanogo, President of the Lorougnon Guédé University in Côte d'Ivoire, is the first woman in Côte d'Ivoire to become a Full Professor of Aquatic Ecotoxicology.

The future is also assured with the younger generation, with many international prize winners and pioneers in their field.

Mrs Gbonon Valérie, Doctor of Biology, carries out research on bacterial resistance to antibiotics. Her work on streptococcus earned her the distinction of being the first Ivorian woman to be awarded the 21st "l'Oréal Unesco International Prize" for Women in Science.

Professor Broualet Espérence is the first woman neurosurgeon in Côte d'Ivoire, the first woman to be awarded the "CAMES agrégation" in Anatomy and Neurosurgery. Professor Céline Nobah Epse Kacou-Wodjè is the first Ivorian woman lecturer in fish farming. Dr Brigitte N'Dri Koné Aya is a pioneer in Ecology and management of savannas by fire in Côte d'Ivoire.

Stéphanie Maubath Carenne Konan, Doctoral student in Computer and Information Sciences at the University Félix Houphouët Boigny in Abidjan, is laureate of the 10th edition of the UNESCO-LOREAL Young Talent Prize for Sub-Saharan Africa. As the list is not exhaustive, these examples are given for information only.

1.4 Proposals for Boosting Girls' Motivation for Science and Technology Education

In the general context of the development problems of the African continent, science and technology should be applied to the problems posed by hunger, disease, ignorance, poverty, and the environment. In other words, the promotion of science and technology education should be based on the realities of the continent and integrate the principles of development.

It would be advisable to define criteria for promotion to scientific academic posts and to ensure that women benefit equitably from such promotions. There is a need to promote the creation of special commissions on women's policy issues in science, engineering, and technology within each university and to encourage women to form networks that can unite female students, teachers, STEM researchers, and managers at both national and inter-African levels.

At the institutional level, especially in the education/training sector, efforts are made through the involvement of the Ministry of higher Education and Science through the "Salon de l'Enseignement Supérieur de Côte d'Ivoire" (SES-CI) and the "Week for the Promotion of Research and Innovation" (SEPRI).

The development of cooperation must be accentuated by open and critical communication at the Ministry of higher Education and Science and by forging strong links between the scientific world and companies.

It will be necessary to set up services to mentor young female scientists, organize a national science day for all students, especially girls, during which opportunities are presented. This type of days, known as career days, is currently organized by the national education system. It would be advisable to promote girls' Science studies High Schools, and girls' polytechnics, to revitalize the association of women scientists by its erection into an Institution of Public Utility, to establish through texts, quotas for young girls entering scientific fields, to develop public–private partnerships at the level of companies, civil society, scientific societies, local authorities, and partners to ensure the supervision of young women scientists until their professional integration. There is also a need to reactivate the memorandum of the local authorities and invite them to build science high schools for girls, to set up a network bringing together all those concerned with science, to strengthen the capacities of guidance counselors, to promote gender budgeting, to addressing the cost of science textbooks or, failing that, making them available in libraries, to revise textbooks to rid them of stereotypes that devalue the girl child, and to present employment opportunities, particularly in science subjects.

At school level, there is a necessity to appoint a teacher responsible for encouraging scientific vocations and advising girls to enter scientific fields, to initiate science clubs in high schools and colleges, and to make science courses accessible through awareness campaigns.

At the social level, there is also a need to grant scholarships and assistance to girls to encourage them to take up scientific subjects, to use the sociocultural services of town halls, and regional councils for awareness-raising activities, to strengthen awareness-raising and communication on scientific subjects, to bring scientific training structures closer to the population, to raise parents' awareness of their role in raising the young girl's awareness, and ask them not to influence the children's choice.

At the pedagogical level, setting up a local supervision for girls in high schools and universities, training teachers in higher education in pedagogy to better articulate scientific learning, encouraging teachers of scientific subjects to promote these subjects for girls, will be necessary.

Dissemination of scientific culture must be done through the media-universal vectors of information. This involves the written press, the audiovisual press which must produce creative programs for the field of scientific fields. These broadcasts will make it possible to stimulate the curiosity of young girls and their families. They will convey the social image of the professionals associated with scientific careers. Conferences must be held by women scientists for young girls, meeting and communication areas must be created, other actors who help to motivate young girls for scientific careers must be involved, namely teachers, civil and academic organizations, parents and volunteers, local communities using local radio stations, and the help of the coalition of women leaders.

2. Conclusion and Recommendation

In short, there is a low representation of girls in STEMs in Côte d'Ivoire. This low representativeness is linked to several factors, which may be cultural, educational, psychological, and economic. As a result, boys and girls choice of education streams cannot be explained solely by a better ability of boys to succeed in scientific disciplines. Guidance decisions fall within a decision-making field that is determined by a number of parameters relating to cultural, the educational, psychological, and economic factors. Numerous efforts are being made by national institutions and especially the Association of Women Researchers of Côte d'Ivoire (AFEMCCI) to encourage young girls to take up scientific vocations.

However, the question of the conformity of scientific and technological education to the interests of girls in our developing countries remains. For, if women are to conquer scientific and technological fields through education and training, it must be admitted that barriers and stereotypes, as well as other prejudices, must be broken down to ensure girls' access to science, taking into account their real interests and not assumed or imposed.

3. Recommendations

- The revitalization of the services in charge of psychosociological follow-up in UFRs to support women scientists at all universities;
- The facilitation access to accurate and reliable information on scientific career opportunities in high schools and universities;
- The creation of a network of actors for the improvement of the flow of scientific information.

References

Acka-Douabele, A. C., & Bih, E. (2006). Impact de la guerre sur l'éducation des filles en Côte d'Ivoire. Actes du Colloque International organisé par ROCARE/FASAF sur « Education, Violences et conflits en Afrique », du 06 au 10 mars 2006 à Yaoundé, Cameroun, 42p. Retrieved from http://www.rocare.org/Bih.pdf

Bandura, A. (1981). Self-referent thought: A developmental analysis of self-efficacy. In J. H. Flavell & L. Ross (Eds.), *Social cognitive development: Frontiers and possible futures* (pp. 200–239). Cambridge: Cambridge University Press.

Blanchard, S., & Vrignaud, P. (1994). Intérêts professionnels et sentiment de compétences. *Questions d'Orientation*, *4*, 31–44.

Bourdieu, P., & Passeron, J. C. (1970). *La reproduction. Éléments pour une théorie du système d'enseignement*. Paris: Ed. de Minuit.

Bouya, A. (1993). *Les filles face aux programmes scolaires de sciences et technologie en afrique. Etude socio-psychologique*. Dakar: UNESCO.

Cosnefroy, L. (2011). *L'apprentissage autorégulé: entre cognition et motivation*. Grenoble: Presses universitaires de Grenoble.

Goubo, R. (2013). *Education et la jeune fille en Côte d'Ivoire*. Paris: Bookelis.

Jacobsen, E. (1991). Adapting mathematics education for the next century. *Impact of Science on Society*, *41*(4), 297–303.

Michaelowa, K. (2000). *Dépenses d'éducation, qualité de l'éducation et pauvreté: l'exemple de cinq pays d'Afrique francophone*. OECD Development Centre Working Papers 157. OECD Publishing, Paris.

Ouattara, K. (2010). Déterminants du projet professionnel des filles de terminale C: cas des filles du Lycee Classique d'Abidjan et du Lycee Mamie Fêtai de Bingerville. In T. Tchombe, Y. Yaro, D. Traoré, & A. Barry (Eds.), *ROCARE* (No. 2, pp. 151–167). Abidjan: Editions Universitaires de Côte d'Ivoire.

Pilon, M. (1996). Genre et scolarisation des enfants en Afrique sub-saharienne. In T. Locoh, A. Labourie-Racapé, & C. Tchit (Eds.), *Genre et développement: des pistes à suivre: textes d'une rencontre scientifique à Paris* (pp. 25–34). Paris: Ceped.

Post-Kammer, P., & Smith, P. L. (1985). Sex differences in career self-efficacy, consideration, and interests of eighth and ninth graders. *Journal of Counseling Psychology*, *32*(4), 551–559. doi:10.1037/0022-0167.32.4.551

Chapter 9

Feminization of Japanese Higher Education and Career Pathway: From "Interruption" to "Upward Mobility"

Yukari Matsuzuka

1. Introduction

For the past 3 decades, a series of government initiatives have been undertaken in Japan to improve gender equality at work and in school. Some progress has been reported through various publications.[1] For example, full-time employment for female workers increased both in number and as a ratio to male workers, and industries and occupations that absorb women have become increasingly diverse and varied.[2] The progress is even more remarkable in the education sector as the rate of women going to higher education exceeded that of men in 2015. It has been noted often that schools are more gender-balanced than workplaces are.[3] Nevertheless, there is a significant disparity between male and female students in the levels and the fields of learning. Although the number of women who take undergraduate programs has increased significantly, women are much less likely than men to proceed to the graduate level. In addition, there is a substantial

[1]Brinton (1993) presents historical observation and analyses over changes in the work environment for female workers in post-war Japan. For statistical unfolding, the Employment Environment and Equal Employment Bureau (1996–2018) published comprehensive reports with summaries in English.

[2]There was a series of governmental initiatives that enabled the progress including the Equal Employment Opportunity Law of 1985, the Amendment of the Child-care Leave Law of 1990, the Basic Law on Gender Equality Society of 1999, and the Act on the Promotion of Women's Participation and Advancement in the Workplace of 2015. The details of the political movement and statistical facts in the labor market for female workers are reported in the White Paper on Gender Equality published by the Gender Equality Bureau Cabinet Office (1996–2019). See the following site for the English summary: Retrieved from http://www.gender.go.jp/english_contents/about_danjo/whitepaper/index.html. Accessed on February 1, 2020.

[3]Gender equality has been a basic principle for schooling in Japan based on Chapter III of the Basic Act of Education enacted right after the World War II.

International Perspectives on Gender and Higher Education, 147–170

doi:10.1108/978-1-83909-886-420201009

difference between men and women regarding their choices of academic areas at both undergraduate and graduate levels. Women are the majority in humanities, education, nursing, and home economics, but they are less likely to be in the fields of natural sciences and engineering. This tendency is observed in other parts of the world but is more apparent in Japan.[4] Hence, the major portion of the government's budget for gender equality in higher education has gone to programs that aim to reduce imbalances in the fields of study.

Meanwhile, it is not clear how these gender disparities in higher education relate to gender inequality in the workplace. Brinton (1993) once remarked that women in Japan had already attained high rates of participation in the economy, but gender differentiation was quite significant in wages, employment status, and occupational role (p. 1). This observation is still true and is largely the reason for low scores on the Global Gender Gap Index for Japan.[5] To explain the inequality, the economics of gender identifies "observable" and "unobservable" factors. Observable factors include years of tenure, experience, education, and training. Unobservable factors include motivation, individual attitude, and discrimination.[6] This paper focuses on observable factors to explain gender inequality in Japan. There is a consensus that differences in wages, employment status, and occupational role between men and women in Japan are due largely to the shorter years of tenure and work experience for women. For some women, shorter tenure is caused by career interruptions due to childbirth and childcare. Many women do not return to full-time work after the interruptions, moving to nonregular and/or part-time workers.[7] For others, short tenure might be their priority to serve their families better at home.[8] Discrimination may also be a factor influencing short tenure, although this paper does not deal with it.[9]

---

[4]Bradley (2000), for instance, found that women are more likely to graduate from education, arts, humanities, social sciences, and law, and men are more likely to graduate from natural sciences, mathematics, and engineering. A very similar but more apparent trend is observed in Japan, which will be discussed in detail under Section 3.

[5]According to the World Education Forum (2019), Japan's gender gap measured by the Global Gender Gap Index is the largest among all advanced economies and has widened over the past years. Japan ranked 121st among 153 countries on the 2019 index, down 11 positions from 2018.

[6]See Ferber and Lowry (1995) or Blau, Ferber, and Winkler (2014) for the formulation in the economics of gender.

[7]See Lee (2004) for the feminization of nonstandard work in Japan and Korea.

[8]For example, Jacobs and Gerson (2004) discuss that once people get married, men are more likely to take jobs with higher allowances even if the work hours are not flexible, while women are more likely to take jobs with flexible work hours even with lower allowance.

[9]It should be noted that what Becker (1957) coined "statistical discrimination" is a serious issue for Japanese women along with their shorter tenure caused by marriage and/or childbirth. Japanese employers consider it a cost if their employees quit after receiving employer-sponsored training, thus female workers are less likely to be hired in or assigned to tenure-oriented positions. For details, see Yamaguchi (2008) for the theory and empirical inquiry into statistical gender discrimination in Japan.

Alleviating these employment issues is a mission assigned to employers, who seem to have been working to allow women to balance work and family. What can and should the higher education community do? Increasing female enrollment in science and engineering is one solution. However, in terms of gender inequality being caused by shorter tenure due to employment interruptions, higher education can help women to prepare for their career pathway tolerant to the interruptions. Such a mission in tertiary education could be carried out through both formal schooling and continuing education programs that offer ongoing career development.

This paper first reviews the progress of female participation in higher education at both undergraduate and graduate levels. It then focuses on gender imbalances in the fields of study at the levels of bachelor's, master's, doctoral, and professional degrees, followed by recent government efforts to reduce the imbalances. The paper will then focus on the labor market, investigating income disparity between men and women, and showing that the main reason for the disparity is the shorter length of employment and frequent turnover of female workers. The investigation continues to find situations where female workers have not suffered from shorter tenure and turnover. It will identify occupations where women have longer tenure and higher salaries, or shorter tenure but higher salaries. Based on these analyses, the paper discusses what the higher education community can do to serve women better by offering skills, knowledge, and a continuous learning environment, enabling women to convert employment interruptions into upward mobility in their career pathways. Concluding remarks will follow.

2. Women in Japanese Higher Education

2.1 Undergraduate

Table 9.1 shows the enrollment of male and female students in Japanese higher education in 2019, including 4-year colleges, 2-year colleges, and national colleges of technology.[10] Overall, the 4-year enrollment has 55.7% male students and 44.3% female students. The 2-year colleges have 11.63% male students and 88.37% female students. National colleges of technology are 5-year schools for students 15 years or older and the last 2 years belong to tertiary education. There are 63 institutions (mostly technical schools) focusing on engineering and mercantile marine studies, with 80.18% male students and 19.82 female students. In total, 54.54% of the tertiary students in Japan are male and 45.46% are female.

Although there are more men than women in Japan's colleges, the rate of female high school graduates who advance to tertiary education has been higher than that of male graduates in the past 5 years. As Fig. 9.1 shows, in 1954, when

[10]Higher education institutions here mean Levels 5 and 6 of the International Standard Classification of Education (ISCED), including 2-year and 4-year colleges (or universities) under the jurisdiction of the Ministry of Education, Culture, Sports, Science and Technology (hereinafter, MEXT).

Table 9.1. Enrollment in Higher Education in 2019.

Type of College	Male	Percentage (%)	Female	Percentage (%)
4-year college	1,625,573	55.70	1,293,095	44.30
2-year college	13,147	11.63	99,866	88.37
National college of technology	45,803	80.18	11,321	19.82
Total	1,684,523	54.54	1,404,282	45.46

Source: MEXT (2019a). *School Basic Survey*.

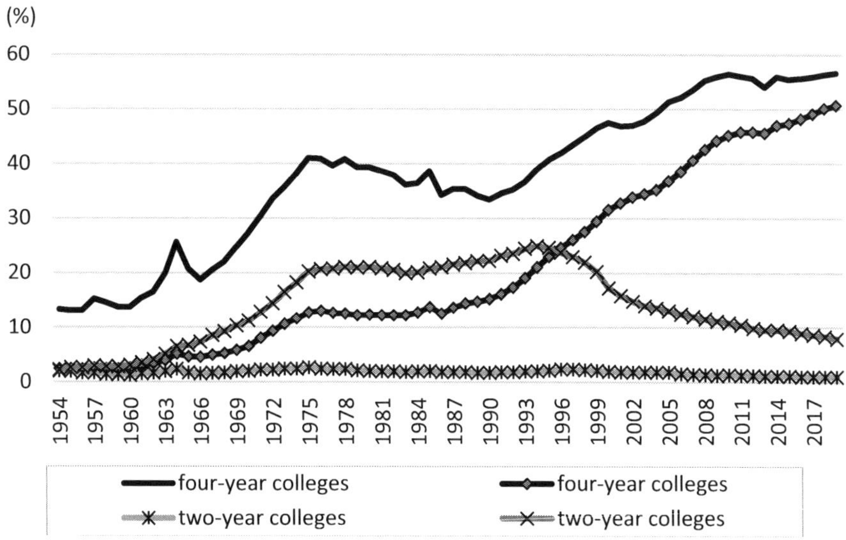

Fig. 9.1. Rate of Admission to 2- and 4-Year Colleges. *Source:* The figure is created by author based on the statistics published by MEXT (2019a).

the Ministry of Education, Culture, Sports, Science and Technology (hereinafter, MEXT) first reported the official statistics on schooling, the rate of female high school graduates admitted into higher education institutions was 4.6% (2.4% in 2-year institutions and 2.2% in 4-year institutions). The rate of male high school graduates admitted into higher education institutions was 15.3% (13.3% in 4-year institutions and 2% in 2-year institutions). In 2019, the rate of female high school graduates admitted into higher education institutions was 58.6% (7.9% in 2-year institutions and 50.7% in 4-year institutions), while the rate of male high school graduates was 57.6% (1% in 2-year institutions and 56.6% in 4-year institutions).

Thus, the rate of entering higher education is higher for women than for men if 2-year and 4-year institutions are counted together. The sharp increases in both male and female entrants between 1965 and 1975 were helped by the decline in the 18-year-old population, which is the denominator for the estimation of the rate of college entrants. The decline of male entrants and the stagnant increase in female entrants between 1975 and 1990 are due to the increase in the 18-year-old population relative to college entrants. Furthermore, the decline in the 18-year-old population since 1992 has contributed to the increase in the rate of higher education entrants for following years.[11]

In terms of the female population, the increasing rate of enrollment in 4-year institutions after 1994 was accompanied by the decreasing rate in 2-year institutions. It is natural to interpret that these two movements are interactive—those who had been going to 2-year institutions are now going to 4-year institutions. The shift in female enrollment from 2-year to 4-year institutions is an important trend for the feminization of Japanese higher education. This transformation has been caused by the flattering wage profile of 2-year college graduates and the long-term consistent decline in the private rate of return to 2-year institutions compared with 4-year institutions.[12] These observations suggest that women have become more conscious of the economic outcome of higher education.

2.2 Graduate Students

In terms of the enrollment at the graduate level, Fig. 9.2 shows changes in the number of 4-year graduates admitted into graduate schools. The number increased constantly for both men and women since the 1980s. The increase was particularly significant between 1992 and 2011. This was largely due to the government's initiative for the quantitative increase in graduate schools and students, inaugurated in 1991.[13] In 1991, 68,739 were enrolled in master's programs and 29,911 in doctoral programs, totaling 98,650 graduate students. In 2000, the number of master's students increased to 142,830 and that of doctoral students increased to 62,481, totaling 205,311. The number continued increasing for another decade and, in 2011, it reached a peak of 272,566. At this point, 13.4% of 4-year graduates were proceeding to graduate schools. This increase is remarkable when considering the demographic trend in the 1990s and 2000s when

[11]A graph that compares the 18-year-old population and higher education entrants since 1955 is attached as Appendix 1.

[12]Hojo (2018) and Shima (1999, 2017) formulated comparative analysis of returns to education and wage profiles by type of schooling. Endo and Shima's (2019) study showed the unique characteristics of Japanese women through inquiries into both direct and indirect economic returns at different levels of schooling.

[13]To develop human resources that can contribute to the various fields in society, the plan was to double the number of graduate schools between 1991 and 2000 and to improve the quality of research and education in the schools (MEXT, 2015). The details of the objectives and plans are described at the following site in Japanese: Retrieved from https://www.mext.go.jp/b_menu/shingi/chukyo/chukyo4/houkoku/1366897.htm. Accessed on February 1.

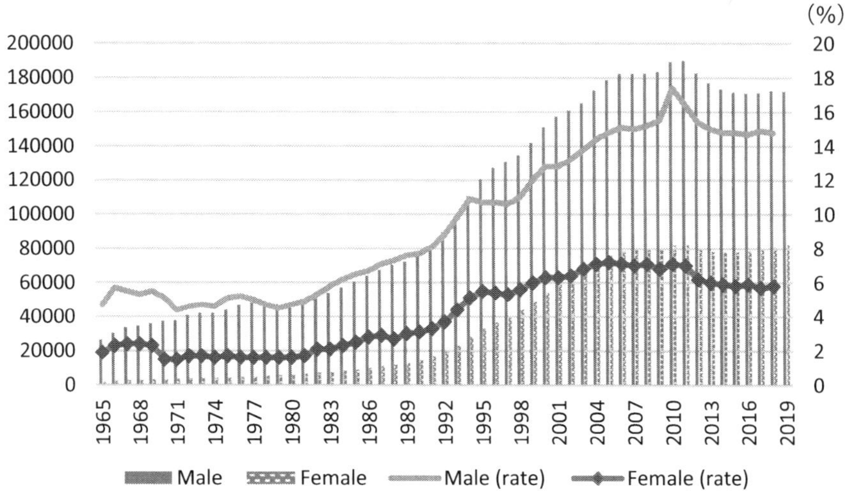

Fig. 9.2. Changes in the Number and Rate of 4-Year Graduates Going to Graduate Schools. *Source:* The figure is created by author based on the statistics published by MEXT (2019a).

there was a constant decline in the college population. Then, since 2011, the entrants into graduate schools have declined. The decline occurred mainly in humanities and social sciences. This could be a backrush of the rapid increase over 3 decades after 1980. However, a close examination shows that the economic effectiveness of additional education varies by field of study and industrial demand.[14] The decline in graduate enrollment may also be due to the lack of substantiality in additional learning initiated by the government, which might have caused the oversupply of those with highest degrees where the labor market has not been ready to absorb them.[15]

A comparison of the long-term trends between male and female enrollment shows that the number and the percentage have constantly increased for both men and women. However, unlike the undergraduate level, the enrollment of women at the graduate level has not caught up with that of men. The long-term trend in the percentage of female graduate students shows that in 1965 when the statistics first became available, the percentage of female graduate students was 7.53%. It reached 10% in 1978, 20% in 1994, and 30% in 2006, showing a constant and significant increase. Nonetheless, since then, the rate of female enrollment in graduate schools has barely increased, reaching only 32.37% in 2019 (MEXT, 2019b).

[14]For the empirical analysis of economic returns to graduate schooling, see Murata and Shimoyama (2018).

[15]Kariya (2011) formulated the nature and meaning of increasing graduate enrollments in education and society from the perspective sociology of education.

It is important to note that the decline in the number of entrants and enrollment in graduate schools in the 2000s and the 2010s was most significant in the fields of humanities and social sciences, while those in physical sciences and engineering were moderate or even increasing in some areas.[16] This trend is important in the feminization of graduate schools because the majority of female graduate students are enrolled in humanities and social sciences and very few are in physical science and engineering. This issue will be discussed in detail under Section 3.

3. Gender Imbalances in the Field of Study

3.1 Imbalances in Bachelor-level Enrollment

Fig. 9.3 shows the number of students in bachelor's programs in 2019 by field of study. More female students than male students were enrolled in the fields of humanities, health, home economics, education, and arts, while more male students than female students were enrolled in social sciences, physical science, engineering, and agriculture.

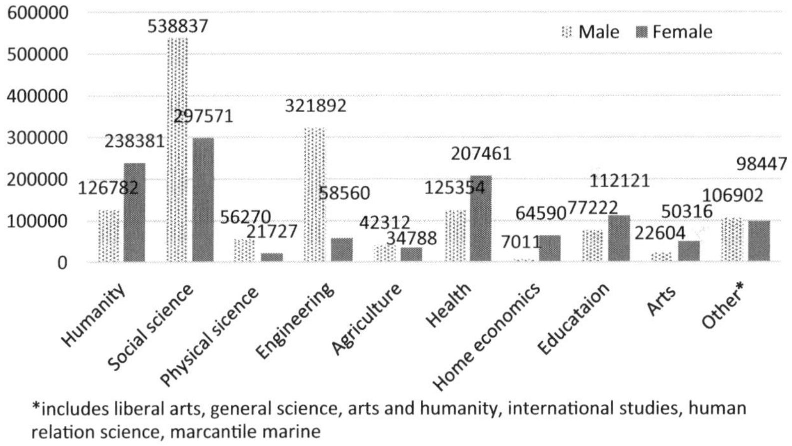

Fig. 9.3. Enrollment by Field of Study (Bachelor's). *Note:* * includes liberal arts, general science, arts and humanity, international studies, human relation science, and marcantile marine. *Source:* The figure is created by author based on the statistics published by MEXT (2019a).

[16]The situation is thoroughly discussed in National Institute of Science and Technology Policy (2020).

3.2 Imbalances in Master's-level Enrollment

Imbalances in the enrollment by field of study became even more conspicuous at the advanced level of study. Fig. 9.4 shows the number of students in master's programs in 2019. In terms of the fields with more female than male students and vice versa, the same picture as in the bachelor's program can be seen. More women than men were enrolled in humanities, health, home economics, education, and arts, while more men than women were enrolled in social sciences, physical science, engineering, and agriculture.

3.3 Imbalances in Doctoral-level Enrollment

Imbalances in the enrollment by field of study increased even further at the highest academic level. Fig. 9.5 shows the enrollment figures in doctoral programs in 2019. In terms of the fields with more women than men and vice versa, we can see a similar picture as that of the bachelor's and master's programs. The fields of humanities, home economics, and arts had more women than men, while the fields of social sciences, physical science, engineering, and agriculture had more men than women. The difference from the bachelor's and master's programs is that while female enrollment was higher than male enrollment in health and education in both bachelor's and master's programs, male enrollment in these fields was higher at the doctoral level. This is because some areas of specialty, such as Pharmacy and Dentistry, mostly aiming at educating students to become

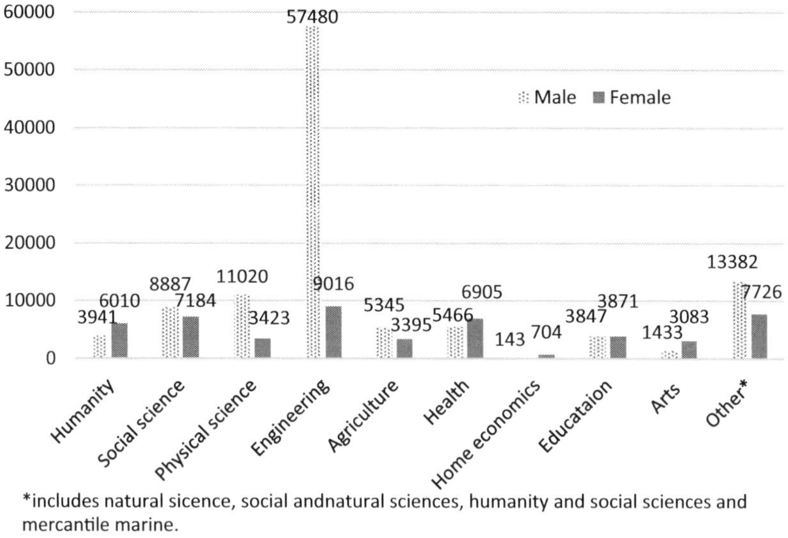

Fig. 9.4. Enrollment by Area of Study (Master's). *Note:* * includes natural science, social and natural sciences, humanity and social sciences, and mercantile marine. *Source:* The figure is created by author based on the statistics published by MEXT (2019a).

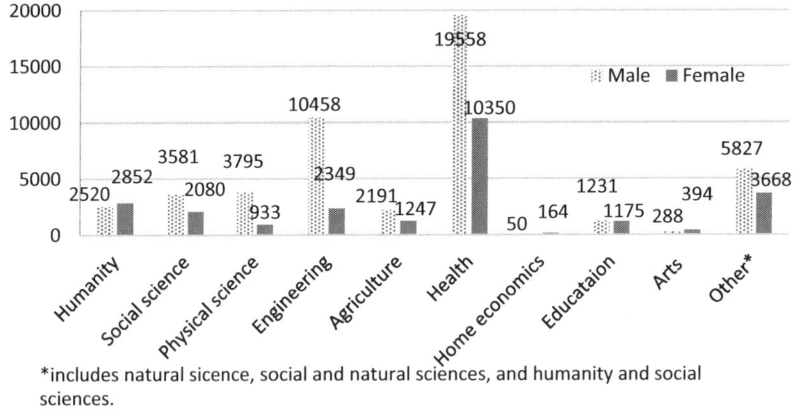

Fig. 9.5. Enrollment by Area of Study (Doctor). *Note:* * includes natural science, social and natural sciences, and humanity and social sciences. *Source:* The figure is created by author based on the statistics published by MEXT (2019a).

dental hygienists, were dominated by women in bachelor's and master's programs, but did not exist at the doctoral level.

3.4 Imbalances in Professional Schools

Fig. 9.6 shows the enrollment by field of study in professional schools in 2019. In terms of the fields with more women than men and vice versa, we can see a similar picture as that of the bachelor's and master's programs. The fields of humanities, home economics, and arts enrolled more women than men, while the fields of social sciences, physical science, engineering, and agriculture had more male students than female students. The difference with the bachelor's and master's programs was that while female enrollment was higher than male enrollment in the fields of health and education in both bachelor's and master's programs, male enrollment was higher in education and was very close to female enrollment in health at the professional school level. This is because, in education, there are teacher-training programs included as professional programs and all teachers (both men and women) are encouraged to take the programs. In health, license-offering programs for Pharmacy and Dentistry have been taken by both female and male students.

3.5 Efforts to Reduce the Imbalances

As explained in the introduction, the Gender Equality Society Basic Law is a regulatory base in Japan for the promotion of gender equality. There has been a series of progress reported since the law was inaugurated, particularly in labor and employment regulations. In the area of higher education, major changes took place in 2018 when the government delivered various statements and initiatives by

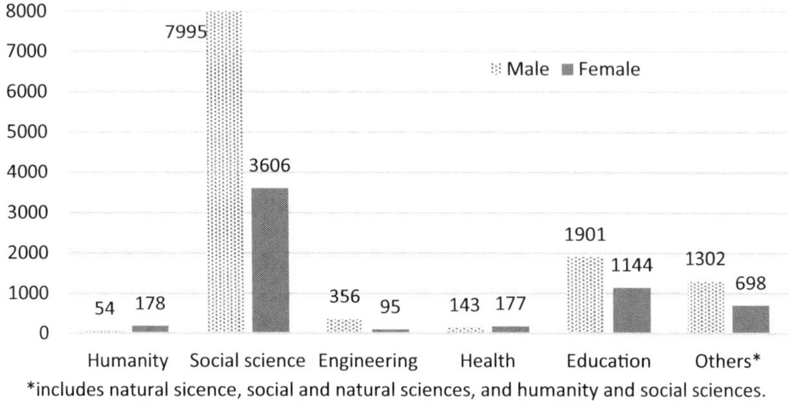

Fig. 9.6. Enrollment by Field of Study (Professional). *Note:* * includes natural science, social and natural sciences, and humanity and social sciences. *Source:* The figure is created by author based on the statistics published by MEXT (2019a).

foreseeing "the age of 100 years of life," where "the revolution of human development" is needed for all groups of society from childhood to old age and from male to female.[17] Related to the issues discussed in the above section, the inequality was summarized as follows:

- Significant lack of female enrollment in science and engineering programs
- Lack of female enrollment at master's and doctoral levels
- Both of the above explain the fewer researchers and other highly skilled professionals in workplaces.

To address these problems, a concrete initiative was developed, and a national budget was allocated. The initiative was titled "The promotion of gender equality in scientific technologies and academic field," consisting of three actions. The following shows the list of actions and budget allocation to MEXT and the Cabinet Office for the 2019 fiscal year:

(1) Increasing researchers in scientific technologies and academics, with a fiscal budget of €7,438,124 allocated to MEXT[18]

[17]The concepts, plans, and some results have been reported in a special report "Tayo na Sentaku o Kano ni suru Manabi no Jujitsu (Enrichment of Learning that Enables Diverse Choices)" White Paper on Gender Equality (Gender Equality Bureau Cabinet Office, 2019).
[18]The estimation is made at the currency rate of 1 EUR = 124.980 JPY as of August 7th, 2020.

(2) Preparing and maintaining the research environment favorable to female researchers and technicians, with a fiscal budget of €8,755,695 allocated to MEXT
(3) Promoting choices for female students and pupils to study in science and engineering fields and developing the human resource in science and engineering, with a fiscal budget of €18,108,232 allocated to MEXT and €157,097 to the Cabinet Office.

In terms of Action (1), the target number of female researchers in natural sciences was set to be 30% of all researchers in the field. The action included the development of a support system and a work environment that enables female researchers to balance work and life. It is noteworthy that the action also features research and enlightenment activities that promote interests among female students and their parents in the area of science and technology for their career options. Action (2) aims to enable universities and other research organizations to support and maintain female researchers, titled "Initiative to realize a diversified research environment." The specific scheme is the "Restart Postdoctoral Fellowship (RPD)" program that supports and facilitates female researchers to return to work after their leave for childbirth and childcare. Action (3) includes events and research projects organized by or through the Cabinet Office and the Japan Science Technology Agency (JST) as well as the MEXT. They organize seminars, internship programs, and other gatherings with industry and academics where female researchers and students come together for information exchange, share research work, and take special classes on scientific experimentation. Research projects should investigate facts and issues surrounding female students and propose ways to develop schemes and actions to increase the number and proportion of female researchers in the areas of science and engineering.

4. Characteristics in the Labor Market

The undersupply of female scientists and technicians is certainly an issue that must be resolved in higher education. Nonetheless, the labor market has many other issues and factors that the higher education community has to consider to improve the environment and conditions of female workers. This section reviews issues in the labor market to clarify what higher education can and should do to address the issues related to women in the workplace. I first review the income disparity between men and women in Japan. I then focus on the length of employment, which largely explains gender income disparity in Japan. The interruption of female employment due to childbirth and childcare is a major characteristic of the Japanese labor market, thus special attention will be paid to the turnover of female workers.

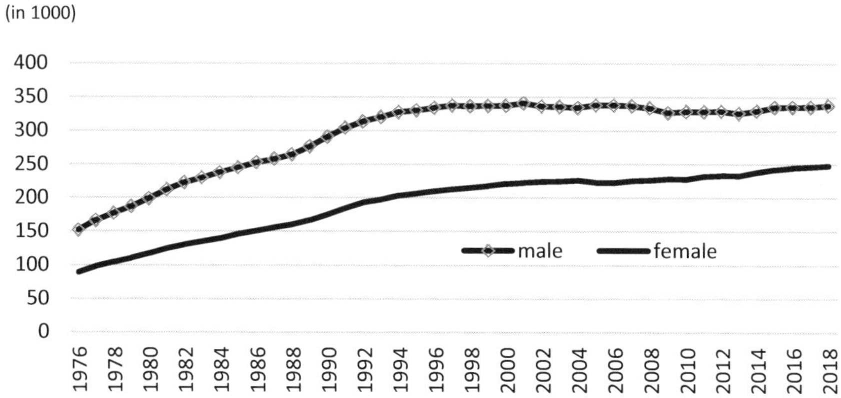

Fig. 9.7. Changes in Average Scheduled Salary for Male and Female Workers. *Source:* The figure is created by author based on the statistics published by the Ministry of Health, Labour, and Welfare (2019a).

4.1 Income Disparity

Compared with other developed economies, Japan still has a significant income disparity between men and women. In Japan, the monthly scheduled salary, instead of the annual salary, is used as an indicator of one's wage. According to the Basic Statistical Survey for Wage Structure by the Ministry of Health, Labour and Welfare, the average scheduled salary of female workers was 36% lower than that of male workers in 2018. The average monthly salary of male workers (whose average age was 43.6 years old and average number of years worked was 13.7 years) was 337,600 yen, while the average monthly salary of female workers (whose average age was 41.4 years old and average number of years worked was 9.7 years) was 247,500. Surprisingly, this wage disparity has been persistent for the past 4 decades, as Fig. 9.7 shows. Between 1976 and 1996, the gap between Japanese male and female workers in terms of the monthly scheduled salary widened, then the gap somehow decreased, but it is still significant.

Many previous studies on gender wage inequality in Japan concur that the inequality is explained by the length of employment as most Japanese firms adopt the seniority payment system.[19] The length of employment for Japanese female workers is largely affected by the interruptions of their career pathway due to childbirth and childcare. In addition, the type of employment is a strong determinant of the length of employment as women are more likely than men to take part-time/temporary jobs. Actually, the employment interruptions and part-time/temporary status for female workers are interrelated or even identical. After career interruptions, many women do not return to their previous job and, if they

[19]Studies from comparative perspectives such as Kalleberg and Lincoln (1988) are useful to understand the unique characteristics of the Japanese labor market.

return to the labor market, many of them take part-time/temporary jobs, which lower their average tenure as well as wages. Thus, the following section focuses on turnover based on the length of employment.

4.2 Turnover as a Major Reason for Short Female Tenure

As discussed above, of all employed workers in 2018, the average age of female workers in Japan was 41.4 years old, and their average number of years of work was 9.7. The average age of male workers was 43.6 years and their average number of years worked was 13.7. The 4-year gap in the ages of the early 40s is significant. This shorter tenure of female workers is partly due to the interruption of employment due to childbirth and childcare and partly because female workers in Japan are more likely than male workers to be temporary and/or term-limited part-time workers. Fig. 9.8 shows the recent turnover trend for male and female workers expressed by the rate of hiring and leaving.[20] In 2018, the rate of hiring for female workers was 18.5%, while that for male workers was 12.9%. The rate of leaving for female workers was 17.1%, while that for male workers was 12.5%. For the past almost 4 decades, the rates of turnover for female workers were between 16% and 23% and those for male workers were between 10% and 15%. These figures have never crossed—women quit and return to work consistently more often than men.

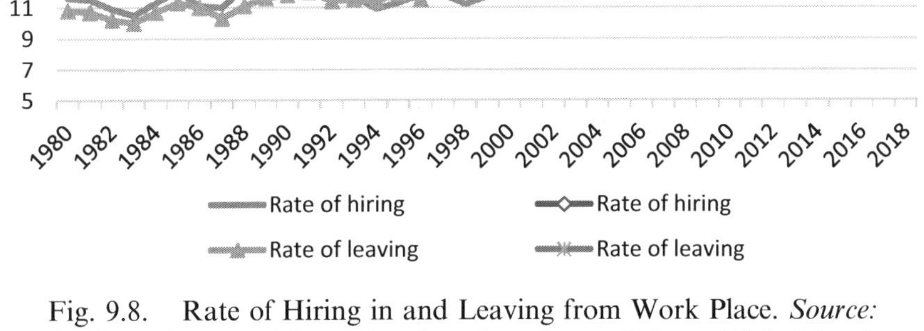

Fig. 9.8. Rate of Hiring in and Leaving from Work Place. *Source:* The figure is created by author based on the statistics published by the Ministry of Health, Labour, and Welfare (2019b).

[20]The denominator is the total workforce at the beginning of the fiscal year.

It is important to discuss the Japanese women's high turnover in more detail. First, many women quit working due to childbirth. After that, some women return to the labor market, but many of them do not return to the same place they worked previously. Others remain at home and, at some point, might restart working as part-time or temporary workers. If the woman has a moderate- to high-income husband, she has to be careful not to earn too much to reach the tax bracket where her husband, as head of the family, must pay extra tax, which can be higher than the net amount his wife receives from her part-time job. Then, she has two possible solutions. One is to work part-time for hours short enough to avoid giving her husband an extra burden. As nonregular workers are legally entitled to become regular after working for 5 years, many employers do not renew contracts for the sixth year. Thus, she repeats the cycle. Another solution is to return to a job that pays her high enough to avoid harming her husband's and her family's account. For a woman who is committed to getting a regular job, the second solution is more reasonable.

Nonetheless, for the second solution, women need an "enabler," that is, the "skills" that would be accepted by employers upon her return from the break. Thus, the type of skill matters. Becker (1993) defines two types of skill (one is productive in a specific firm; another, in many firms). The first one (firm-specific skill) is useful at a specific firm, thus those who have more of this type of skills have an incentive to stay at the same firm. The second type (what Becker termed "general skills") is portable to other firms and is thus tolerant to turnover. As these skills are occupation-specific, this rest of this paper will focus on the relationship between occupations, length of tenure, and skills needed for the occupations.

4.3 Analysis by Occupation

Analysis in this section is to explore occupations favorable to women in Japan. I will identify occupations that allow Japanese women (1) longer tenure and higher salary, and (2) shorter tenure but higher salary. Findings from the analysis will lead us to Section 5 where I will examine the type and level of education required for the occupations favorable to women, expecting to find out what higher education can offer for the improvement of female career pathways.

4.3.1 Longer Tenure with High Salary

Longer tenure with higher salaries can be realized for women who can stay with the same employers for longer. With other things being constant, if their employment is less likely to be, interrupted by, for example, childbirth and/or childcare, their salaries would be higher than those whose employment is interrupted. To find longer tenure occupations with higher salaries, the differences in the average salary and in the average tenure between male and female workers were estimated by occupation. Data for tenure and salaries were taken from the Basic Statistical Survey for Wage Structure published by the Ministry of Health, Labour and Welfare (2019a). I used 129 occupations defined as small occupational categories for the estimations. The mean of the male–female difference in average tenure was 2.61, with a standard deviation of 3.866. The average monthly salary of female workers was 247.500 yen. Then, occupations with longer tenure and higher salaries were selected using the following criteria:

- Occupations where the male–female difference in the average tenure is below one standard deviation under the mean (in this case, −1.256).
- For the salary, occupations with an average monthly scheduled salary higher than the average monthly scheduled salary in all occupations (247.5 [247,500 yen]).

Table 9.2 shows occupations that met the above criteria. "Age" represents the average age of workers in respective occupations when the survey was conducted. "Tenure" represents the average number of years the respondents had worked in the organization when the survey was conducted. "Weekly work hours" are the average hours worked. "Monthly pay" is the average amount of monthly scheduled salary and "annual pay" includes the scheduled monthly salary, overtime work allowance, and a special allowance called a "bonus" (usually paid twice a year). The occupations are listed from the top, by monthly scheduled salary.

The lawyer, certified public accountant, real estate appraiser, aircraft crew, social insurance consultant, and power generation/substation specialist occupations were selected as occupations with longer tenure with higher salaries. Within this group, there are two different types of occupations in terms of the relationship between age, tenure, work hours, and monthly and annual pay. For the lawyer, real estate appraiser, and aircraft crew occupations, the average tenure for female workers is longer than for men *and* the salaries of women are higher than those of men. For a certified public accountant, social insurance consultant, and power generation/substation specialist, the average tenure for female workers is longer *but* the average salaries of women are lower than those of men. "Hours worked" appear slightly higher for men than for women, but the difference is not large enough to explain the wage difference. Thus, although all the listed occupations have longer tenure with higher salaries compared with female workers in other occupations, tenure is more fairly reflected in the former occupations.

4.3.2 Shorter Tenure but Higher Salaries

The selection was based on the following criteria:

- Occupations where the male–female difference in average tenure is above 0.5 standard deviation higher than the mean (in this case, 4.543). This means that male average tenure is 4.543-year longer than female average tenure.
- For the salary, occupations in which the average monthly scheduled salary is higher than the average monthly scheduled salary in all occupations, which is 247.5 (247,500 yen).

Table 9.3 shows occupations that met the criteria. The occupations are listed from the top, by monthly scheduled salary.

Table 9.2. Occupations with Longer Tenure and Higher Salary.

	Age		Tenure		Weekly Work Hours		Monthly Pay (000)		Annual Pay (000)	
Occupation	**Male**	**Female**	**Male**	**Female**	**Male**	**Female**	**Male**	**Female**	**Male**	**Female**
Lawyer	35.2	36.9	6.2	8.6	171.0	157.0	504.7	570.2	7,728.4	7,575.6
Certified public accountant	38.2	40.5	10.1	12.1	163.0	157.0	502.7	442.9	9,140.4	8,037.7
Real estate appraiser	48.8	33.2	3.5	5.5	160.0	146.0	350.3	402.0	6,396.0	6,684.8
Aircraft crew	36.0	35.8	4.4	12.0	139.0	143.0	354.8	391.6	4,351.2	6,154.3
Social insurance consultant	45.9	56.7	11.4	16.4	175.0	176.0	379.1	331.7	5,336.8	4,586.8
Power generation/substation specialist	38.7	44.5	15.7	18.6	154.0	153.0	320.7	247.5	5,847.6	4,073.7

Source: This table is developed by author based on statistics published by the Ministry of Health, Labour, and Welfare (2019a).

Table 9.3 Occupations with Shorter Tenure but Higher Salary.

Occupation	Age		Tenure		Weekly Work Hours		Monthly Pay (000)		Annual Pay (000)	
	Male	Female	Male	Female	Male	Female	Male	Female	Male	Female
Aircraft pilot	43.1	35.6	16.1	3.7	148.0	152.0	1,474.9	911.6	20,542.4	11,816.2
Reporter	41.8	36.2	15.9	11.2	157.0	156.0	472.2	395.6	8,169.5	6,967.7
First-class architect	50.3	41.2	16.3	10.9	172.0	166.0	424.5	338.6	7,399.5	5,570.3
Railway driver	41.5	32.9	20.9	10.1	146.0	140.0	349.1	311.6	6,595.9	5,515.7
Engineer	44.0	36.3	13.4	6.4	164.0	158.0	347.3	270.8	5,723.9	4,257.3
Train conductor	38.9	29.4	17.6	7.1	152.0	142.0	320.7	261.5	6,007.6	4,736.6
Dental hygienist	50.5	34.8	22.5	5.8	176.0	167.0	358.0	256.1	6,309.6	3,628.6
Commercial large truck driver	48.6	46.2	12.1	6.5	176.0	176.0	282.3	251.6	4,579.6	3,985.6

Source: This table is developed by author based on statistics published by the Ministry of Health, Labour, and Welfare (2019a).

Aircraft pilot, reporter, first-class architect, railway driver, engineer, train conductor, dental hygienist, and commercial large truck driver were the shorter tenure occupations with higher salaries for female workers. A closer look at the relationship between wage and tenure with other data shows that in these occupations, women are, on average, much younger than men. Therefore, although workers earn significantly higher salaries than women do, the difference in age between male and female workers explains the difference in the amount of salary.[21]

While employment interruptions due to childbirth and childcare are the major determinants of lower salaries for female workers, the former occupations allow women to return to their previous job easily while the latter cases welcome mid-career women. In both cases, the market value of female workers is less likely to depreciate, and the listed occupations tend to require professional or technical skills. Changes in demand for occupations may change the salaries, but offering skills that do not depreciate in the career pathway of female workers would be an important solution for higher education to contribute to equal employment opportunities.

5. Solution in Higher Education

In Section 3, we have reviewed that the Japanese government and tertiary institutions have been working to increase the participation of female students in science and engineering. Such an initiative is important to reduce the gender gap in the targeted academic and occupational area. However, more areas of study can and should focus on improving the career pathway of women. To the extent that those areas require professional, technical, and/or advanced knowledge and skills, the improvement of women's career pathway relies much on higher education. If the skills and knowledge required in the career pathway are such that employers do not sponsor the workers, the role of higher education becomes even more important.

Thus, this section discusses the role of education in the occupations identified above as that of providing more gender-balanced working conditions. Tables 9.4 and 9.5 show the level of education required or necessary to work in the occupations listed in the previous section, i.e., occupations that allow longer tenure and higher salaries, and shorter tenure but higher salaries for female workers. The Japan Statistics Bureau offers information on the level of education required for 81 occupational categories. As the previous investigation was based on 129 occupational categories, the occupations selected in the previous inquiry were regrouped along with the 81 categories. In Tables 9.4 and 9.5, the first columns are the occupations that allow female workers longer tenure and higher salaries

[21]To confirm this observation, statistical significance has to be tested using the regression of the difference in wage by the difference in tenure, age, work hours, and all other available explanatory variables, which will be the subject of a future study.

Table 9.4. Education for Occupations with Longer Tenure and Higher Salary.

Occupation	Occupational Category	Education: 4-Year and Up	Education: Any Postsecondary
Lawyer	Legal workers	85.71%	90.83%
Certified public accountant	Management, finance, and insurance professionals	74.97%	87.04%
Real estate appraiser	Other specialist professionals	58.74%	82.50%
Aircraft crew	Customer service workers	16.53%	40.75%
Social insurance consultant	Management, finance, and insurance professionals	74.97%	87.04%
Power generation/ substation specialist	Stationary and construction machinery operators	19.08%	31.93%

Source: This table is developed by author based on statistics published by Japan Statistics Bureau (2019).

and shorter tenure and higher salaries, respectively. The second columns show the occupational categories in which the occupations in the first columns fit. The third columns show the level of education required in the respective occupational categories. "Four-year and up" means that the occupations require more than 4 years of education, from a bachelor's degree upward. "Any postsecondary" indicates that those with any postsecondary degrees can be employed in the occupations. Junior colleges, national colleges of technology, and specialized training colleges are included in this category.

Table 9.4 shows that four out of six occupations, including lawyer, certified public accountant, real estate appraiser, and social insurance consultant, require higher education (with more than 50% of at least 4-year education and more than 80% of postsecondary education). These occupations also require an official license. In Table 9.5, four out of eight occupations, including reporter, first-class architect, engineer, and dental hygienist, require a high level of education (with more than 50% of at least 4-year education and more than 80% of post-secondary education). First-class architect and dental hygienist also require an official license.

The above tables show that occupations that allow the preferred career pathway for female workers require a higher level of education, some of which

Table 9.5. Education for Occupations with Shorter Tenure but Higher Salary.

Occupation	Occupational Category	Education: 4-Year and Up	Education: Any Postsecondary
Aircraft pilot	Ship and aircraft operators	26.39%	49.81%
Reporter	Authors, journalists, editors	76.59%	88.11%
First-class architect	Professional and engineering workers	54.62%	88.87%
Railway driver	Railway drivers	19.09%	30.15%
Engineer	Engineers	64.21%	82.35%
Train conductor	Other transport workers	14.59%	27.39%
Dental hygienist	Professional and engineering workers	54.62%	88.87%
Commercial large truck driver	Motor vehicle drivers	9.83%	21.44%

Source: This table was developed by author based on statistics published by Japan Statistics Bureau (2019).

also require official licensing. These findings correspond with the theory formulated by Becker (1993) about general and specific skills. According to Becker, "general skills" are those skills that are productive not only in a specific firm but also in other firms. For example, dental hygienists can be productive both in a specific dental clinic or hospital and in any other dental clinic and hospital that provides dental care. Hence, the productivity and wages of dental hygienists do not decrease after changing employers.[22] In theory, skills for these occupations are paid for by workers, not by employers, and in-house training sponsored by employers is not aimed at developing general and portable skills.

Hence, higher education is expected to develop general, portable, and occupation-specific professional and/or technical skills. Such skills development

[22]On a different note, occupations such as car retailing are disadvantageous to female workers. The average tenure for car retailers is 12.8 years for men and 6.7 for women and their average schedule salary in 2019 was 312,900 yen for men and 239,800 yen for women. This might be due to what Becker (1957) defines as "taste discrimination," where both sellers and buyers think that selling cars is a "man's job" and women are given an insignificant role.

can be offered through formal schooling including bachelor's, master's, and doctoral programs. It can also be offered by higher education institutions through continuous education programs. The recent government initiative that targets "the age of 100 years of life" focuses on lifelong learning for older workers and female workers. By using this scheme, Japanese higher education can advance its feminization from school to work for upward mobility of the female career pathway.

6. Conclusion

Japan has experienced remarkable progress toward equality of education, particularly in terms of enrollment in higher education. At the same time, there are significant differences in academic fields that male and female students enroll in. The science and engineering fields reveal the disparity. The government and tertiary institutions have been delivering various programs to reduce the disparity. To fill out the enrollment gap in specific unbalanced areas is certainly a process toward the feminization of higher education. This paper focused on the interactions between higher education and the labor market. It analyzed the current labor market performance of female workers and suggested how the higher education community should act to improve the performance. The examination focused on the gender gap in tenure as it is a key determinant of wage disparity between male and female workers in Japan. In fact, shorter tenure is unavoidable for most women because the main reason is career interruption due to childbirth and childcare.

This paper defined two types of occupations as preferable for female workers: (1) occupations with longer tenure and higher salaries and (2) occupations with shorter tenure but higher salaries. The first type allows women to return to their previous job easily and the second welcomes mid-career women on a full-time basis, both of which cases the market value of female workers is less likely to decrease. The study found that most of these occupations require a high level of education, suggesting that meeting the skills demand in these occupations is what higher education can contribute to the equalization of labor market opportunities for female workers. Furthermore, occupations with shorter tenure with higher salaries tend to require skills that are occupation-specific rather than firm-specific and the development of such skills is more likely to rely on institutional schooling or training, not on employers. For the enhancement of equal opportunities in the labor market, offering programs to develop highly professional and portable skills seems to be a feasible and effective role for higher education.

This paper suggests that feminization in Japanese higher education could contribute to women better by understanding the mobile nature of their work experience and thus offering programs that enable women to turn employment interruptions into upward mobility in their career pathways.

References

Becker, G. S. (1957). *The economics of discrimination*. Chicago, IL: University of Chicago Press.

Becker, G. S. (1993). *Human capital* (3rd ed.). Chicago, IL: University of Chicago Press.

Blau, F. D., Ferber, M. A., & Winkler, A. E. (2014). *The economics of women, men, and work* (7th ed.). Boston, MA: Pearson.

Bradley, K. (2000). The incorporation of women into higher education: Paradoxical outcomes? *Sociology of Education*, *73*(1), 1–18.

Brinton, M. C. (1993). *Women and the economic miracle: Gender and work in postwar Japan*. Los Angeles, CA: University of California Press.

Employment Environment and Equal Employment Bureau. (1996–2018). Hataraku Josei no Jitsujo. [Facts of women in workforce.] Employment Environment and Equal Employment Bureau, Tokyo, Japan: Japan Ministry of Health, Labour and Welfare. https://www.mhlw.go.jp/bunya/koyoukintou/josei-jitsujo/19.html (available in Japanese as of August 10, 2020)

Endo, S., & Shima, K. (2019). Empirical study on the rate of return to education in Japan: Focusing on the trends and differences in lifestyle of women. *Seikatsu Keizaigaku Kenkyu*. [*Journal of Life and Economy*.], *49*, 41–55.

Ferber, M. A., & Lowry, H. M. (1995). The sex differential in earnings: A reappraisal. In J. Humphries (Ed.), *Gender and economics* (pp. 429–439). Aldershot; Brookfield, VT: Edward Elgar.

Gender Equality Bureau Cabinet Office. (1996–2019). Danjo Kyodo Sankaku Hakusho. [White paper on Gender Equality]. Gender Equality Bureau, Tokyo, Japan: Cabinet Office, Government of Japan. English summaries. http://www.gender.go.jp/about_danjo/whitepaper/r01/zentai/html/honpen/b1_s00_00.html (available in Japanese as of August 21, 2020 Summary in English is available in the following site: http://www.gender.go.jp/english_contents/about_danjo/whitepaper/pdf/ewp2019.pdf (as of August 21, 2020)

Gender Equality Bureau Cabinet Office. (2019). Tayo na Sentaku o Kano ni suru Manabi no Jujitsu. [Enrichment of learning that enables diverse choices.] White Paper on Gender Equality.

Hojo, M. (2018). Gakureki Shuekiritsu ni tuiteno Kenkyu no Genjo to Kadai. [Current status and issues on studies in return to education.] *Nihon Rōdō Kenkyū Zasshi*. [*Monthly Journal of the Japan Institute of Labour*.], *694*, 29–38.

Jacobs, J. A., & Gerson, K. (2004). *The family and public policy. The time divide: Work, family, and gender inequality*. Cambridge, MA: Harvard University Press.

Japan Statistics Bureau. (2019). Employment status survey, https://www.e-stat.go.jp/en/stat-search/files?page=1&toukei=00200532 (as of August 21, 2020)

Kalleberg, A. L., & Lincoln, J. R. (1988). The structure of earnings inequality in the United States and Japan. *American Journal of Sociology*, *94*, Supplement: Organizations and Institutions: Sociological and Economic Approaches to the Analysis of Social Structure, S121–S153.

Kariya, T. (2011). *The Japanese forms of credential inflation and their effects on university education: How has the value of degrees changed in the era of 'universal access' to university education?* Discussion Paper Series. Tokyo, Japan: University of Tokyo Institute of Social Science Panel Survey Project. No. 48.

Lee, J. (2004). Taking gender seriously: Feminization of nonstandard work in Korea and Japan. *Asian Journal of Women's Studies*, *10*(1), 25–48.

MEXT. (2015, September 15). *Mirai o Kenin suru Daigakuin Kyouiku Kaikaku: Shakai to Kyodoushita "Chino professional" no Ikusei*. [*Graduate education reform that leads the future: The development of "knowledge professionals" with society*.] Report by Central Council of Education (Section of Higher Education), https://www.mext.go.jp/b_menu/shingi/chukyo/chukyo4/houkoku/1366897.htm (available in Japanese as of August 21, 2020).

MEXT. (2019a). School basic survey. Retrieved from https://www.mext.go.jp/en/publication/statistics/index.htm for the summary of statistical data since 1950.

MEXT. (2019b). Daigakuin o secchi suru daigaku. Daigaku no Gakkousu, Daigakuin Zaisekishasu. [Number of universities that have graduate schools and number of graduate students]. School Basic Survey, https://www.e-stat.go.jp/stat-search/database?page=1&layout=datalist&toukei=00400001&tstat=000001011528&cycle=0&tclass1=000001021812&statdisp_id=0003147060 (available in Japanese as of August 23, 2020).

Ministry of Health, Labour, and Welfare. (2019a). Basic statistical survey for wage structure. Japan Ministry of Health, Labour, and Welfare, https://www.e-stat.go.jp/stat-search/files?page=1&layout=dataset&toukei=00450091&tstat=000001011429 (available in Japanese as of August 23, 2020).

Ministry of Health, Labour, and Welfare. (2019b). Survey on employment trends. Japan Ministry of Health, Labour, and Welfare, https://www.e-stat.go.jp/stat-search/files?page=1&toukei=00450073&tstat=000001012468 (available in Japanese as of August 23, 2020).

Murata, O., & Shimoyama, A. (2018). The diffusion of higher education and the work situation: Analysis using the employment status survey. *The Journal of Economics of Kwansei Gakuin University*, *72*(3), 83–100.

National Institute of Science and Technology Policy (2020). *Japanese science and technology indicators 2020: NISTEP Research Material,* No.295, NISTEP: Tokyo. The report is available in Japanese at: https://nistep.repo.nii.ac.jp/?action=pages_view_main&active_action=repository_view_main_item_detail&item_id=6700&item_no=1&page_id=13&block_id=21 (as of August 11.2020)

Shima, K. (1999). Economic Analysis of Students' College Choice: Focusing on Private Rate of Return. *Kyoiku Shakaigaku Kenkyu*. [*The Journal of Educational Sociology*.], *64*, 101–121.

Shima, K. (2017). Rate of return to university education: Focusing on national versus private university and university ranking. *Daigaku Keiei Seisaku Kenkyu*. [*Journal of Research on University Management and Policy*.], *7*, 3–15.

World Economic Forum. (2019). *Global gender gap report 2020*. Geneva: World Economic Forum.

Yamaguchi, K. (2008, May). Danjo no Chingin Kakusa Kaisho eno Michisuji Tokeiteki Sabetsu no Keizaiteki Fugouri Rironteki Jisshouteki Konkyo. [Path to solve gender wage inequality: Theoretical and empirical grounds for economic irrationality over statistical discrimination.] *Nihon Rōdō Kenkyū Zasshi*. [*Monthly Journal of the Japan Institute of Labour*.], (574).

Appendix 1

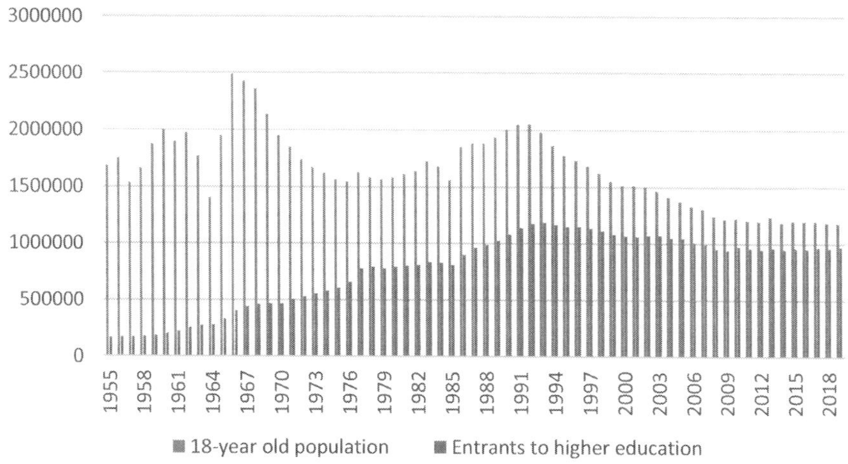

Fig. 9.A1. 18 years old population and higher education entrants

Chapter 10

Women in Higher Education in India: Historical Influences, Contemporary Narratives, and the Way Ahead

K. M. Joshi and Kinjal V. Ahir

1. Historical Chronicle of the Status of Women in India

The status of women during the ancient Vedic period (c.1500–c.500 BCE) was that of respect and dignity, as referred in the ancient literature "Rigveda." Various traditions like *swayamwar* (whereby women choose their groom), remarriage of widow, monogamy, inheritance of wealth of the deceased by unmarried daughters, freedom to dance and sing, etc., endowed self-respect to women. Women were encouraged to participate in religious ceremonies, acquire highly intellectual knowledge, and become teachers of great admiration (for example, Gargi, Maitraey, and Jayanti). Consecutively, with evolution and recognition of certain annexures to *Vedas* like the *Brahmanas (Aitareya Brahmana)*, *Upanishads*, *Smritis (Manusmriti)*, and *Sutras* (*Dharmasutras* evolved during 500 to 200 BC), the role of women got confined to patriarchal hegemony with restricted education, and her prime task directed to serve the male. The "Sati" tradition (whereby a widow voluntarily or forcefully was surrendered to the pyre of the demised husband) was another ruthless practice of the period. *Varna system* (class system) later divided the society into four *varnas* or classes, which plagued the society and infused caste system. Unfortunately this prevails even today in a different and partial form. During the early Medieval Period, women were married as early as between the age of 6 to 8, she was denied education, but was respected at home, and had property rights. The Medieval era was dominated by Muslim rulers in India. There are examples of diligent and courageous female rulers in both Hindu and Muslim reigns like Razia Sultana (1236–1240), Chand Bibi, Tarabai, and Rani Ahilyabai. These were efficacious female administrators and political influencers both as wives and daughters. During this period, several unethical practices such as child marriages, sati tradition and its honoring, restricted widow remarriages, lack of education for women, subsuming role of women in society and family, and dowry in the name of the traditional "*Stridhan*" gained prominence.

International Perspectives on Gender and Higher Education, 171–191

doi:10.1108/978-1-83909-886-420201010

During the colonial rule, the lack of dignity of women was empathetically challenged, largely by Western-educated liberal Indian men. The women's movement during this phase can largely be categorized into two components, one with "social cause" and another with the cause to "achieve freedom and sovereignty for India." Raja Ram Mohan Roy, founder of *Brahmo Samaj* in 1882, in Bengal was highly instrumental in making Sati tradition illegal, besides his efforts for abolishing ethnic and social discriminations. Ishwar Chandra Vidyasagar and Maharishi Karve promulgated support for widow remarriages. Justice Ranade and Bhandarkar, founders of *Prarthana Samaj* in 1867, predominantly focused on education for women by sponsoring the same. Dayanand Saraswati founded *Arya Samaj* in 1867, for equality among boys and girls, and opened many schools for girls. An inquiry into women's rights movement cannot be entirely elucidated without the freedom struggle in India. Mahatma Gandhi was able to mobilize women in the freedom struggle against British rule particularly for the *Satyagraha Movement* in 1919 and *Quit India Movement* of 1942. Their participation in the freedom struggle permitted them to move out of their household duties and were seen as serious contributors in the freedom struggle even in a patriarchal society. Besides participating in the nonviolent freedom struggle, women were also trained in the use of weapons and nursing to fight in the freedom struggle by joining *Rani Jhansi Regiment*, an exclusive women's wing of Subhash Chandra Bose's *Indian National Army* to fight against the colonial rule (Aggarwal, 2019; Anonymous, 2015; Mondal, 2019; Srivastava, 2019).

Women's suffrage was granted since the first election of independent India in early 1950s (Biswas, 2018). Many movements in the postindependence period were not directly related to women's issues, but women's participation in such movements addressed social issues (*sati*, dowry, alcohol consumption among men, and resulting domestic violence), political, economic (landless laborer's movement in Telangana, antiprice rise movement in 1970s, evolution of SEWA), and even environmental issues (*Chipko* movement, against deforestation whereby tribal people embraced the trees in a symbolic manner to suggest that before cutting the trees they should cut them). Elaborate narratives and literature can be found related to women's movement in India during postindependence era, some of which include Aggarwal (2019), Chadha (2014), Kapur (2019), Pande (2018), Arora (2017), Mainwal (2014), and Gull and Shafi (2014). In the post-independence era, the success achieved by women in India in various walks of life is noticeable (Kapur, 2019; Mainwal, 2014; Pandey, 1987).

2. Status of Women in India during Contemporary Times

According to the 2011 Census, as cited in MOSPI (2019), the sex ratio for India was 943 and women comprised 48.5% of the total population. The sex ratio in the rural area has been historically high as compared to the urban area. But in recent past, there has been a decline in the sex ratio in the rural area and improvement in the urban area. This has narrowed the gap between rural and urban sex ratio since 1951. Amidst cases of female infanticide and sex-specific abortions in favor of male child, the child sex ratio in the age group of 0 to 6 years was 918. The sex ratio was highest for Christians (1,023) followed by Buddhists (965), Jains (954), Muslims (951), Hindus (939), and lowest for Sikhs (903). About 10% of the total households were headed by women from July 2011 to June 2012 (MOSPI, 2019).

2.1 Status of Women's Health in India during Contemporary Times

Women's mean age during the marriage was between 21 and 22.2 during 2012–2016 and was not below 20.8 even for the rural area. The fertility rates for mothers with less than primary education (2.4), primary education (2.3), middle education (2.1), class 10th (1.9), class 12th (1.6), and graduate and above (1.5) for the year 2016 reflects the reduction in the total fertility rates of mother with rising levels of education. An inverse relationship between the level of education and fertility rates of mothers was observed (MOSPI, 2019).

Life expectancy at birth has been increasing for both the genders, but it has been consistently higher for women as compared to men with 69.6 years and 66.4 years, respectively, in 2016. Infant mortality rate (IMR) reduced during 2007–2016 for both women and men; IMR for girls was slightly higher at 36 as compared to boys at 33 for the year 2016. About 50% of women between the age group 15 and 49 were observed to be anemic during 2015–2016. 53.5% of married women between the age group 15 and 49 were using some methods of family planning. The Usual Monthly Per Capita Consumption Expenditure survey for 2014 highlighted that in the urban areas, except the highest fifth quintile, for all the rest of the four quintiles, the medical expenditure on men was greater than that on women. The medical expenditure for rural areas was observed to be higher for men as compared to women for both first (lowest) and fifth (highest) quintiles. The average medical expenditure on women was higher for second, third, and fourth quintiles in rural areas (MOSPI, 2019).

Barooah (2011) in his study for India concluded that the likelihood of child malnutrition reduced if the mother was literate as compared to the ones who were not literate. Child malnutrition was found to be comparatively lower due to more effective use of healthcare institutions by literate women.

2.2 Status of Political Participation of Women in India during Contemporary Times

The participation of women in the legislature, executive, and judiciary can play a pivotal role in strengthening the status of women in India. During the period 2016–2018, about 12% of the Central Government Council members comprise women. Women comprise only 6 out of 25 Cabinet Ministers and 3 out of 49 Ministers of State in 2018 in India. Although percentage of electors in General Election has increased, it remained low for both women (65.5%) and men (67%) during the 16th General Election. Percentage of voter's turnout across various states for women remained between 57% and 88%. Women members elected or nominated to Rajya Sabha (upper house of the Parliament) were barely 11% of the total members in 2016. With a 50% reservation policy at the level of local bodies, i.e., *Gram Panchayat*, women comprised 46% of elected representatives in the Panchayats in November 2016 (MOSPI, 2019).

2.3 Legislative Provisions for Protection of Women's Rights and Security in India

Indian legislature provides for various provisions for the protection of women's rights, security, and dignity. Some of the significant legislatures include, *the Immoral Traffic (Prevention) Act, 1956*, (which makes prostitution illegal and particularly forcing a child in prostitution); *the Hindu Succession Act, 1956*, (which allows daughters of the deceased to claim succession over father's property equally as sons); *the Dowry Prohibition Act, 1961*, (prohibits giving and receiving dowry); *the Maternity Benefit Act, 1961*, (with the amendment in the act in 2017, the Act has a provision for full pay leave for maternity benefits for a duration extended up to 26 weeks, which can be availed before or after the childbirth); *the Medical Termination of Pregnancy Act, 1971*, (which allows under specific conditions the termination of pregnancy by government-approved medical practitioners); *the Equal Remuneration Act, 1976*, (which provides for equal remuneration and not discriminate between different genders); *the Commission of Sati (Prevention) Act, 1987*, (which prohibits performing the tradition of *Sati* forcibly or voluntarily and glorification or honoring *Sati* practice in any form); *the Pre-Conception and Pre-Natal Diagnostic Techniques (Regulation and Prevention of Misuse) Act, 1994,* (which prohibits sex determination largely to control sex-specific abortion against female fetus); *the Protection of Women from Domestic Violence Act, 2005* (protecting women against being victim of domestic violence); *the Prohibition of Child Marriage Act, 2006*, (which prohibits the marriage of girl before the age of 18 years and for boys below the age of 21 years); *the Sexual Harassment of Women at Work-place (Prevention and Protection) Act, 2013*, (provides protection against sexual harassment at workplace); etc. (Chaturvedi, 2017; Indian Women Welfare Foundations, 2009). In spite of several acts and legislative protection, the crime against women has not declined (MHA, 2019; Ramanuj, 2015; Roy, 2019). Around 7% of the total crimes (4,831,515) were committed against women (338,954) in 2016 (MOSPI, 2019). In the judiciary, only 3 out of 24 Supreme Court judges were women. For none of the big states, the percentage of female judges in State High Courts exceeded beyond 20% of the total judges (MOSPI, 2019).

2.4 Currents Status of Women in Education Prior to Higher Education in India

As per the latest Census, literacy rates for women have remained low at 64.63 as compared to men at 80.88%. However, there has been a remarkable improvement in rural female literacy rate and reduction in the gender gap in literacy rates in rural area (MOSPI, 2019). Level-wise enrollment across all categories depicts low enrollment for women as compared to men (MHRD, 2018, p. 8). A consistent rise in the number of women per 1,000 men enrolled at different levels of education, namely, primary, upper primary, secondary, and senior secondary, was observed. But the data reveal that at different levels of higher education, the number of women was observed to be lesser than that for men.

The various reasons for not enrolling in education for women belonging to the age group of 5–29 years were largely associated with their participation in household activities, financial constraints, no tradition in the community to attend schools, and the school distance from the residence. Besides marriage, these reasons were also the major causes for dropout among women. Average annual dropout rates were high for primary levels of education, lower for upper primary, and again very high for the secondary level of education. Average expenditure per student pursuing general education was higher for men than women at the primary, upper primary, secondary, and senior secondary education levels. But at the level of higher education, the expenditure for women on an average was higher than that for men. Gender Parity Index (GPI) for all levels of education has shown a prodigious positive progress (MOSPI, 2019).

3. Gender and Job Market in India

A significant objective to pursue higher education is to seek better employment. Therefore, the demand for higher education is a derived demand for both men and women. The job market prospects motivate and determine the participation in higher education for both men and women.

According to the latest census, the Workforce Participation Rate for women was 25.5% and 53.26% for men. Worker Population Ratio (number of persons employed per 1,000 population) in 2015–2016 was 25.8 for women and 73.3 for men. Labor Force Participation Rate (number of persons in labor force per 1,000 persons) in 2015–2016 was 27.4 for women and 75.5 for men. Despite the Equal Remuneration Act in India, disparity in the salary earnings for men and women persists. For all the occupations with all levels of education combined, the average salary earned per day in rural areas was INR 201.56 for women and INR 322.28 for men, whereas the same in urban areas was INR 366.15 and INR 469.87, respectively (MOSPI, 2019).

It has been found that the increase in the level of schooling has positive impact on earnings by women in the urban informal sector (Asha Latha, 2012). The inequality in wages and other employment linked problems that women face in informal and unorganized sector like agriculture, domestic work, handloom weaving, and beedi (indigenous hand-rolled cigarette) manufacturing among others have been highlighted in several studies (Kaila, 2012; Yadav, Chandradeep, & Barsa, 2012).

The number of women entrepreneurs are growing in India despite the difficulties that many of them encounter. The problems they face include lack of sufficient skills, knowledge, and training, lack of funds, inefficient communication, lack of awareness of various schemes for women entrepreneurs, insufficient networking and business ties, risk intolerance, patriarchal society–induced lack of confidence of facing risks, balancing between work and life responsibilities, pressure to save at the cost of self-consumption, and constraints from family (M. Das, 2013; S. Das, 2013; Rao, 2011; Sahu, 2013; Shukla & Chatterjee, 2013). With the changing nature of job market, women have started participating in the skill up gradation and imbibing appropriate technical knowledge.

4. Women in Higher Education in India: Pertinent Facts

Various aspects related to higher education can be considered to measure the success of higher education in any country. These aspects comprise of institutional growth, access, equity, efficiency, and staff. This section contemplates all these features in context of women in Indian higher education.

In terms of institutional infrastructure, three types of higher education institutions are found in India, namely, Universities, Colleges, and Stand-alone Institutions. First, "Universities" are degree-awarding institutes established under an Act of Parliament or State Legislature and award their own degree. Second, "Colleges" are institutions affiliated to the Universities and cannot award a degree of their own. The third, "Stand-alone Institutions" offer only Diploma courses.

Considering the historical patriarchal norms in the society against coeducation, separate universities and colleges have been established and grown over time in the higher education in India. Out of a total of 993 universities in India, 16 women's universities across 13 states of India enroll only women students. On the other hand, out of 39,931 colleges in higher education in India, 11.04% of colleges are exclusively devoted to women (MHRD, 2019).

Access to higher education is an important measure to assess the success of higher education. The absolute enrollment of male students in higher education institutes in India in 2018–2019 was 19.2 million and that of female students was 18.2 million. Gross Enrollment Ratio (GER) for higher education in India for men increased phenomenally over 8 years from 20.8 in 2010–2011 to 26.3 in 2018–2019. Correspondingly, the GER for higher education in India for women registered a faster growth with a rise from 17.9 to 26.4 for the same period. GPI in higher education (the ratio of GER for females by GER for males) ascended to one (1) in 2018–2019, implying parity in access to higher education between males and females in higher education (MHRD, 2019).

It is important to ascertain the equity between men and women at various levels of higher education. Even though there exist a little discrepancy, largely the enrollment of women as percentage of total enrollment was to quite extent adequate at various levels of higher education (48.63% at all levels of higher education), like Diploma (33.2%), Undergraduate level (49.03%), Postgraduate level (56.42%), and PhD (43.81%) (MHRD, 2019).

An explicit gender-specific choice of discipline can be observed in higher education in India, which is referred by few authors as "genderization of higher education" (Joshi & Ahir, 2016a). The overall enrollment of women has increased substantially. The enrollment of women in "Engineering and Technology" as compared to various disciplines was noticeably abysmal at undergraduate level (29%), postgraduate level (37%), and in PhD (31%). Even among "Stand-alone Institutions," it was observed that professional courses like polytechnic (18%) and business administration (40%) registered lesser female enrollment. But the female enrollment share was very high in the traditionally women-dominated disciplines like "nursing" (86%) and "teacher training" (63%). Barring "Engineering and Technology," in most of the disciplines like Arts, Science, Commerce, Education, and Management, the enrollment of women was about 50% or above both at undergraduate and postgraduate levels (MHRD, 2019). While looking at the demand for selected disciplines, gender leaning decisions in favor or against disciplines may be attributed to the societal and cultural factors.

One of the measures of efficiency in higher education is the outturn or the number of students successfully passing out. Considering the amount of resources invested in educational achievement, the number of students passing out from the system is considered as a measure of efficiency. The percentage share of women passing out of various undergraduate and postgraduate disciplines was higher compared to percentage share of women enrolled as compared to that for men (MHRD, 2019). It can thus be deciphered that once in higher education, the likelihood of passing is higher for women as compared to men.

The composition of higher education system has staff as one of the significant stakeholder. The staff comprise both teaching and nonteaching staff. The share of female staff has an impact on the participation of women in higher education in a strict and rigid patriarchal society. In the year 2018–2019, the share of the female teaching staff was 42.2% in Indian higher education. The share of female teaching staff in colleges was 76% and in universities 58% (MHRD, 2019). It is noteworthy that there are positive interventions in the form of reservations in jobs including teaching jobs in the public sector. Women's reservation in government jobs is also legally provided for, in states like Gujarat (GoG, 1997).

In 2018–2019, women comprised 65.46% of total Tutors, 42.6% of Assistant Professors, 36.83% of Associate Professors, and 27.26% of Professors. Therefore, visibly as we proceed upward in the hierarchy of teaching staff, the percentage share of women declines. In terms of nonteaching staff, about 33% of the total staff comprised women in 2018–2019 (MHRD, 2019).

5 Factors Influencing the Women's Access to Higher Education: Some Discourses, Narratives, and Anecdotes

Ample literature exists regarding various aspects related to governance, efficiency, quality, internationalization, access, and equity in higher education in India (Agarwal, 2006; Agrawal, 2011; Altbach, 1993, 2009; Joshi & Ahir, 2013, 2014, 2015, 2016b, 2017; Joshi, Ahir, & Desai, 2018; Psacharopoulos, 1994; Tilak, 2011). However, discussions related to one of the basic detrimental aspects still seems to be limited in the existing literature, namely the reasons responsible for the decision related to women's enrollment or discontinuation in higher education (Madan, 2012 being exceptional). Hence, an attempt was made to understand the motivating and demotivating factors that influenced the decisions for women to pursue higher education using primary data collection. Observations from secondary data sources as stated in the above sections are hereby triangulated using two methodologies to understand the factors that influence access to higher education in India for women. Firstly, women who had discontinued pursuing education after higher secondary (did not enroll in higher education) were asked the reasons for the said decision using the unstructured personal interviews. Secondly, women currently pursuing higher education were asked about the factors that made them participate in the higher education. Both the methodologies were canvassed at a higher education hub, Vallabh Vidyanagar in Gujarat, a western state of India from December 2019 to January 2020. The conclusions drawn are based on and may be restricted to the area surveyed. However, important insights drawn from the survey can have a strong resemblance to similar observations in a large part of the country. Narratives of both the methodology are described in detail further.

5.1 Narratives by the Women Who Dropped Out of Higher Education

The women who had discontinued their studies after higher secondary education or its equivalent (higher secondary is equivalent to ISCED level 344 as per UIS, 2012) and did not pursue higher education were interviewed. A total of 50 women were interviewed. 10 women each belonging to five different age groups, 20–30 years, 30–40, 40–50, 50–60, and 60 and above were interviewed. The objective for surveying women belonging to different age cohort was to find the varied reasons during the past 5 decades for the discontinuation of the studies. The respondents were informed in the beginning that their names shall be kept anonymous. It was found that the most common reason across age groups was marriage, closely combined with associated customs, traditions, and maternal responsibilities. Almost 7 out of 10 women mentioned this as a reason for discontinuation across all age groups. Nonfavourable economic conditions were also mentioned as a reason for not pursuing higher education. The reasons for discontinuation of studies after higher secondary have not changed much over the last 5 decades. Few very specific anecdotes were also mentioned and have been discussed further to understand the causes of discontinuation of studies by women after higher secondary education.

In one instance, a respondent completed her undergraduate degree in Science through the financial assistance received in form of scholarship. However, the procedure for the scholarship takes time before which the fees are generally required to be paid. She somehow managed finance during her undergraduate program in time, but for the master's degree she could not manage fees because of the deferred scholarship disbursement and hence discontinued her studies. One of the respondent also described how her friends, relatives, and well-wishers extended financial assistance to pursue school education till secondary level (lower secondary is equivalent to ISCED level 244 as per UIS, 2012). However, the guilt of seeking help and obligation from others and its consequences restrained her from pursuing higher education.

It has also been reported that in many circumstances, education for boys was given preference in comparison to that of girls. One respondent also mentioned that the reason for discontinuation of her education was her parents' anticipation of marriage expenditure. It was presumed by the parents that expenditure on higher education on daughters would leave insufficient financial resources to incur expenditure to perform her marriage ceremony. Therefore, spending money for marriage was preferred. It was also mentioned that a societal attitude prevailed that investment in the education of the daughters would bear no returns for the maiden family, and so it was not encouraging to invest in the daughter's education. On the other side, it was assumed that the son's education would bring returns to the family forever, thereby motivating the family to facilitate son's education.

In one case, the mother of a female student had an extreme medical condition, whereby the mother was required to stay in the hospital for a long duration. Higher education in India has a provision for student's leave due to his/her medical situations but not for the family members' medical requirements. In the particular case being discussed, since the respondent was required to take care of the mother who was admitted in the hospital for a long time, her absence from the institute led to low attendance. As a consequence, she was not permitted to appear in the examination. The deteriorated financial condition also subsequently added to the cause for discontinuation of the study. Some girls were burdened with responsibilities of household chores since there was no one in the family to do the same due to the death of the mother. As per the Indian tradition, the customs following the death in a family can last up to 15 days, causing the absence of students for a longer duration. Other reasons included social responsibilities like taking care of younger siblings or the sick or physically or mentally challenged family members, which was largely expected to be done by women rather than men.

Rural societies are very closely interwoven with traditions and thus exemplify the intersectionality associated with access to higher education for the women. The rural areas are characterized by rigid traditional mindset and thus affect the access to higher education of women. It was unanimously mentioned by the respondents that if any girl of a village married without informing or taking consent of the parents while pursuing higher education, it would bring shame to the family. Further it was expected to create a deep negative impact for other girls to pursue higher education, out of the fear of similar consequences perceived by their parents. Even if any parent or family would be supportive of educating their daughters, such incidents would act as a strong deterrent against enrollment and access to higher education for willing students. Delays in returning from studying were questioned, even if the delays were due to participation in the activities of the college.

Various crimes against women also acted as a strong deterrent against allowing women to pursue higher education at far off distances, whenever there was a lack of higher education infrastructure in the nearby vicinity. In such situations, safety of the women during the daily commutation to pursue higher education was a major concern, with fears of crimes like abduction or rape. Parents of the girl students fear for the safety of their daughters. This was a primary reason to allow girls to pursue education only till the level which was available in the vicinity. Subsequently, the girls had very little choice of subjects and had to select whatever was offered in the vicinity. They were not allowed to pursue higher education at far off distances either by commuting or staying in hostels out of the fear for their security. Many women who wished to study at distant places found hostel expenses prohibitive. Some of the respondents also mentioned that their parents perceived that the age at which they were in higher education was a tender age, and girls could be vulnerable and immature to succumb to wrongdoings. Hence, girls were insisted to stay with parents and pursue higher education in the vicinity.

For two sisters in a family, the reason for dropout was the death of the father who dropped and picked them from the school. After the father's death, the financial situation changed, and no facility of commutation was available to cover the long distance to the school. This compelled them to drop out of school itself.

Some of the respondents expressed that few parents were too possessive and extremely pampering and believed that lodging and boarding facilities in hostels were not at par with facilities at their home. In view of this, they preferred to educate their daughter within their residential location. In view of the marriage of the daughters, some parents preferred to keep the daughters with them until marriage instead of putting them in hostel. They believed that by staying at home the girls are likely to spend as much happy family time as possible with the maiden family before the marriage.

A few women mentioned that failure in the examinations during the initial phases of higher education was also a reason for not continuing further education. Few women dropped out of higher education, simply due to a lack of interest in pursuing higher education. It was also reported that many girls dropped out of education due to better prospects of alternate earnings, particularly getting government jobs, prospects of operating beauty parlor, sewing/tailoring success, or to pursue their hobbies. One of the respondents dropped out of higher education due to poorer economic condition and opened a beauty parlor at home. For her, the opportunity cost of pursuing higher education as compared to operating a beauty parlor was much higher.

In some communities, women were not allowed to pursue higher levels of education since the men in those communities were not much educated. Consequently, during matchmaking, society could ridicule men that he was lesser educated than his wife. In that situation, the male ego in a patriarchal society was hurt. To avoid such situations during matchmaking, women were not allowed to pursue higher education. In a specific case, a girl was engaged to a nonresident Indian (NRI) and so was expected to shift abroad with the husband after marriage. Her in-laws convinced her that she would not be required to work further in the foreign country and as a consequence she quit the studies. Some also dreaded that educated women would be dominating, would question and argue more for genuine or not genuine demands, and thus not be obedient in the smooth functioning of the institution of the family. In some cases, the marriage date was intentionally fixed during the examination time so that the student would not be able to appear for her exams and subsequently drop out of education.

Some elderly people in the maiden family of girls would not see any benefit of women pursuing higher education while she was expected to be ultimately involved in household chores or at best engage in agricultural activities. So they felt that instead of wasting time in pursuing higher education, they rather learn household chores or agricultural activities that would be helpful to them after their marriage, as would be expected of her then. For some women, the timing of higher education institutes was colliding with the routine time of household chores which was expected to be done during definite morning hours. Sweeping, moping, and washing clothes and utensils are associated with cleanliness, which is further associated with piousness in prayers. Therefore, it was expected that these daily chores were completed in the morning itself, so that prayers could be offered in cleaner atmosphere. If the time of household cleanliness collided with the time of the higher education institute, it would be a deterrent to pursue higher education. The problem was similar for pursuing higher education in afternoon shift since the lunch was expected to be served hot and freshly cooked and thus the time collided with the duration of higher education institute.

Few respondents mentioned that the husband, girl's extended family members, and her in-laws believed that since the husband's earning was adequate, the wife need not study. The pursuance of higher education was strongly and exclusively associated with job-seeking outcomes. Such people were completely oblivious to the social benefits of pursuing higher education, and thus saw no merit in women pursuing higher education. The social advantages like rearing and educating children in better manner, or taking care of household finances in a better manner, becoming capable to take care of certain banking formalities or paying bills, and similar other social benefits were not considered. It was also stated by some respondents that permitting women to do job after marriage was seen as a social stigma on male members of the family who were ridiculed with lack of capability to earn sufficiently. In such circumstances, men would have to face allegations that men lacked capability to earn so as to seek help from educated wife by allowing her to work for an economic reward in the job market. Such belief was observed not only for unskilled work done by women in the job market but also for skilled work.

Another female who completed her graduation and currently belongs to the age group of 50–60 years had to face a lot of struggle to complete her higher education. She was compelled by the in-laws' family and society to drape a *sari* after marriage (sari is a traditional Indian attire whereby about 6 meters of cloth is draped in a particular manner), even while going to the college. As she had to travel by train to reach the college, she would go to the women's room at the railway station, change *sari* to a more comfortable *salwar kameez* (an Indian attire with a long overcoat and partitioned loose jeggings with a 2-meter long scarf), which was reasonably comfortable for the long travel and during studies. On her return, she would again go to the railway station women's room, put on the *sari*, and return home. Even today few female students can be found wearing a *sari* while pursuing higher education, mostly after their marriage, either willingly or as per the expectation from the family and society. Few female students hesitated to go to bigger cities to pursue higher education due to hesitation regarding the variations in culture and atmosphere in bigger cities as compared to their small hometown or villages.

5.2 Narratives by the Women Who Were Pursuing Higher Education

Focused group discussions in groups ranging from 8 to 12 women participants were conducted for those pursuing Master's degree. The selected women participants had already completed 3 years at undergraduate level. The objective of the discussion was to understand the factors that motivate women to pursue postgraduate education. Focused group discussions were conducted in three fields of higher education, based on their higher share in total enrollment (MHRD, 2019), namely humanities, commerce, and sciences. The respondents included students who paid low fees (government-subsidized fees) as well as those who paid self-financed (user charges) higher fees. As conveyed, the self-financed fees were three times higher than the government-subsidized fees for each semester. In India, the guardian of the student generally pays fees even at higher levels of education and not the student. The majority of the respondents from the humanities group belonged to rural areas (8 out of 10 respondents' permanent residence was in the rural area). Contrary to respondents pursuing humanities, the majority of respondents in the groups of commerce and sciences belonged to urban areas. About 10 girls out of 12 girls belonged to the urban areas in the sciences and all girls in commerce discipline belonged to urban areas. The respondents were informed in the beginning itself that their names shall be kept anonymous, and they had a choice of whether to disclose or conceal their names. They volunteered to participate after knowing the purpose of research. They were first asked to write factors that motivated them to pursue higher education. Then the discussion was opened and the moderator scripted the discussions.

5.2.1 Focused Group Discussion in Humanities

The focused group discussion with the humanities group in which the majority of the girls belonged to rural areas exhibited peculiar characteristics of rural socioeconomic environment. The education level of parents and in-laws was a significant factor that affected the participation decision of the women. Instances were cited where mothers were not educated, but they wanted their daughters to live an economically better and self-reliant life, particularly after their marriage. They believed that if their daughters were not educated, they may be compelled to join agricultural activities or some menial activities and were likely to suffer and lead poor life. The educated mothers had strong conviction that it was necessary to provide higher education to their daughters for their future. In few cases where mothers were apprehensive to allow their daughters to pursue higher education, the fathers motivated and compelled their daughters to pursue higher education, convincing mother and other family members. For a few women who were engaged or committed or married, their parents left the decision regarding the continuation of higher education on the in-laws of the girls. In certain exceptional cases, the married female students were both motivated and facilitated by in-laws to continue or pursue further studies. The highly educated and successful parents became an inspiration for their daughters and created an environment for them to participate and perform well in higher education.

Many female participants proudly stated that their families did not discriminate between them and their brothers for enrolling in education at any levels. In a narration, a girl described how her mother and grandfather forced her to study despite weak economic position. The girl lost her father at a very young age. Her mother was a daily wager, but her mother and her grandfather's efforts made her a role model for other girls of the village. Her performance became an exemplar for four girls from her extended family to pursue higher education. She also mentioned how her mother, grandfather, and extended family members accepted that she can have male friends in the college too. Besides, in two separate cases, the strong support of the friend to undertake higher education was the biggest stimulus to continue education.

In case of one girl student, her father was the head of the community. He wanted to set a role model for the daughters of other community members and so strongly pushed for her daughters' education.

In contrast to the reasons for dropouts, in some instances, pursuing higher education was the eligibility criteria for marriage. In certain communities, if a girl was educated, it increased her prospects of getting a better match for marriage. They would also take pride in the education and would in fact mention the qualifications of the bride and the groom even on the marriage invitation cards. Particularly in some cases if the female was highly educated, it would also increase the chances of getting proposals for marriage from abroad, from the NRIs, and this was also one of the motivational factor to pursue higher education.

A big number of respondents informed that subsidized tuition fees and transportation facility were very influential in their decision to take up further education. Some of the States are currently providing free transportation for female students. Three girls stated that they were using three connecting crowded public transport conveyance to reach the higher education institute. They described the daily commute as "very tiring," but they continued to study due to the support in the form of subsidy. A girl also mentioned that due to merit she could get admission in a public university, where the fees were subsidized. She expressed that she could not have pursued higher education in the absence of subsidized fees since high fees were unaffordable for her family.

Few female students were highly self-motivated for further education, and some considered higher education as a symbol of higher status in the society. Some of them viewed merit in pursuing higher education for better job prospects, to earn well, and thereby contribute to the socioeconomic status of the family. Three respondents mentioned that their parents believed that higher education was associated with social status and recognition in the society, and hence they allowed their daughters to pursue higher education. The motivation from teachers who taught them at the previous levels of education was also mentioned as the reason to pursue higher education.

A girl specifically mentioned that her parents believed that pursuing higher education was closely associated with the better understanding of how to live with a broader perspective and comprehend the issues faced in life. A girl herself wanted to explore the world and wanted to understand how the world was progressing. She enrolled for further education in expectation that such acquaintance might take place while pursuing higher education.

In spite of several reasons for the discontinuation of further education or dropout, there have been multifold reasons for those who continued the journey of their education. The positive factors that influenced women to pursue higher education include availability of higher education infrastructure in the vicinity, equal opportunities for boys and girls in the family, support and appropriate guidance from elder siblings – both from elder brothers and sisters – and better economic conditions. It was pleasant to note that at least two girls mentioned curiosity to seek knowledge as an influential factor for pursuing higher education.

5.2.2 Focused Group Discussion in Sciences

As mentioned previously, most of the respondents in the group pursuing science were from the urban areas. Majority of them wanted financial independence through a career after the higher education studies. Many expressed their sentiments by saying that "*I would not like to beg for my wants to anyone.*" Women perceived that pursuing higher education increased the possibility of gaining highly rewarding employment in the job markets and would thus mitigate any financial risk that might arise in their future life, even after their marriage. One of the girls wanted to pursue higher education due to the inspiration from the elder sibling who could get a government job by studying well. In India, it is a taboo that government jobs offer lifelong financial safety and continues to aspire many to pursue government jobs.

Few girls mentioned that pursuing higher education was also becoming mandatory out of societal pressure, whereby those not pursuing higher education were looked down upon, and so they studied. Majority of girls (8 out of 12) explicitly mentioned that due to an improvement in their lifestyle, their expenditures had become exorbitant. They would not like to compromise on their living standards but would instead like to earn enough to be able to afford to continue living that lifestyle in the future too. Hence, they were confident that after accomplishing a degree of higher education, they would be able to choose a career for themselves with which they would be able to self-sponsor their growing needs. They accepted that most of their luxurious needs have now become necessities like mobile, its unlimited internet data usage, makeup, fashionable clothes, accessories, and a party-like lifestyle.

One of the girls mentioned specifically that she had observed that women engaged in only household work were not seen with appreciation and respect. The household chores were not viewed to be anything special. Instead, if a female was a working female, her appreciation at work motivated her. Her appreciation at the office also inclined the family members to both appreciate and respect her.

She further believed that the same relatives who demotivate both the women and their families to permit women to pursue higher education and even try to malign her image in the society and family return to the family and the women for financial and societal support, once the women has achieved substantial social and financial success. A girl pursuing her Master's in Mathematics said, "*It was just for the parents to stand by the girl firmly while she pursued her dream and then the critiques themselves respect the girl and their family.*"

Few girls also aspired for professional goal achievements and satisfaction of accomplishing a higher degree. Four girls aspired to pursue PhD degree to gain the title of "Doctor" affixed before their name. Girls also believed that with higher levels of education, one acquires greater knowledge which assists in taking correct decisions both at professional and a personal level too. This opinion was similar to that expressed in the discussion in humanities too albeit expressed differently. Most of the girls believed that they had proven their intelligence by scoring very well in the previous levels of education and so they deserved to further education. They insisted that their higher education investment was the best utilization of the financial resources of their parents. At least six girls pursued higher education due to their interest in the subject, which they agreed was possible due to the faith of their parents. One of them told,

> Parents' motivation and facilitation, particularly undeterred financial support was mostly imperative to pursue higher education for almost all women. Either illiterate or highly educated families, parents proved to be the driving force to pursue the dreams of achieving the higher education for the girls.

Some also shared that their employment would be a support to the family during the time of crisis, which would not be possible if they were not educated. A girl also iterated the common understanding that "*an educated girl benefits two families.*" A parallel common belief in the Indian culture persists that a girl's maiden family and the family that she is married to will benefit if she was educated. Few female students believed that if they pursued higher education it created a "demonstration effect" in the society, thereby motivating other girls and their parents to allow their daughters to pursue higher education.

5.2.3 Focused Group Discussion in Management

Management is treated as a professional course (with relatively higher fees, relatively more exposure to job market in the form of internships, and hands-on training unlike traditional courses) and the group comprised female students pursuing Masters of Business Administration under both government grant-in-aid program (subsidized by the government) and self-finance program (with higher fees). Some of the reasons were similar to the above groups, like need to be financially independent (mentioned explicitly as "*I would like to swipe my own debit or credit cards to buy cars, clothes, mobiles,*" "*Shopping was a stress-buster, but certainly wanted to bear myself the burden of this stress-buster by earning salary used for shopping, Do not want to live life after marriage on the mercy of family members*"), expectations and encouragement from family and parents (since acquiring education was treated as an inevitable status symbol that one must acquire that would bring pride to parents and families), besides being ambitious (expressed by one of the respondents as "*Mediocrity is nowhere celebrated,*" suggesting that one has to be ambitious to surpass mediocrity). One shy girl, when prompted to speak, firmly uttered that

> I wish to complete the MBA program as desired by my parents and help them both financially and emotionally even after marriage. I desire to fulfil my duty towards my parents. The MBA degree will give me wings to remain financially independent instead of relying on the husband to make my parents happy.

Pursuing higher education was enforced on some girls as an outcome of higher performance in their 12th board exams or in some competitive exams before baccalaureate, which further resulted in greater expectations for their performance in higher education. A girl currently in MBA program explained how parents entrust their thoughts:

> I scored good marks in higher secondary and wanted to study pure science. But my father said that the pure science has no value or respect in society and it was for those who score low. Despite non liking for engineering, I was forced to study engineering.

A respondent elucidated that acquiring a higher education degree explicitly provides the job market a signal regarding the superiority of the candidate in the highly competitive job market. She also mentioned that working at the top level of management would enable her to be a decision-maker rather than instruction receiver from seniors/bosses. In order to reach the higher levels of managerial decision-making, it was important to undertake relevant education.

Negative sentiments toward being *only a homemaker* were reiterated by this group too, suggesting that society respects working ladies more than homemakers. Since the respondents had explicitly observed this in society, they wanted to assure that they worked in job markets instead of being an exclusive homemaker.

The group further suggested that a lot of motivation to become ambitious comes from educational institutes and the ecology provided by such institutes. It was categorically mentioned that their female professors were role models for them to learn how to manage work–life balance, which would further assist them to fulfill the expectations of both the workplace and families after marriage. Surprisingly, only selected girls considered higher education for the sake of seeking knowledge for forthcoming life. Many girls mentioned that education makes recipient smarter, more self-aware, and makes their lives fruitful and purposeful. A girl suggested that higher education was an opportunity to delay marriage. The respondents unanimously agreed that patriarchal domination has reduced over some time but was still prevalent in certain forms. To eradicate the same, to achieve equality, and to be role models for other girls in their families and society, they were motivated to study for their equal rights.

6. Conclusion

Higher education is seen as a catalyst for an upward socioeconomic movement in particular for the disadvantaged groups/gender. Indian higher education has witnessed the absolute growth of women participation during the last 2 decades. GPI reveals the parity achieved in the Indian higher education. Although the female enrollments have increased dramatically, but the female enrollment in traditionally "male-dominated" disciplines, and programs, still exhibits disparity. When gender disparity is imbibed in the social construct, the realms of access to higher education, and the leverage that can be derived from the same is bound to be affected. Various governmental policy initiatives like differentiated fees, incentives for accommodation, and transportation have contributed in improving the enrollment of the female. Besides this, India has exclusive universities and colleges for women.

While societal norms are changing, the pace certainly needs to be augmented and continued till gender neutrality becomes the "*new normal.*" Also, the gap needs to be reduced between two different societal setup, whereby certain societies are already gender neutral and those that are still dominated by historical patriarchal norms, limiting the progress of women in higher education and in job market. A feminist movement led by masses of the men can prove to be highly successful. The support of men at home and the workplace can generate gender neutrality. This unequivocal move will assure a more equal and just society.

Parental and family support has proven to be the most enduring impetus or constraint to pursue higher education for women. Many policy interventions like "*beti padhao, beti bachao*" (educate daughters, save daughters), selfie with daughter, etc., are great nudges to celebrate the pride of educating girls and honoring daughters. It should be assured that these policies do not remain restricted to the urban conglomerates only. The rural community should be more addressed through such initiatives. Various narratives described in the chapter highlight the intricacies involved in assuring improved access to higher education by women. Identification of causes to pursue or drop out of higher education for women being the first stage, apposite policy initiatives can assure improved access to higher education for women. The commitment and determination of the country to assure gender neutrality in various aspects of higher education would go a long way in enhancing the status of women and thereby advance the condition of the nation as was believed by Dr B.R. Ambedkar, Chairman, Constitution Drafting Committee of India, "*I measure the progress of a community, by the degree of progress which women have achieved....*"

References

Agarwal, P. (2006). *Higher education in India: The need for change*. ICRIER Working Paper No. 180. Indian Council for Research on International Economic Relations, New Delhi.

Aggarwal, M. (2019). Women's movements in India: Forms and main national organizations. History Discussion. Retrieved from http://www.historydiscussion.net/essay/womens-movements-in-india-forms-and-main-national-organisations/1801. Accessed on December 20, 2019.

Agrawal, T. (2011, September). *Returns to education in India: Some recent evidence*. Working Paper WP-2011-017. Indira Gandhi Institute of Development Research, Mumbai. Retrieved from http://www.igidr.ac.in/pdf/publication/WP-2011-017.pdf. Accessed on June 24, 2012.

Altbach, P. G. (1993). The dilemma of change in Indian higher education. *Higher Education*, *26*, 3–20. doi:10.1007/BF01575104

Altbach, P. G. (2009, June 5). The giants awake: Higher education systems in China and India. *Economic and Political Weekly*, *44*(23), 39–51. Retrieved from https://www.epw.in/journal/2009/23/special-articles/giants-awake-higher-education-systems-china-and-india.html. Accessed on January 1, 2020.

Anonymous. (2015). Women's movement in India. Sociology. Retrieved from https://socioguide.blogspot.com/2015/11/womens-movement-in-india.html. Accessed on December 12, 2019.

Arora, B. (2017). Negotiating structural inequalities in post-independence India: The case of deserted women and widowhood in Indira Goswami's *Neel Kanthi Braja* and *A Saga of South Kamrup*. *Society and Culture in South Asia*, *3*(1), 1–23. doi: 10.1177/2393861716674546

Asha Latha, D. (2012). *Women in urban informal sector* (p. 182). New Delhi: Akansha Publishing House. ISBN:978-81-8370-314-7.

Barooah, V. K. (2011). Maternal literacy and child malnutrition in India. In M. Pal, P. Bharati, B. Ghosh, & T. S. Vasulu (Eds.), *Gender and discrimination: Health and nutrition status and role of women in India*. New Delhi: Oxford University Press. ISBN:978-0-19-807664-3.

Biswas, S. (2018). Did the British Empire resist women's suffrage in India? *BBC News*, February 22. Retrieved from https://www.bbc.com/news/world-asia-india-43081429. Accessed on January 14, 2020.

Chadha, A. (2014, May 25). Political participation of women: A case study in India. *OIDA International Journal of Sustainable Development*, *7*(2), 91–108. Retrieved from https://ssrn.com/abstract=2441693

Chaturvedi, V. (2017). Top 10 legal rights every woman should know. Retrieved from https://www.quora.com/What-is-the-history-of-womens-rights-in-India. Accessed on December 14, 2019.

Das, M. (2013). Problems and prospects of women entrepreneurs in India. In S. K. Chaudhary (Ed.), *Women empowerment through entrepreneurs in India* (pp. 115–132). New Delhi: Avon Publications. ISBN:978-93-8183-900-3.

Das, S. (2013). Development of women entrepreneurship in India: Problems and prospects. In S. K. Chaudhary (Ed.), *Women empowerment through entrepreneurs in India* (pp. 305–321). New Delhi: Avon Publications. ISBN:978-93-8183-900-3.

GoG. (1997). *Gujarat Civil Services (Reservation of posts for Women) Rules, 1997*. Notification No. GS/97-13-CRR-1096-2213-/G.2. General Administration Department, Sachivalay, Gandhinagar. Retrieved from https://gpsc.gujarat.gov.in/Archieved/pdf/GR-for-Woman-reservation.pdf. Accessed on December 12, 2019.

Gull, R., & Shafi, A. (2014, May). Indian women's movement after independence. *International Research Journal of Social Sciences*, *3*(5), 46–54. ISSN:2319-3565. Retrieved from http://www.isca.in/IJSS/Archive/v3/i5/10.ISCA-IRJSS-2014-66.pdf. Accessed on January 11, 2020.

Indian Women Welfare Foundations. (2009). Women specific legislations: Laws and Acts. Retrieved from http://www.womenwelfare.org/laws_acts.html. Accessed on December 12, 2019.

Joshi, K. M., & Ahir, K. V. (2013). Indian higher education: Some reflections. *Intellectual Economics*, *7*(1), 42–53.

Joshi, K. M., & Ahir, K. V. (2014). Higher education in India: Reflections on changing landscapes. In K. M. Joshi & S. Paivandi (Eds.), *Higher education across nations* (pp. 412–456). New Delhi: B.R. Publishing Corporation. ISBN: 9789350501368.

Joshi, K. M., & Ahir, K. V. (2015). The state of higher education governance in India: A perspective. In K. M. Joshi & S. Paivandi (Eds.), *Global higher education: Issues in governance* (pp. 262–314). New Delhi: B.R. Publishing Corporation. ISBN: 9789350502235.

Joshi, K. M., & Ahir, K. V. (2016a). Equity in Indian higher education: Issues and challenges in access and participation. In S. Paivandi & K. M. Joshi (Eds.), *Equity in higher education: A global perspective* (pp. 55–82). New Delhi: Studera Press. ISBN:978-93-85883-06-4.

Joshi, K. M., & Ahir, K. V. (2016b). Higher education growth in India: Is growth appreciable and comparable? *Higher Education Forum*, *13*, 57–74.

Joshi, K. M., & Ahir, K. V. (2017). Quality assurance in Indian higher education: An unfinished agenda. In S. Georgios, K. M. Joshi, & S. Paivandi (Eds.), *Quality assurance in higher education: A global perspective* (pp. 127–144). New Delhi: Studera Press. ISBN:978-93-85883-27-9.

Joshi, K. M., Ahir, K. V., & Desai, B. S. (2018). The awaited rise of the sleeping elephant: Trajectories of creating world-class universities in India. In M. Rabossi, K. M. Joshi, & S. Paivandi (Eds.), *In pursuit of world class universities: A global experience* (pp. 59–90). New Delhi: Studera Press. ISBN:978-93-85883-64-4.

Kaila, H. L. (2012). Stress and coping among women managers in Indian organizations. In R. P. Yadav, K. Chandradeep, & Barsa (Eds.), *Women workers in India* (pp. 113–130). New Delhi: New Century Publications. ISBN:978-81-7708-295-1.

Kapur, R. (2019). Status of women in post-independence India. Research Gate. Retrieved from https://www.researchgate.net/publication/330220960_Status_of_Women_in_Post-Independence_India/citation/download. Accessed on January 13, 2020.

Madan, S. (2012). Aspects of gender bias in India. In S. Madan (Ed.), *Economic development and status of women in India: The case of Haryana* (pp. 54–117). New Delhi: Serials Publications. ISBN:978-81-8387-529-5.

Mainwal, S. (2014, April). Changing status of women in modern India: A sociological study. *International Journal of Engineering and Management Research*, *4*(2), 288–290. ISSN:2250-0758. Retrieved from http://www.ijemr.net/DOC/ChangingStatusOfWomenInModernIndiaASociologicalStudy(288-290).pdf. Accessed on January 12, 2020.

MHA. (2019). *Crime in India, 2018. Statistics* (Vol. 1, pp. 195–294). New Delhi: National Crime Records Bureau, Ministry of Home Affairs, Government of India.

MHRD. (2018). *Educational statistics at a glance*. New Delhi: Department of School Education and Literacy, Statistics Division, Ministry of Human Resource Development, Government of India.

MHRD. (2019). *All India survey on higher education: 2018–19*. New Delhi: Department of Higher Education, Ministry of Human Resource Development, Government of India.

Mondal, P. (2019). Women's movements in India: Pre-independence women's movements. Retrieved from http://www.yourarticlelibrary.com/essay/womens-movements-in-india-pre-independence-womens-movements/32975. Accessed on December 14, 2019.

MOSPI. (2019). *Women and men in India, 2018 (a statistical compilation of gender related indicators in India)* (No. 20). New Delhi: Social Statistics Division, Central Statistics Office, Ministry of Statistics and Programme Implementation, Government of India.

Pande, R. (2018, November 14). The history of feminism and doing gender in India. *Revista Estudos Feministas*, *26*(3), e58567. doi:10.1590/1806-9584-2018v26n358567. Retrieved from https://www.scielo.br/scielo.php?script=sciarttext&pid=S0104-026X2018000300905&lng=en &tlng=en. Accessed on January 12, 2020.

Pandey, B. (1987, March). Post-independence educational development among women in India. Paper presented in the Seminar on 'Women in Changing Society' at the Centre for Women's Development Studies, University of Hyderabad. Retrieved from https://www.cwds.ac.in/wp-content/uploads/2016/09/Post-Independence-Educational.pdf. Accessed on January 11, 2020.

Psacharopoulos, G. (1994). Returns to investment in education: A global update. *World Development*, *22*(9), 1325–1343.

Ramanuj, M. (2015). Sexual harassment in India's educational institutions and how to stop it. Retrieved from https://blog.ipleaders.in/sexual-harassment-in-indias-educational-institutions-and-how-to-stop-it/. Accessed on January 2, 2020.

Rao, P. D. (2011). *Women entrepreneurs and socio-economic development*. New Delhi: Serials Publication. ISBN:978-81-8387-424-3.

Roy, A. (2019). 2018: The year when #MeToo shook India. *The Economic Times*, June 1. Retrieved from https://economictimes.indiatimes.com/magazines/panache/2018-the-year-when-metoo-shook-india/2018-the-year-of-metoo-in-india/slideshow/66346583.cms. Accessed on January 14, 2020.

Sahu, A. P. (2013). Social entrepreneurship: A blending of economic and social value. In S. K. Chaudhary (Ed.), *Women empowerment through entrepreneurs in India* (pp. 83–114). New Delhi: Avon Publications. ISBN:978-93-8183-900-3.

Shukla, T. N., & Chatterjee, C. (2013). Microfinance and women empowerment. In S. K. Chaudhary (Ed.), *Women empowerment through entrepreneurs in India* (pp. 45–66). New Delhi: Avon Publications. ISBN:978-93-8183-900-3.

Srivastava, P. (2019). Status of women in India: Ancient, medieval and modern, sociology. Sociology Discussions. Retrieved from http://www.sociologydiscussion.com/status-of-women/status-of-women-in-india-ancient-medieval-and-modern-sociology/13526. Accessed on December 13, 2019.

Tilak, J. B. G. (2011). *Trade in higher education: The role of the General Agreement on Trade in Services (GATS)*. Fundamentals of Educational Planning – 95. Paris: UNESCO, International Institute for Educational Planning.

UIS. (2012). *International Standard Classification of Education ISCED 2011* (p. 22). Canada: UNESCO Institute for Statistics. ISBN:978-92-9189-123-8.

Yadav, R. P., Chandradeep, K., & Barsa. (2012). *Women workers in India*. New Delhi: New Century Publications. ISBN:978-81-7708-295-1. Retrieved from https://files.eric.ed.gov/fulltext/EJ1099426.pdf. Accessed on December 11, 2019.

Chapter 11

Feminization of Higher Education in Iran: Paradoxes and Complexities

Saeed Paivandi and Yasmin Nadir

1. Introduction

Four decades after the Cultural Revolution in Iran in June 1980, which marked the beginning of Islamization of education, women constitute a significant portion of university student population, reversing gender balance in their favor, contrary to general expectations. For many, this was an unusual outcome since, it was assumed, Islamization would equate a decline in – if not a total barrier to – women's socioeconomic participation particularly in education and the labor market. In today's Iran, however, women's education beyond secondary levels is not an exception but a norm similar to many countries in the region and elsewhere.

Much academic attention has thus far attempted to unpack the complexities and paradoxes inherent to the feminization of higher education, which this chapter builds on and nuances. Beginning with a brief statistical review of women's enrollment at universities since the 1970s examined in relation to their rather curtailed participation in the job market, we try to summarize the change and provide a picture of the link between feminized higher education on the one hand and a male-dominated labor market on the other. The statistical review severs as a starting point to then critically map the existing literature on women in higher education and offer nuanced conceptions that would enrich the existing frameworks.

To do that, we narrow our focus to two clusters of scholarship that thematically diminate current debates: women's motivations, aspirations, and decision-making to pursue postsecondary education and Islamization of (higher) education as part of the wider structures that impact their progress in the society. We argue that, in unpacking the complexities and paradoxes inherit to these processes, the existing literature in most part is restricted in its methodological and theoretical approaches, particularly as some authors tend to underappreciate the forces, changes, and politics beyond the State and society that influence the formation of women's subjectivities as well as the Islamization of education. We emphasize that analysis should be situated in the larger contexts of the globalizing world that (in)form Iranian women's aspirations to pursue postsecondary studies on the one hand and

International Perspectives on Gender and Higher Education, 193–212

doi:10.1108/978-1-83909-886-420201011

influence education and its Islamization on the other, both shaping each other dialectically. We argue that Iranian women's ideals and motivations are not separated, but linked to and influenced by the "spirit of time" (Hegel, 2012) that is the global gender awareness raised through various media and mediums. The Islamization project, since the Cultural Revolution in 1980, that in most part defines the structure and content of the education system, needs to be understood as incorporating this spirit in contradictory ways.

Far from monolithic understandings, we offer an insight into the *contradictions* in the formation of women's motivations as well as the Islamization of education, as they are also implicated in the globalizing world and are formed in relation to it – in terms of expected and unexpected impacts and meanings – not isolated from it. This chapter invites nuanced methodological approaches and theoretical understandings beyond disciplinary binaries and singular analytical scopes to look at the complexities and the casual power of feminization of higher education in Iran as situated in the globalized world.

2. Women in Iranian Higher Education: A Very Brief History

The early modern educational institutions at secondary and postsecondary levels – inaugurated in 1851 – were exclusively designed for boys, so were the pioneering specialized schools such as School of Political Sciences – linked to Foreign Ministry – and the School of Medicine (Kardan, 1957; Naraghi, 1992) that were established at the time. The advent of the Constitutional Revolution (1906) followed by the establishment of the Pahlavi's (1925–1979), however, opened a new chapter in the history of education for women. For the first time, the Higher Council of Education in 1922 proposed education for girls and boys alike in primary and secondary schools. Since then, inclusion of women at all levels of education has gradually, but surely, expanded (Naraghi, 1992; Paivandi, 2006).

In 1934, University of Tehran – Iran's first modern university – was inaugurated – with 1,034 students – followed by the inauguration of College for Teacher Training (1935) which formally allowed girl students to enter higher education. Women teachers were trained for girls' high schools which slowly grew in number (Kardan, 1957; Menashri, 1992). Predominantly from upper classes – particularly belonging to Iranian aristocrats and less-conservative families – a few women also traveled to Europe or the Middle East to pursue their education. Between 1930 and 1940, Hashemian (2010) notes, at least 46 women went to France, Belgium, Germany, Switzerland, or Lebanon to study. The first group of women were also admitted to University of Tehran in 1940 (Menashri, 1992, p. 105), and 6 year after the first female doctor graduated from the same university. The later decades witnessed noticeable and steady increase in the number of women enrolled at universities ranging between 25% and 30% throughout the 1950s, 1960s, and early 1972s.

Inspired by a vision for an industrialized modern country, Mohammad Reza Shah's educational development plans expanded in scope and structure, thanks to the oil boom of mid-1970s. The annual Ramsar Educational Conference organized under the direct presidency of the Shah was an important step to determine and evaluate higher education policy for such a vision. As such higher education and inclusion of girls in it remained a high priority (Menashri, 1992; Naraghi, 1992), strengthened by the 1974 law which offered free academic studies for boys and girls (Menashri, 1992, p. 250). With an average annual growth rate of 6%, the 1970s saw an increase in the number of students enrolled in higher education in the country which exceeded the capacity of Iranian universities. Even the administration of *Konkour* turned into a real obstacle. If in 1961 almost 36% of pupils – having finished their secondary studies – could enter higher education, in 1979 only 12% could (Naraghi, 1992).[1] As such many had to go elsewhere – mainly Europe and the United States – to start or continue their higher education. According to UNESCO (1982) at the end of the 1970s, Iran ranked the first country in the world to send student's abroad, increasing from 13,600 in 1970 to 74,640 in 1979 – i.e., an average annual increase of 19% – of which 68% studied in the United States. Female enrollment at universities, prior to the popular uprisings of 1978–1979 against the Shah, reached a historical peak of 31% (SCI, 1982).

Relatively absent from antimonarchy discourse in 1979 was the restructuring of education in line with Islam. The victory of the Revolution led by Ayatollah Khomeini, however, brought an *Islamic educational revolution* – as stated by the Ayatollah – to the front lines struggles for nation building and state formation.[2] The monarchic education system in general, and Social Science in particular, were declared as anti-Islamic, unreliable, and *Westoxicated*; a concept developed as a postcolonial critique of Western influence in Iran.[3] Hence, their Islamization was paramount both as a religious duty and a political necessity (Hamdhaidari,

[1]A university entrance exam where candidates are ranked according to their grades. In Iran, the exam became centralized at the national level from 1969.

[2]Cited in Report of the Headquarters of the Cultural Revolution 22nd of Khordad 1359 to 22nd of Bahman 1362 (Gozaresh-e setad-e enqelab-e farhangi az 22 khordad 1359 ta 22 bahman 1362) Islamic Republic of Iran, Headquarters of the Cultural Revolution.

[3]Some intellectuals had begun to develop a critical discourse on the influence of Western on educational system in terms of its structure and content. This intellectual movement was mainly initiated by Muslim academics and personalities like Ali Shariati (1933–1977) et Jalal Al-e-Ahmad (1923–1969). The new Islamist discourse sought to reintroduce Islamic values to modern education and fight against the influence of Western culture. Jalal Al-e-Ahmad, essayist and Iranian intellectual, began in the 1960s to criticize the education system. The work of Al-e-Ahmad, published in 1962, entitled "occidentality" (Gharbzadegui), reflects the mentality of emerging Islamist movements from this period who considered the West as the cause of all the misfortunes of their country and those of the Third World. A chapter of his book is devoted to education and universities considered by the author as Westernized institution. For him, the university was influenced by the West as a goal "the training of men of occidentality." Al-e-Ahmad thought that the curriculum had "no presence of tradition, no trace of the past culture, any course in ethics or philosophy, no link between yesterday and tomorrow, between home and school, East and West" (Nikpey, 2001; Paivandi, 2012a).

Agahi, & Papzan, 2008; Paivandi, 2006, 2012a). The well-established educational infrastructure that the revolutionaries inherited from the Pahlavis made the change possible. Like many other institutions, education was a highly centralized system that was financed, administrated, and monitored by the central government. It, hence, made it rather easy for the clerical power to devise, dictate, and implement their plans from above. Primarily set up as a means to fight and eliminate competing political actors within the system and clamp down on the political turmoil at universities, a 3-year radical Islamization-homogenization project known as the Cultural Revolution began in 1980 through which higher education was closed and purged from political competition (Hamdhaidari et al., 2008; Mojab, 1991).

In addition to substantial changes that were made to academic curriculum and the restructuring of staff, new institutes of higher education were established following the reopening of universities in 1983 to respond to the sociodemographic demand for postsecondary education.[4,5] *Daneshgah-e-Azad-e-Eslami* (Free Islamic University) – a pseudo-private institute – was inaugurated in Tehran in the same year with 3,000 students but soon expanded to dozen other cities. In the years that followed, the expansion in the provision of higher education accelerated, and new institutes such Payam-e-Nour distant learning were set up. As such, the post Revolution Iran, as noted, witnessed a rapid growth in the number and diversity of institutes of higher education, against the expectations.

3. Feminization of Higher Education: Overall Trends and Changes

As observed, women's increased enrollment in higher education under the Islamic Republic was a process that rooted in Pahlavi's educational development plans (Malekzadeh, 2011; Menashri, 1992; Salibi, 2010), but materialized in decades after the Revolution of 1979 particularly since 1990s. In 2018, a total of nearly 3.6 million students, including 1.7 million girls, studied at different universities which are generally categorized into four main types: public universities which include almost 18% of the total number of students with a female student rate of 52%; Islamic Azad University which accommodates 40% of students in the country and a rate of 41% female population; Payam-e-Nour (the distance learning university) network with nearly 18% of total student population and female student rate of 64%. Other private institutes or short-term professional training enablements accommodate the remaining 28% and female student rate of 40%. There are moreover eight women-exclusive universities, e.g., *University of Al-Zahra*, *University of Hazrate Masume* – specializing in law, business administration,

[4]According to an estimation (Paivandi, 2006), more than a third of teachers and 16% of students have left university or have been expelled by the commissions set up during the Cultural Revolution (1980–1982).

[5]Drawing on data from the Statistical Center of Iran, Malekzadeh (2011, p. 187) demonstrates how the increase in rural female literacy rates in 1970s, carried over to 1980s and 1990s, creates a "momentum" for women in higher education.

accounting and English translation – which play a very marginal role in the higher education system in Iran, but nonetheless contribute to the increase in the number of female students.

Overall, it is estimated that from 1979 to 2018, the number of students increased, approximately 8% per year on average depending on the decade and the gender: Over the past 40 years, the number of students multiplied 21 times in total with a considerable increase in female student population which is 31 times bigger than that of the prerevolution year. As can be seen in Table 11.1, the growth rates are significantly higher for girls for two consecutive decades between 1990 and 2009. The rapid growth allowed girls to close the historical gender gap with men in 2000s; 51% in 2002 and 52% in 2006. Current figures, however, as the table shows, indicate a slight decline to 48% in 2018, which might relate to gender quotas in certain fields of study.[6] Table 11.2 provides a comparative record of the student population growth prior and after the Revolution calculated per 100,000 inhabitants.

In 2016, there were 4,850 students per 100,000 inhabitants, compared to only 530 in 1976. The growth is significantly greater for women: 4,751 students per 100,000 inhabitants in 2016 compared to only 287 in 1976 (i.e., 17 times greater). Against early assumptions, the expansion of higher education has largely benefited women, who were, for the most part, marginalized in previous eras to the extent regard it as "democratization" of education in Iran (Rahbari, 2016; Shams, 2016). It was in 1999 that for the first time the number of women admitted to Universities in *Konkour* exceeded the number of men. The gendered rebalancing of higher education enrollment, has also been coupled by the relative increase in the number of women researchers, in predominantly male-dominated fields since the inception of modern education in the country. However, significant disparities persist where women's access to certain field and faculties remain restricted particularly (but not only) in engineering.

Overall, the change in women's participation in different fields and levels of study, over the past four decades, can be mapped as follows: Medical Sciences, Humanities, and Social Sciences are predominantly feminized. 60% of the student population in these fields are now women compared to 40% in 1970s and 1980s. In Experimental Sciences and Arts, on average, women constituted two out of three students after the year 2000, compared to nearly one in three in the 1970s and 1980s. Disciplines such as Agronomy, Veterinary Medicine, and Engineering Sciences which accommodated less than 5% of female students' population in 1970s and 1980s witnessed a considerable change. In Agronomy and Veterinary Medicine, on average, women constituted 52% of students in the 2000s. In

[6]In order to contain the growth of girls in certain technical and scientific fields, the government tried to set up a quota system from the mid-2000s. Debates over gendered quotas in Iran are divers and competing, particularly as they related to the balance between higher education and the needs of the labor market and the way it contributes to the reproduction of the male-dominated structures (see Alizadeh & Danesh, 2017). Our understanding of the existing literature points to the need for more in-depth analysis of the complexities of changing quota systems, especially as factual data are not easy to access at times.

Table 11.1. Girls' Enrollment in Higher Education.

Year	Average % Women	Average Annual Growth Rate	
		Women	Men
1970–1979	29%	10%	9%
1980–1989	31%	4%	5%
1990–1999	36%	22%	13%
2000–2009	50%	11%	9%
2010–2018	48%	−2%	0%

Source: SCI (1977, 1982, 1992, 2002, 2011, 2018).

Table 11.2. Number of Students in 100,000 Populations.

Year	Women	Men
1966	64	171
1976	287	622
1986	207	475
1996	1,557	2,402
2006	4,280	3,752
2016	4,751	5,175

Source: SCI (1977, 1982, 1992, 2002, 2011, 2018).

engineering Sciences, during the same period, on average, only one student in four was a woman. Gender balance, at different stages of study, remains in favor of women at undergraduate levels at 51% followed by PhD at 48% and master's levels at 46%, demonstrating a close competition between man and women to access education beyond bachelor's degree (SCI, 2019).

4. Higher Education and the Job Market: An Overview

As noted thus far, Iran is gradually becoming an atypical and complicated case with regard to the connection between the higher education and the job market (Ghanei-rad, 2004; Majbouri, 2013; Noroozi & Alemi, 2003; Rezai-Rashti, 2011; Rezai-Rashti & Moghadam, 2011). While recent studies indicate an "inverse relation" between higher education and employment, whereby "people with higher education, receive 9% lower salaries compared with those without higher education" (*Financial Tribune*, 2017), there has been a persistent and worsening imbalance between the labor market and the number of university graduates,

Table 11.3. Educational Level of the Active Literate Population in Iran.

Level of Study	1996		2016	
	Women	Men	Women	Men
Elementary	36%	46%	22%	24%
Secondary	27%	28%	11%	26%
End of secondary	22%	15%	19%	26%
Higher education	15%	11%	48%	24%
Total	100%	100%	100%	100%

Source: SCI (1977, 2016).

mainly women, who remain unemployed. Table 11.3 provides a comparative overview.[7]

As shown, the increase in the number of female graduates has generated a growing feminized pressure on the labor market where one in two women has a higher education qualification.

Iranian women's labor force participation has, historically, been low; 13% in 1976, 9% in 1996, and 15% in 2016 (SCI, 2018). The data clearly demonstrate acceleration after an initial decline in the first 2 decades post the revolution of 1979: 1.45 million in 1976, 1.3 million in 1986, 2 million in 1996, and 5 million in 2016. Among active women, 20% work in public services (education, health, administration), 31% as specialists, 10% in services, and 15% in traditional sectors (agriculture, crafts) compared to only 24% for men. The considerable growth in the category of "specialists" – reserved in Iranian statistics for skilled jobs – clearly shows that women graduates of higher education tend to occupy an increasingly important place in the labor market and there is an increasing competition between men and women in this sector.

According to the latest details on labor force data (SCI, 2019), a total of 5.3 million women, i.e., 16% of the female population over the age of 10, were active in the labor market in 2018, of whom 1.01 million were unemployed with the overall female unemployment rate of 19% compared to 10% for men in the same year. The relative weight of women in the job market is close to 20%, i.e., one in five workers in Iran is a woman. The unemployment rate is particularly high for women under the age of 30; 37% for the population below 25 – compared to 24% for men – and 34% for those between 25 and 29 – compared with 22% for men – in 2018. According to SCI data, nearly 30% of women – 12% of men – graduates (excluding the medical sector) were unemployed in 2018 compared to 13% of women – 8% for men – who did not complete their secondary education.

[7]For the purposes of this chapter, we rely on the official statistics by the Statistical Center of Iran (SCI), noting that there are inconsistencies and inadequacies of data provided by different sources on women's participation in the labor market, as also observed by other researchers. See Moghadam (2009); **Fallah** Haghighi et al., (2018); **Foroutan** (2013); Lashkari (2007).

Analyzing data for the second-quarter of the fiscal 2015–2016, Behnia et al. (2015 cited in Donyay-e-Eqtesad 2018) further illuminate that 40% of Iran's unemployed "fall into the long-term unemployment category [...among which] women's share is 52 percent" (Donyay-e-Eqtesad 2018). Their research also documents that among the unemployed female population, 70% have higher education credentials and that educated women in urban areas have less at 50% chance in finding a job (Behnia et al., 2015).

5. Women's Motivations and Demand for Higher Education: A Review and Critique of the Existing Literature

The establishment of the Islamic Republic based on a particular understanding and application of the Shi'a jurisprudence post the Revolution of 1979 raised serious concerns over the trajectories of democracy and inclusion in the country, especially the status of women, among other social groups and minorities. In the context of the deteriorating sociopolitical climate – both internally and externally – as well as the worsening economic condition in the first decade of the revolution coinciding with the war with Iraq (1980–1988) – women's persisting and increased admission/completion of their further and Higher Education (HE) post 1988 were highly unexpected for many. Apart from an initial drop off in the immediate aftermath of revolution, women's HE admission has steadily grown ever since, ultimately reversing the gender gap in their favor by early 2000s. While for those less familiar with the story, the continued upward trend may be a surprise, in today's Iran, women's education beyond secondary level is the norm similar to many countries in the region and elsewhere (Karnameh Haghighi & Akbari, 2005; Rahbari, 2016; Rezai-Rashti & Moghadam, 2011; Salibi, 2010; Shams, 2016; Shavarini, 2005; Tayebinia & Rahmani, 2016; Zahiri Nia & Behroozian, 2012).

Taken as an expression of agency, much scholarly interest thus far has been placed on the dynamics of women's motivation, unpacking their aspirations and desires for further education and the way their choices are (in)formed in relation to the ideological orderings of the State in education and beyond (Mehran, 2009; Shavarini, 2005, 2006). In Shavarini's analysis (2005), for instance,

> ...the desire for higher education [on the one hand] illuminates the challenges facing women in Muslim nations and *the ways in which Muslim women are using this institution to change their social status* [...creating] a sphere of hope, a refuge, and a place to experience limited freedom beyond restrictive family environments; an asset that can increase a woman's value [...] a vehicle that can earn respect and a right that may make possible financial. (p. 329, emphasis added)

In this type of analysis, women's access to educational opportunities at the university level is primarily important as a claim to human rights. Their persistent and increased enrollment/completion is then interpreted as a manifestation of their resistance against the ideological State, successfully pushing the boundaries of their social inclusion (Hoodfar & Sadr, 2009). Entangled in identity politics, higher education for women is then understood as the space for claim-making within and beyond education. In Tayebinia and Rahmani's words (2016), it points to a renewed drive for the realization of self, means for empowerment, and a fight for recognition and development. Higher Education makes women "captivity-aware," Shavarini (2009) argues. It is thus essential for demands of transformation. As such postsecondary education for women completes the wider debate on social change in Iran (and the Middle East) illuminating the struggle between women – as a proxy for a dynamic society – pursuing modern values and norms against the Islamizing policies of the Islamic Republic (Bayat, 2009).

A theoretical tension within the existing literature relates to the quality of higher education on the one hand (Ghanei-rad, 2004) and the extent to which HE in its own right, – disconnected from a meaningful link to further development opportunities particularly advancements in a labor market marked by limited employment trajectories – on the other can serve as a vehicle for gender justice.[8] As echoed in much of anthropological or sociological research thus far, increased enrollment at universities is a gendered response to restricted choices already available to women in the Iranian society; "women have nothing to do but to study" (Shavarini, 2006). Seeking a level of freedom from the conservative family environments, going to universities for many women increases the chances of meeting a potential partner and "experiencing the intangibles" (Shavarini, 2005, p. 430) also giving them some social prestige in a society where education is considered highly important. While offering an important emancipatory potential – including relative freedom in mobility as many students travel to other cities for their education – a university degree also "increase[es women's] worth for marriage" (Shavarini, 2005), an effective tool to negotiate *mehrieh*, a bride price; "the higher the bride's educational attainment," Rezai-Rashti and Moghadam's study notes "the higher the *mehrieh*" (2011, p. 436).[9]

Revealing the internal paradoxes inherent to their motivations and decision-making, methodologically moreover, Iranian women's aspirations to pursue higher education are predominantly analyzed in relation to the gender regime of the Islamic Republic. There seems to be very little attention paid to the complexities in the construction of motivations and choice-making processes as influenced by the regional and global changes in the discourse on woman's rights, itself shaped by wider transformations in political economy and emerging feminist movements. This is a significant knowledge gap we argue, as it limits the analyses

---

[8]Debates over the quality of higher education in Iran particularly (but not only) as influenced by Islamization of curriculum and its limited meaningful connection to labor market and country's development are diverse. A thorough and critical analysis is a research in its own right and is beyond the limits and scope of this chapter.

[9]According to the tradition of *Mehrieh* derived from an ancient Islamic practice of dowry, a future husband undertakes during his marriage to pay a sum of money or gold coins (or other objects and goods) to his wife in case divorce. In the *Mehrieh* tradition, the families of the wife and the husband who agree on the amount of the Mehrieh, before the wedding.

to the internal socioeconomic and political dynamics as though they are disconnected from the changes in the globalized world. Given the rise and expansion of social media platforms – including advancements in technologies and means of communications – moreover, we need to learn more about the complex ways in and through which (the formation of) women's desires for education and employment are influenced by factors beyond the boundaries of the Islamic Republic. Comparing women's labor force participation – in the context of larger "neo-liberal policy turn" – in Tunisia, Jordan, and Iran, Moghadam (2005) correctly refers to the spread of "global feminism" in the Middle East and beyond, arguing for their combined impact on the formation of social demands to improve women's socioeconomic status, an important part of which is their equal access to educational opportunities.

With limited analytical connection with the complex global processes, Aghajanian, Tashakkori, Thompson, Mehryar, and Kazemipour (2007), for instance, adopt a more historical approach tracing the "tenacity" of women's modern values of education and labor market participation to the late Pahlavi King's westernizing-modernizing projects particularly since 1960s. The emphasis and attention to women's education, they argue, were fostered by Mohammad Reza Shah (1941–1979) and later strengthened through the post Iran–Iraq war reconstruction policies (1989–1997) and the reform movement of early 2000s (1997–2004). They thus suggest "continuity" in women's educational attainment despite the imposition of gendered limitations in various ways over the past four decades. While necessary, the "historical" explanation still remains selective and disconnected from the global changes at the time and years that followed. It thus does not capture the dynamics of social transformations that partly manifested in and through the growth in the demand for higher education on the one hand (Ghanei-rad, 2004) and the expansion in its provision on the other, both having implications for women's (motivation and decision) to attain educational qualifications and participate in the labor market. To this complexity, sociodemographic studies (Esfahani & Shajari, 2012), for instance, add the decline in the fertility rates particularly between 1986 and 2006 and the increase in the average age of marriage for women, themselves influenced by the increase in women's educational attainment, as factors that played a significant role in shaping their motivation and decision to study postsecondary levels.[10,11] The complex combinations of contributing factors, thus, form women's decisions and aspirations as well as the choices and chances that are made available to them.

6. Problematizing Islamization: Nuanced Conceptions and Critiques

Islamization may be one key policy that has been highly contested even among the revolutionaries as early as the establishment of the Islamic Republic. The

[10]Rate of demographic growth; 3.9% in 1986, 1.6 in 2006, and 1.2 in 2016 (SCI, 2016).
[11]19.8 years in 1986, 22.5 in 2006, and 23 in 2016 (SCI, 2016).

competing republicans and authoritarians groups within the emerging State understood Islamization in greatly different veins, either as

> ...an essential complement to the process of democratization [...] a cultural and intellectual rejuvenation via the medium of an Islamic 'liberation' or an elemental competent in the 'ritualization and institutionalization' of the State ideology. (Ansari, 2003, p. 224)

For the authoritarians, Ansari notes, "this ideological project could not be a matter of choice. The people had voted for an Islamic Republic in which 'Islam' was obviously the senior partner" (Ansari, 2003, p. 224). With the gradual and violent triumph of the authoritarian strand Islamization constituted a vital aspect of the State identity and project of nation-state building (partly) implemented in and through the country's higher education and the schooling system, legitimizing the Islamic character of the political system.

Cultural Revolution (1980–1983) – which sought to purge political competition, dissidents, and nonconformists from educational and cultural institutes and later on from the society at large – marks the official start of the process of Islamization in higher education. While the dynamics of Cultural Revolution – which progressively expanded to include all of the cultural policies of the country ever since (Moradi, 2001; Mojab, 1991) – have been extensively debated, Islamization itself, both as a State policy and political–ideological discourse, remain a controversy in academic circles and beyond.

Methodologically on the one hand, Islamization is understood *in contrast* with the Pahlavi's (rather) secular educational policies and programs which were oriented toward industrialization and modernization focused on the creation of a skilled work force. As part of the Shah's growth and development plans, emphasis was placed on liberation of women particularly since 1960s through reform in family laws, voting rights, increased access to education, and employment opportunities (Naraghi, 1992). In opposition to the development pathway by the Pahlavi's then, Islamized education under the rule of Ayatollah Khomeini, in much of the existing analysis, *marks a discontinuation in a historical process*. In her award-winning book, *Jewells of Allah*, Nina Ansari (2015) best summarizes such conception of Islamization as follows:

> Khomeini aimed to dismantle the Shah's educational system and infuse Islamic ideology into every aspect of Iran's academic environment. Given the Islamic Republic's *preeminent objective logic dictates* that the strategy would be to *revert back to the traditional Maktab*[12] schooling system. (p. 100, emphasis added)

[12]For some explanation on *Maktab* see Paivandi (2012).

Against the Pahlavi's modern and modernizing education, Islamization in such understanding of Islamization thus appears to equate *a throwback to premodern era*, even though the governments post the revolution never demonstrated such tendencies and wish to reestablish *Maktabs*. The throwback, in this type of conception, would primarily be expected in women's status, especially manifested in their restricted access to public spaces and opportunities particularly education and employment.[13] Anything other – women's increased enrollment at universities in our case – would then be regarded as an "unusual course of action" (Ansari, 2015) an anomaly or "paradox" (Mehran, 1990; Mir-Hosseini, 1999; Shams, 2016).

In explaining the *unexpected*, Shavarini (2005) emphasizes the "Islamic packaging" of education which contributed to the growth in the provision of education under the Islamic Republic, even "democratizing women's secondary education" (Karnameh Haghighi & Akbari, 2005) by lifting the religious–cultural barriers for the conservative strata's through gender segregation, mandatory hijab, and the imposition of an Islamized curriculum (Ansari, 2015; Hamdhaidari et al., 2008). As such Mir-Hosseini (1999) talks about Hijab as passport emphasizing the way Islamization facilitated women's access to education especially among religious-conservative groups. Much anthropological research provides such analysis to explain the growth in female education post 1979 despite pressures.

Examined, not in contrast, but *as a continuation* of a historical process, whereby the revolutionary State utilized the well-functioning education system constructed by the Pahlavi's and expanded it (Amuzegar, 1993; Malekzadeh, 2011; Menashri, 1992), Islamization is also understood in terms of its *ideological content*. It is defined as the "strict enforcement of religious laws in all sphere of life" (Mehran, 2003, p. 272) and the imposition of the State's particular Islamic ideology – including a corresponding gender regime – in education and beyond for nation-state building purposes. This literature primarily examines Islamization in its *immediately observable traits* especially (but not only) in gender segregation, mandatory hijab, and the increase in number and budget of religious institutes – including higher education as well as the imposition of religious discourse in academic and school curriculum particularly in Social Sciences (Behdad, 1993; Paivandi, 2015).

Expanding this analysis, many also conceptualize Islamization in terms of *the dynamics of the State ideology*, manifested, for instance, in the complex quota systems put in place and their limited and unequal sociopolitical and economic involvement and space for progress (Afshar, 1997; Bahramitash, 2003; Parvazian, Gill, & Chiera, 2017; Rahbari, 2016). Islamization in this conception is critiqued as a fundamental hindrance to democracy and gender justice as it reduces women's status to second-class citizens and defines their role many as care-givers in the traditional family structures and gendered socioeconomic spaces (Moghadam, 2005).

---

[13]As argued by Paivandi, the model put forward by the Islamic Republic was the type of "Islamic" schools similar to Alavi and Kamal before the revolution; a modern curriculum but Islamized through an Islamic reading of the world. It was Shariati who spoke of Maktabs understanding it as a "demodernized" model rather than a traditional one (Paivandi, 2006).

Following the era of Reconstruction and Reform (1989–2004) after the end of war with Iraq analysis of Islamization of (higher) education began to notice modifications, corresponding to the wider policies of the governments as well as the internal politics of the State (Alkhansa, 2018; Malekzadeh, 2011; Moghadam, 2015; Rezai-Rashti & Moghadam, 2011). In this process, growing scholarly attention has been paid to the shift from pro-poor free educational policies of 1980s into a neo-liberal (pseudo) privatized fee-based education to date (Moghadam, 2005, 2015).[14,15] Since then, provision of education (at all levels) – as a means to create a skilled and educated labor force – has been foreseen in all National Development Plans in line with the ideological policies of the Islamic Republic with specific implications for women. While the dynamics of the neo-liberalist education combined with Islamization has, to our knowledge to date, not been extensively examined, there is emerging literature that offer nuanced analysis of the concept. Critiquing the predominant assumption in much of the existing debates thus far – that portrayed Islamization as a coherent, static, and homogenized project – the emerging literature points to internal tensions and contradictions within Islamization as a State ideology and the changing practices that accompanied it over the past 40 years (Hamdhaidari et al., 2008).

Building on the theoretical understanding of nation and state formation as an ongoing hegemonic process (Gramsci, 1971) and the complexities as well as contradictions inherent to the functions of institutions which are themselves implicated in competing ideological forces within the system, nuanced understandings of Islamization has been introduced to the literature (Alkhansa, 2018; Malekzadeh, 2011). In this conception as succulently put by Malekzadeh, Islamization in Iran since 1980 is "an uneven process frequently compromised by material limitations and the hesitation of State leaders to act" (2011, p. 106). Taking a historical approach to the study of the schooling system under the Islamic Republic and the ideological as well as material/economic struggles within the system, Islamization in Malakzadeh's conception is analyzed as a "*contradictory product* produced by a new regime as it took an uneven path towards achieving its ideological goals, stumbling often along the way" (Malekzadeh, 2011, p. 106). Far from a one-on-one relation between, a homogenized autocratic State on the one hand and a coherent ideological Project - production on the other, this understanding offers a complex image of Islamization which appears to be substantially lacking thus far, particularly in the study of Iran's higher education and women's place within it.

Conceptualizing Islamization as such, we argue, offers useful insights not only in terms of the internal politics within the Islamic Republic but also opens the theoretical as well as methodological possibilities to situate its analysis in the wider context of shed light on its dynamic modifications in Iran as a player in

[14]Some authors have considered this type of institution to be semiprivate because of their membership in state-controlled sectors. We chose the term pseudo-private because the forces inside the State which created, and monitor, remain controlled by the State actors, even though the main part of their costs are covered through fee-paying students.

[15]Currently, 75% of higher education remain fees-based (CSI, 2019).

the globalized world across time. As has been noted extensively thus far, anti-imperialist discourses particularly that against the United States and the West more generally constitute an important component of Islamization in Iran and beyond. The ideological struggle against the influence of the West, the dangerous other, remains elemental in defining and consolidating Islamization since 1979 and the inception of the Cultural Revolution. Fne of Rohani's main achievements was signing UNESCO's '2030' document in 2016 for immediate integration into the country's educational system. It was, however, strongly resisted by Ayatollah Khamenei, who emphasised; This UNESCO 2030 document is not something that the Islamic Republic will surrender to. It's wrong to sign some document and then quietly go ahead and implement it. That's absolutely forbidden. Ayatollah Khameini's order to stop the implementation of the document was announced in the wake of the presidential campaign in 2017.[16]

As such, we argue that analysis of Islamization of education should remain highly mindful of the larger context particularly in relation to international contexts, e.g., the impact of US foreign policies or the West in general as well as growing Islamism in the region. This is an important gap in the existing literature, without which the analysis of Islamization and its concomitant impact on women's access to socioeconomic opportunities remain rather simplistic, highly underdeveloped and significantly disconnected from wider contexts.

7. Discussion by Way of Conclusion

Modern education which predated the Pahlavi's (1925–1979) gradually developed into a consolidated and well-functioning system to modernize and industrialize the country, creating a momentum for education that carried over and exponentially grew under the Islamic Republic. Against general assumptions, the Islamized systems of schooling and higher education post-1979 did not equate a throwback to the premodern era, especially – as many expected – symbolizing in women's restricted and declining access to educational opportunities. By early 2000s, higher education in Iran was – by and large – feminized as evidence shows.

[16]On UNESCO's 2030 document see (1) http://english.khamenei.ir/news/4796/Iran-won-t-submit-to-agendas-like-UNESCO-2030-Ayatollah-Khamenei and (2) https://www.radiofarda.com/a/f3-khamene-vs-unesco/28474271.html. Following the political turmoil with the US peaking with the killing of Iranian Qassem Soleimani in Iraq on January 3, 2020, a specific content is approved by Hassan Rohani – Iran's President – on January 22, 2020 to be added to school and academic textbooks titled "Crimes and Conspiracies of America." See the link in Farsi https://www.irna.ir/news/83643963/%D8%B1%D9%88%D8%AD%D8%A7%D9%86%DB%8C-%D9%82%D8%A7%D9%86%D9%88%D9%86-%D8%AA%D8%B9%DB%8C%DB%8C%D9%86-%D8%B3%D8%B1%D9%81%D8%B5%D9%84-%D8%AC%D9%86%D8%A7%DB%8C%D8%A7%D8%AA-%D9%88-%D8%AA%D9%88%D8%B7%D8%A6%D9%87-%D9%87%D8%A7%DB%8C-%D8%A2%D9%85%D8%B1%DB%8C%DA%A9%D8%A7-%D8%AF%D8%B1-%DA%A9%D8%AA%D8%A8-%D8%AF%D8%B1%D8%B3%DB%8C.

While widely celebrated, this rather unexpected outcome remains a controversy in academia and beyond. A growing body of literature points to the impact of the Islamic Republic's gender ideology – within its wider political economy – on the socioeconomic status of women; their limited access to certain fields of study, professional opportunities, and advancement within the system of higher education as well as unequal participation in the labor market among others. Focusing particularly on the literature that examines feminization of higher education in light of women's agency – especially their motivations and decision-making – and in relation to Islamization of education, this chapter offered a critical thematic mapping of the scholarship thus far. We argued that, in unpacking the complexities of these processes, the existing literature in most part is restricted in its methodological and theoretical approaches, particularly as it excludes Iran from forces and changes beyond the State. We emphasized that more analytical attention needs to be paid to the *global processes* that have (in)formed Iranian women's aspirations to pursue postsecondary studies on the one hand and influenced education and its Islamization on the other, both shaping each other dialectically.

The growing awareness and demand for women's rights and gender justice globally continue to inform and shape women's individual and collective motivations, decisions, and mobilization to pursue higher education. Maybe more than ever, the image of a modern woman in today's Iran is closely linked to (some form of) participation in postsecondary education and the labor market. They constitute two significant aspects of women's identities in the globalizing world even among conservative groups; empowerment and independence. Analyzed mainly *in opposition* to the ideology of the Islamic Republic – which as argued seeks to reinforce traditional gender roles – the dominant literature limits the debate to an *in-country struggle between women and the State*. Our theoretical and methodological critique of such analysis is that it does not examine Iranian women's ideals and aspirations as linked to and influenced by the "spirit of time" (Hegel, 2012) that is the global gender awareness raised through various media and mediums, in addition to emerging feminisms – including indigenous understandings and women's rights movements – in Iran, the region and beyond. Their force, we argue, continues to construct women's subjectivities – as individuals and collectives – shaping their motivations and dynamics of decision-making to pursue further education and demand recognition and gender justice through various means.

We see the same theoretical and methodological narrowness in much of the analysis of the education system and its Islamization. Well before its official inception in and through the Cultural Revolution in 1980s, Islamization – in intellectual and political discourses – was shaped in opposition to Western culture and values particularly that of the US and its corresponding gender ideology. Islamization has thus never been separated from the world, but closely linked to it. Women have since remained a proxy in this ideological battle. Islamization and its impact on women, therefore, have wider dimensions, complexities, and paradoxes, beyond a project restricted to the internal politics of a religious State and its gendered imposition of norms and values on the female population. Such conception appears to be lacking in the existing analysis. While opposing it, the

Islamized (higher) education, we argue, has paradoxically incorporated elements of the global gender awareness. Islamization, as a hegemonic project, does not take place in a vacuum, it is continually formed in relation to larger processes and social dynamics inside and outside the Iranian society.

Recent subtle changes in school curriculum, where prominent women – such as late Professor Maryam MirzaKhani, the Iranian women mathematician – are depicted as inspirational role models, are just one such example.[17] Through such depiction, the Islamized curriculum ironically promotes the image of a successful modern woman – a national heroin and an international icon – motivating young girls to pursue a similar path in higher education and compete in a masculine field. This is while reaching such a high level of success would be highly unlikely for women in Iran given gendered biases and limitations among other important factors. We argue that understanding Islamization, as influenced in relation to the global processes *both accommodating and rejecting it*, sheds lights on its complexities in and beyond the politics of the nation-state and helps conceptualize it as a changing, uneven, and contradictory hegemonic project.

From a sociological viewpoint, feminization of higher education in Iran, as extensively argued, have simultaneously taken place with feminization of unemployment and larger gender injustice in the country. Together with the expansion of (higher) education and women's increased access to it, there is a growing understanding of gendered restrictions on them partly rooting in biases and discriminations in Iran's legal frameworks and policies that restrict their progress and autonomy. Combined with the global awareness and push for gender justice – as noted earlier – and in the context of a weakened economy and shrinking spaces for development and expression of dissent at home – the increase in the number of educated women poses an important challenge to the status quo. One can interpret the growing dissatisfaction as expressed in the increase in brain drain among educated women who pursue their ideals abroad as also observed. The difficult and deteriorating social pressure on youth particularly women coupled with worsening economic problems and crisis in employment prospects is shown to have contributed to a real desire for immigration among girls.[18] The Islamic Republic is losing its human capital as well as its decades' long investments in education creating potentially an active opposition. Over the past 40 years, as observed, resentment has accumulated and is surfacing in and through various means and movements led by and for women in Iran and outside. Feminization of higher education maybe Islamic Republic's Achilles heel and a significant force in pushing back the existing gendered limits for a more inclusive and just society. The importance of this predicament deserves nuanced methodological approaches and theoretical understandings beyond disciplinary binaries and singular analytical scopes to look at the complexities and the casual power of feminization of higher education in Iran as situated in the globalized world.

---

[17]Mirzakhani was honored with the Fields Medal, the most prestigious award in mathematics in 2014, and became the first woman and the first Iranian to obtain this international prestigious prize.

[18]Fouroutan and Sheykh's (2017) study shows 54% for girls as compared to boys 38%.

References

Afshar, H. (1997). Women and work in Iran. *Political Studies*, *45*(4), 755–767.

Aghajanian, A., Tashakkori, A., Thompson, A., Mehryar, A. H., & Kazemipour, S. (2007). Attitudes of Iranian female adolescents toward education and nonfamilial roles: A study of a postrevolutionary cohort. *Marriage & Family Review*, *42*, 49–64.

Alizadeh, A., & Danesh, P. (2017). Sociological analysis of gender quotas in higher education of Iran. *Motaleat Zanan*. [*Women's Studies*.], *15*(1), 7–32 [Persian].

Alkhansa, Y. (2018). *Selective histories: Living and teaching in Iran under the Islamic republic*. Ph.D. thesis, University of Sussex, Brighton.

Amuzegar, J. (1993). *Iran's economy under the Islamic republic*. London; New York, NY: I.B. Tauris.

Ansari, A. M. (2003). *Modern Iran since 1921: The Pahlavis and after*. London: Pearson Education Limited.

Ansari, N. (2015). *Jewels of Allah: The untold story of women in Iran*. Los Angeles, CA: Revela Press.

Bahramitash, R. (2003). Islamic fundamentalism and women's economic role: The case of Iran. *International Journal of Politics, Culture, and Society*, *16*, 551–568.

Bayat, A. (2009). *Life as politics: How ordinary people change the Middle East*. Stanford, CA: Stanford University Press.

Behdad, S. (1993). Islamization of economics in Iranian universities. *International Journal of Middle East Studies*, *27*, 193–217.

Behnia, M., Alavian, A., & Fareq-Bal., A. (2015). Job Market Review in the Years 2013 and 2014 (Baresi-ye-Vaziat-e- Bazar-e-Kar dar Salhay-e- 1392 va 1393) [Persian], Institute Of Higher Education, Management and Planning Research, Office of President of The Islamic Republic, Jul. 2015.

Donyay-e-Eqtesad (2018, January 6). Why doesn't One Feel the Creation of Jobs in the Market? (Chera Eshteqal Zayi dar Eqtesad-e- Iran Ehsas Nemishavad?) [Persian]. Retrieved: https://www.magiran.com/article/3687417

Esfahani, H. S., & Shajari, P. (2012). Gender, education, family structure and the allocation of labour in Iran. *Middle East Development Journal*, *4*, 1–40.

Fallah Haghighi, N., Mahmoudi, M., & Bijani, M. (2018). Barriers to entrepreneurship development in Iran's higher education: A qualitative case study. *Interchange: A Quarterly Review of Education*, *49*, 353–375.

Financial Tribune. (2017). Inverse relation of higher education, employment prospects. *Financial Tribune*, August 7. Retrieved from https://financialtribune.com/articles/economy-domestic-economy/69863/inverse-relation-of-higher-education-employment-prospects. Accessed January 2020.

Foroutan, Y. (2013). Family–work dilemma of female migrants: Patterns and strategies. *Migration and Development*, *2*, 173–190.

Fouroutan, Y., & Sheykh, M. (2017). The trend of international immigration among Ferdowsi University students. Jameh Shenasi nahadhai ejtemai [The Sociology of Social Institutions], *4*(10), 61–79.

Ghanei-rad, A. (2004). Inharmonious development of higher education, unemployment and immigration. *Fasl Nameh Refahe Ejtemai*. [*Journal of Social Wellfar*.], *15*, 252–314 [Persian].

Gramsci, A. (1971). *Selections from prison notebooks*. New York, NY: International Publishers.

Hamdhaidari, S., Agahi, H., & Papzan, A. (2008). Higher education during the Islamic government of Iran (1979–2004). *International Journal of Educational Development*, *28*, 231–245.

Hashemian, A. (2010). The first women who did their university studies abroad. *Rahavard Journal*, *28*, 148–162 [Persian].

Hegel, G. W. F. (2012). In J.-P. Lefebvre (Trans.), La Phénoménologie de L'esprit [Phenomenology of Spirit]. Paris: Groupe Flammarion (1ère Edition 1807).

Hoodfar, H., & Sadr, S. (2009). Can women *act* as *agents* of a *democratization* of *theocracy* in Iran? Research Report. United Nations Research Institute for Social Development, Geneva.

Kardan, A. M. (1957). *L'organisation scolaire en Iran (histoire et perspective)*. Thèse présentée à l'Université de Genève, Geneva.

Karnameh Haghighi, H., & Akbari, N. (2005). The study of women's participation in increasing demand for higher education. *Pajouhesh Zanan*. [*Womens' Research.*], *3*(1), 69–100 [Persian].

Lashkari, M. (2007). Women, higher education and employment. *Peyk-e-Noor*, *5*, 123–134 [Persian].

Majbouri, M. (2013). Female labor force participation in Iran: A structural analysis. *Review of Middle East Economics and Finance*, *11*, 1–23.

Malekzadeh, S. (2011). *Schooled to obey, learning to protest: The ambiguous outbomes of postrevolutionary schooling in the Islamic Republic of Iran*. Washington, DC: Georgetown University.

Mehran, G. (1990). Ideology and education in the Islamic Republic of Iran. *Compare: A Journal of Comparative and International Education*, *20*(1), 53–65.

Mehran, G. (2003). The paradox of tradition and modernity in female education in the Islamic Republic of Iran. *Comparative Education Review*, *47*, 269–286.

Mehran, G. (2009). Doing and undoing gender: Female higher education in the Islamic Republic of Iran. *International Review of Education*, *55*, 541–559.

Menashri, D. (1992). *Education and the making of modern Iran*. New York, NY: Cornell University Press.

Mir-Hosseini, Z. (1999). *Islam and gender: The religious debate in contemporary Iran*. Princeton, NJ: Princeton University Press.

Mojab, S. (1991). The state and university: The "Islamic Cultural Revolution" in the institutions of higher education of Iran, 1980–1987. Ph.D. Thesis, University of Illinois, http://hdl.handle.net/2142/22697

Moghadam, V. M. (2005). Women's economic participation in the Middle East: What difference has the neoliberal policy turn made? *Journal of Middle East Women's Studies*, *1*, 110–146.

Moghadam, V. M. (2009). Undercounting women's work in Iran. *Iranian Studies*, *42*, 81–95.

Moghadam, V. M. (2015). The politics of women and work in Iran. *Iran Nameh*, *30*, 6–32 [Persian].

Moradi, S. (2001). Student movement and supreme cultural revolution. *Andisheh Jame-e*. [*Idea of Society*.], *14*, 26–31 [Persian].

Naraghi, E. (1992). *Enseignement et changements sociaux en Iran du VII° au XX° siècle* [Education and social changes in Iran from the 7th to the 20th century]. Paris: MSH.

Nikpey, A. (2001). *Politique et religion en Iran contemporain. Naissance d'une institution* [Politics and religion in contemporary Iran. Birth of an institution]. Paris: L'Harmattan.

Noroozi, L., & Alemi, Z. (2003). The employability of graduates of higher education, looking at the specific situation of women. Iran Higher Education and Employment, First seminar, University of Tarbiyat Modaress, Tehran [Persian]. Retrieved from https://www.civilica.com/Paper-ESHTEGHAL01-ESHTEGHAL01_005.html

Paivandi, S. (2006). *Islam et Education en Iran. Echec de l'islamisation de L'école en Iran* [Islam and Education in Iran. Failure of Islamization of School in Iran]. Paris: L'Harmattan.

Paivandi, S. (2012). The meaning of the Islamization of the school in Iran. In M. Ahmed (Ed.), *Education in West Asia* (pp. 79–102). London: Bloomsbury.

Paivandi, S. (2015). Interminable querelle de la sécularisation de l'éducation en Iran [Endless quarrel over the secularization of education in Iran.]. Raison Publique, *19*. Retrieved from http://www.raison-publique.fr/article759.html

Parvazian, S., Gill, J., & Chiera, B. (2017). Higher education, women, and sociocultural change: A closer look at the statistics. *Sage Open*, *7*, 1–12.

Rahbari, L. (2016). Women in higher education and academia in Iran. *Sociology and Anthropology*, *4*, 1003–1010.

Rezai-Rashti, G. M. (2011). Exploring women's experience of higher education and the changing nature of gender relations in Iran. In R. Bahramitash & E. Hooglund (Eds.), *Gender in contemporary Iran: Pushing the boundaries* (pp. 61–77). New York, NY: Routledge.

Rezai-Rashti, G. M., & Moghadam, V. M. (2011). Women and higher education in Iran: What are the implications for employment and the "marriage market". *International Review of Education*, *57*, 419–441.

Salibi, J. (2010). Analysis of the growth in admission of women to higher education: Progress and challenges. *Pazuheshnameh Zanan*. [*Women's Studies.*], *1*, 39–64 [Persian].

SCI (Statistical Center of Iran). (1977). *Statistic year book of 1355*. Tehran: Statistical Center of Iran.

SCI (Statistical Center of Iran). (1982). *Statistic year book of 1360*. Tehran: Statistical Center of Iran.

SCI (Statistical Center of Iran). (1992). *Statistic year book of 1370*. Tehran: Statistical Center of Iran.

SCI (Statistical Center of Iran). (2002). *Statistic year book of 1380*. Tehran: Statistical Center of Iran.

SCI (Statistical Center of Iran). (2011). *Statistic year book of 1390*. Tehran: Statistical Center of Iran.

SCI (Statistical Center of Iran). (2018). *Statistic year book of 1396*. Tehran: Statistical Center of Iran.

SCI (2019). A Selection of Labor Force Survey Results - Year 1398. Retrieved from https://www.amar.org.ir/english/Latest-Releases-Page/ID/13026/A-Selection-of-Labor-Force-Survey-Results–Year-1398

Shams, A. (2016). Revolutionary religiosity and women's access to higher education in the Islamic Republic of Iran. *Journal of Middle East Women's Studies*, *12*(1), 126–138.

Shavarini, M. (2005). The femenization of Iranian higher education. *The Review of Education*, *51*, 329–347.

Shavarini, M. (2006). Wearing the veil to college: The paradox of higher education in the lives of Iranian women. *International Journal of Middle East Studies*, *38*, 189–211.

Shavarini, M. (2009). The social (and economic) implications of being an educated women in Iran. *Harvard Educational Review*, *79*, 132–135.

Tayebinia, M., & Rahmani, J. (2016). Newly found motivations in women's changing identities in higher education. *Fasnameh Tahghighat Farhangi Iran*. [*Quarterly Journal of Iranian Cultural Research.*], *9*, 101–129 [Persian].

UNESCO. (1982). *Statistics of students abroad*. Paris: UNESCO.

Zahiri Nia, M., & Behroozian, B. (2012). Comparison of influencing factors for entering men and women at university. *Zan va Jameh*. [*Journal of Woman and Society.*], *5*(4), 69–90 [Persian].

Chapter 12

Women's Empowerment through Higher Education: The Case of Bangladesh

Rumana Ahmed and Nelia Hyndman-Rizk

1. Introduction

In Bangladesh, women's increased participation in higher education over the last decade has failed to improve their labor force participation. Thus, there has been a pervasive decline in employment for those with higher education. Data show that in Bangladesh, for those with a university degree, the overall unemployment rate is 16%, while for females the unemployment rate is 24%, compared to 13% for their male counterparts (Bangladesh Bureau of Statistics, 2015, p. 85). The contrast between higher educational attainment and lower labor force participation is the central anomaly that this exploratory research study addresses. This chapter starts by presenting the theoretical framework and research question. Then the women's education and empowerment debate in developing countries is examined and the context of higher education in Bangladesh. The case of agency development and empowerment at a women's college in Northern Bangladesh is then presented. While the findings section documents the study's view from the field, the discussion section considers the implications of the findings for the broader debate on women's empowerment through higher education. The chapter concludes with a discussion of the research contribution and recommendations that can improve the overall status of women and contribute to women's agency in developing countries like Bangladesh. The contribution the study makes for the development literature is twofold: first by highlighting that there remains an "instrumental" deficiency in women's higher education practice in Bangladesh and, secondly, by identifying "strategic male engagement" as a key facilitator of women's empowerment and agency development.

2. Theoretical Framework and Research Question

Development discourse between the 1960s to 1980s was built on the economic indicators of growth, modernization, industrialization, trade, increasing national income, and poverty reduction, as delineated in the World Bank's

International Perspectives on Gender and Higher Education, 213–230

doi:10.1108/978-1-83909-886-420201012

annual reports. However, since the 1990s, critiques of this model have expanded development to include education and health measures (see UNDP's Human Development Index (HDI)). Also, gender critiques of development have contributed to the gender development index being compiled since 1995. Together, such indexes more completely measure equality and agency development among men and women (Visvanathan, Duggan, Nisonoff, & Wiegersma, 2011, p. 18). However, in the 2000s, women's agency and empowerment was identified as a key gap in the development literature and approach (World Bank, 2012). Two prominent schools of thought emerged, which differed in how to define empowerment in development. For the first group of scholars, empowerment was instrumental to achieving other development goals, while for the second group of thinkers, the intrinsic value of empowerment was emphasized, as being an end unto itself. Empowerment, for the first group of thinkers, is a process of increasing power, conceived through the interaction between two building blocks: agency, "an actor's or group's ability to make purposeful choices' and the opportunity structure," "the broader institutional, social, and political context of formal and informal rules and norms, within which actors pursue their interests" (Alsop, Bertelsen, & Holland, 2006, pp. 11–13). Individual and collective assets determine agency, including capabilities, such as human health, education, social position, identity or leadership status, and psychological assets (self-esteem, self-confidence), and the ability to imagine a better future. The second group of scholars, led by Kabeer (2001) and Ibrahim and Alkire (2007), were inspired by the Capability Approach (CA), developed by Sen (1985). For them, empowerment is the "expansion of agency" (Ibrahim & Alkire, 2007, p. 384) and "the expansion in people's ability to make strategic life choices, in a context where this ability was previously denied to them" (Kabeer, 2001, p. 19). These definitions, however, exclude the institutional factors, which structure agency, because agency is intrinsically valued as an end point (Sen, 1985). For Kabeer (2001), following the work Sen (1999), women should be active agents in the development process, rather than passive recipients of "welfarist" development.

Focusing on the role of education as a key capability, this study asked the central question: *Does higher education improve women's agency development in Bangladesh?* To expand the analysis of the impact of education on the agency development of students, the study applied the framework: "the school/empowerment link" (Ross, Shah, & Wang, 2011), which distinguished between their *instrumental* and *intrinsic* empowerment. Ross et al. (2011) define instrumental empowerment as attaining the practical demands rendered by institutional engagement, such as, the development of numeracy, literacy, and other relevant human capital skills. These skills are instrumental for economic participation. Intrinsic empowerment, on the other hand, is the impact of the educational process on the capability of women to understand their social position and to develop self-efficacy, self-confidence, and psychological resilience (Ross et al., 2011, p. 26). The study explored the performance of students across five determinants and constraints of agency development: quality of education, social norms, household dynamics, laws, legal frameworks and job markets.

3. Trends in Women's Education and Empowerment in Developing Countries

Education in a modern economy is an investment in *human capital* (Olaniyan & Okemakinde, 2008), the return of which benefits both the individual and the nation, through improving women's economic participation. Women's economic involvement has been indicated as being important for their *well-being* and it is an *entitlement*, the lack of which considerably affects women's empowerment and agency development (Sen, 1999, pp. 191–192). Furthermore, the neo-liberal approach of "efficiency and effectiveness" and the prevailing trend of "smart economics" regard the investment in girl's and women's education as an investment in human capital with a possibility of higher a *social return* (World Bank, 2012). Despite debate, significant literature has documented women's greater labor force participation or income earning potential (Sen, 1999, p. 191), and improved human capital (Agnihotri, Palmer-Jones, & Parikh, 2002; Kishor & Gupta, 2004; Qian, 2008). While R. T. Jensen (2010) finds that the acceleration of women's economic opportunity can encourage access and investment in human capital for women (Jensen, 2010, p. 23). Beaman, Duflo, Pande, and Topalova (2012) show that women's participation in leadership positions can influence young women's aspirations and educational attainment. Taking evidence from India, R. Jensen (2012) concludes that women's economic participation positively correlates with their delayed marriage and fertility behavior, owing to the resulting growth in career aspiration, thus, extending education or post-school training. Through the review of the debates on economic development and women's empowerment, Duflo (2012) found a link between economic development and gender equality. In poor economic conditions and opportunity structures, women are more disadvantaged than men, because economic development benefits women by removing their disadvantage and reducing gender inequalities (Duflo, 2012, p. 1053).

Moreover, at a national level, a positive correlation has been found between the proportion of highly educated workers in the labor force of a country and that country's per capita income (Holland, Liadze, Rienzo, & Wilkinson, 2013). This correlation shows that workers with more education are less likely to fall into the trap of unemployment or low-income jobs. However, the literature finds that tertiary graduates from either developed or emerging economies benefit most from this matrix (Nunez & Livanos, 2010; Schomburg & Teichler, 2007). Less is known, however, about the corresponding dynamics in the developing world. It is the tertiary graduates who are most likely to remain unemployed, rather than the less educated or uneducated. The lag in labor force participation by educated workers in the lower-middle income or developing economies highlights a mismatch between human capital and human productivity. The links between growing educational levels and unemployed graduates in developing countries could be caused by the following factors: poor demand for, but a strong supply of skilled labor, a lack of job-relevant skills, or the higher expectations of graduates that keep them from entering low-paid or less-recognized jobs (Key Indicators of the Labour Market, 2015). Sex segregation in the labor market, feminized labor in low-skilled, low-paid jobs, and wage differentials between men and women still persist. Eswaran and Malhotra (2011) argue that women's empowerment, through expanding economic opportunities, is helpful for their well-being, increases their autonomy, and delays when they marry, but can also increase the incidence of domestic violence (Eswaran & Malhotra, 2011, p. 1258). Applying a similar framework in urban areas of Bangladesh, Heath (2012) finds a similar correlation between greater economic opportunities and domestic violence, especially among women with less education or who were married young. Moreover, in Bangladesh, women's increased participation in higher education over the last decade has failed to improve their labor force participation. Thus, there has been a pervasive decline in their socioeconomic status to the effect that their dependence persists. This contrast between women's educational attainment and limited economic participation motivates the present study to explore and understand whether pursuing higher education can ensure women's empowerment and agency development in Bangladesh.

4. Higher Education and Development in Bangladesh

After independence in 1971, Bangladesh became heavily dependent on foreign aid. Though limited in mineral resources, it capitalized on two endowments: land and labor. Bangladesh has also been able to reduce dependence on foreign aid (Helal & Hossain, 2013). Bangladesh has achieved the fastest growing economic status among the countries of the Asia-Pacific region (second fastest in the world) with a GDP growth rate of 7.9% (Asian Development Bank, 2019). A South Asian country, Bangladesh is the eighth most populous country in the world, it is expected to reach a population of 170 million by 2020. Bangladesh has achieved most of the Millennium Development Goals (MDGS-8) ahead of time; outstanding progress was made in areas, such as poverty alleviation and gender parity in primary and secondary level education, to name a few. Regarding the Sustainable Development Goals (SDGs-17) considerable achievement has been recorded in several areas. In a global ranking on women empowerment Bangladesh ranks 48, with a score of 0.721, which is significantly better compared to other South Asian countries (General Economics Division, 2018).

In the development literature, Bangladesh has featured prominently, as a result of the ready-made garments (RMG) industry since the 1990s (Rahman & Islam, 2013). The country is characterized by cheap labor and, thus, is less prone to unemployment. However, examining the "U-shape" effect for female labor force participation in India, Mehrotra and Parida (2017) found that less education and low skilled women's work opportunities are eroding on the face of growing mechanization in agriculture and rising capital intensity in manufacturing sectors. Rahman and Islam (2013) found a negation of the U-shaped hypothesis, however, in case of the labor supply in Bangladesh, compared with India, as Bangladesh has witnessed a steady growth in female labor force participation, even in the agricultural sector, in line with other export-oriented industrialized countries. Micro-finance projects since the 1980s and the proliferation of garment industries in the mid-1990s have mainly targeted rural women, or those associated with more vulnerable work, such as domestic or construction labor as their first jobs. But such informal employment hardly offers long-term solutions for poverty reduction since the survival capacity of these industries are often under challenge from international commitment and competition (Kabeer & Mahmud, 2004, pp. 147–148). Moreover, such a "top-down" distribution approach keeps women as *passive recipients*, thus, requiring "bottom-up" agitation to transform women to be *active agents* of development programs (Moser, 1993). Using the link between paid work and women's empowerment within Bangladesh, Kabeer, Mahmud, and Tasneem (2011) described women's job opportunities in four categories: (1) paid work outside the home, (2) paid work within the home, (3) unpaid subsistence production or expenditure-saving work within the home, and (4) economic inactivity. The study concluded that employment outside the home and mostly in the "formal sector" usually helps women grow their decision-making capability and strengthen their "voice" through agency (Kabeer et al., 2011). Therefore, along with educational attainment, independent incomes through women's participation in the formal sector are entitlements for their empowerment and agency development.

However, the primary concern in educating girls, since independence, was to train them into "enlightened motherhood" (Chanana, 1994), in line with the welfaristic economic model, to provide them with a female friendly career, that would not interrupt "the second shift" (Hochschild & Machung, 2012). The ideology of enlightened motherhood was reoriented with the introduction of neoliberal educational policies, with Education for All (EFA) and the Female Stipend Program (FSP) being introduced in 1982. The FSP sought to increase girls' educational participation, especially to the secondary level, to limit early marriage in rural areas and popularize the use of contraceptives to reduce pregnancy (Herz, 1991; Khandker & Samad, 2013; Thein, Kabir, & Islam, 1988). Though causality is difficult to establish, data suggest that the stipend program was successful in improving secondary school enrollment for girls. However, while FSP is not a stand-alone program for achieving gender parity in education, it certainly aids the mutually dependent goals of universal access and gender equity and improved the standards and led to more relevant secondary education.

Moreover, increasing the level of women's education does not necessarily improve women's bargaining power to challenge patriarchy (Arends-Kuenning & Amin, 2001). Neither does it confirm the increase in labor force participation, as noted above. To counter patriarchy and gendered norms, agency development offers promise, because the state is obligated to inform women about their options and impose restrictions on inequality in public schools and, thus, ensure that females' capabilities and gender justice are fully achieved (Nussbaum, 2001). Such development, therefore, supports and, in turn, relies upon other project interventions, such as improving access, especially in remote areas, improving quality, such as in teaching quality and making curriculum relevant, and developing institutions so they are monitored and evaluated (Aikman & Unterhalter, 2005; Mahmud, 2003, p. 5; Tembon & Fort, 2008; Unterhalter, 2007). Women's higher education offers a unique environment to examine the nexus between education and agency development.

5. A Women's College in Northern Bangladesh: A View from the Field

This study examines the case of a women's college in Northern Bangladesh, to explore what female students thought about their own empowerment and agency development through participating in higher education. This research study was part of a Masters of Philosophy thesis in the School of Business, at the University of New South Wales, Canberra, in 2017. A qualitative research design was regarded appropriate for this research project, since it allows an interpretation to give meaning to participants' words, pictures, or any emergent ways of expression (Creswell, 2007). Following obtaining an ethics approval from the Human Research Ethics Committee, this research was conducted in a women's college in Northern Bangladesh. The women's college is one of the affiliates of Bangladesh National University, which is the fifth largest university in the world by enrollment (more than 2 million students in 2,154 affiliated colleges or other institutions) (Bangladesh National University, Undated). At the time of data collection, the college was mainly offering Honors degrees in six subjects: English, economics, Bangla, political science, social work, and Islamic Studies, along with an HSC in arts, commerce, social science, and natural science. The women's college is equipped with almost all the necessary facilities, such as a science and computer laboratories, a multimedia classroom, library, mosque, and canteen. As a researcher who is a native Bangladeshi, born and brought up in Northern Bangladesh, the first author is familiar with the language, culture, and prevalent social practices.

5.1 Methodological Approach

The research strategy was an embedded case study (Yin, 2014) to explore and understand women's experience of higher education and the resulting empowerment in a public Women's College from Northern Bangladesh. Using purposeful sampling in general and convenience sampling (Creswell & Poth, 2017; Palinkas et al., 2015), a cohort of 20 students (among the total of 1,671), 10 from first year and 10 from the fourth-year Honors program, were invited to participate in in-depth interviews. Therefore, the sample is indicative not representative; however, when the research objective is to understand the life worlds of the participants, the researcher needs to identify a sample from whom he/she can gain the most insight (Merriam, 2002, p. 48). The majority (n = 55%) of respondents were from the villages and union councils from 13 *upozilas* (subdistricts) surrounding Dinajpur and were between 19 and 22 years of age. Each interview spanned from 30 to 40 minutes, asking semistructured questions (in the respondents' first language, Bengali) and were open-ended in nature (Bryman & Bell, 2007).

5.2 Data Analysis Procedures

While data collection techniques involved in-depth interview and observation, thematic analysis was conducted as the primary data analysis technique.

Furthermore, secondary data sources were also used to cross-check the findings (Bryman & Bell, 2015). In the first stage, all recorded interviews were professionally transcribed and then translated from Bengali to English over a period of 1 month. The transcripts were then thematically coded (Bryman & Bell, 2015, p. 595), resulting in five primary themes: educational experience, reflections on social norms, household dynamics, legal awareness, and job market aspirations. The coding followed the principles of thematic analysis, whereby the data were coded until no new information was found and data saturation was reached (Bryman & Bell, 2007). Let us now examine the findings of the study.

5.3 Research Findings

This section presents the research findings. The analysis highlights the performance of students across five determinants and constraints of agency development: quality of education, social norms, household dynamics, laws and legal frameworks, and job markets. Let us now look at each area more closely.

5.4 Educational Quality

The case study women's college only offers subjects from arts/social science group in Honors level, mostly due to the lack of government funds and a shortage of quality teachers at the higher levels, as informed by the Principal. Farida, a first-year student of Islamic Studies, lives in Dinajpur proper in the heart of the town and felt that doing Honors in Islamic Studies would limit her job market value as she responded with a sigh,[1]

> Selecting the Arts group, I used to feel myself luckier than my brother studying in Science, as I was saved from joining several private tuitions; but now I realize the loss, my subject and my institution is both incompetent to make a better place for me in the job market, maybe I will be married off soon and then a career will be an optional choice!

Questions were raised about single-sex schooling. Tania was in her final year of an Honors degree in political science, she exclaimed,

> From childhood, I have seen my father as a conservative guardian who never celebrated the idea of free mixing between boys and girls, thus, me and all my elder sisters have always been studying in single sex schools, in that case we had to choose from the subjects offered in such institutions.

[1]Pseudonyms have been used for qualitative data analysis to de-identify the participants on ethical grounds.

The student's stereotyped subject selection and sex-segregated study led us to question them about their father's reasons for sending them to higher education. This led to the question; Do male guardians primarily view education as a means for preparing their daughters for the job market, or as a means to build social status, which attracts a better husband in the marriage market? Different viewpoints were found among participants. For less educated and lower-middle class families, sending girls to study in competitive subjects and in better institutions, with better job market prospects, is not only a financial burden, but it can lead them to aspire for careers that are not always welcomed. Achieving a suitable marriage match might be harder, because a woman being more qualified or career-oriented is not acceptable in patriarchal societies that fear them gaining better bargaining power. Thus, sending daughters or wives to a women's college might convince patriarchal guardians that it is a safer venture than a co-educational college, because the former challenges the *status quo* less.

While questions were asked about their satisfaction through higher education, Armin was cynical about the curriculum, which she said is sexist and teaches female students to behave in ways that promote patriarchal norms and keeps them in a cocoon without metamorphosis. Nity had a different view as she thought that her life has changed a lot compared to her illiterate or less educated associates, many of whom are already mothers of one or two children. Putul, a first-year economics student, also found that education had magical effect on her life. She aspired to be a banker with her economics degree. Trisha's words reflected the empowerment that education can and should render women:

> There are still short falls in the education system and curricula, which needs to be more reflective, and should have some practical applications rather than based on rote learning. Practical involvement has given me more confidence to grow as an empowered woman.

Along with educational success, she had gained practical experience through voluntary service in different NGOs. She has mobility to the extent of traveling abroad with an NGO and gained independent income from her cattle farm in her village, which resulted from the proper use of a loan from the Grameen Bank.

5.5 Reflections on Social Norms and Household Dynamics

We found that 95% of the students came from the union councils, or rural areas, to reside in campus hostels. However, most of the girls denied being discriminated against at home. For most of them, the treatment they receive, compared to their brothers at home and male counterparts in society, is what is required to give them social protection. They believe patriarchy, instead of maintaining the *status quo*, is rather a form of protection, which guides them in life. Some participants, for example, Prity and Trisha, came from remote areas, where women's education is rarely welcomed. They acknowledged their fathers' insight and support to help them reach so far. Shila expressed similar gratitude for her brother's cooperation. The only married respondent, Fatima explained her experience as follows:

> I have seen that if the husband, the second guardian, is favorable enough, then the wife's qualification can be regarded positively, and though household pressures are there for the wife, mostly the husband's positive attitude towards a wife's career is very helpful.

Those who think discrimination does prevail in their families, argued that it was not directly the result of male figures, but rather of their mothers, who restrict them from walking on certain tracks, which are socially ascribed as being *unsuitable* for girls. They think that the lack of education of their mothers and the persistence of this value system (social roles) affects the boys in their later life, who regard women as vulnerable and less competent to walk alone in society.

However, 90% of the respondents felt that their decision-making capability has not only improved through educational retention, but also from the acceptance of their family, because they were thought to have a mature understanding derived from their level of education. About 85% of the respondents felt they had a voice in family affairs, which shows the unequivocally positive effect of higher education.

5.6 Limited Legal Awareness

Research respondents for this study were either unaware or highly critical about the legal system in Bangladesh, to them laws are "by the male and for the male." The prevailing social practice of regarding females as the weaker sex, highly restricts women's mobility, premarital relationships and so on. Young girls traveling to and from schools and colleges are also protected from predacious males and crimes as heinous as sexual harassment and violence, to even rape and suicide. Many respondents had experienced street harassment, as Prity expressed:

> Just behind the college there is a small market and even in broad day light a girl is not safe from the evil eyes and filthy comments of the men there. Several times I felt a shiver ran down my marrow to walk past that spot. Then I can realize why my parents want me to remain segregated from the boys. Without a male guardian, none or nothing could protect a girl or a woman from these hyenas.

Perhaps street harassment is the most vicious of the modern-day crimes, especially in the urban areas; it hinders the process of bringing the girls out of the home and into the public sphere, as they seek education. The prevalent laws and legal practices are often unable to help victims substantially and they are left with humiliation and possible consequences like suicide.

Though mostly unaware of the legal system and laws protecting women, some respondents recollected certain violations of laws related to being unpaid or underpaid. Though most respondents agreed that personal income is most important for women's self-esteem and independence, none thought that income alone would eradicate the prevalence of violence against women (VAW). Some respondents lamented about being ineligible for property rights, whereby women have been left dependent and incapable of starting their own business. Mention was also made of Muslim and Hindu property laws, which favors males over females in terms of distributing land property and assets. However, all acknowledged that, without having any required information transparency, raising awareness and establishing strong governance and monitoring systems, laws are not equipped to ensure justice in society.

5.7 Job Market Aspirations

Respondents for this study, even in their fourth year, were comparatively less motivated to start a career, as most expected to marry after finishing their study. Most respondents saw marriage, child-rearing responsibilities, housekeeping, and looking after aged in-laws as the most prominent barriers to joining the labor force. Therefore, any economic participation will depend on the attitude of their future in-laws. Most of them must secure the male guardians' permission; higher educational attainment was not the only consideration for economic participation. Rani, a fourth-year economics student, reflects on the role of males in controlling the life course of women in their households:

> Actually, permission is not in the sense of a restriction, but it is kind of a discussion to choose the wrong from the right and as we are dependent on males from the beginning of our life it tends to be our habit to seek the decision from the head of the family. We never feel we can control our life until we are forced to do so for example, someone is divorced or their husband is dead.

Respondents who were confident to build a career (only a 30%) are either driven by financial hardship or to support their parents, thereby, challenging the traditional view of "son preference." Such women were aware of the growing trend of human development that regards all humans as capable of proving their worth within the right provisions. The most common job aspiration among respondents was a primary school teacher (35%), followed by lecturers in tertiary colleges (25%), then NGO workers (15%), bank or/and public employees (10%), and other suitable jobs (5%).

Limited IT literacy and the capability of majority of the respondents (even in fourth year) not only point to the existence of *digital divide* in women's higher education practice in Bangladesh but also indicate a lack of one of the crucial skills required by the modern job market. As informed by the participants, not so much due to infrastructural insufficiency, rather the curricula and course design in arts/commerce degrees rarely develop computer literacy among students. Boys or men, however, being more mobile and because they are expected to be job market candidates, build their IT capability. Nevertheless, it was noticeable that respondents who participated in some income earning, either from their first- or fourth-year study, were more mature and their self-confidence was more positive than for women without any external income. Following are the summaries of the findings:

Quality of education: As for the intrinsic empowerment, improvement was found at the individual level; however, constraints remain at the societal level. Furthermore, instrumental empowerment needs further attention.

Socio-cultural norms: The study found that female students are expected to adhere to the *status quo*, particularly the social roles as determined by the formal and informal institutions of culture, society, and religion.

Household dynamics: Higher education has improved the respondents' decision-making role in their families.

Law and legal frameworks: Respondents were either unaware or highly critical about the legal system in Bangladesh, to them laws are "by the male and for the male."

Job market: Respondents for this study even in their fourth year were comparatively less motivated to start a career as most expected to marry after finishing their study.

5.8 Discussion

Since the major share of the college's student quota are students coming from surrounding *upozilas*, 95% respondents for this study were from rural areas, where profound gendered norms and patriarchal formal and informal institutions guide household dynamics. Nevertheless, female students entered higher education, because of individual capability and their families' willpower. It was likely, therefore, that their instrumental achievement through higher education would merely result in credentialism, if not accompanied by *a fair deal* in realizing greater economic participation, such as a job in the formal sector. Otherwise, improving education may risk only deferring the age of marriage, reducing fertility rates, but increasing the frustration among graduate women. Such an opportunity is likely to tarnish the family's view of the effectiveness of a girls' education, as it can result in a potential loss in human capital and a waste of capability. Several discrepancies in instrumental matters were ascertained through this research: subjects are stereotyped; study is segregated; curricula are deficient; rote learning is used; and generic skill development, motivation for career development, and ICT training are deficient. As such, the instrumental empowerment through higher education among this cohort is limited.

As for the intrinsic empowerment, we found that the female students had developed their skills in decision-making, often by contributing to family matters and their individual advancement. They have extended their mobility outside the home, and their improved self-confidence was reflected in their capability for self-management of themselves and their education. Two patterns of self-realization were identified: Trisha, Putul, Paboni, and Fatima viewed the world from a collectivist life experience and had internalized the patriarchal socio-cultural context. However, Armin, Tania, or Prity had engaged a radical feminist view that attributes women's overall subordination to patriarchy, from father and brother in their youth, to husband in their adulthood, and to their sons during their aging (Moser, 2003, p. 42). Their gravest realization was that elderly female figures, either in their own home or in their in-laws' house, were the supervisors for the patriarchy and the head of the household. Notably, respondents like Trisha, Putul, Paboni, and Fatima were more advanced in their empowerment and agency development, being influenced by higher education and personal income. Armin, Tania, or Prity's economic dependence on males (as family heads) was yet to be experienced. In a collectivist society like Bangladesh, where patriarchy is the gatekeeper for the formal and informal institutions and guides the household context, these women proceeded with heightened self-confidence to effect difference in their own lives and surroundings. This openly demonstrates their intrinsic empowerment through higher education.

As discussed earlier, Bangladesh has a more traditional socio-cultural structure, entailing an agrarian economy and a rural base patriarchy, central to a culture characterized by collectivism and accepted systems of marriage. In such circumstances, *woman's emancipation* (Molyneux, 1985, p. 245), whereby they are empowered over their gendered roles, is inconsistently mediated by different levels of liberal attitude, either from her parents or in-laws. In Bangladesh, the entire socio-cultural practice determines that finance sustains the power of patriarchy. This practice is characterized by son-preference, men's accredited gender role as a breadwinner, and patriarchal formal and informal opportunity structures to ensure that men earn *trust, treatment, and training* to develop agency from birth. Conversely, women's gendered roles of "homemaking" and the prevalent gender discrimination pattern, consequently, obligate them to follow such social norms. The entire socio-cultural practice sustains the power of patriarchy through reproducing patriarchy economically. However, for the women involved in education, two exceptions beside their gender roles can negotiate and contribute to the possibility of their *strategic emancipation*, rather than empowerment and agency development, as such: women's "capability through educational performance" and women's "capability to contribute in the family income."

This study identified the trinity of *trust, treatment, and training* from key males (i.e., fathers, brothers and husbands) as a way to negotiate with and through males to positively engage them to help women in their families negotiate the existing barriers to their empowerment and agency development imposed by patriarchal socio-cultural norms, household dynamics, and law and legal frameworks. The factual description of *trust, treatment, and training*, as experienced from the interviews, would further crystallize the point.

Trust: Trisha was one among the interviewees unraveled as an example of empowered women; her educational performance, self-realization, commitment and contribution to her family and society, her mobility, social network, personal income – all have broadened the periphery of her strategic emancipation, which will with time grow further. To demonstrate her success at developing her agency, Trisha said, *I had to convince my parents, mainly father, what I am doing is not going to conflict with their (society's, as they belong to it) interest.* This signifies that women firstly need to convince their parents (mainly fathers) that they are capable of progressing through education, like the boys in a family and that this progress offers nothing that is socially unacceptable. Earning this *trust* is the most important component in her strategic emancipation, since the journey begins from here. Developing countries like Bangladesh are still conservative enough, at least in the rural and less educated circumstances, to let their women leave their gendered roles. With education, they can only grow if permitted to do so within the individual circumstances and surroundings, which might considerably vary.

Treatment: Earning *trust* from the patriarchal head of the household leads to favorable *treatment* from them, as Prity expressed: *I could never stand on the ground I am on now without my father's support and inspiration.* This also demonstrates how important it is for a girl's strategic emancipation to receive positive support from the male head of household that says, "carry on, I will be there with you."

Training: Last but not the least, in a society governed by patriarchy, it is highly important that they *train* the girls to follow the right track, which along with reducing challenges, ensures social security. As the only married women, Fatima clarifies understanding when she demonstrates how positive and crucial *training* is to women's strategic emancipation:

> I was married off when I was in year 12; I passed the Higher Secondary Certificate (HSC) after my marriage. Now I have a nine month old daughter. Both my husband and I look after her. We run our own tutorial business at home and my husband admitted me into this college in political science, because he himself has an MA in the same subject and thus can help me with my study. Together we want to go further in our careers and we want to raise our daughter with a proper education.

Strategic emancipation: The essence of collaborative coexistence between males and females in their family formation is assumed by the theory of *complementary needs* (Brubaker, 2016). Bangladeshi patriarchal cultural norms rely on male's and female's ancient mutual interest and contribution, where woman's role is established as "carer" in nurturing children, maintaining family, and looking after the elderly persons, whereas the man's role is as "provider" through protecting his family's existence and supporting the members financially. The radical feminist realization, driven by individualistic Western ideals, runs contrary to social norms where patriarchy is the supreme religion and social and economic order based on the "principle of inequality" (Singh, 2007). In individualist societies, every person is his/her own boss, while the power dynamics in collectivist societies often go with the more experienced, capable, and economically strong family member if the matter requires a financial decision. The mother is often sought to solve household-related problems, whereas the father or elder brother addresses matters that pertain to the outside world, but often the decision is derived through mutual discussion. In a collectivist and patriarchal culture like Bangladesh, where family and household tend to be the most reliable asylum for women providing them with social, economic, and emotional support; adherence to either Western feminism or a utopian dream of a classless society would mean losing their primary source of support or extended forms of violence against women.

Women's growing capability through education and independent income can earn the right to a position at the discussion table, as was explained from the experience of Trisha, Fatima, or Putul. Nevertheless, Prity, Tania, or Armin criticized their family and their society's male-biased attitudes. We argue that such criticisms mystify the entire socialization process, however, which more traditional societies, like Bangladesh, would reasonably refute and might, instead, lead to domestic violence. Thus, rather than empowerment, as such, women's growing capability through education and economic participation, with the support of key males in their families, can lead them toward their "strategic emancipation" at the individual level, through which they can aim to improve women's collective agency development. Putul's words support this notion:

> I have received a scholarship all through my educational experience; I am an idol to many of the villagers as they seek my reference to give lessons to their daughters. The way I talk, the ways I dress myself have become a model of a real student. Even my parents also think that I will never make a wrong decision as education has trained me to walk on the right path.

She further exclaimed,

> I teach math, Bangla, and English to the students of year 8 in an NGO operated school in our village, and the school authority loves me a lot for my performance. I also teach in private tuitions. With my personal income I buy things for my parents, help them in their needs even I maintain my own bank account. My parents also feel that being educated is worthwhile; in future I want to work in some banks as my subject economics will create that opportunity for me.

Putul, a student of first-year economics, reflects how the combination of "capability through educational performance" and "capability to income earning" mediate deep-rooted social norms and pave the way for women's strategic emancipation. While she faced many socio-cultural and economic predicaments in her journey, the trinity of *trust, treatment, and training* confirmed her better socio-economic platform than others. Putul aspires to a bright future, which she would achieve if she could steadily follow the track of higher education and economic independence supported by her father or future husband. Fig. 12.1 illustrates the rungs of the ladder that Putul has already crossed while targeting empowerment through strategic emancipation.

Fig. 12.1 shows that, while Putul's education and income experience are likely to see her overcome the socio-cultural practice of educating women less, without the positive support of *trust, treatment, and training* from her father, it would have been difficult for her. Thus, underscoring the contingency factors and compromising situations that any girl has to cope with, this study found that instrumental empowerment through higher education needs further attention, because it empowered girls intrinsically, at least at the individual level. However, constraints remain at the societal level. While barriers are still prevalent in opportunity structures, both in formal and informal institutions, active participation and positive engagement of male family members (e.g., fathers, brothers or husbands) can potentially enhance girls' capabilities, empowerment, and agency development. It is

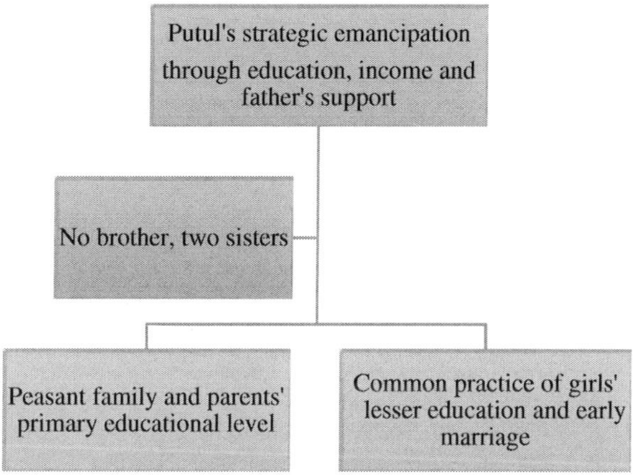

Fig. 12.1. Conceptual Scheme of How Putul Achieved Strategic Emancipation.
Source: As in (Ahmed, 2017, p. 171).

a matter of facilitating the application of the endowments and capabilities they have developed through higher education.

6. Conclusion and Contribution

The present research explored women's higher education practice and inequalities in women's labor force participation in Bangladesh. The study asked, *does higher education improve women's agency development in Bangladesh?* If higher education empowers women (both instrumentally and intrinsically), it should ensure their labor force participation and, in turn, their agency development. However, this development narrative was challenged by this study, because it assumes the harmonious coexistence between opportunity structures, both formal and informal. Rather, for the women in this study, higher education led to their *intrinsic* empowerment, through growing their self-reliance and self-realization, however, their *instrumental* empowerment was incomplete, as their education did not sufficiently prepare them for the demands of the job market. Furthermore, there remain loopholes in the socio-economic and patriarchal construct; which could more fruitfully be utilized to overcome the impediments to women's empowerment and agency development in Bangladesh. Since the collectivist culture, religion, and social restrictions in Bangladesh have given men dominance and status over women, the present study advocates for women's strategic emancipation, a middle pathway, which seeks the positive engagement of key males, for a more sustainable approach. A key contribution of this study is to highlight the importance of intrinsic and instrumental educational empowerment, along with male engagement, so that men can be strategic enablers of women's agency development in Bangladesh, rather than social impediments blocking the way.

References

Agnihotri, S., Palmer-Jones, R., & Parikh, A. (2002). Missing women in Indian districts: A quantitative analysis. *Structural Change and Economic Dynamics*, *13*(3), 285–314.

Ahmed, R. (2017). *Learning through higher education: A case study on the role of education in improving women' s empowerment, agency development and labour force participation in Bangladesh*. (Master of Philosophy), University of New South Wales, Canberra, Australia. Retrieved from http://unsworks.unsw.edu.au/fapi/datastream/unsworks:46530/SOURCE02?view=true

Aikman, S., & Unterhalter, E. (2005). *Beyond access: Transforming policy and practice for gender equality in education*. Oxford: Oxfam.

Alsop, R., Bertelsen, M. F., & Holland, J. (2006). *Empowerment in practice: From analysis to implementation*. Washington, DC: World Bank Publications.

Arends-Kuenning, M., & Amin, S. (2001). Women's capabilities and the right to education in Bangladesh. *International Journal of Politics, Culture, and Society*, *15*(1), 125–142.

Asian Development Bank. (2019, April). Asian Development Outlook (ADO) 2019: Strengthening disaster resilience. Retrieved from https://www.adb.org/publications/asian-development-outlook-2019-strengthening-disaster-resilience

Bangladesh Bureau of Statistics. (2015). *Labour force survey Bangladesh 2013*. Dhaka: Bangladesh Government Press. Retrieved from http://www.bbs.gov.bd

Beaman, L., Duflo, E., Pande, R., & Topalova, P. (2012). Female leadership raises aspirations and educational attainment for girls: A policy experiment in India. *Science*, *335*(6068), 582–586.

Brubaker, J. (2016). Complementary needs theory. In C. L. Shehan (Ed.), *The Wiley Blackwell encyclopedia of family studies, 4 Volume Set*. Hoboken, NJ: John Wiley & Sons.

Bryman, A., & Bell, E. (2007). *Business research methods*. Oxford: Oxford University Press.

Bryman, A., & Bell, E. (2015). *Business research methods*. NewYork, NY: Oxford University Press.

Chanana, K. (1994). Social change or social reform: Women, education and family in preindependence India. In C. C. Mukhopadhyay & S. Seymour (Eds.), *Women, education and family structure in India* (pp. 35–58). Boulder, CO: Westview Press.

Creswell, J. W. (2007). *Qualitative inquiry and research design: Choosing among five approaches* (2nd ed.). Thousand Oaks, CA: SAGE Publications.

Creswell, J. W., & Poth, C. N. (2017). *Qualitative inquiry and research design: Choosing among five approaches* (4th ed.). Thousand Oaks, CA: SAGE Publications.

Duflo, E. (2012). Women empowerment and economic development. *Journal of Economic Literature*, *50*(4), 1051–1079.

Eswaran, M., & Malhotra, N. (2011). Domestic violence and women's autonomy in developing countries: Theory and evidence. *Canadian Journal of Economics*, *44*(4), 1222–1263.

General Economics Division. (2018). *Sustainable Development Goals: Bangladesh progress report 2018*. Dhaka: Government of the People's Republic of Bangladesh.

Heath, R. (2012). *Women's access to labor market opportunities, control of household resources, and domestic violence*. World Bank Policy Research Working Paper (6149). Retrieved from http://documents1.worldbank.org/curated/en/661101468156874780/pdf/WPS6149.pdf

Helal, M., & Hossain, M. A. (2013). Four decades of economic development of Bangladesh: An assessment. *Journal of the Asiatic Society of Bangladesh*, *58*(2), 335–362.

Herz, B. (1991). *Letting girls learn: Promising approaches in primary and secondary education* (Vol. 133). Washington, DC: World Bank Publications.

Hochschild, A., & Machung, A. (2012). *The second shift: Working families and the revolution at home* (reprint, with new preface ed.). New York, NY: Penguin Group.

Holland, D., Liadze, I., Rienzo, C., & Wilkinson, D. (2013). *The relationship between graduates and economic growth across countries*. BIS Research Paper 110. Retrieved from https://assets.publishing.service.gov.uk/government/uploads/system/uploads/attachment_data/file/229492/bis-13-858-relationship-between-graduates-and-economic-growth-across-countries.pdf

Ibrahim, S., & Alkire, S. (2007). Agency and empowerment: A proposal for internationally comparable indicators. *Oxford Development Studies*, *35*(4), 379–403.

Jensen, R. (2012). Do labor market opportunities affect young women's work and family decisions? Experimental evidence from India. *The Quarterly Journal of Economics*, *127*(2), 753–792. doi:10.1093/qje/qjs002

Jensen, R. T. (2010). Economic opportunities and gender differences in human capital: Experimental evidence for India. Retrieved from http://164.67.163.139/Documents/areas/ctr/marschak/w16021.pdf

Kabeer, N. (2001). Resources, agency, achievements. In A. Sisask (Ed.), *Discussing women's empowerment* (Vol. 3, pp. 17–57). Stockholm: Sidastudies.

Kabeer, N., & Mahmud, S. (2004). Rags, riches and women workers: Export-oriented garment manufacturing in Bangladesh. In M. Carr (Ed.), *Chains of fortune: Linking women producers and workers with global markets* (pp. 133–164). London: Commonwealth Secretariat.

Kabeer, N., Mahmud, S., & Tasneem, S. (2011). *Does paid work provide a pathway to women's empowerment? Empirical findings from Bangladesh*. IDS Working Paper 375. Retrieved from https://www.lse.ac.uk/gender/assets/documents/research/choice-constraints-and-the-gender-dynamics-of-lab/Does-paid-work-provide-a-pathway-to-womens-empowerment.pdf

Key Indicators of the Labour Market. (2015). Education and labour markets: Analysing global patterns with the KILM. Retrieved from http://www.ilo.org/wcmsp5/groups/public/—dgreports/—stat/documents/publication/wcms_424077.pdf

Khandker, S. R., & Samad, H. (2013). *Microfinance growth and poverty reduction in Bangladesh: What does the longitudinal data say?* Retrieved from http://beta.findevgateway.org/sites/default/files/publications/files/mfg-en-paper-microfinance-growth-and-poverty-reduction-in-bangladesh-what-does-the-longitudinal-data-say-mar-2013.pdf

Kishor, S., & Gupta, K. (2004). Women's empowerment in India and its states: Evidence from the NFHS. *Economic and Political Weekly*, *39*(7), 694–712.

Mahmud, S. (2003). *Female secondary school stipend programme in Bangladesh: A critical assessment*. Retrieved from https://www.researchgate.net/profile/Simeen_Mahmud/publication/268254362_Female_secondary_school_stipend_programme_in_Bangladesh_A_critical_assessment/links/56af172608ae19a385171049.pdf

Mehrotra, S., & Parida, J. K. (2017). Why is the labour force participation of women declining in India? *World Development*, *98*, 360–380.

Merriam, S. B. (2002). Introduction to qualitative research. In S. B. Merriam (Ed.), *Qualitative research in practice: Examples for discussion and analysis* (1st ed., pp. 1–17). San Francisco, CA: Jossey-Bass.

Molyneux, M. (1985). Mobilization without emancipation? Women's interests, the state, and revolution in Nicaragua. *Feminist Studies*, *11*(2), 227–254.

Moser, C. O. N. (1993). *Gender planning and development: Theory, practice and training*. London; New York, NY: Routledge.

Nunez, I., & Livanos, I. (2010). Higher education and unemployment in Europe: An analysis of the academic subject and national effects. *Higher Education*, *59*(4), 475–487.

Nussbaum, M. (2001). *Women and human development: The capabilities approach* (Vol. 3). Cambridge, MA: Cambridge University Press.

Olaniyan, D., & Okemakinde, T. (2008). Human capital theory: Implications for educational development. *Pakistan Journal of Social Sciences*, *5*(5), 479–483.

Palinkas, L. A., Horwitz, S. M., Green, C. A., Wisdom, J. P., Duan, N., & Hoagwood, K. (2015). Purposeful sampling for qualitative data collection and analysis in mixed method implementation research. *Administration and Policy in Mental Health and Mental Health Services Research*, *42*(5), 533–544.

Qian, N. (2008). Missing women and the price of tea in China: The effect of sex-specific earnings on sex imbalance. *The Quarterly Journal of Economics*, *123*(3), 1251–1285.

Rahman, R. I., & Islam, R. (2013). *Female labour force participation in Bangladesh: Trends, drivers and barriers*. Retrieved from http://www.oit.org/wcmsp5/groups/public/—asia/—ro-bangkok/—sro-new_delhi/documents/publication/wcms_250112.pdf

Ross, H. A., Shah, P. P., & Wang, L. (2011). Situating empowerment for millennial schoolgirls in Gujarat, India and Shaanxi, China. *Feminist Formations*, *23*(3), 23–47.

Schomburg, H., & Teichler, U. (2007). *Higher education and graduate employment in Europe: Results from graduates surveys from twelve countries* (Vol. 15). Berlin: Springer Science & Business Media.

Sen, A. (1985). Well-being, agency and freedom. *The Journal of Philosophy*, *82*, 169–221.

Sen, A. (1999). *Development as freedom* (1st ed.). New York, NY: Anchor Books.

Singh, S. (2007). Deconstructing 'gender and development'for 'identities of women'. *International Journal of Social Welfare*, *16*(2), 100–109.

Tembon, M., & Fort, L. (2008). *Girls' education in the 21st century: Gender equality, empowerment, and economic growth*. Washington, DC: World Bank.

Thein, T., Kabir, M., & Islam, M. (1988). *Evaluation of the female education scholarship program supported by the Asia foundation*. Washington, DC: USAID.

Unterhalter, E. (2007). *Gender, schooling and global social justice*. London; New York, NY: Routledge.

Visvanathan, N., Duggan, L., Nisonoff, L., & Wiegersma, N. (Eds.). (2011). *The women, gender, and development reader* (2nd ed.). London; New York, NY: Zed Books.

World Bank. (2012). World development report 2012: Gender equality and development. The World Bank, Washington, DC. Retrieved from https://siteresources.worldbank.org/INTWDR2012/Resources/7778105-1299699968583/7786210-1315936222006/Complete-Report.pdf

Yin, R. K. (2014). *Case study research: Design and methods* (5th ed.). Thousand Oaks, CA: SAGE Publications.

Chapter 13

Women's Access to Brazilian Higher Education: The Case of the Federal University of Santa Catarina

Silvana Rodrigues de Souza Sato,[a] *Mariele Martins Torquato,*[a] *and Ione Ribeiro Valle*[a]

The education of women is a recent phenomenon in history. For centuries, the woman was idealized as a character in the family situation of subordination and dependency of the father and the husband, being the right to education, historically neglected to them. In this way, for a long time, women have dedicated themselves to a private space and, consequently, have been far removed from a formal education. According to Aries (1981, p. 190), "in addition to domestic learning, girls were not, as it were, receiving any education. In families where boys went to school, they learned nothing." This was also the case in Brazil. According to Duarte (2000), during the colonial period, the number of schools in Brazil was very small. Only convents and seminaries were concerned to offer instruction to those who sought them out. However, their number was insufficient to change "substantially the customary cultural indulgence" (Duarte, 2000, p. 293). Based on large rural property and slave labor, the Brazilian economy paid little attention to formal education for men and no attention to women. Social stratification and the patriarchal family model favored a power structure founded on the authority of man. For Ribeiro (2000), the Iberian cultural tradition, brought from Portugal to the Brazilian colony, considered the woman an inferior being, so there was no need to teach her to read and write. Other factors were also important for disregard of women's education, such as the Church's monopoly on education and the action of the Society of Jesus, which advocated male dominance, as well as dogmatic forms and state authority

With the coming of the court, the situation gradually changed. From a common feeling that the nineteenth century represented the peak of civilization for the

[a]All authors are members of the Education and Training of Educators Research Group in Santa Catarina (GPEFESC) and the Pierre Bourdieu Sociological Research Laboratory (LAPSPB).

International Perspectives on Gender and Higher Education, 231–248

doi:10.1108/978-1-83909-886-420201013

bourgeois society, everyone seemed to agree that it was no longer possible to accept that the population was in such opposite situations, for while some held all the privileges and powers, others lived in an absurd situation of inferiority. Gradually, a new perspective emerged, manifested by opinions expressed in newspapers that society would not evolve if there were not also the concern with the education of women and the ability to participate with men in the progress and techniques of science. With the Independence of the country, in 1822, the Brazilian society began to present a more complex social structure. As a result of immigration and economic diversity, the demand for education has increased and is now seen by the intermediate social strata as a tool for social ascension. In this new context, on the part of the leaders of the country, the concern with the feminine education, especially for the economic elite, appears. Early empire legislators established that primary education should be state-owned and extended to girls. However, these classes should be governed only by women. Due to the shortage of qualified teachers and the lack of interest on the part of the parents toward the education of the daughters, the feminine education was reduced to the read and write and covered a reduced percentage of students.

In the first half of the nineteenth century, the first institutions for the teaching of women emerged, but this was a dual teaching framework with strong gender distinctions. Women had primary education focused on moral and social content, aimed at improving the role of mother and wife. Secondary education was restricted, for the most part, to the teaching profession, that is, to the training of primary school teachers. Despite these advances, women remained excluded from the highest levels of education during the nineteenth century. If access to elementary education was difficult for women, higher education was only male, leaving women excluded from the first higher education. Only in 1881, by means of an imperial decree, women were granted the right to enroll in higher education. However, secondary education was expensive and essentially male, and normal courses did not empower women into colleges. In the movement of resistance to the current norms, some women were pioneers and overcame strong obstacles. This is the case of Rita Lobato Velho Lopes, the first woman to obtain a medical degree in Brazil in 1887. Romanelli (2001) points out that, during the nineteenth century and the first half of the twentieth century, the exclusion of women from secondary education made it difficult entry into higher education. As we can see, gender duality and segmentation were present in the Brazilian educational system, from the earliest initiatives aimed at schooling the population: women had the lowest rates of literacy and had restricted access to the highest levels of education. At the beginning of the twentieth century, the female presence in secondary and higher education, however, increased in a much lower proportion than that of men. Between 1907 and 1912, the female presence in secondary schools represented a quarter of the total number of students and in higher education, women did not reach 1.5% of the total number of students in the Federal District, where there were the best educational rates in the country (Table 13.1).

We can observe that the most significant advances in women's education occurred after the revolution of 1930. It is worth mentioning the participation of the Brazilian Association of Education (ABE) in this process, in which

Table 13.1. Number of Students Enrolled in Secondary and Higher Education Federal District: 1907–1912.

	Secondary Level			Higher Level		
Year	**Men**	**Women**	**% Women**	**Men**	**Women**	**% Women**
1907	3,721	1,221	24.7	2,455	32	1.3
1909	4,596	1,460	24.1	3,323	39	1.2
1912	7,165	2,145	23.0	3,630	53	1.4

Source: Statistics of the twentieth century (Beltrão & Alves, 2004).

education, both feminine and masculine, plays the role of indispensable tool for "progress of the country." It was the so-called period of "enthusiasm for education," which aimed to "invest in the assembly of a school apparatus that would ensure the organization of the nation through the organization of cultures" (Carvalho, 1997, p. 116).

The 1930 revolution, by redirecting Brazilian development to the domestic market and to the industrial urban sector, made it possible to create the first mass public policies, especially for urban populations. The first demands of industrialization influenced the expansion of education, but as the expansion of capitalism did not take place on an equal basis throughout the national territory, the greatest expansion of school demand only developed in regions where capitalist relations were more advanced. Thus, during the so-called Pact Populist (1945–1964), the school system began to suffer strong social pressure, due to demands for greater access to education. However, because of the agreements of the ruling elite, the "aristocratic" character of the school was maintained, with concrete consequences for the democratization of education. It is important to note that only in 1961, through the Law on Guidelines and Bases (LDB) of the Brazilian Education, did the equivalence of all the medium-level courses were guaranteed, enabling women who had the teaching profession to compete for a vague in higher education.

The choice of methodological procedures is always linked to the research problem. The main question of this proposal is to understand if there were changes in the access of women to the Federal University of Santa Catarina (UFSC), through the analysis of the gender variable of the enrolled and classified in the vestibular competitions (2001–2015). The self-declared sex of the candidates is of paramount importance for the understanding of the prolongation of the studies and also in the relation with the professional choices. To compose this research, we used the socioeconomic questionnaires answered by the candidates at the time of enrollment in the selections.

The quantitative approach was present throughout this longitudinal study. Bardin (2011), in describing differences between quantitative and qualitative analysis, says that the former "is based on the frequency of appearance of certain elements" (p. 144). But even if the author points to a path of use of both forms or, moreover, defends the qualitative analysis, it does not fail to emphasize that the quantitative approach "obtains descriptive data by means of a statistical method. Thanks to a systematic discount, this analysis is more objective, more faithful, and more accurate, since observation is better controlled" (p. 145). We bet on the content of this statement and made use of the Microsoft Excel Program that helped us to tabulate the data, verify the hypothesis of research, formulate categories of analysis, and achieve results.

The proposal presented here is an introduction that deals with the historical panorama on women's access to education and, more precisely, at the higher level. In the sequence we present the profile of the student according to the sex variable to Brazilian higher education. Shortly thereafter comparisons were made regarding the enrollment and classification of women and men at the Federal University of Santa Catarina. Questions about enrollments in Higher Education Institutions (HEIs), administrative dependencies of them, and shifts attended by the students added up in the analysis undertaken. The last part of the proposal provides empirical data on the access of candidates who enrolled and qualified in the most popular courses of UFSC between 2001 and 2015.

1. The Profile of Ingressants in Brazilian Higher Education: Women in Highlight, Less at UFSC

In the year 2014, we had in Brazil 55.5% of women and 44.5% of men among the population in general. However, in the age of higher education (20–24 years), the population is divided into 50%, thus on the profile of students at this level of education, considering several variables such as sex linked to enrollment in higher education; enrollment by administrative category; enrollment by turns; and enrollment by sex in the most sought-after courses in Brazil and the Federal University of Santa Catarina. The mobilization of these variables seemed relevant to us to better understand the participation of women in this stage of education.

During the period from 2008 to 2012, the participation of women, both among those enrolled in the entrance examinations and among the candidates who have access to the Brazilian Higher Education, here denominated entrants, presented higher rates than the men. Census data show a significant superiority of female students, representing 55.4% of the total student population at this level of education (Fig. 13.1).

However, in the federal educational institutions, the difference between men and women is smaller, due to their strong presence in the Federal Institutes and Federal Centers of Technological Education (CEFETs), where the courses are traditionally linked to the masculine universe. Even so, women's participation grows, making the difference small, since men figure in 51.5% of the specific vacancies of the courses of technologists. Analyzing the private institutions, where the greatest expansion of higher education occurred, the difference between men and women is greater, and this number reaches approximately 29.6% of female superiority. The administrative categories are the majority, corresponding to 51.5% in federal institutions, 54.5% in state, 56.2% in municipal, and 56.4% in private institutions.

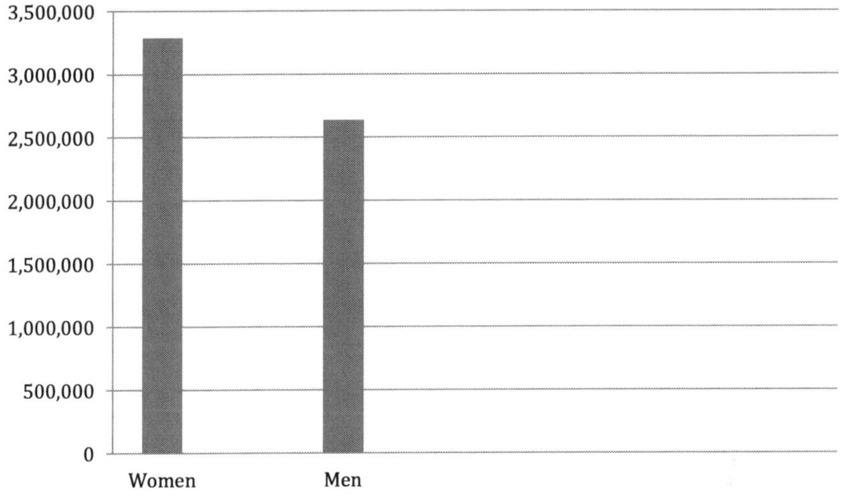

Fig. 13.1. Number of Enrollments in Face-to-Face Courses in Institutions of Higher Education, According to Sex—Brazil—2012. *Source:* INEP/MEC (2012).

In Brazil, women constitute a majority in higher education in all administrative categories, as a result of a series of strategies that have long been attempting to be better recognized and to respond to their new social roles. Thus, women have strongly assumed responsibilities in family composition: data from the IBGE (2011) indicate that 37.4% of families have women by reference. We still understand that it is relevant to point out that 18.5 million women support their families in the country. This paradigm shift in which men have traditionally been providers has been demanding from women a great deal of effort to increase their income, since 31% of female-headed households live on a monthly income of up to a half per capita minimum wage, while in male-headed households this percentage drops to 26.8%. The struggle of women thus includes the search for the expansion and extension of schooling, with the aim of equalizing and/or compensating for the lags found in the labor market, where women occupy the same positions as men, women earn less. Other references come from the educational and family relationships, since women are blamed for the school performance of their children and they are expected to follow and guide them in school processes. The United Nations Educational, Scientific and Cultural Organization (UNESCO) and the United Nations Children's Fund (UNICEF) encourage schooling of women in developing countries, as their studies point to the relationship between better school performances of children with the maternal school levels.

The results obtained in higher education derive from the strategies that women adopt throughout their lives, in order to cover all stages of schooling. The dynamics of women in Brazilian higher education demand a significant analysis, as it is currently observed a movement that, while maintaining elements of the traditional trajectories in courses considered feminine, such as degrees and middle positions in the areas of health, such as nursing, psychology, among others, they stand out expressively for male careers.

With regard to college courses, demographic censuses reveal that, more and more, students are looking for evening grades. However, we highlight the participation of women in this choice. Of the total number of women enrolled in higher education, 62% now attend night classes. A change of paradigm is observed here, since data prior to 2002 show that women's night shift demand was low. This reality was tied to the almost exclusivity of the care of the children, exercised by the women and demanding of them to be in the home at night. Changes observed in this sense have allowed men also to exercise this activity, releasing them for the entrance into nocturnal studies, and it is important to emphasize that more than 50% of the women students of the nocturnal higher education are mothers (IBGE 2014). The finding of the largest number of female students in the Brazilian university in the night period demonstrates the possibility of the increase of the choice of the courses by the women, since there is more offer in this shift of said male courses. The so-called female courses (pedagogy, nursing, pharmacy) are more concentrated during the daytime in public institutions. It is necessary to emphasize that students of the night period are, as a rule, those that conciliate work and studies, situation that focuses on their real possibilities of learning. Thanks to a series of studies, we know that there is a conflicting relationship between these students and the academic knowledge, among them, the lack of ability with oral and written expression, the aversion to dense texts, processes that can result in a lack of education expected from university education. Although this is not at the core of our interests, what we want to demonstrate is that there is an additional effort for these students, who certainly accumulate formal work and studies, a significant part of private work still, most of the time, tied to the feminine as demand. Regarding the profile of the students, it refers to the fact that women are entering, more and more, in baccalaureate courses. Differently from what was seen until the 1980s, when they entered almost exclusively undergraduate courses and subareas of health, organizing careers, although they were a majority, remained in subordinate positions, while the male minority organized trajectories of leadership positions, as shown by studies on the teaching career.

If the course of Pedagogy is still the most sought-after course for women, 93.4% (Table 13.2) and this option, such as Campos and Silva (2002), Valle (2003), pronounced with important contributions that link this choice to the condition of women in patriarchal model societies, the counterpoint is in the search for courses such as administration and law, positioned in our table as second and third options, which configure a new reality of Brazilian academic scenarios. These professions (law and administration), characteristically, were occupied substantially by men, which is reflected very much in the positions of prestige of a country. For example, in public administration only recently women hold seats in power and in the political sphere, Brazil had its first woman president only in 2010, preceded by 35 men since the proclamation of the republic, indicating the process of masculinization of the command, in counterpoint the

Table 13.2. Ten Courses with the Highest Enrollment of Women and Men—2012—Brazil.

Women Enrollments			
Women	**Enrollments**	**Men**	**Enrollments**
Pedagogy	556,283	Administration	372,893
Administration	460,149	Law	345,999
Law	391,272	Civil Engineering	143,868
Nursing	198,872	Accounting Sciences	132,017
Accounting Sciences	181,157	Computer Science	108,874
Social service	157,242	Production Engineering	90,266
Personal Management/ Human Resources	135,067	Mechanical Engineering	75,936
Psychology	131,786	Training of Physical Education professionals	71,293
Physiotherapy	81,982	Electrical engineering	67,303
Pharmacy	72,342	Logistics management	61,054

Source: INEP/MEC (2012).

feminization of subalternity. In the private sector, they represent only 9% of the management positions of the largest companies. In the judiciary, the participation between men and women is also no different, since the representativeness of women in relation to the spaces of power and decision are insignificant. In addition, this percentage decreases gradually according to the higher instances and positions provided by indication, according to IBGE (2011). In this context, the importance of the numbers on the agenda is analyzed, which show that even though the second and third options are the administration (56.5%) and law (54.2%) courses for female participants, they are still in greater numbers, if compared to the first male option. In this context, it is important to note that men take an average of 4–5 years to complete the courses of administration and law and women take 5 years, according to ENADE (2012), but when computed the national average of completion of all higher education, women tend to complete faster than the incoming men. Thus, we can infer that there is a difficulty related to careers considered masculine, corroborating this idea, we can observe that the movement of women in engineering courses is very low, since among the ten most sought-after courses in Brazil, women do not appear in any of the four engineering majors in the entrance of men.

2. Arriving at the UFSC and Observing the Dynamics of Women

The Federal University of Santa Catarina has the peculiarity of being distinguished from the other Brazilian institutions by the smaller admission of women. In order to better understand this phenomenon, we mobilized the data "enrolled in the vestibular" and "new entrants by sex in the UFSC," in addition to the same categories of analysis investigated and used in the macro Brazilian reality: enrollment by sex; enrollment per shift; and courses in the institution.

2.1. UFSC Enrollment by Sex

In the year of 2010 we carried out a study in partnership with Valle, Sato, and Besen (2010) on the enrollment indexes and classifications of women and men in the UFSC between the years of 1981 to 2009. During the first years, men represented the majority of the number of enrollments (59.3% in 1981). The difference between the number of men and women enrolled in the vestibular decreased gradually until reaching a certain stability. Between 1990 and 1994 the number of male and female applications accounted for approximately 50% of applications. Since 1995, we have seen a significant change in enrollment that will reverberate to the present day: the number of women enrolled grows with the growing number of general applications in the competitions.

However, it was the men who presented the best performance; they get the highest ratings. This trend has been easing over the investigation period. If they represented 59.3% of those classified in 1981, in 2009, they occupied 53.6% of the total number of places. We highlight the year 1996 in which women occupied for the first and only time the largest number of university chairs: 53% of the total.

The continuity of the research shows that in the vestibular competitions of the UFSC, women continue to enroll in greater numbers. However, it is men who get the highest ratings. We can observe the phenomenon described in Fig. 13.2.

From 2001 to 2007, candidates for university positions registered around 52% and men 48%. In the next 4 years (2008–2012), women's applications gained more force, reaching 54% of the house, against 46% of the male applications. Thus, from 2007 to 2012, the difference between the number of women and men doubles by four percentage points to eight. In the last 3 years (2013–2015), we have had few changes, although the difference persists, it is lower: six percentage points. If the number of registrations of women is always greater than that of men, in relation to the classifications, the movement goes in the opposite direction, since the men are classified in greater number than the candidates, which can be verified in the figure above. Between 2001 and 2006, male and female grades ranged from 53% to 56% for men and 47% for women and 44% for women. But from 2007 to 2013, the difference in sex census figures narrowed as if in 2007, the difference was eight percentage points more than male classifications in 2013 falls to two percentage points, almost equaling the number of classifications between men and women. In the last 2 years (2014 and 2015), a number of male classifications resumed growth, distancing itself again from women. Highlights for the year 2015: 59% of the total number of places were occupied by men.

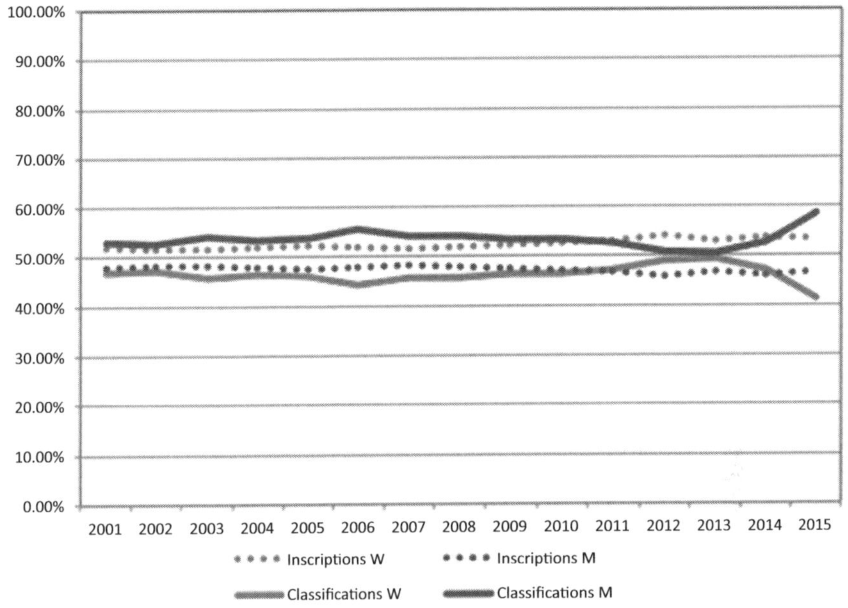

Fig. 13.2. Relation of the Number of Enrolled and Classified in the Vestibular Competitions of the UFSC According to the Sex. *Source:* Data from socioeconomic questionnaires COPERVE/UFSC (2001–2015), Sato (2018).

2.2. The Dynamics of Women per Shift at UFSC

Unlike the Brazilian general framework, UFSC night classes are attended mostly by men. Even when it comes to courses offered in two periods, the female presence is always less. Of the 20 evening courses offered by the institution, they represent only 30% of the students. These data lead us to consider that this option makes it even more difficult for women to enter, even in view of the fact that most night courses have less competition for admission, there are other factors for choosing the female graduations (Table 13.3).

2.3. The Female Audience in the Most Sought-after Courses at UFSC

Among the ten courses most sought by women in UFSC, there are those who do not correspond to the table, namely administration and law and in others considered as male courses. This is surprising, because there is an imagination that in the South of Brazil, women have better cultural levels and there are official data that have better economic conditions, which in some way should affect the possibilities of transit between other courses. But what was visualized in the research was contrary movement: the maintenance of traditional choices

Table 13.3. Most Wanted Courses in the UFSC by Men and Women between the Years of 2008 and 2012.

Courses with Greater Participation Female	Courses with Greater Participation Male
Pedagogy	Computer Science
Nutrition	Computer Engineering
Nursing	Electronic Engineering
Social service	Control Engineering and Automation
Executive Secretary	Mathematics and Scientific Computing
Spanish Lyrics	Mechanical Engineering
Speech Therapy	Electrical Engineering
Psychology	Information System
French Lyrics	Physics
Portuguese Lyrics	Production Engineering

Source: Coperve/UFSC (2013).

within the old patriarchal milestones of choices and classification in academic courses. One information present in the data that seems relevant is that only half the courses chosen by women work at night in the UFSC, in counterpoint to the most sought-after courses by men, who mostly work full-time (as is the case of graduations of engineering) or are available only at night. Thus, it remains to question how much the institutional organization contributes to this reality and, still, how much it prevents the entrance of the most popular layers in the public university. Is the UFSC working for the maintenance and reproduction of social inequalities and patriarchal bases, or does this institution disregard the possible demands of less elitist sectors of the population when it comes to entering the higher level?

3. The Presence of Women in the Five Most Popular Courses at UFSC

For a long time, different studies have shown that Brazilian public universities are historically considered to be elitist because they provide reproduction and continuity of studies more for certain class fractions than for others. In this same vein are the courses of greater demand and therefore our focus of analysis turned to them. If, according to Langouët (2002), the democratization of education occurs when individuals from different social groups coexist in the same educational spaces, the great question we seek to answer regarding the gender variable is whether at least a similar number of men and women are registering and classifying for the most popular courses at UFSC?

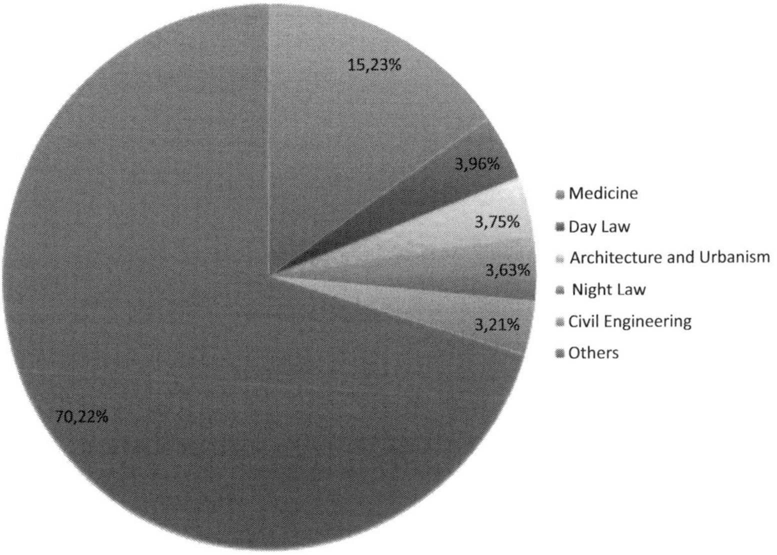

Fig. 13.3. Percentage of Enrollments in the Courses of Greatest Demand of UFSC between the Years 2001 and 2015. *Source:* Data collected on the COPERVE/UFSC website (2001–2015) – Sato (2018).

In the universe of 506,214 enrollments that the university received between 2001 and 2015, the courses of greatest demand, that is, those that the applicants to a university more enrolled were the following, in descending order: Medicine, Day, Architecture and Urbanism, Night Law and Civil Engineering. Together these graduations totaled about 30% of the total enrollment, with emphasis on the Medicine course, which represents half of this percentage (Fig. 13.3).

Reflecting on the sexual inequalities revealed in the marked differences in the school trajectories of men and women always requires reaffirming that the history of school institutions was not common to both sexes. For a long time, classrooms were occupied by the eldest son of the family and only a long time later by the daughters. Past customs and conditions imposed on women delayed access to literacy and teaching, and when they were able to reach school, their courses were shorter than those of men. Studies have demonstrated the consequences of differential treatment of men and women in access to education, as well as the opening of school doors for both sexes after education claims for all Brazilians mainly in the years 1968 and in the country's redemocratization in 1980, as we have already mentioned in the introduction of this work.

However, Baudelot and Establet (2009) emphasize that thinking about social justice and the effectiveness of a school system cannot be based only on factors such as differences in results between social classes or countries of origin of students, but also on inequalities between the sexes. As a result of years of exclusion from school reserved for men or condemnation to studies aimed at the status of mothers and/or wives, women have occupied little of the training spaces for a long time. But as educational researches and particularly this study have shown, in the last 40 years, the female public has begun to look more for educational establishments, including universities, such as the UFSC. But the reflection of history is revealed at the moment of choosing a professional career with a consequence on the registration and classification in undergraduate courses. As much as today we can emphasize the greater demand of women for university education, our research shows that it is men who are able to access this level of education in greater numbers and that, in addition, some professional careers remain closed to them. Therefore, as the authors above state "if the differences have decreased [between men and women], they are far from disappearing" (p. 99).

3.1. Medicine and Day Law: Female Inscriptions and Male Classifications

Between the years of 2001 and 2015, graduation in Medicine has always been more required by the female audience. The average number of registrations made by women was 62.2% and that of men was 37.8%, and over the period, they started to apply more (9%). The contrary movement occurred in the analyzed data regarding the classifications. In 10 of the 15 years surveyed, men ranked higher than women. What we can see in the figure below (Fig. 13.4).

In relation to the classifications of men and women in the medical course, we can characterize them in two stages, which oscillate: 2001 to 2008, phase in which more men are classified (2001, 2002, 2003, and 2005), best represented phase by women (2004, 2006, 2007, and 2008). With emphasis on the years 2002 and 2005, in which the men classified, respectively, 28% and 24% more than the number of women. The year 2008 highlights the fact that the percentage of women classified is 18% more than men. The second stage shows the great presence of men who were approved and classified in the course. From 2009 to 2015, in 2014 alone, there are practically the same number of men and women classified (50% for each sex), and in all other years the highest percentage was for men. The high percentage of men's classification in 2009 and 2010 stands out, in this order 66.3% and 62.3%.

As in the medical course, in the daytime law, women ran in ever higher numbers than men, on average 60% of women candidates versus 40% men. The distance between the sexes becomes smaller as regards the classification, when we observe that in 15 years, approximately 50% (average) of each sex can access university chairs. But unlike the inscriptions, the number of women and men classified fluctuates quite depending on the year.

As stated above, the highest number of entries has always been made by women rather than men. But at the beginning of the period covered, 2001, the percentages of entries between women and men were closer. Especially after the year 2008, they were moving away and the number of female applications increased considerably.

From 2001 to 2007, the number of registrations made by women was 55% on average, while that of men was around 45%. As of 2008, there was a greater

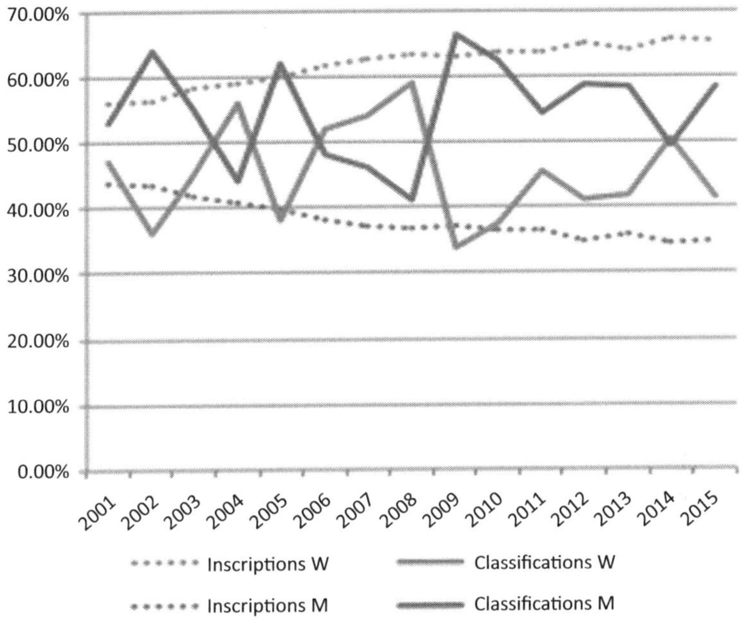

Fig. 13.4. Inscriptions and Classifications of Women and Men in the Medical Course. *Source:* Data collected in the socioeconomic questionnaires of COPERVE/UFSC (2001–2015), Sato (2018).

demand by the female public, marking a growth of 8% between 2008 and 2012. In the next phase, this demand declined somewhat (from 65.4% to 62.8%) but continues high.

The highest indexes were obtained by men, between the years of 2001 and 2007. Between 2008 and 2012, the highest percentage of classified was women, except for 2011, the year in which 51% of the classified were declared male. From 2013 to 2015, women ranked highest in 2 years. It should be noted that in the years 2004 and 2006, the percentages of men classified were close to 60% and that in the other years these percentages between the sexes were very close, even if at one point one ranked more than the other. Another issue observed was that in the first years of the period (2001–2007), men ranked more than women, a fact that reverts in recent years, with the exception of the years of 2011 and 2014. But in the overall performance of 15 years, the men ranked more in the second most searched course by the candidates to the positions of right.

3.2. Architecture and Urbanism: A Female Graduation

The women were the ones that made the most inscriptions in the course of Architecture and Urbanism during the studied period. In the first phase, the percentage of female applications rose between 67% and 71.4%. In the following two steps, the percentage has always been above 70%, reaching the percentage of more than 74% in the years 2010, 2012, and 2013.

Unlike the previous two courses, there was a large presence of women in the competition classification lists, but what differs from the moment of the inscriptions was that they occupied more university seats in the first phase than in the later ones (from 2001 to 2015, there was a decrease of 17.6% in the participation of women). Between 2001 and 2007, the percentages of women's classification reached high rates between 66% and 79.7%. In the second phase (2008–2012), in the first 2 years and in the penultimate, the annual percentage always exceeded 70% of female approval, remaining in another 2 years, around 63%. Noteworthy for the year 2012, the lowest percentage of female classification of the period occurred (58.3%). Between the years of 2013 and 2015, there is a reduction in the classification of women. The indexes ranged from 66% to 60%.

The data analyzed still show the continuous, but sometimes oscillating, elevation of the masculine public that managed to be classified in greater percentages for the Architecture and Urbanism course, mainly from 2012 to 2015, in which the success percentages of these candidates reached about 40% per year.

3.3. Night Law and Civil Engineering: Courses with a Male Profile

In most of the years investigated, men enrolled in higher numbers for the Night Law course. From 2001 to 2007, in 6 years, the largest number of applications was male (between 53% and 57%). In the year 2006, there was practically a division in the total number of registrations, 50.86% were made by women and 49.14% by men.

The second phase (2008–2012) again was marked by the largest number of male entries. Of the 5 years of this stage, in three the men applied for more, between 50.6% and 56.2%. In 2011, the number of registrations of men and women was practically the same (49.64% and 50.36%, respectively). From the year 2012, women came to predominate in the scenario, reaching between 54.3% and 56.7% of the total enrollment. Different table was drawn regarding the classifications, with the exception of the year 2014, in the others always the largest number of successful in the contests was of men.

The data that represent the male classification for the Night Law course show some instability but register high performance percentages. From 2001 to 2007, the percentages fluctuate by 20% (72.5% to 52.5%). At this stage, we find the lowest percentage of female classification: 27.5% (2001). Still, in 2005 and 2006, in these 2 years, we had the lowest rates of men entering the course (52.5%); consequently, a greater approximation between men and women occurred in the first phase of the survey. In the second stage, men ranged from approximately 58% to 72%. From 2012 to 2013, there was a decrease of almost 9% in the men's classification, a decrease that is accentuated from 2013 to 2014, plus 9%. But in the last year of the survey, the male classifications returned to mark great growth: 17.8%.

Another course that has always received the largest number of applications made by men and, also, have always managed to rank in higher numbers than women was the fifth most sought of the institution, Civil Engineering. However, it was observed that there was a movement of reduction of the demand for this graduation by the men during the studied period, less than 11.3%, and in a smaller percentage (approximately 4%), as the classifications.

The reduction in the number of applications by men was more evident in the second and third phases. Between 2001 and 2007, male enrollments were around 75% and 78%, and there were decreases in the year 2002 and 2007 to the approximate house of 73%. In the year 2008, they grew again, 77.9%. This increase does not persist in later years. From 2008 to 2009, there was a drop of more or less 8% in male enrollments and a 3.5% increase by 2012. In the first 2 years of the last stage, the reduction continues, reaching 61% of enrollments made by men in 2014. In 2015, there was an increase of 5.6% in male applications for the Civil Engineering course. That is, if from 2008 to 2014, there was a reduction in demand for graduation by men, in that period the female demand increased by 16.6%.

If, as we have seen, women are enrolling more for Civil Engineering chairs in the last 8 years of this research, the advance in the objective chance of attending the undergraduate degree did not follow the same indexes, since they were not able to classify themselves in the same proportion as have signed up. From 2001 to 2007, we had a completely irregular stage in the number of classifications, from 7 years, in four the rankings were around 26% to 32% and in the other three, they fell to the percentages between 12.7% and 16%. The second phase was the only one in which there was an increase of almost 10% (from 23% to 32.6%) and in the latter occurred again a fall in the classifications of women.

It should also be noted that in only 3 years women have managed to reach over 30% of the total classifications for the Civil Engineering course (2005, 2007, and 2010). In addition, the male ranking figures never fell from the high mark of 67.3%, reaching 87.2% in the year 2002.

In summary, through the treatment of the data referring to the sex self-declared by the enrollees and classified in the most popular courses of the UFSC, we can affirm that regarding the similarities between the two groups, there were many more permanencies than changes throughout the studied period. When analyzing the data of all the candidates, we confirmed the largest number of registrations being performed by women, and the ratings have always been more successful for men. The same occurred in the courses of Medicine and Day Law, that is, the female public is more enrolled in these degrees, but it is the men that access more to the university chairs. The increase in enrollments and female classifications after 2007/2008 in the last year should be noted.

The Architecture and Urbanism course has always received more applications and, consequently, more approvals from women. What has been changing in the last phase (2013–2015), since the men began to demonstrate better performances in the competitions for this graduation, even though they did not surpass the classification indices of the women.

As for the inscriptions in the courses of Night Law and Civil Engineering, contrary movement occurred, since it is the men that are enrolled in greater numbers. We emphasize that in the last years of the survey, women are also looking for more than these two courses, which increased the percentage of enrollment of candidates of this sex. However, the classification rates of men in the Night Law degree were always higher than those of women, except in 1 year, 2014. And in the Civil Engineering course, from 2008, we observed a higher demand and classification of the group female. But the increase in registrations is much more evident than the classification of the candidates.

Democratizing access to higher education is an important but not a defining part of social justice in education. This is the synthesis of this study, which, when mapping the studies on the access of women to the university level, observed that there is an important contribution of researchers indicating that the female choices of the offered courses are not random choices, since the socioeconomic condition and partners often define its positions and provisions in the field of professions. Although traversed by the historical bias of patriarchal traditions, when they enter higher education, there is an empowerment of the feminine that increases their prestige in family, political, and labor relations. Thus, feminist studies reveal the difficulties of reconciling access to higher schooling in the face of the imposition of preestablished roles in marriage and motherhood.

The disparities in the time of enrollment and classification in different university courses between the sexes allow us to evaluate the dynamics of the formation of women who, in this context, have specific contexts in which their movements use the expansion of the higher education system to enter the spaces with force which directly affect the hierarchies of courses and accesses within the administrative categories, referring to old patriarchal milestones and, at the same time, flowing into previously exclusive spaces for men.

Our studies allow us to observe that gender struggles in this field are very directly associated with class struggles, because for women, the highest admission courses are those with low social and economic value, such as the Pedagogy course UFSC. As we have seen, in spite of the important expansion of the opportunities of higher education registered in the last years in Brazil, the inequalities persist. They appear in different forms, particularly as regards the situation of women in higher education. When we use as an illustration the micro reality of UFSC, we note that this university differs significantly from other higher education institutions in the country. In the UFSC, despite higher enrollment of women in vestibular exams, their admission is lower than that of men. We are called attention, for example, to the fact that they remain firm in the entrance to the Pedagogy course, without flowing to the other areas, as it happens in the national scene. In the analysis of the organization of the institution it was possible to see that the non-offer of this graduation in the night can be one of the factors that affect the lower admission of women in the UFSC, since the profile of these students happens at a later age, and by women already in the labor market, which would lead to inscriptions in the night.

We can infer that the UFSC aggravates social reproduction, as we observe the movement of women in the interior does not realize the meager gains observed in the macro system. That is, if in the national scenario there is a flow in baccalaureate courses and with higher valuations such as administration and law, the same did not occur in the research institution, what prevails in the UFSC is the historical linking of its services with "the heirs."

In general, the vestibular competitions of the UFSC, of the studied period, have always received, in greater number, inscriptions of women. In contrast, it was the men who scored the most. When we treat the data referring to all the courses of the institution, we confirm the absence of variations with respect to the variable sex in the inscriptions and classifications. However, as we investigate the category in the five most sought-after courses, we note a greater democratization in some grades in recent years. In the course of Architecture and Urbanism, we began to have more number of inscriptions and masculine classifications. On the other hand, there was an increase in the number of women enrolled and classified in Civil and Law courses of the night shift. That is, these findings help us to note that there are some changes in women's access to UFSC's most sought-after courses, as well as the provision of free pre-university courses and affirmative action policies. These actions contribute to the greater female presence in federal higher education in Santa Catarina.

References

Aries, P. (1981). *História Social da Criança e da Família* [*Social History of the Child and Family*]. Rio de Janeiro: Zahar.

Bardin, L. (2011). *Análise de conteúdo* [*Analysis of content*]. Tradução [Translation]: Luís Antero Reto, Augusto Pinheiro. São Paulo: Edições 70.

Baudelot, C., & Establet, R. (2009, March). *L'elitisme républicain: L'école française à L'épreuve des comparaisons internationales* [*Republican elitism: The French school in the test of international comparisons*]. Paris: Éditions du Seuil et La République des Idées.

Beltrão, K. I, & Alves, J. E. D. (2009). The Reversal of the gender Hiatus in 20th Century Brazilian Education. Cad. Pesquisa (online). Vol. 39, no. 136, pp. 125–156. Available in: http:/www.metas2015.unb.br/Documentos/Educação%20Universal/Reversão%20do%20hiato%20de%20genero%20na%20%educacao.pdf. Accessed on June 28, 2014.

Campos, M. C. S. S., & Silva, V. L. G. (Eds.). (2002). *Feminização do magistério: vestígios do passado que marcam o presente* [*Feminization of teaching: vestiges of the past that mark the present*]. Bragança Paulista: EDUSF.

Carvalho, M. M. C. (1997). In W. P. Costa & H. C. Delorenzo (Eds.), *A Década de 1920 e as Origens do Brasil Moderno* [*The 1920's and the Origins of Modern Brazil*]. São Paulo: UNESP.

COPERVE/UFSC (2013) (Permanent Entrance Exam Commission). Higher Education Census and Statistics, UFSC – 2008, 2009, 2010, 2011e 2012. Available in: http:www.coperve.ufsc.br. Accessed on June 22.

Duarte, C. L. (2000). Nísia Floresta Brasileira Augusta [Brazilian Writers of the 19th Century]. In Z. L. Muzart (Ed.), *Escritoras Brasileiras do Século XIX*. Florianópolis: Mulheres.

ENADE (Exame Nacional de Cursos). (2012). Censo 2012 [Census 2012]. Retrieved from http://download.inep.gov.br/educacao_superior/enade/manuais/manual_enade_2014.pdf. Accessed on July 29, 2014.

IBGE (Instituto Brasileiro de Geografia e Estatística). (2011). Censo 2011 [Census 2011]. Retrieved from http://www.ibge.gov.br/home/estatistica/economia/perfilmunic/2011/. Accessed on July 29, 2014.

IBGE. (2014). (Brazilian Institute of Geography and Statistics). Demographic Census of Brazil (CENSUS) 2010. Available in: http://www.ibge.gov.br/home/estatistica/economia/perfilmunic/2010/. Accessed on July 29

INEP/MEC. (2012). Censo e Sinopse Estatísticas do Ensino Superior [Census and Synopsis Statistics of Higher Education], INEP/MEC – 1933, 1945, 1960, 1965, 1970, 1980, 1990, 1995, 2000, 2001 e 2012. Retrieved from http:www.inep.gov.br. Accessed on August 25, 2013.

Langouët, G. (2002, July/December). A escola francesa se democratiza, mas a inserção social torna-se cada vez mais difícil [The French school is democratized, but social insertion becomes more and more difficult]. *Revista Perspectiva* [*Perspectiva Magazine*], Florianópolis, *20*(Especial), 85–106.

Minayo, M. C. S., & Sanches, O. (1993, July/September). Quantitativo-qualitativo: oposição ou complementaridade? [*Quantitative-qualitative: opposition or complementarity?*] *Caderno de Saúde Pública*, Rio de Janeiro, *9*(3), 237–248.

Ribeiro, A. I. M. (2000). Mulheres educadas na colônia [Women educated in the colony]. In E. M. T. Lopes, L. M. F. Faria, & C. G. Veiga (Eds.), *500 anos de educação no Brasil* [*500 years of education in Brazil*]. Belo Horizonte: Autêntica.

Romanelli, O. (2001). *História da educação no Brasil (1930/1973)* [*History of Education in Brazil (1930/1973)*]. Petrópolis: Vozes.

Sato, S. R. S. S. (2018). *Movimentos de Democratização do Acesso: análise do perfil dos inscritos e classificados à Universidade federal de Santa Catarina em perspectiva longitudinal (2001–2015)* [*Access Democratization Movements: analysis of the profile of those enrolled and classified at the Federal University of Santa Catarina in a longitudinal perspective (2001–2015)*]. Tese de Doutorado, Universidade Federal de Santa Catarina, Florianópolis.

Valle, I. R. (2003). The Era of professionalization: Training and socialization of the teaching staff from 1st to 4th grade. Florianópolis: Cidade Futura.

Valle, I. R., Sato, S. R. S., & Besen, D. S. (2010). Who obtains the best classifications indices in the UFCS entrance exams (1981–2009): Men or Women? In: VIII Research Meeting on Education in the Southern Region, Londrina. Proccedings of the event. Londrina: ANPEd Sul., 1–18.

Chapter 14

Access and Gender Equity in Colombian Higher Education: From Aspirations to Success

Lina Uribe-Correa and Aldo Hernández-Barrios

1. Method

In order to analyze the state of gender participation in higher education and its recent evolution, we use quantitative indicators from several national databases provided by the Colombian Ministry of Education (SNIES, SPADIES, and OLE), as well as by UNESCO Institute of Statistics, CEPAL and OECD.

In conducing this analysis, we take into account the conceptual framework, categories, and some of the relevant indicators provided by Uribe-Correa (2012) in regard to the concept of *access*. Access implies the extent to which it covers not only the entry point to higher education but also the permanence of individuals to successfully complete their academic programs. According to Uribe-Correa (2012), the concept of access includes the categories of *coverage, equity, retention*, and *graduation*. We join the categories of coverage and equity (bearing in mind that the main topic of this chapter is gender participation in higher education). In addition, we incorporate other indicators that account for insertion of women and men to the labor market (*salary* and *employment rates* – the latter by using a *proxy*, which is the population of graduates that contribute to the social security system). We include some other indicators not comprised in Uribe's research that are available within UNESCO data, and account for the above-mentioned categories. We have studied all these categories taking into account gender differences. We approach the analysis from different periods according to data availability, 2018 being the last year for most of the analyses. Reliable data are available until the year 2016 for those indicators referring both to retention in higher education and success in the labor market.

We use aggregated data from official databases by UNESCO Institute of Statistics, CEPALSTAT and Education at a Glance (OECD, 2019). We also utilize aggregated data for the descriptive analyses from SNIES, SPADIES, and OLE (Colombian Ministry of Education's Databases). We employ microdata by SNIES to address a statistical association analysis, seeking to identify degrees of

International Perspectives on Gender and Higher Education, 249–272

doi:10.1108/978-1-83909-886-420201014

association between gender and other relevant variables to study participation in higher education.

The following table describes the categories, indicators, variables, and sources that we consider for the analysis (Table 14.1).

The following part describes the databases used in order to study recent developments regarding women's participation in higher education and subsequent success within the labor market.

SNIES: SNIES is the National System of Higher Education Information; it captures census statistics of aspirants and students in each higher education institution (HEI) registered before the Ministry of Education. Databases available for this analysis correspond to the 2016–2018 period; the period of analysis for graduates was 2009–2018. The database is configured regarding each academic program within each HEI in a specific period, and separated by the number of women and the number of men reported as applicants, aspirants admitted, first-time students, graduates, and enrollees. For the statistical association analysis, we have rearranged data to establish individuals as the unit of analysis, which also entailed a condensation of the annual databases available into one file. As a result, four different databases were reorganized (applicants, acceptances, first-time students, and graduates); this allowed us to establish levels of association between relevant variables. Additionally, we present some aggregated data offered by the Ministry of Education reports based on SNIES.

SPADIES: SPADIES is the System for Prevention and Analysis of Dropout in Colombia. This system tracks each individual who has accessed higher education since 1998, following the status within HEIs until his/her graduation or abandonment. SPADIES also allows to collect socioeconomic data for each student, institution, academic program, and social group (e.g., by income or mother's education level) as well as to identify any students who are beneficiaries of any aid (financial, academic, or other types of aid). Periodic reports from Colombian HEIs fed this information system, which is managed by the Colombian Ministry of Education. We use this database to analyze *retention and attrition* by gender, with the variables: *dropout rate and graduation rate.*

OLE (Labour Market Observatory): The OLE is an observatory that follows graduates in the labor market, focusing on salary and formal employment rates. To do so, the OLE leverages on the information originated within the national social security system. This database shows averages of entry salary for graduates from each academic program, institution, geographical area, public or private sectors, types of institutions, and levels of education, as well as the number of graduates in each category. It also presents such data by economic sectors. We used the OLE to analyze *salary and employment* by gender, accounting for the variables *entry salary* and *formal employment rate.*

UNESCO Institute of Statistics: This institute offers a variety of information and data regarding the *Sustainable Development Goals*. The themes relevant for this analysis are Education and Equity. Multiple sources contribute data from each country; the most common sources for Colombia are as follows: National Household Surveys, the National Population Census, and Reports by the Colombian Information Systems. We use UNESCO indicators to analyze

Table 14.1. Categories, Indicators, and Databases Used for the Analysis of Gender Participation in Higher Education.

Categories	Indicators	Variables	Source of Authors' Information on Outcomes
Coverage and equity	Enrollments	Applicants Acceptances First-time students Enrollments (national, by levels of education, and by fields of knowledge)	SNIES – Colombian Ministry of Education – Microdata
		Enrollment growth	SNIES – Colombian Ministry of Education – Aggregated National Data
		Enrollment share of females and males enrolled in higher education by gender and by fields of knowledge Share of enrollments by gender and by fields of knowledge regarding the total population in each field Enrollment share of females and males enrolled in tertiary education and by levels of education (ISCED) Share of enrollments by gender and by levels of education (ISCED) regarding the total population in each level Gender parity index of enrollments	UNESCO Institute of Statistics
	Changes in enrollment by	Net enrollment rates by income quintiles (20–24 age cohorts)	CEPAL Statistics

Table 14.1. *(Continued)*

Categories	**Indicators**	**Variables**	**Source of Authors' Information on Outcomes**
	family income levels	Gap in enrollment rates by income quintiles (20–24 age cohorts) Variation in enrollment rates by income quintiles (20–24 age cohorts) 2008–2018	
Retention and graduation	Changes in attrition	Dropout rates	SPADIES, Colombian Ministry of Education
	Changes in graduation	Graduation rates Share of graduates by fields of knowledge Share of graduates by levels of education (ISCED) Gender parity index for graduates	SPADIES, Colombian Ministry of Education UNESCO Institute of Statistics
Salary and employment	Salary Employment	Entry salary by gender Formal employment rates by gender	Reports by the Labour Market Observatory, Ministry of Education, and OECD (Education at a Glance)

Note: The table above is the author's adaptation of the study developed by Uribe-Correa (2012) regarding gender and including other indicators to complete the framework.

descriptive data on *enrollments* by gender about fields of knowledge, and levels of education (ISCED).

CEPALSTAT: This database owned by the Economic Commission for Latin America and The Caribbean (United Nations) offers over 2,000 indicators and measures that are comparable internationally coming from Latin American and the Caribbean countries. Information and data from Colombia come mostly from National Household Surveys. We use CEPAL education statistics concerning net attendance rates by income quintiles (for the 20–24 age cohort) to analyze the breach between sexes and the variation of such indicator within a decade (2008–2018).

OECD Indicators of Education Systems (INES): The INES provide data on the performance of country systems, regarding nations that are members of OECD as well as nonmember G20 nations. This allows for data comparison across countries, and to access historical data within one nation. Indicators relevant to this work are those related to "the output of educational institutions and the impact of learning on economic and social outcomes" to analyze the percentage of women's salaries vis-à-vis men's salaries. All of the OECD indicators are available in Education at a Glance – a yearly publication (OECD, 2019).

1.1 Characterization of the Colombian Higher Education System

One of the most prominent features of the Colombian higher education system is diversification in types of institutions, varying across the country in size, complexity, types of founders, fees, and quality, inter alia. Such variety has allowed access to a significant number of students from different backgrounds increasing coverage for the relevant age cohort and across income quintile groups.

By 2018, 298 HEIs comprised the system, of which 72% were private. Since 1975, both private institutions and enrollments have been the majority as compared to the public sector. For decades, higher education enrollees in Colombia grew deriving from a strengthened and dynamic private sector; and private enrollments grew constantly. However, the trend shifted since 2005 as the result of a mix of public policies applied since 2002, which generated an upsurge of matriculations in public HEIs. The public sector accounted for 74.3% of enrollment increase between 2002 and 2010, with mixed results among public universities and SENA – the national apprenticeship institute – that upgraded a part of its programs to higher education level (Uribe-Correa, 2012).

While the share of private institutions within the higher education market has continued to be almost the same through the years, private enrollment participation suffered a downturn. Today's participation is similar for public and private institutions, since half of higher education students are in public institutions.

Enrollment growth has been constant in recent years. In 2010, there were 1,674,021 enrollees. With a 44% growth, Colombian higher education population achieved 2,408,041, in 2018 – accounting for 52.01% of enrollment rate for the 17–21 age cohort (SNIES, 2019a). Such rate also grew by 15 % ca. within the last 8 years.

Nevertheless, the rhythm of enrollment expansion recently experienced a deceleration as a result of different factors. Some of them imply a deterioration of affordability for families, and an increase of the unemployment rate in the country. Other causes for the slowing down of enrollments are changes in public policy programs such as the elimination of the "*Ser Pilo Paga*" program (Being Smart Pays Off), as well as the decline of the 15–19 age cohort which passed from 11.8%

of the Colombian population in 1973 to 8.7% in 2018, according to DANE's census (DANE, 2019). The system has 38,000 less enrollees between 2017 and 2018.[1]

The number of graduate students was limited to 173,079 in 2018, and doctoral students only amounted to 6,225 during the same year. The great majority of students in higher education in Colombia are in undergraduate programs; 69.7% are enrolled in university education instead of technical or technological programs (short-cycle education).

By 2018, the Colombian system included 86 universities, 138 university institutions, 48 technological institutions, and 30 professional technical institutes, offering 10,952 academic programs, under surveillance and quality control by the Colombian Ministry of Education.[2] These types of HEIs do not reflect the types of higher education they are permitted to offer. Colombian law allows universities and university institutions to offer technical and technological education; technical and technological institutions are allowed to offer university education after a process named "redefinition." It implies an authorization by the Ministry of Education to offer programs and degrees by cycles in subsequent order, starting with technical or technological education, then with university education, and finalizing with a graduate program (*technical o technological specialization*), all of them related to a specific and unvaried field of knowledge or profession throughout the cycle.

Act 30/1992 defined technical and technological education as a part of higher education, and Act 749/2002 further outlines the extent of the types of education that lead to a professional degree. Technical education undertakes to generate skills based on practical knowledge for individuals to execute specific activities within the labor market, in productive and service-related sectors. Act 30/1992 defines technical education as one that trains for instrumental and operational occupations. Technical education confers a "technical professional" degree in the relevant field of knowledge, and its programs have a duration ranging from 1 to 2 years.

According to the legislation, technological education comprises a more innovative stand than technical higher education. Technological graduates are enabled to design, build, implement, control, and transform means and processes in order to solve problems across the industry. Such type of education may involve management training, leading to a degree of "technologist in…" after completing 2.5 to 3 year-long programs.

Technical and technological education has traditionally been regarded as one of a lesser statuses when compared to university education. According to (1998),

[1]The program provided grants to 40,000 low-income students with the top scores in the National Standardized Test.

[2]Colombian legislation has distributed institutions in four groups in regard to their "academic character": universities, university institutions (or technological schools), technological institutes, and technical institutes. Whereas the difference between technological and technical is visible concerning the type of education, the dissimilarity between universities and university institutions (or technological schools) is subtler. Definitions of both of them in Act 30/1992 appear to be blur and nonmutually excluded, showing universities more prone and capable for high quality in scientific research than university institutions. However, such a difference is not as apparent in practice.

this type of education was perceived as third-class training for the poor since as early as the 1960s. Public policy from 2002 has been oriented to increase coverage by means of both increasing places at public universities and upgrading vocational training to technological-level education by SENA.[3] At the same time, the Colombian government launched intensive campaigns toward an increase of the prestige of technical and technological education assisted by the World Bank as the main partner for financial aid.

Contextually, public campaigns for this type of education resulted in an increase of more than 270,000 new enrollments between 2002 and 2010. SENA contributed by expanding higher education to 40.9% of new enrollees during this period. Technical and Technological Education represents 30% of today's enrollment share – 4% less than in 2010, with almost 732,000 enrollees.

The Colombian government has abided by the perspective of international agencies such as the World Bank and OECD, considering that short-cycle programs respond directly to the needs of the industry and connect graduates rapidly to the labor market. However, the Colombian society – and even the Ministry of Education – see technical and technological education as the lowest levels of the pyramid within the higher education system. Additionally, those who graduate from 1.5to 3 year higher education programs receive lower salaries on average than those graduating from university education (4–5-year programs), according to the Labor Market Observatory of the Colombian Ministry of Education (2019). In this vein, it is relevant to explore the participation of women by levels of education or academic degrees.

1.2 Participation of Colombian Women in Higher Education

The year 1935 saw the first woman to ever access higher education in Colombia, in a period of fights for women's rights. Before that time, women had very limited educational opportunities and were mostly oriented to arts and crafts or activities permitted to women, such as elementary teachers – learned during high school – for the most privileged females considering status and location. Many women would not even complete secondary studies, which was a requisite to enter universities.

Since 1930, Colombian women organized themselves to promote equality of participation not only in education. This resulted in diverse groups of reforms adopted by liberal governments after a conservative period (Ramírez, 2010). López-Pumarejo was the Colombian President who promulgated a decree to open university studies to women in 1934. It should be mentioned that women in Colombia were not granted the right to vote until as late as 1954, when a legislative act approved by a National Constituent Assembly was passed.

From the 1930s onward, women have actively partaken in higher education. According to Ramírez (2010), Colombian women were the center of multiple cultural changes during the second part of the twentieth century. Such changes represented a silent cultural revolution that influenced new features of personal and social life of women (Ramírez, 2010). The trend onward was consistent:

[3]The public national vocational training center that receives compulsory contributions from corporations through parafiscal taxes.

Women were gaining a share in higher education, to the point where they surpassed male enrollments: the enrollment share of women in higher education was 18.2% in 1960, and it skyrocketed to 23.2% in 1965, 36.4% in 1975, 48.7% in 1985, and 51.7% in 1990 (Valdéz & Gomariz, 1993). Throughout the 1990s and the first decade of the twenty-first century, this share kept slightly higher than men each period, and during the last 8 years (2010–2018) participation of women has grown from 51.6% to 53.0% (SNIES, 2019a).

1.3 Characterization of Gender Participation in Colombian Higher Education

Participation of women in higher education in Colombia has been prominent through the years. Women have had greater enrollments in absolute and representative terms, and they have shown better enrollment rates than men. This trend is common within the group of OECD countries where Colombia has been invited to be a member, and Chile and Mexico are already the only members within the group of Latin American countries (Costa Rica is in the process of adhesion).

In Colombia, the gross enrollment ratio in HE for women increased from 52.2% to 59.7% from 2013 to 2018; a 2% growth versus men, which went from 45.4% to 51.1% (UNESCO, 2019). A higher enrollment ratio can also be observed for women; over 8% by 2018.

It is important to specify that women have outnumbered men within the Colombian population in general. According to the last population census (DANE, 2019), 51.2% are women and 48.8% are men in Colombia (2018). Nevertheless, for the youth ranging 15–19 years old, women represent 4.26% of the population versus men – 4.46% of the Colombian populace. For the 20–24 age cohort, women are 4.43% versus 4.49% of men (DANE, 2019). The conclusions show that although women in the relevant age cohorts are less in number than men in the Colombian population, females have better presence in higher education than males do. According to most recent data, the system includes 1,275,663 women (53.0%) and 1,132,378 men (47.0%). In 2010, women represented 51.6% of the total population in higher education (SNIES, 2019a).

The dynamic of access also shows a continued trend of women entering the higher education system in a larger number than men, regardless of their age upon arrival. Women also have a better net entry rate, which measures the percentage of female or male new entrants to higher education (technical, technological, or university programs) of the total female or male population of the age of entry into higher education.[4,5]

[4]Net entry rate to first tertiary programs for all ages according to UNESCO "Students who, during the course of the reference school or academic year, enter a program at a given level of education for the first time, irrespective of whether the students enter the program at the beginning or at an advanced stage of the program." Retrieved from http://data.uis.unesco.org/#.

[5]In some other countries different from Colombia, there are Masters' Long First Degree (LFD) that count toward this indicator. As stated, this is not the case in Colombian Higher Education.

Table 14.2. Net Entry Rate to First Tertiary Programs for All Ages (Percentages).

Year	2013	2014	2015	2016	2017	2018
Male	55.90	34.75	40.48	49.37	45.13	40.20
Female	60.08	38.15	44.43	54.29	50.06	43.75

Note: The source of the table above is the author's elaboration using UNESCO Institute of Statistics (2019).

Table 14.2 depicts net entry rates to first tertiary programs by gender. Better measures are determined for women each year for the 2013–2018 period. It also shows fluctuating entry rates for both sexes over the years analyzed, and deteriorated between 2013 and 2018. This might be associated to a deceleration in enrollments in general in higher education in Colombia, as a result of the factors mentioned already.

The Gender Parity Index (GPI) for new entrants is another indicator that measures relative access to tertiary education for females and males. A GPI closer to 1 demonstrates equal access to both sexes. A GPI greater than 1 shows greater gains for women than men. The GPI is calculated by dividing the value of the net entry rate for females by the value of said indicator for males. Results in Colombia also show greater improvements for women as compared to men, ranging from 1.07 to 1.11 each year from 2013. Such indicator is consistent with the gross enrollment parity index, which fluctuates between 1.15 and 1.17 (UNESCO, 2019).

Analyzing gender participation in detail in regard to entrance, enrollment, and graduation, it is found that women are underrepresented in several fields of knowledge. Particularly, women are less prone to enroll in certain fields traditionally conquered by men.

The percentage of women students enrolled in higher education, in the field of Information and Communication Technologies, was only 24.5% in 2014 and is even lower in 2018 – 20.7%. This percentage is followed by the participation share of women in Engineering, Manufacturing, and Construction programs (32.9% in 2014 and 33.7% in 2018). Women are also underrepresented in Services, and Art and Humanities, but account for the majority in Education; Social Science, Journalism, and Information; Business, Administration and Law; and in Health and Welfare, where they account for a total 71.0% (2014) and 71.5% (2018).

As for the group of studies in Natural Science, Mathematics, and Statistics, enrollments are almost equitable for both sexes. However, disaggregating Mathematics from the others, women represent only 31.4% of the total students enrolled for the first semester of 2018 (SNIES, 2019b), and Statistics alone is only of 31.9%.

Within the spectrum of specific disciplines, it is relevant to describe the participation of women in Nursery. The presence of women is significantly higher than men in Colombia. Nursery has traditionally been deemed to be as a second-class profession if compared to Medicine, in Colombia and other countries alike. During the first semester of 2018, 20,077 women enrolled in Nursery programs compared to 4,544 men (SNIES, 2019b). According to Errasti-Ibarrondo, Arantzamendi-Solabarrieta, and Canga-Armayor (2012) society and the field of work itself do not recognize Nursery as an independent field but is regarded as an inferior profession likened to medicine, mainly because it is perceived as a profession related to "tasks." Sanhueza-Alvarado (2015) conclude – based on a literature review that analyzed job characteristics of the nursery profession – that lack of sufficient healthcare personnel leads to an all too frequent increase of workload for nurses – sometimes to reach the double. The aforesaid authors found that gender has marked the profession under patriarchy, bringing inequality both in salary and responsibilities. Their care skills and attitudes give them such a role similar to that of a housewife.

However, if women enrollees surpass men in nursery, they also exceed men enrollments in Medicine: 28,431 and 19,430, respectively (2018). This is relevant, in that it proves that women have taken over health disciplines in a wide range. Women's enrollment is more than double (2.3 times) men's enrollment in health science programs in an ample spectrum including Nursery, Nutrition, Dental Studies, Speech Therapy, Physiotherapy, and other undergraduate programs (SNIES, 2019b). Within other knowledge fields – and specifically regarding enrollments in social sciences – there also are other feminized professions in Colombia such as Psychology, Sociology, and Social Work.

The Colombian Ministry of Education conducted a joint work with the Research Group on Interdisciplinary Studies on Gender at Universidad Nacional (n.d.). They found horizontal segregation, and state that there are "feminine careers" linked to care work. These careers are not completely valued by the society in its symbolic sphere nor in physical assets, despite being highly relevant to social welfare (Colombian Ministry of Education, n.d.) (Table 14.3).

Table 14.3. Percentage of Female Students Enrolled in Higher Education by Fields of Knowledge.

Years	**2014**	**2018**
Education	63.6	62.8
Arts and humanities	47.3	48.9
Social sciences, journalism, and information	68.4	70.0
Business, administration, and law	60.8	60.0
Natural sciences, mathematics, and statistics	50.5	49.6
Information and communication technologies	24.5	20.7
Engineering, manufacturing, and construction	32.9	33.7
Agriculture, forestry, fishery, and veterinary	41.9	45.5
Health and welfare	71.0	71.5
Services	43.4	42.6

Note: The table above is the author's elaboration using UNESCO Institute of Statistics.

The percentage of graduates who are female by fields of knowledge is consistent with the share of female enrollment in terms of gender disparity. Two out of 10 graduates from information and communication technology programs are women in 2018, and the number decreased by one female graduate as compared to 2014. Three women out of 10 graduates are in the fields of Engineering, Manufacturing, and Construction, while four women out of 10 graduated from Agriculture, Forestry, Fishery, and Veterinary as well as Service Programs. Female graduates are a minority in STEM programs: 33.4% compared to 66.6% men by 2018, and the distribution has remained very similar within the last 5 years.

The participation of female graduates of the total number of graduates in STEM fields contrasts with the percentage of female graduates from other areas such as Education (68.6%); Social Sciences, Journalism and Information (70.6%); Business, Administration and Law (62.7%), and Health and Welfare (72.1%). We found a moderate association between gender and fields of knowledge as well as gender and specific disciplines through the statistical association analysis exhibited hereinafter (Table 14.4).

Disparities are also present by level of education, particularly in women's enrollment within doctoral programs, reaching only 39.8% as compared to men in 2018 (60.2%) 1% higher than in 2013, according to UNESCO's International Standard Classification of Education (UNESCO, 2019). We also found a slight association between educational degree and gender within the analysis of SNIES microdata, which is presented below (Table 14.5).

Table 14.4. Percentage of Female Graduates from Tertiary Education by Fields of Knowledge.

Years	**2014**	**2018**
Education	67.4	68.6
Arts and humanities	51.3	50.6
Social sciences, journalism, and information	68.7	70.6
Business, administration, and law	62.1	62.7
Natural sciences, mathematics, and statistics	52.0	54.2
Information and communication technologies	31.1	23.3
Engineering, manufacturing, and construction	33.7	34.6
Agriculture, forestry, fishery, and veterinary	41.3	44.7
Health and welfare	73.1	72.1
Services	42.8	42.8
STEM	34.2	33.4
Non-STEM	62.3	63.0

Note: The source of the table above is the author's elaboration by using UNESCO Institute of Statistics.

Table 14.5. Percentage of Female Students in Tertiary Education by Levels of Education.

	Years	2013	2018
Short cycle: technical and technological	ISCED 5	49.6	48.0
Bachelor's education	ISCED 6	54.0	55.0
Masters and equivalent level	ISCED 7	55.2	55.1
Doctoral programs	ISCED 8	38.8	39.8

Note: The source of the table above is the author's elaboration by using UNESCO Institute of Statistics.

Regarding graduates, the lowest number of women can be found within ISCED 8 level: less than 4 out of 10 graduates from doctoral programs are women. Men graduates, in contrast, are underrepresented in ISCED 6 and ISCED 7 (bachelors, and aggregated masters' and specialization's programs), and are overrepresented in short-cycle programs.[6]

According to the *Labour Market Observatory*, earnings for graduates from this latter type of programs are lower than those for graduates from university education. Graduates from technical programs held an employment rate of 63.1% in 2016, compared to persons with technological degrees (71.8%), and for university graduates (79.9%) (Moreno-Cifuentes & Huertas-Erazo, 2019) (Table 14.6).

Data are steady when we analyze the share of female enrollees in doctoral programs of the total population of women in higher education, which was 1.9% (2018), as compared to 3.3% for men of the total male enrollment. This shows greater gains for men through the last 5 years (UNESCO, 2019).

Another relevant overall indicator for equity is enrollment rate by income groups. Findings have shown that income is a predictor for access, retention, and academic success (McDonough & Fann, 2007). We found from the analysis of CEPAL (2019) indicators that between 2008 and 2018, enrollment rates by income quintiles in Colombia has remained uneven. This shows a significant gap between the poorest and richest population regardless of gender. The net enrollment rate for both sexes is 4.2 times for quintile 5 than it is for quintile 1 and for each sex, although the rates have been traditionally higher for women than men within each quintile group. During the decade, the greatest expansion of higher education attendance has occurred in the middle class – quintiles 3 and 4 – for both sexes, with a variation in enrollment rates of 4.1% and 3.9%, respectively, from 2008 to 2018. Women's enrollment surpassed that of men in almost all income quintiles in 2008 as well as in 2018, except for males coming from quintile

[6]Specialization is a 1-year graduate program in Colombia that drives to a degree as "Specialist in…." This is the lower level of graduate education within the country.

Table 14.6. Percentage of Female Graduates from Tertiary Education by Levels of Education.

	Years	2013	2018
Short cycle: technical and technological	ISCED 5	50.6	51.5
Bachelor's education	ISCED 6	57.9	59.0
Masters and equivalent level	ISCED 7	57.3	56.9
Doctoral programs	ISCED 8	39.6	38.4

1 that surpassed women's enrollment in 2018. In addition, enrollment rate for males in such quintile 1 was lower in 2018 than that of women.

By gender, the most prominent achievements are evident in middle-class women: the increase of female enrollment rate grew 6.1% for quintile 4 and 4.5% for quintile 3 during that period, with lower growth for men within these income quintiles (2% and 3.5%, respectively). For the poorest quintiles, the male enrollment rate growth was higher than females in the 2008–2018 period. The gap of male enrollment between the poorest and the richest students in 2008 was 34.1%, while it decreased to 27.8% in 2018. However, there was a reduction of the enrollment rate from 2008 to 2018 for quintile 5. Regarding women enrollment rates, the gap in 2008 between quintiles 5 and 1 was 36.3%, while it closed at 32.5% in 2018, also having a reduction in 2018 for quintile 5 (Table 14.7).

1.4 Statistical Association Analysis

Using microdata provided by SNIES (SNIES, 2019c), we ran both chi-Square and Cramer's V tests in order to identify associations between gender (woman and man) and other relevant variables such as (a) institutional sector (public and private), (b) type of institution (university, university institution, technological institute, or technical professional institution), (c) education level (undergraduate and graduate program), (d) academic degree (doctoral, master, bachelor, technological, and technical), (e) field of knowledge (by Colombian Ministry of Education's aggregation), (f) specific discipline of academic program, and (g) modality of teaching (face-to-face, distance, and online). Calculations addressed the population of applicants, those admitted, and first-time students for the period 2016–2018, as well as graduates for the 2009–2018 period.

According to SNIES, 6,556,107 individuals applied for admission at higher education between 2016 and 2018 (47.2% women and 52.8% men). Half of applicants (50.9%) were admitted within different academic programs at HEIs. 3,218,586 were rejected, from which a majority of 53.8% were women compared to unadmitted men (46.2%). From those who were admitted, 77.6% effectively enrolled (2,590,012 students).

Table 14.7. Net Enrollment Rates for the 20–24 Age Cohort by Gender and Income Quintiles for the Years 2008 and 2018.

	Quintile 1		**Quintile 2**		**Quintile 3**		**Quintile 4**		**Quintile 5**	
Year	**Female**	**Male**	**Female**	**Male**	**Female**	**Male**	**Female**	**Male**	**Female**	**Male**
2008	11.2	10.4	14.5	10.5	17.8	15.6	26.6	24.8	47.4	44.5
2018	12.2	13.5	15.5	14.2	22.3	19.1	32.7	26.8	44.7	41.3
Variation from 2008–to 2018	1	3.1	1	3.7	4.5	3.5	6.1	2	−2.7	−3.2

Note: The source of the table above is the author's elaboration by using CEPAL (2019).

Table 14.8. Associations between Gender and Variables of the Study.

		χ2*	df	Cramer's V
Applicants Period 2016–2018	Gender and field of knowledge	439,172.61	8	0.259
	Specific discipline	720,469.79	54	0.349
Admitted students Period 2016–2018	Institutional sector	21,980.81	1	0.081
	Modality	13,650.43	2	0.064
	Academic degree or level of education acquired	15,645.88	5	0.069
	Field of knowledge	238,522.98	7	0.267
	Specific discipline	3,922.49	54	0.343
First-time students (enrolled in the first course) Period 2016–2018	Institutional sector	20,333.07	1	0.089
	Modality	20,333.07	2	0.068
	Academic degree or level of education acquired	12,468.90	5	0.069
	Gender and field of knowledge	194,391.87	7	0.274
	Specific discipline	323,012.38	54	0.353
Graduates Period (2016–2018)	Institutional sector	18,296.08	1	0.072
	Modality	28,382.73	2	0.09
	Academic degree or level of education acquired	24,241.49	5	0.083
	Gender and field of knowledge	226,431.30	7	0.253
	Specific discipline	445,836.42	55	0.358

Note: Author's calculations by using SNIES microdata. * $p < 0.05$.

We found moderate associations (significant chi-square test and Cramer's V > 0.10, see Table 14.8) between the variables of gender and field of knowledge as well as between gender and specific disciplines or academic programs for the whole analyzed groups: applicants, admitted aspirants, and enrollees in the first course within the higher education system (2016–2018), and for graduates between 2009 and 2018.

We identify consistent moderate associations that exhibit more cases than expected among women in the population of applicants, admitted students, first-time students, and graduates within the following fields of knowledge under the denomination of knowledge groups by the Colombian Ministry of Education: Education Sciences, Health Sciences, Social and Human Sciences, and Management and Economy. In contrast, the number of men is higher than expected in Mathematics and Natural Sciences; Engineering and Architecture; Fine Arts; and Veterinary Science and Agronomy.

Regarding specific disciplines, women (applicants, admitted, in first courses, and graduated) present more cases than expected in the programs of Bacteriology, Chemistry, Economy, Education, Environmental Health, Liberal Arts, Anthropology, Library Science, Management, Engineering, Microbiology and Biology, Modern Languages, Linguistic, Literature, Nursing, Nutrition and Diet, Dental Therapy, Optometry and other Health Science; Fine Arts, Political Science, International Relations, Psychology, Accounting, Public Health, Social Communication, Journalism, Sociology, Social Work, Surgical Instrumentation, and Therapies.

Considering men, the programs with larger number of male graduates than expected are Advertising, Agriculture and Livestock, Engineering, Agronomy, Architecture, Biomedical Engineering, Chemical Engineering, Civil Engineering, Design, Electrical Engineering, Electronic and Telecommunications' Engineering, Engineering of Mines, Metallurgy, Forestry Engineering, Agricultural Engineering, Geography, History, Geology and other Natural Science, Industrial and Food Engineering, Industrial Engineering, Law, Mathematics, Statistics, Mechanical Engineering, Medicine, Music, other kinds of engineering, Philosophy, Theology, Physics, Representative Arts, Sports, Physical Education and Recreation, Telematics, Computing Engineering, Military or Police Training, Veterinary Medicine, Visual Arts, and Animal Science.

We identified some other associations of lower strength than the ones explained already (significant chi-square test and Cramer's V values between 0.05 and 0.09, see Table 14.8) referred to gender and institutional sector (public and private), level of education or academic degrees, and modality of teaching (face-to-face, distance, and online). A lower percentage of men admitted in (48.2%) and graduated (44.7%) from HEIs than women is found; the number of men admitted to public institutions is higher than expected (52.4%), as well as the number of men enrolled (52.9%) and graduated from public HEIs (50.5%). In contrast, women appear to have a higher participation than expected in private universities.

Considering the level of education achieved of the total population of graduates between 2009 and 2018, 47.0% completed a bachelor's degree, 25.6% a technological degree, 5.4% a technical degree, 18.0% earned a grad specialization course, 3.8% a master's degree, and 0.1% a doctoral degree. In both first-time course and graduation, there is a number of cases greater than expected in bachelor's degrees and grad specialization courses. We also found such a pattern in the data presented by UNESCO. Nevertheless, it is important to clarify graduate programs in Colombia includes not only master's degrees but grad specialization courses, having a greater proportion of the population enrolled in the first one.

With respect to the modality of teaching, face-to-face education shows greater percentage of students enrolled of the total students in higher education in Colombia (84.5%), followed by distance education (13.4%), and online education (2.1%). We found a small association between gender and the modality of teaching, showing a higher number of women initiating and graduating distance and online education than expected. Contrastingly, men participate in face-to-face programs in a larger quantity than expected.

1.5 The Attrition Analysis

According to the analysis of SPADIES data, we found that the cumulative dropout rate reached 49.5% for the total population in higher education between 2009 and 2018. Men are more highly impacted than women are, since the highest percentage of dropouts are men (54.5%) of the group who abandoned the system. Men also hold the majority in percentages of those who drop out regarding each modality of teaching; they account for 55.0% of dropout cases in face-to-face education, 63.5% in distance programs, and 70.6% in online higher education. Contrariwise, women show greater attrition in technical education (66.8%).

Female dropout cases are prominent in two main fields of knowledge: Agronomy and Veterinary (58.6%), and Engineering, Architecture, and Urbanism (57.8%). The latter is still a program that men abandon significantly (60.7%), along with mathematics and Natural Science (61.1%). Social Science and Humanities has the lowest dropout rates among men (43.6%) and Health Science is also the lowest for women (43.7%).

Concerning specific disciplines, there is alignment for both sexes within academic programs related to Mathematics and Statistics, Physics, Computing Engineering, and Telematics. Such phenomenon might be related to knowledge areas that comprised STEM fields with particular levels of complexity. Percentages of cumulative dropout rates at those fields range from 66.9% and 73.5%. There are certain common patterns of lower dropout rates between males and females regarding some academic programs such as Military and Police Training, Nursery, and Nutrition and Diet.

1.6 After Graduation

Although the Colombian labor market opened the doors to feminization within the different layers of the occupational structure (some to a greater extent than others), a significant imbalance is present regarding salary. Women earn on average less than men do for joint levels of higher education and fields of knowledge, equal to 88.1% male salaries (the average salary for men was $2.128.156 vs $1.874.206 for women by 2016) (Labour Market Observatory, 2019). According to OECD, women's earnings as a percentage of men's earnings among Colombian graduates from higher education in 2017 was 81.0%. Colombia ranked seventh in the list of countries with greater percentage for women across OECD countries, following Costa Rica, Belgium, Slovenia, Spain, Turkey, and Luxembourg (OECD, 2019). It is relevant to describe that none of the countries reported in Education at a Glance has reached salary equality for men and women. Costa Rica has the best performance with 97% of women's earnings as a percentage of men's earnings (OECD, 2019).

This trend of gender imbalance is equal in Colombia for each level of education, taking into account both undergraduate and graduate degrees. According to data from the Labour Market Observatory by the Colombian Ministry of Education, the salary gap is larger in absolute terms for women holding master's degrees, followed by doctoral degrees, and grad specialization courses. The lowest gap in entry salary occurs at technical degree levels. This trend of lower salaries for women compared to men across all education levels covers at least 6 years prior to 2016, according to the availability of data (Colombian Ministry of Education, 2017a) (Table 14.9).

As for "feminized" professions, we found that women holding Nursery degrees earn on average 92.2% of men's salaries; female Medicine degree holders earn 93.8% of men's compensation; and Nutrition and Diet graduates get 92.6% of the payment offered to male professionals in the same filed of knowledge. Women earn less than men in Psychology (88.4% of men average salary), Education (87.0%), Management (87.3%), Computing Engineering (88.0%), and Library Science (90.1%), inter alia. In some other disciplines, women earn better than men, as is the case of Bacteriology (108.6%), and Math and Statistics (116.6%).

In contrast to salary, employment rates are higher for women than men holding university degrees and graduate degrees. The exception here is doctoral degrees between 2011 and 2013, as women held lower employment rates than men did during this period.

Regarding technical and technological degrees, men tend to have higher employment rates than women. This is related to the fact that men enroll in these levels of higher education in larger proportions than women do (Table 14.10).

1.7 Colombian Public Policy in Regard to Gender

Colombian public policy has advocated for disadvantaged groups to access higher education in order to promote equity initiatives. However, the majority

Table 14.9. Average Entry Salary by Gender by Level of Education (2016 – Colombian Pesos).

		Men	**Women**	**Gap**
Undergraduate	Technical degree	1,109,223	1,019,499	−89,724
	Technological degree	1,262,620	1,058,534	−204,086
	University degree	1,933,266	1,696,532	−236,734
Graduate degrees	Grad specialization degree	3,468,971	2,995,509	−473,462
	Master's degree	4,449,513	3,600,292	−849,221
	Doctoral degree	6,702,221	6,112,408	−589,813

Note: The table above is the author's elaboration from the Labour Market Observatory (2019).

Table 14.10. Employment Rate by Gender and Level of Education (2016 – Percentages).

		Year 2012			Year 2014			Year 2016		
		Men	**Women**	**Variation**	**Men**	**Women**	**Variation**	**Men**	**Women**	**Variation**
Undergraduate	Technical degree	67.7	62.3	−5.4	69.1	64.7	−4.4	65.6	60.8	−4.8
	Technological degree	70.3	66.0	−4.3	74.3	70.4	−3.9	73.3	70.5	−2.8
	University degree	78.9	79.3	0.4	80.5	80.8	0.3	79.5	80.2	0.7
Graduate degrees	Grad specialization degree	91.0	93.9	2.9	90.5	93.8	3.3	87.5	92.9	5.4
	Master's degree	92.1	92.5	0.4	92.1	93.9	1.8	93.6	94.9	1.3
	Doctoral degree	95.6	88.9	−6.7	92.9	97.0	4.1	96.2	96.6	0.4

Note: The table above is the author's elaboration using data from Labour Market Observatory (Colombian Ministry of Education, 2017a).

of these initiatives have focused on attributes other than sex (e.g., income and geographical location). Public universities are committed to allotting quotas for indigenous people. Diverse national initiatives call HEIs to privilege admission to Afro-descendent communities, individuals who are victims of the armed conflict, and persons in condition of disability, among others. Implementation of these initiatives is entirely up to HEIs, in pursuance of the principle of autonomy.

The recent 2016–2026 Decennial Education Plan vows "to build a society in peace based on equity, inclusion, respect to ethics and gender equality" (Colombian Ministry of Education, 2017b, pp. 6). The plan foresaw an important strategy to achieve its objective: to develop and strengthen national and regional financial sources toward inclusion of people in conditions of vulnerability, to guarantee access, retention, and graduation in higher education. The Colombian government aligned its goals with the relevant Sustainable Development Goals: to assure egalitarian access for all men and women to technical and university education.

The Decennial Education Plan proposes indicators to measure advancements regarding gender: enrollment parity index, and graduation parity index. Two more indicators might include a gender perspective yet in an implicit fashion: gross enrollment ratio for rural population and graduates of masters' and doctoral programs.

The 2018–2022 National Development Plan – "A Pact for Colombia, A Pact for Equity" established as an objective to foster inclusive education with quality. Colombia also follows the Iberian–American goals in education; one of them is to accomplish equality in education by overcoming all forms of discrimination.

All of the objectives and strategies above are part of the strategic frame set forth by the Colombian Ministry of Education (2018). Additionally, the former administration issued specific public policy guidelines in 2012 to increase gender equity. As a result, a strategy was launched to encourage educational supply with a differential focus for women in technical, technological, and university education. A more specific strategy within these guidelines is to promote initiatives toward professional orientation for women to increase their enrollment in those fields of knowledge in higher education that have traditionally been "masculine" (Alta Consejería Presidencial para la Equidad de la Mujer, 2012, pp. 139). During the 2016–2018 period, the Ministry of Education and the Interdisciplinary Research Group on Gender at Universidad Nacional developed a project called "Gender Approach and Identities toward Policy Guidelines of an Inclusive Higher Education." This project included a diagnosis of gender and sexual diversity in the Colombian higher education system, a conceptualization frame for an analysis to establish action strategies, and recommendations to include gender perspectives into higher education policy (Colombian Ministry of Education, n. d.).

Nevertheless, gender policy does not translate in clear and concrete public policy efforts and actions to increase enrollment and graduation of women in specific disciplines and fields of knowledge where they are underrepresented – including doctoral programs. At the same time, public policy efforts to increase participation of men where they are the minority are not tangible in Colombia, whereas it is a clear objective in some OECD countries: "while many countries have promoted higher education attainment for men and provided incentives to pursue higher education, men have not responded. This may be partly due to critical years before tertiary education, when boys are more likely to struggle academically, repeat a grade, or drop out of school" (OECD, 2019, p. 198).

Interestingly, the Colombian Society of Mathematics launched a Gender Equity Commission that promotes and stimulates women enrollment in this field. The Colombian Society of Mathematics committed to create and award grants, scholarships, and calls oriented toward women and math studies. They develop alliances with national and international organizations to endorse women participation in science. The Colombian Academy of Science has a group that encourages women to become involved in STEM fields in education, who are working to connect girls and boys from school to develop abilities in math, technology, and science. They are working to reveal the factors that have stimulated the women participation gap in STEM studies, and to issue recommendations to parents and the society in general, seeking to eliminate barriers and have more women students and graduates from those fields.

2. Conclusions

The participation of Colombian females in higher education has grown during the last 85 years, since the first woman ever accessed higher education in 1935. The turning point came in the early 1990s, when women's enrollment became higher than men, and the trend has persisted to the present. This trend has also continued if we analyze enrollment rates by gender and income quintiles, enrollments in university undergraduate, and specializations' programs, as well as in certain fields of knowledge. Nevertheless, the imbalance of women's presence exists within specific fields of study such as Information and Communication Technology programs, Engineering, Manufacturing, and Construction, and in general, in STEM fields. We also found a moderate association between field of knowledge and gender using the chi-Square association test regarding aspirants who were admitted, entrants, first-time students, and graduates as well as between gender and specific disciplines on such variables. In addition, we found some statistical association regarding gender and academic degree (or education levels acquired) as well as between gender and modality of education (face-to-face, distance, or online education) considering the same variables. Concerning education levels, descriptive statistic also showed lower participation of women in doctoral programs.

Our findings are consistent with the trend found for the average of OECD countries, in that "women are underrepresented in science, technology, engineering and mathematics (STEM) but over-represented in health and welfare"

(OECD, 2019, p. 192). Our findings also fit OECD indicators for country members, where the share of women has passed that of men at ISCED 6 and ISCED 7 but not at the doctoral level (OECD, 2019). Contrastingly, the percentage of female doctoral graduates in Colombia is lower (38.4%) than the range of OECD countries (48–52%).

Regarding the pathway from aspiration to graduation from higher education, it is relevant to conclude that half the individuals who apply are admitted at Colombian HEIs, and 77.0% thereof actually enroll. Only half the individuals who enroll complete their programs and obtain educational degrees. As a consequence of this dynamic, only about 25% of the number of aspirants indeed graduate from higher education in the Country. Men are most widely affected with the attrition phenomenon, as they have higher overall dropout rates, in general, by modality of teaching and education levels, with the exception of technical professional education. The abandonment of STEM programs is similar between men and women, and is of a great magnitude.

Concerning participation in the labor market, Colombian women have occupied a larger number of places but they still earn less than men in general, in all levels of education. This pattern is repeated within diverse fields of knowledge and specific disciplines, showing that there is an imbalance that has been hard to overcome.

As for public policy, Colombia has incorporated gender equity in higher education as a purpose within national plans and has adhered to global and regional objectives. Nevertheless, specific government actions have not been palpable referring to particular public efforts to increase women's participation in fields or levels where they are underrepresented, or to foster men's enrollment wherever they are the minority. The majority of government-level endeavors have focused on diagnosis and guidelines toward the encouragement of HEIs to establish institutional policies in this regard. Professional and Science Associations have shown concern about gender equality in populations of higher education students, and graduates, specifically in STEM, and have made efforts to promote gender balance.

References

Alta Consejería Presidencial para la Equidad de la Mujer. (2012). *Orientations for national public policy of gender equity for women*. Bogotá.

CEPAL. (2019). CEPALSTAT Bases de datos y publicaciones estadísticas. Estadísticas e Indicadores. Retrieved from https://estadisticas.cepal.org/cepalstat/web_cepalstat/estadisticasIndicadores.asp?idioma=e

Colombian Ministry of Education. (2017a). *Anuario estadístico de la educación superior colombiana* [*Statistical yearbook of Colombian higher education*]. Bogotá: Imprenta Nacional de Colombia.

Colombian Ministry of Education. (2017b). *Plan decenal de educación 2016–2026* [*Decennial plan of education 2016–2026*]. *El camino hacia la calidad y equidad* [*A pathway toward quality and equity*]. Bogotá: Oficina Asesora de Comunicaciones. Retrieved from http://www.plandecenal.edu.co/cms/media/herramientas/PNDE%20FINAL_ISBN%20web.pdf

Colombian Ministry of Education. (2018). *Marco estratégico institucional 2019–2022* [*Strategic institutional framework 2019–2022*]. Bogotá: Colombian Ministry of Education. Retrieved from https://www.mineducacion.gov.co/1759/articles-382974_recurso_3.pdf

Colombian Ministry of Education. (n.d.). *Enfoque e identidades de género para los lineamientos política de educación superior inclusiva* [*Approach and gender identities for policy orientation towards an inclusive higher education*]. Bogotá: Colombian Ministry of Education. Retrieved from http://www.equidadmujer.gov.co/Documents/Lineamientos-politica-publica-equidad-de-genero.pdf

DANE. (2019). *National population and housing census 2018*. Retrieved from https://www.dane.gov.co/index.php/estadisticas-por-tema/demografia-y-poblacion/censo nacional-de-poblacion-y-vivenda-2018/cuantos-somos. Accessed on January 18, 2019.

Errasti-Ibarrondo, B., Arantzamendi-Solabarrieta, M., & Canga-Armayor, N. (2012). The social imaginary of nursery: A profession to know. *Anales del Sistema Sanitario de Navarra*, *35*(2), 269–283. doi:10.4321/S1137-66272012000200009

Gomez, V. M. (1998). Alternate needs to the traditional university in Colombia. In L. E. Orozco (Ed.), *Higher education, global challenge and national response*, (pp. 10–14). Bogotá: Universidad de Los Andes.

Labour Market Observatory. (2019). *Vinculación laboral de recién graduados. Entry labour entailment of graduates.* Bogotá: Colombian Ministry of Education. Retrieved from http://bi.mineducacion.gov.co:8380/eportal/web/men-observatorio-laboral/tasa-cotizacion-por-sexo

McDonough, P., & Fann, A. J. (2007). The study of inequality. In P. Gumport (Ed.), *Sociology of higher education. Contributions and their context* (pp. 53–93). Baltimore, MD: The Johns Hopkins University Press.

Moreno-Cifuentes, L., & Huertas-Erazo, D. A. (2019). *Monitoring higher education graduates 2017*. Bogotá: Colombian Ministry of Education, Observatorio Laboral de la Educación.

OECD. (2019). *Education at a glance 2019: OECD indicators*. Paris: OECD Publishing. doi:10.1787/f8d7880d-en

Ramírez, M. H. (2010). Las mujeres en la construcción de la nación colombiana [*Women in the built of the Colombian nation*]. Presented at the Cátedra Bicentenario de la Independencia 1810–2010. Universidad Nacional de Colombia, Manizales.

Següel-Palma, F., Valenzuela-Süazo, & Sanhueza-Alvarado, O. (2015). El trabajo profesional de enfermería: revisión de la literatura [The professional work of nursery: a literature review]. *Ciencia y Enfermería*, *21*(2), 11–20. doi:10.4067/S0717-95532015000200002

SNIES. (2019a). Resumen de indicadores de gestión [*Summary of management indicators*]. Perfil Nacional [National profile]. Retrieved from https://www.mineducacion.gov.co/sistemasinfo/Informes/212350:Resumen-de-indicadores-de-Educacion-Superior. Accessed on December 19, 2019.

SNIES. (2019b). Matriculados 2018 [*Enrollments 2018*] [Database]. Retrieved from https://www.mineducacion.gov.co/sistemasinfo/Informacion-a-la-mano/212400:Estadisticas

SNIES. (2019c). Inscritos. Admitidos. Matriculados Primer Curso. Graduados. [*Applicants, enrollees, first time students, and graduates*] [Database]. Retrieved from https://www.mineducacion.gov.co/sistemasinfo/Informacion-a-la-mano/212400:Estadisticas

UNESCO Institute of Statistics. (2019). Equity: 4.3.2 gross enrolment ratio for tertiary education by sex (administrative data). Retrieved from http://data.uis.unesco.org/Index.aspx. Accessed on January 20, 2020.

Uribe-Correa, L. (2012). *Access to higher education in Colombia: An assessment of public policy and outcomes*. Doctoral dissertation. Albany: State University of New York, University at Albany.

Valdes, T., & Gomáriz, E. (1993). *Colombia. Mujeres Latinoamericanas en cifras* (pp. 61) [*Colombia. Latin-American women in figures* (pp. 61)]. Madrid: Instituto de la Mujer. Ministerio de Asuntos Sociales de España y Facultad Latinoamericana de Ciencias Sociales. FLACSO. Retrieved from https:// biblio.flacsoandes.edu.ec/shared/biblio_view.php?bibid56321&tab5opac

Chapter 15

Women in Canadian Higher Education: The Paradox of Gender Parity and Equity

Shirin Abdmolaei and Goli M. Rezai-Rashti

1. Introduction

Despite the once strong opposition to women's participation in Canadian universities (see Gillett, 1998), the past several decades has seen a dramatic shift in the gendered makeup of higher education as women have steadily outnumbered men in university enrollment and completion rates. Between the 1965 and 1966 school year, statistics showed that approximately 61,190 women were enrolled in full-time undergraduate studies. By 1970, this jumped to 101,190; women making up nearly 36.6% of undergraduate enrollment. In 1983, women accounted for 47.4% of full-time undergraduate enrollment (Guppy, Balson, & Velluntini, 1986). And since the early 1990s, women in Canada have accounted for a majority of full-time students enrolled in undergraduate programs while the proportion of women enrolled in graduate degrees has been steadily increasing. In 2006, 32.5% of women between the ages of 25 and 34 had either a bachelor's degree or graduate degree. Within a decade, this percentage rose to 40.7% by 2016 (Statistics Canada, 2017), a point by which women accounted for approximately 56.2% of all postsecondary enrollment (Statistics Canada, 2018). Statistics show that women outnumber men in university completion rates in every Canadian province (Turcotte, 2011).

Despite the incredible gains and strides women have made in Canadian higher education, findings and outcomes reveal a multitude of mixed and contradictory results. While women are surpassing male enrollment and graduation rates, their entrance into traditional male disciplines, such as science, technology, engineering, and mathematics (STEM), still lags behind men (Andres & Adamuti-Trache, 2007; Zarifa, 2012). Women exceed men in undergraduate degrees, but their enrollment in advanced levels of education decreases by each degree, demonstrating that women are less likely than men to obtain graduate degrees (Ferguson, 2016). And despite women's higher rates of postsecondary attainment, this has not manifested in their overall participation in the labor market, and women do not always reap the financial rewards of university degrees the way their male counterparts do, either. Men continue to have, on average, higher incomes than

International Perspectives on Gender and Higher Education, 273–290

doi:10.1108/978-1-83909-886-420201015

women and participate at much higher rates than women in the labor force; statistics demonstrating that as of 2019, only 61.4% of women participate while 70.1% of men do (Boudarbat & Connolly, 2013). Women also continue to be underrepresented in leadership roles and upper-ranked positions in the workplace, within and outside of higher education (Erwin & Maurutto, 1998; Glauser, 2018; Hideg & Shen, 2019).

When we problematize the common trend of speaking about women through a universalist lens, we also see significant racial, ethnic, and socioeconomic differences between women in terms of access to, and success in, higher education, including what disciplines they are more likely to enroll in, as well as their representation in the labor force and upper-ranked positions in the workplace (see Abada, Hou, & Ram, 2009; Bailey, 2016; Chui, 2011; Collins & Magnan, 2018; Davies, Maldonado, & Zarifa, 2014; Finnie, Childs, & Wismer, 2011; Henry & Tator, 2009; Krahn & Taylor, 2005; Michalski, Cunningham, & Henry, 2017; Richardson & Cohen, 2000; Wang, 2013). Moreover, despite the illusion of gender parity in Canadian higher education, women continue to experience barriers, discouragement, harassment, and underrepresentation on the basis of their gender prior to and during their university studies (Acker & Wagner, 2019).

In this chapter we will be reviewing existing literature which provides an overview of contemporary issues and trends relating to the feminization of Canadian higher education. This chapter begins by discussing the feminization of education and the "panic" over boys' underachievement before moving on to examining the fields of study women are both overrepresented and underrepresented within higher education. Next, in our effort to complicate essentialized notions of women, we demonstrate the different rate to which women access and participate in higher education by race and ethnicity while highlighting the implications of socioeconomic barriers. Finally, we discuss the paradoxes of gender equity and women's educational success by drawing attention to their participation in the labor force. While countries such as Canada have been hailed for their success in advancing women's participation and achievement in higher education, we aim to complicate the notion of equity as it extends to women and minorities throughout this chapter. A closer examination of Canadian women in higher education in this present chapter will illustrate the structural and persistent patterns of difference, racism, exclusion, and sexism, together demonstrating the paradoxes of gender parity and equity.

2. Feminization of Education, Backlash, and Boys' Underachievement

Although attempts to understand the causes and factors explaining the higher enrollment of women in higher education has been subject to extensive studies in OECD countries such as the United States, there surprisingly exists a comparatively limited number of studies which have examined the Canadian context. Nonetheless, the feminization of education in Canada has been the focus of discussion in recent years. Some scholars have considered cognitive, biological, and physical differences between boys and girls from a young age as a determining factor in school performance between boys and girls and have subsequently suggested the need for state intervention to change school curriculum. For example, Frenette and Zeman (2007) found that there were notable differences between boys and girls during the elementary and high school years which can account for the gender gap in Canadian universities. The authors found that girls outperformed boys on standardized testing and overall school marks, and these factors, coupled with study habits and parental expectations, accounted for 58.9% of the gender gap in university participation, suggesting that girls' academic performance in elementary and high school may be central to understanding the greater participation of women in university. Other researchers have argued that women's increasing participation in education has been a response to the women's movement of the 1960s while connected to the demands of the labor market.

Interestingly, the success of girls and women in education has also pointed to one of the great paradoxes of gender equity in liberal democracies across the Western, English speaking world: significant backlash and "panic" over the feminization of education at the expense of male students. As the feminization of education has been a source of anxiety and worry over the underachievement of male students, since the 1990s, Canada has raised concerns over the underachievement of boys in literacy, which sparked policy interventions by provincial governments (Martino & Rezai-Rashti, 2012a).[1] In Ontario, for example, it is believed that this trend started when standardized testing and test-based accountability was introduced as means to measure student performance in literacy. This move to metrics and datafication created debates among educational scholars over whether boys' lower marks in standardized literacy tests required policy intervention (for a critique see Lingard, Mills, & Weaver-Hightower, 2012). The concern over boys' literacy resulted in provincial governments introducing several explicit and implicit policies to overcome this gender achievement gap. These measures included recruiting more male teachers to improve boys' literacy in an effort to close the gender achievement gap. Although there is no specific policy on male teachers' recruitment, Martino and Rezai-Rashti's (2012b) research in elementary schools revealed that administrators' perceptions and hiring practices are still focused on racial and gender similarities between teachers and students in order to minimize the gender achievement gap (Rezai-Rashti & Martino, 2017).

In their Equity and Inclusive Education Strategy (2009), which was designed to focus on marginalized groups in education, the Ontario Ministry of Education identified boys as one of these subjugated groups. Interestingly, alongside other designated marginalized groups who had historically and systematically encountered "biases, barriers, and power dynamics that limit our students'

---

[1]Canada is the only country with no national system of education and each province has autonomy over policies and procedures relevant to their provincial contexts.

prospects for learning, growing, and fully contributing to society" (2009a, p. 11), boys were given a marginalized status in education:

> Our government is committed both in raising the bar for student achievement and to reducing the achievement gaps. Recent immigrants, children from low-income families, Aboriginal students, *boys*, and students with special education needs are just some of the groups that maybe at risk of lower achievement. (Ontario Ministry of Education, 2009a, p. 5, emphasis added)

This statement in the policy document about boys' underachievement was a result of accountability-driven policies as a basis for presenting boys as a disadvantaged group in the same way as students with special needs:

> Evidence consistently shows that some groups of students tend to face barriers to learning…*Boys*, for example, often lag behind girls in reading, and the ministry has funded teacher inquiry and research and provided teacher training and resources to help boost boys' reading skills. Students with special education needs also have complex and unique educational requirement. (Ontario Ministry of Education, 2009a, p. 14)

Martino and Rezai-Rashti (2012a) have problematized the gender achievement gap that has perceived boys as "the new disadvantaged," arguing that (i) "decontextualized achievement data in the form of high stakes testing become the only measure of student performance"; and (ii) the focus on single category of gender as a basis for disaggregating test score data means that other forms of inequalities such as race and social class are not addressed (p. 423).

In an effort to improve boys' literacy in Ontario, in 2004 and 2009, the Ontario Ministry of Education initiated two guidelines: "*Me Read? No Way!*" and "*Me Read? And How!*"—both of which were practical guides intended to help improve literacy for boys and were widely distributed to teachers, administrators, and faculties of education across the province. While these guides include "boy friendly" literature in elementary schools to encourage boys to read more "non-feminine" literature to help better literacy rates among male students, an implication of these guides has been its not-so-subtle subscription to a particular notion of gender equity and a "*feminized*" education system that has been failing boys. It is also important to note that the results of standardized tests are still presented by gender on the websites of schools and testing organizations to highlight the lower literacy rates of boys while simultaneously emphasizing the feminization of education.

While the feminization of education and the underachievement of boys have perhaps been sources of anxiety and "panic" in Canada and have been addressed by varying provincial governments across the country, what is really missing in the discourses of failing boys and the feminization of education has been the need to interrogate which boys and which girls are underachieving. This is to avoid essentialization and universalization of gender and educational achievement.

3. Fields of Study by Gender

Although women account for the majority of undergraduate enrollment in Canada, women are predominately enrolled in social science and humanity programs (Hango, 2013b). Business, management, marketing, health professions, and education also account for almost half (47%) of female degree holders (Ferguson, 2016). Although women have been making significant leeway into disciplines such as law, dentistry, and medical fields, there has been little progress in other disciplines which have been historically reserved for men, particularly science, technology, engineering, and mathematics (STEM) (Andres & Adamuti-Trache, 2007; NSERC Chairs for Women in Science and Engineering, 2018; Statistics Canada, 2017). According to Acker and Oatley (1993), one of the most frequently addressed issues regarding gender and education has been the split between art and science. The focus of most literature has been to understand females' underrepresentation in mathematics, physical sciences, engineering, computer studies, and related fields from elementary to postsecondary education.

The underrepresentation of women in STEM has been subject to much discussion over the course of the last several decades in Canada (Canadian Committee on Women in Engineering, 1992). The publication of the Science Council of Canada's *The Science Education of Women in Canada: A statement of concern* in 1982 was among the first efforts by the federal government to acknowledge the underrepresentation of girls in science and mathematics in high school. Keen on understanding this gap and prompted by economic incentives, governments, school boards, postsecondary institutions, and businesses have promoted and initiated projects intended to increase the interest of young girls and women in mathematics and sciences and to encourage their pursuits of careers in such fields (Gadalla, 2001). Despite these efforts, and nearly 40 years later, little progress has been made (Wall, 2019); statistics showing that while 33.1% of men enroll in a STEM program in higher education, only 17.8% of women do (Finnie & Childs, 2018).

Hango (2013a) observed that in 2011, women accounted for approximately 66% of all graduates between the ages of 25 to 34 in a non-STEM program. Comparatively, only 39% of women of the same age group graduated from a STEM program. Although the participation rate of women in biological sciences and agriculture is growing, there has been little increase in enrollment and completion rates in fields such as economics, engineering, computer science, and physics, while engineering and applied sciences are among the disciplines which see the highest rate to which male students enroll (Andres & Adamuti-Trache, 2007). Women who did graduate from a STEM program were largely concentrated in science and technology (59%), while only 23% of women graduated from engineering and 30% graduated from computer science (Hango, 2013a). Although some advancement have been made over the course of the last several decades, the rate to which women graduate from a STEM program still remains low with minimal gains. For example, in 1992, women graduates in architecture, engineering, and a related program stood at 17.5% and rose only to 22.2% in 2008. In mathematics and computer and information sciences, the percentage of women graduates actually declined, from 35.2% in 1992 to 30.4% in 2008. The number of women graduating from all other fields, including non-STEM fields, increased in most programs (Turcotta, 2011).

However, perhaps the most surprising takeaway from our overview of existing research is that despite women having the grades and test scores to pursue mathematics and science in higher education, they choose to enroll in STEM fields at a considerably lower rate than their male counterparts (Finnie & Childs, 2018; Hango, 2013b). A study conducted by Hango (2013a) found that among female students who perceived their mathematics skills and grades to be excellent, only 47% chose to pursue a STEM program in higher education compared to 66% of boys with similar responses. Gender stereotyping, socialization, and a lack of female representation in these fields have been identified as social and structural factors which may explain why girls and women often become discouraged and disengaged from STEM fields and are less likely to enroll in a STEM program in higher education (see Canadian Committee on Women in Engineering, 1992; Council of Canadian Academies, 2012; also see Dutta, 2019; Gadalla, 2001). Not all those who enroll in a STEM field in their first year of undergraduate studies graduate from a STEM program, either. As Wall (2019) contends, a critical concern regarding women in STEM is whether they will remain in it throughout their undergraduate degrees. Although some studies from the United States have found that women are less likely to complete a STEM degree than men—reasons being that women often grow uninterested in the curriculum, feel isolated due to the low numbers of female students in their programs, are subjected to unfair treatment, and experience a lack of female representation—very few comparative studies have been undertaken in Canada. In their effort to fill this gap, Wall's (2019) study found that women who started off in STEM in 2010 were nearly twice as likely (23%) than men (12%) to switch to a non-STEM degree, most leaving by the second year of their undergraduate studies. While the author found that only 66% of women persisted in STEM, more women (36%) completed their studies within the expected completion time as opposed men (25%).[2] In a separate study conducted on the educational pursuits of 91 female science students in Canada, Erwin and Maurutto's (1998) longitudinal study discusses both the reasons why women chose to pursue science in university and the barriers and obstacles which impeded their educational trajectories while in university. Success in mathematics and science courses in high school, including support from parents and teachers, encouraged most female participants in their study to pursue STEM in university (also see Dooley, Payne, Steffler, & Wagner, 2017; Hango, 2013a). However, by the second year of their undergraduate studies,

[2]In most Canadian provinces, a typical undergraduate degree is completed in 4 years. The only exception is Québec, where students must complete a 2-year CEGEP program prior to beginning their undergraduate degrees, which usually takes 3 years to complete.

nearly half of participants' grades dropped to a C+ average or lower while only 25% had their scholarships renewed, and many failed to posses the grades needed to continue their education in science or pursue advanced degrees. A significant number of students also dropped at least one course while more than half (53%) considered switching to a different program. Interestingly, those who were majoring in mathematics, physics, and computer science were more likely to switch to another science program or had switched to a non-science major. Women who were in biology and psychology were less likely to switch to another major.

The authors also found that working-class and Black students, who worked more hours during the school year in their sample, were less academically successful and were more likely to drop out, which speaks to the intersections of structural inequities which impede upon low-income, racialized women's success in STEM as well as in higher education more generally. The findings of this study also found that lower levels of self-confidence and increased anxiety among participants emerged by the second year of their undergraduate studies as they grew more uncertain about their futures. Lack of female role models in the form of faculty and professors, experiences with gender discrimination, and concerns for safety on campus were also discussed as additional barriers that female students in Erwin and Maurutto's study faced, impeding their continuation in STEM.

Walton, Logel, Peach, Spencer, and Zanna's (2004) study of women's experiences in selective engineering programs in Canada found that participants in programs with low female representation struggled. In comparison to their male counterparts, women described feeling overwhelmed, expected to be less successful, and performed worse in their classes. Given the lack of underrepresentation and negative stereotypes, female students in predominately male disciplines often deal with psychological challenges. Yet the authors' testing of two intervention methods aimed at alleviating the effects of the "chilly climate"—the social-belonging intervention and the affirmation-training intervention—helped women develop a sense of belonging in male-dominated fields and helped women cope with stress which arose from marginalization. However, while the interventions were promising, the authors also argue that STEM settings need to be improved in order to eliminate sexism and include more female representation in STEM, writing that

> …a community of women may reduce social marginalization and the need for specific intervention. Efforts to increase the representation of women in STEM thus go hand-in-hand with efforts to help women function well in male-dominated STEM settings as means to promote gender equality. (p. 483)

Given the findings of the above studies, perhaps it is unsurprising, then, that the number of women participating in the sciences declines with each level of education. The number of women receiving a degree in a STEM field also decreases by every degree type (NSERC Chairs for Women in Science and Engineering, 2018). The percentage of female students who earned a master's degree in the natural sciences and engineering from 2005 to 2014 was approximately 37%, while only 32% of women received one at a doctoral level (Natural Sciences and Engineering Research Council of Canada, 2017). However, statistics show that women's enrollment in natural sciences and engineering at a master's level has increased by 55% over the past decade, while doctoral enrollment has increased by 102% (Corporate Planning and Policy Directorate, 2010). Broken down by fields, 34% of women earned a doctorate in physical and life sciences, 15% in architecture and engineering, and 21% in mathematics, computer, and information sciences. In some non-STEM fields, women account for more than half of the doctorates earned, such as education (62%) and psychology (67%). Almost half of the doctorates received in health and related fields were earned by women (49%), while women in humanities obtained 43% of doctoral degrees. Only 39% of women received a doctorate in the social sciences (Ferguson, 2016).

4. Racialized Women and Socioeconomic Disparities

Canada is among one of the most diverse countries in the world. In 2011, Canada had a foreign-born population of approximately 6,775,800 people which represented 20.6% of the total population—the highest among the G7 countries.[3] While more than 200 ethnic identities were reported to the 2011 National Household Survey, visible minorities represent 19.1% of the total Canadian population. The largest visible minority groups in Canada compromise of South Asians, Chinese, and Black-Canadians, together accounting for 61.3% of the visible minority population (National Household Survey, 2011). In a country as racially, ethnically, and socioeconomically diverse as Canada, there are considerable variations in the rate to which Canadians access and complete higher education. Recent studies have shown that visible minorities who are either children of immigrants or came to Canada as children participate in postsecondary education at a higher rate than non-immigrant White Canadians, and it has been observed that East Asian, South Asian, and Middle Eastern-Canadian students maintain a significant advantage in terms of postsecondary attainment and are more likely to pursue higher education (Finnie & Mueller, 2010; also see Abada et al., 2009; Childs, Finnie, & Mueller, 2017; Picot & Hou, 2011). In a study conducted by Krahn and Taylor (2005), their findings revealed that visible minority youth have high educational aspirations and most intended on pursuing at least one post-secondary degree. While university participation rates of first-generation immigrants stand at approximately 57% and 54% for second-generation immigrants, only 38% of non-immigrants attend university (Childs, Finnie, & Mueller, 2017).

Visible minority women who were born in Canada are more likely than other women and men to hold a university degree. About 44.7% of Canadian-born visible minority women between the ages of 25 to 54 had a university degree,

[3]The Group of 7 or G7 refers to the eight most industrialized nations in the world, which includes Canada, France, Germany, Italy, the United Kingdom, Japan, United States, and the United Kingdom.

compared to 25.8% of women who were not a visible minority. About 47.7% of visible minority women born in Canada were also more likely than Canadian-born visible minority men (38%) as well as visible minority immigrant men (41.2%) to have a university degree (Hudon, 2016). Racialized women in Canada also enroll in fields of study not generally chosen by women. The National Household Survey conducted by Statistics Canada in 2011 found that visible minority women were more likely to study business, management, and public administration, while they were also more likely to study a STEM field compared to their non-immigrant White female counterparts (also see Birani & Lehmann, 2013; Finnie & Childs, 2018; Natural Sciences and Engineering Research Council of Statistics Canada, 2017). The Corporate Planning and Policy Directorate (2010) found that one explanation for the increase in the number of women in the natural sciences and engineering has been through immigration. Female visible minorities, which includes Canadian-born and immigrants between the ages of 25 and 34, accounted for 4 in 10 female university STEM degree holders, averaging 41% of women within this age group who hold a STEM degree. They accounted for 65% of women holding a mathematics and computer science degree, 54% of engineering degrees, and 30% of science and technology degrees (Ferguson, 2016). While visible minority women participated in disciplines such as education and personal, protective, and transportation services at a substantially lower rate than non-visible minority women, they participated in health and related fields, agriculture, natural resources and conservation, and social and behavioral sciences to roughly the same extent (Hudon, 2016).

All ethnic groups in Canada have experienced an overall improvement in the levels to which they access and complete higher education (Davies et al., 2014). Although racialized women, on average, are making incredible strides in Canadian postsecondary education, systemic racism, socioeconomic vulnerabilities, and inequitable educational practices impede the educational paths of many visible minority groups, particularly Indigenous peoples, Black students, and low-income Canadians, who access and complete university at a considerably lower rate than other minority groups (Abada et al., 2009; Abada & Tenkorang, 2009; Birani & Lehmann, 2013; Collins & Magnan, 2018; Davies et al., 2014; Finnie et al., 2011; Krahn & Taylor, 2005; Michalski et al., 2017; Richardson & Cohen, 2000; Wang, 2013). Although the children of immigrants tend to have a much higher rate of university attendance and completion, this does not appear to extend to the children of Filipino immigrants. Despite the very high levels of postsecondary education of Filipino parents, Filipino youth have among the lowest rates of university graduation in the country (Kelly et al., 2014).

Systemic barriers rooted in a history of colonialism and racist social structures have presented considerable obstacles for Indigenous peoples in Canada. Wang (2013) found that high dropout rates during the K-12 years, low expectations of Indigenous youth, discrimination, and lack of social and financial support have deterred Indigenous peoples from pursuing higher education. Statistics revealed that in 2016, only 10.9% of Indigenous peoples between the ages of 25 to and 64 had a bachelor's degree or higher (Statistics Canada, 2017). However, following the trend that we have been observing in Canada, Indigenous women pursue university at a much higher rate than Indigenous men. In 2011, 13% of women received a university degree while only 8% of men did (Indigenous and Northern Affairs Canada, 2011).

Similar patterns appear to exist for Black Caribbean students as well, who experience the lowest university completion rates among visible minorities in the country (Abada et al., 2009). In their study of Black students in Toronto, Robson, Anisef, Brown, and George (2018) found that Black students were less likely to be enrolled in academic courses in high school in comparison to other racial groups, and with Latinos, they were among the lowest averages. Black female students, however, were one and a half times more likely to pursue university than Black males. In the province of Ontario, younger Black women between the ages of 25 and 24 are 9.5% more likely to have a university degree than Black women between the ages of 45 to and 54, but younger Black men are less likely to have a university degree than older Black men (Parkins, 2018). Nonetheless, as Neeganagwedin (2013) writes, Black women in Canada have a "history of marginalization" (p. 239) within Canadian educational contexts, where a Eurocentric curriculum and institutionalized barriers manifested in educational contexts present obstacles for Black women, which needs to be taken into account when considering the lower rates to which Black women participate in university in comparison to other women in the country. Indeed, the complexities of postsecondary attainment in Canada require further exploration of a number of intersectional reasons which may explain not only gendered differences but also generational differences within various racial and ethnic communities.

Access to higher education in Canada has expanded to all students regardless of their socioeconomic statuses given the expansion and availability of financial aid to all students with financial needs. However, Christophides, Cirello, and Hoy's (2001) and Drolet's (2005) studies have found that students who come from high-income households are still more likely to attend university while parental income is an important factor for university participation (also see Andres, Adam-Trache, Yoon, Pidgeon, & Thomsen, 2007). Research has also shown that the sort of education received in elementary and secondary school may provide some reasons into the obstacles and underrepresentation that students face. In a study of the postsecondary pathways of second-generation Haitian youth in Québec, Collins and Magnan (2018) found that a lack of parental and institutional help, emerging from occupying a lower socioeconomic status, as well as a lack of social and cultural capital, had implications for their education and their ability to navigate the education system.

5. Postsecondary Educated Women in the Labor Force

The changing student body in Canadian higher education has undoubtedly resulted in subsequent shifts in the labor market. In 2009, 58.3% of women were employed, nearly doubling from 1976 (Ferraro, 2011), and for university educated women between the ages of 25 to and 54, their participation in the labor force rose from 15.7% in 1990 to 29.3% in 2008, while their wages have been substantially increasing as well. As McMullen, Gilmore, and Le Petit (2010) observed, among postsecondary graduates, women are more likely to work in the health sector, government services, and education—the latter of which women make up by nearly double the teaching force than men in secondary, primary, and preschool levels (Turcotte, 2011)—while men continue to work largely in the sciences, management, and fields related to manufacturing. However, the authors note that between 1996 and 2006, there have been significant advancements for women in architecture, engineering, and the sciences.

Although women have been outnumbering men in university attainment, this has not necessarily resulted in higher employment earnings over men, despite similarities in terms of degree, level of education, and age. For example, in 2005, it shows that for workers between the ages of 35 to and 39 with a degree in medicine, dentistry, and veterinary medicine or optometry, the ratio between the incomes of men and women was 0.89 with men receiving $70,000 on average while women received $62,317 (Turcotte, 2011). A recent analysis of tax filings and educational attainment among publicly funded colleges and universities starting in 2010 found that just after one year of graduating from university, women earn an average of $5,700 or 12% less than men. This widens to 25% 5 years after graduation, with women making an average of $17,700 less than men across all disciplines (Finnie, Miyairi, Dubois, Bowen, & Amery, 2019). This points to how discrimination in the labor market begins early during the hiring stage.

While STEM programs are often marketed as providing higher wages for graduates, labor market outcomes substantially differ depending on gender. Hango (2013a) found that in 2011, the unemployment rate for men with a university degree from a STEM program was 4.7% while it was 7.0% for women. They also found that the yearly salary for women with STEM degrees and non-STEM degrees was not much different, although men who graduated from a STEM field did receive more than men with non-STEM degrees. This could partly be explained by the findings of the 2006 consensus which found that for university degree holders between the ages of 25 to and 44 years old, more women as opposed to men with a STEM degree were likely to work in the social sciences, education, health, business, finance, and administration while men occupied positions that were mostly in management and natural and applied sciences (Corporate Planning and Policy Directorate, 2010). According to these data, it appears that "there exists a higher 'leakage rate' out of NSE-related [natural sciences and engineering] occupations for women as compared to men" (Corporate Planning and Policy Directorate, 2010, p. 32). Another reason for the income disparity between men and women in STEM fields has to do with the gender wage gap. Studies have shown that women between the ages of 25 to and 29 who worked full-time earned approximately 85 cents for each dollar earned by a male, although this also depended on their level of schooling (Turcotte, 2011). Research by Boudarbat and Connolly (2013) also found that female graduates in any field make on average 6–14% less than men do. In Ontario, Parkins (2018) found that female university graduates in health, education, and teaching earn 96% of the income of their male counterparts, but women in science only receive 88% of what men make while women in engineering make only 84% of what men make.

In the context of the university, despite the average earnings of university professors increasing between 2005 and 2015, statistics show that the gender age gap stands at 17.5%, with men earning approximately $110,713 per year on average while women only receive $91,366. However, the gap between non-racialized and racialized women professors is staggering. While non-racialized women receive 82 cents for every dollar earned by a non-racialized male, racialized professors receive only 68 cents to that of every dollar earned by a non-racialized male (Canadian Association of University Teachers, 2018). Moreover, racialized and Aboriginal academics experience higher rates of unemployment than their White colleagues, which points to discriminatory hiring patterns and larger structures of gender and racial inequity (also see Canadian Association of University Teachers, 2018).

Although women are graduating from university at much higher rates than men, and while the labor market is indeed diversifying, representation remains low for women in senior management positions (Cooke-Reynolds & Zukewich, 2004; The Conference Board of Canada, 2018b). In 2006, women compromised of only 37% of all senior manager positions (Drolet, 2011). Efforts have been made to combat the underrepresentation of women in senior roles across a variety of sectors. In 2010, the Canadian Board Diversity Council set a goal of having at least 30% of women represent Financial Post 500 Companies (FP500) by 2018 (The Conference Board of Canada, 2018b). However, only one-quarter of all seats on the FP500 boards are currently held by women, and many FP500 organizations do not have any representation of women on their boards. Although progress has been stagnant, it is slowly changing. In 2001, women only held 10.9% of the seats, while in 2018, they held 24.5%.

Nonetheless, women's representation remains low and even lower for women who are visible minorities—despite the rate to which visible minority women participate in fields such as business and STEM disciplines. Among the companies listed on the Toronto Stock Exchange (TSX60), 17 out of the 60 largest companies had women make up 30.5% of board members while only 6.35% were visible minorities. In the medical field, Glauser (2018) found that while 41% of Canadian physicians are women, out of 26 members who sit on the Ontario Medical Association (OMA) board of directors, only 8 are women. Glauber has attributed this to the existence of bias against women, familial obligations, and the "confidence gap" between women and men. Trends in university faculty positions also show gendered and racial disparities. Indeed, women are holding more full-time faculty positions and senior leadership appointments in Canadian universities than a decade ago. But a study conducted by Universities Canada (2019) found that while women in leadership positions are nearly proportionate to men, gender parity appears to be more consistent among deans in the arts, social sciences, and humanities; data showing that women hold 50% of these positions. However, their representations as deans in health and STEM faculties are substantially lower, showing that women make up 34.4 % of health faculties while only 28.6% of STEM faculties across the country. Findings also reveal that women account for 48.5% of Assistant Professor positions, compared to 27% of Full Professor positions, while racialized women are the most underrepresented among professors and university instructors (Canadian Association of University Teachers, 2018). Racialized faculty remain disproportionately underrepresented; data revealing that while 44.1% of White women hold senior positions, only 3.6% of racialized women do (Universities Canada, 2019; also see; Henry et al., 2017).

6. Conclusion

In this chapter we reviewed existing literature on the contemporary situation of women in Canadian higher education. Since the early 1990s, women in Canada have accounted for a majority of full-time students enrolled in undergraduate programs, while the proportion of women enrolled in graduate degrees has also been increasing. However, the success of women in Canadian higher education has been mixed and paradoxical. The educational success of girls prior to attending postsecondary has been identified as one of the determining factors explaining the overrepresentation of women in higher education. Prompting concern and "panic," there has been considerable backlash to what has been characterized as the feminization of education and the underachievement of boys, the latter of whom have been imagined to be "the new disadvantaged" (Martino & Rezai-Rashti, 2012a) vis-à-vis the educational achievements of girls. And in higher education, while women are in fact surpassing male enrollment in higher education, their entrance into traditional male disciplines, such as science, technology, engineering, and mathematics (STEM), is still greatly lagging behind men, while those who pursue a STEM degree do not always complete their degrees, which speaks to the social and structural barriers that often impede upon women's educational success and opportunities. Moreover, despite women's higher rates of postsecondary attainment, their advanced levels of education have not manifested in the labor market, with the wealth gap showing that men, on average, have higher incomes than women. Women also continue to be underrepresented in positions of leadership and upper-ranked positions.

The multi-racial, multi-ethnic, and socioeconomic diversity of Canada further complicates the representation of women in higher education. Although research shows that women are underrepresented in traditional male disciplines, immigrant and visible minority women in Canada access these disciplines, including university more generally, at much higher rates than their White counterparts. However, racialized women are less likely than White women to occupy senior leadership positions in the workplace. And while immigration and gender parity have transformed the social makeup of Canadian higher education, research has found that systemic racism, socioeconomic vulnerabilities, and inequitable educational practices impede certain minority groups and working-class Canadians from accessing higher education while also hampering their opportunities to complete their postsecondary studies. Further research is needed in order to problematize speaking of women in higher education through essentialized narratives in an effort to understand their different experiences with regards to accessing and completing higher education, including their representation in the labor market and workforce.

References

Abada, T., Hou, F., & Ram, B. (2009). Ethnic differences in educational attainment among the children of Canadian immigrants. *The Canadian Journal of Sociology*, *34*(1), 1–28.

Abada, T., & Tenkorang, E. (2009). Pursuit of university education among the children of immigrants in Canada: The roles of parental human capital and social capital. *Journal of Youth Studies*, *12*(2), 185–207.

Acker, S., & Oatley, K. (1993). Gender issues in education for science and technology: Current situation and prospects for change. *Canadian Journal of Education*, *18*(3), 255–272.

Acker, S., & Wagner, A. (2019). Feminist scholars working around the neoliberal university. *Gender and Education*, *31*(1), 62–81.

Andres, L., & Adamuti-Trache, M. (2007). You've come a long way, baby? Persistent gender inequality in university enrolment and completion in Canada, 1979–2004. *Canadian Public Policy*. [*Analyse de Politiques*.], *33*(1), 93–116.

Andres, L., Adamuti-Trache, M., Yoon, E., Pidgeon, M., & Thomsen, J. P. (2007). Educational expectations, parental social class, gender, and postsecondary attainment: A 10 year perspective. *Youth & Society*, *39*(2), 135–163.

Bailey, K. (2016). Racism in the Canadian university: Indigenous students' experiences. *Ethnic and Racial Studies*, *39*(7), 1261–1279.

Birani, A., & Lehmann, W. (2013). Ethnicity as social capital: An examination of first-generation, ethnic-minority students at a Canadian university. *International Studies in Sociology of Education*, *23*(4), 281–297.

Boudarbat, B., & Connolly, M. (2013). The gender wage gap among recent post-secondary graduates in Canada: A distributional approach. *The Canadian Journal of Economics*, *46*(3), 1037–1065.

Canadian Association of University Teachers. (2018). *Underrepresented & underpaid: Diversity & equity among Canada's post-secondary education teachers*. Canadian Association of University Teachers. [*Association canadienne des professeures et professeurs d'université*.] Ottawa, Canada. Retrieved from https://www.caut.ca/sites/default/files/caut_equity_report_2018-04final.pdf

Canadian Committee on Women in Engineering. (1992). *More than just numbers*. Ottawa, ON: Canadian Committee on Women in Engineering. Retrieved from https://www3.carleton.ca/cwse-on/webmtjnen/repomtjn.html

Childs, S., Finnie, R., & Mueller, R. E. (2017). Why do so many children of immigrants attend university? Evidence for Canada. *Journal of International Migration and Integration*, *18*(1), 1–28.

Christofides, L. N., Cirello, J., & Hoy, M. (2001). Family income and postsecondary education. *The Canadian Journal of Higher Education*. [*La revue canadienne d'enseignement supérieur*.], *31*(1), 177–208.

Chui, T. (2011). *Immigrant women*. Ottawa, ON: Statistics Canada. Catalogue no. 89-503-X. Retrieved from http://www.oaith.ca/assets/files/Publications/Government%20Documents/Women_In_Ca nada_6thReport/WmCanada_ImmigrantWm.pdf

Collins, T., & Magnan, M. (2018). Post-secondary pathways among second-generation immigrant youth of Haitian origin in Quebec. *Canadian Journal of Education*. [*Revue Canadienne de l'éducation*.], *41*(2), 413–440.

Cooke-Reynolds, M., & Zukewich, N. (2004). *The feminization of work*. Ottawa, ON: Statistics Canada. Catalogue no. 11–008. Retrieved from https://www150.statcan.gc.ca/n1/en/pub/11-008-x/2003004/article/6806eng.pdf?st=U_RHaAcH

Corporate Planning and Policy Directorate. (2010). *Women in science and engineering in Canada*. Natural Sciences and Engineering Research Council of Canada, Ottawa, ON. Retrieved from https://www.nserc-crsng.gc.ca/_doc/Report-Rapports/Women_Science_Engineering_e.pdf

Council of Canadian Academies. (2012). *Strengthening Canada's research capacity: The gender dimension*. Council of Canadian Academies, Ottawa, ON. Retrieved from https://cca-reports.ca/reports/strengthening-canadas-research-capacity-the-gender-dimension/

Davies, S., Maldonado, V., & Zarifa, D. (2014). Effectively maintaining inequality in Toronto: Predicting student destinations in Ontario universities. *Canadian Review of Sociology*. [*Revue canadienne de sociologie*], *51*(1), 22–53.

Dooley, M., Payne, A., Steffler, M., & Wagner, J. (2017). Understanding the STEM path through high school and into university programs. *Canadian Public Policy*, *43*(1), 1–16.

Drolet, M. (2005). *Participation in post-secondary education in Canada: Has the role of parental income and education changed over the 1990s?* Ottawa, ON: Statistics Canada. Catalogue no. 11F0019MIE— No. 243. Retrieved from http://www.publications.gc.ca/Collection/Statcan/11F0019MIE/11F0019MIE2005243.pdf

Drolet, M. (2011). Why has the gender wage gap narrowed? *Perspectives on Labour Income*, *32*(1), 3–13. Statistics Canada. Retrieved from https://www150.statcan.gc.ca/n1/en/pub/75-001-x/2011001/pdf/11394-eng.pdf?st=crMyfh_r

Dutta, R. (2019). Point of view: I face sexism as a young, female engineer, but I have hope. *CBC News*, December 5. Retrieved from https://www.cbc.ca/news/canada/montreal/i-study-engineering-montreal-polytechnique- 1.5382596

Erwin, L., & Maurutto, P. (1998). Beyond access: Considering gender deficits in science education. *Gender and Education*, *10*(1), 51–69.

Ferguson, J. S. (2016). *Women and education: Qualification, skills and technology*. Ottawa, ON: Statistics Canada. Catalogue no. 89-503-X. Retrieved from https://www150.statcan.gc.ca/n1/pub/89-503-x/2015001/article/14640-eng.pdf

Ferraro, V. (2011). Paid work. In *Women in Canada: A gender-based statistical report* (pp. 111–136). Ottawa, ON: Statistics Canada. Catalogue No. 89-503-X. Retrieved from https://www150.statcan.gc.ca/n1/pub/89-503-x/89-503-x2010001-eng.pdf

Finnie, R., & Childs, S. (2018). Who goes to STEM disciplines? Evidence from the youth in transition survey. *Canadian Public Policy*, *44*(S1), S43–S55.

Finnie, R., Childs, S., & Wismer, A. (2011). *Under-represented groups in postsecondary education in Ontario: Evidence from the youth in transition Survey*. Toronto, ON: Higher Education Quality Council of Ontario.

Finnie, R., Miyairi, M., Dubois, M., Bonen, T., & Amery, B. (2019). *How much do they make? New evidence on the early career earnings of Canadian post-secondary education graduates by credential and field of study*. Ottawa, ON: Education Policy Research Initiative and Labour Market Information Council.

Finnie, R., & Mueller, R. E. (2010). They came, they saw, they enrolled: Access to post-secondary eduction by the children of immigrants. In R. Finnie, M. Frenette, R. E. Mueller, & A. Sweetman (Eds.), *Pursuing higher education in Canada: Economic, social, and policy dimensions* (pp. 191–216). Montréal, QC; Kingston, ON: McGill-Queen's University Press.

Frenette, M., & Zeman, K. (2007). *Why are most university students women? Evidence based on academic performance, study habits and parental influences*. Ottawa, ON: Statistics Canada. Catalogue no. 11F0019MIE—No. 303. Retrieved from https://www150.statcan.gc.ca/n1/en/pub/11f0019m/11f0019m2007303eng.pdf?st=vdIWIIS7

Gadalla, T. M. (2001). Patterns of women's enrolment in university mathematics, engineering and computer science in Canada, 1972–1995. *The Canadian Journal of Higher Education*. [*La revue canadienne d'enseignement supérieur.*], *31*(1), 1–34.

Gillett, M. (1998). The four phases of academe: Women in university. In J. Stalker & S. Prentice (Eds.), *The illusion of inclusion: Women in post secondary education* (pp. 36–47). Halifax, NS: Fernwood Publishing.

Glauser, W. (2018). Rise of women in medicine not matched by leadership roles. *Canadian Medical Association Journal*, *190*(15), E479–E480.

Government of Ontario. (2009). *Ontario's equity and inclusive education strategy*. Retrieved from http://www.edu.gov.on.ca/eng/policyfunding/equity.pdf

Guppy, N., Balson, D., & Vellutini, S. (1986). Women and higher education in Canadian society. In J. Gaskell & A. McLaren (Eds.), *Women and education* (pp. 171–192). Calgary, AB: Detselig Entreprises.

Hango, D. (2013a). *Gender differences in science, technology, engineering, mathematics and computer science (STEM) programs at university*. Ottawa, ON: Statistics Canada. Catalogue no. 75 -006-X. Retrieved from https://www150.statcan.gc.ca/n1/en/pub/75-006-x/2013001/article/11874-eng.pdf?st=qgDHK5jQ

Hango, D. (2013b). *Ability in mathematics and science at age 15 and program choice in university: Differences by gender*. Ottawa, ON: Statistics Canada. Catalogue no. 81-595-M—No. 100. Retrieved from https://www150.statcan.gc.ca/n1/en/pub/81-595-m/81-595-m2013100-eng.pdf?st=Cw

Henry, F., Dua, E., James, C. E., Kobayashi, A., Li, P., Ramos, H., & Smith, M. S. (2017). *The equity myth: Racialization and indigeneity at Canadian Universities*. Vancouver, BC; Toronto, ON: UBC Press.

Henry, F., & Tator, C. (2009). *Racism in the Canadian university: Demanding social justice, inclusion, and equity*. Toronto, ON: University of Toronto Press.

Hideg, I., & Shen, W. (2019). Why still so few? A theoretical model of the role of benevolent sexism and career support in the continued underrepresentation of women in leadership positions. *Journal of Leadership & Organizational Studies*, *26*(3), 287–303.

Hudon, T. (2016). *Visible minority women*. Ottawa, ON: Statistics Canada. Catalogue no. 89-503-X. Retrieved from https://www150.statcan.gc.ca/n1/en/pub/89-503-x/2015001/article/14315-eng.pdf?st=aksCofH2

Indigenous and Northern Affairs Canada. (2011). Indigenous post-secondary education by gender in 2011. Retrieved from https://www.aadnc-aandc.gc.ca/DAM/DAM-INTER-HQ-AI/STAGING/texte-text/aB-PSE-Gender-2011_1452097153982_eng.pdf

Kelly, P., Austria, J., Chua, J., de Leon, C., Esguerra, E., Felipe, A., … Tupe, E. (2014). *Promoting post-secondary pathways among Filipino Youth in Ontario*. Filipino Youth Transitions in Canada. Retrieved from https://ycar.apps01.yorku.ca/wp-content/uploads/2014/01/fytic-ohcrif-2014.pdf

Krahn, H., & Taylor, A. (2005). Resilient teenagers: Explaining the high educational aspirations of visible minority youth in Canada. *Journal of International Migration and Integration*, *6*(3–4), 405–434.

Lingard, B., Mills, M., & Weaver-Hightower, M. B. (2012). Interrogating recuperative masculinity politics in schooling. *International Journal of Inclusive Education*, *16*(4), 407–421.

Martino, W., & Rezai-Rashti, G. (2012a). *Gender, race, and the politics of role modelling: The influence of male teachers*. New York, NY; London: Routledge.

Martino, W., & Rezai-Rashti, G. (2012b). Neoliberal accountability and the politics of boys' underachievement: Steering policy by numbers in the Ontario context. *International Journal of Inclusive Education*, *16*(4), 423–440.

McMullen, K., Gilmore, J., & Le Petit, C. (2010). *Women in non-traditional occupations and fields of study*. Ottawa, ON: Statistics Canada. Catalogue no. 81-004-X. Retrieved from https://www150.statcan.gc.ca/n1/pub/81-004-x/2010001/article/11151-eng.htm

Michalski, J. H., Cunningham, T., & Henry, J. (2017). The diversity challenge for higher education in Canada: The prospects and challenges of increased access and student success. *Humboldt Journal of Social Relations*, *1*(39), 66–89.

National Household Survey. (2011). *Immigration and ethnocultural diversity in Canada*. Ottawa, ON: Statistics Canada. Catalogue no. 99-010-X2011001. Retrieved from https://www12.statcan.gc.ca/nhs-enm/2011/as-sa/99-010-x/99-010-x2011001-eng.pdf

Natural Sciences and Engineering Research Council of Canada. (2017, October). *Women in science and engineering*. Retrieved from https://www.nserc-crsng.gc.ca/_doc/Reports-Rapports/WISE2017_e.pdf

Neeganagwedgin, E. (2013). Narratives from within: Black women and schooling in the Canadian context. *Alberta Journal of Educational Research*, *59*(2), 226–246.

NSERC Chairs for Women in Science and Engineering. (2018). Analysis of the distribution of gender in STEM fields in Canada. Retrieved from https://www.sfu.ca/content/dam/sfu/wwest/Documents/WISEReport2017_final.pdf

Ontario Ministry of Education. (2009a). *Ontario equity and inclusive strategy*. Toronto, ON: Queens Printer for Ontario.

Parkins, A. (2018). *Education: Gains and gaps in attainment and earnings*. Toronto, ON: Mowat Centre. Retrieved from https://tspace.library.utoronto.ca/bitstream/1807/99426/1/Parkin_2018_Education_Gains.pdf

Picot, G., & Hou, F. (2011). *Preparing for success in Canada and the United States: The determinants of educational attainment among the children of immigrants*. Ottawa, ON: Statistics Canada. Catalogue no. 11F0019M. Retrieved from https://www150.statcan.gc.ca/n1/en/pub/11f0019m/11f0019m2011332-eng.pdf?st=

Rezai-Rashti, G., & Martino, W. (2017). Black male teachers as role models: The homogenizing impulse of gender and racial affiliation. *American Educational Research Journal*, *47*(1), 37–64.

Richardson, C., & Cohen, N. B. (2000). Post-secondary education programs for aboriginal peoples: Achievements and issues. *Canadian Journal of Native Education*, *24*(2), 169–184.

Robson, K., Anisef, P., Brown, R. S., & George, R. C. (2018). Under-represented students and the transition to post-secondary education: Comparing two Toronto cohorts. *Canadian Journal of Higher Education.* [*Revue Canadienne d'enseignement supérieur.*], *48*(1), 39–59.

Science Council of Canada. (1982). *Who turns the wheel? Processing's of a workshop on science education of women in Canada (1981)*. Prepared by J. Ferguson. Ottawa, ON: Science Council of Canada.

Statistics Canada. (2017). Education in Canada: Key results from the 2016 consensus. *The Daily*, November 29. Retrieved from https://www150.statcan.gc.ca/n1/daily-quotidien/171129/dq171129a-eng.pdf

Statistics Canada. (2018). Canadian postsecondary enrolments and graduates, 2016/2017. *The Daily*, September 18. Retrieved from https://www150.statcan.gc.ca/n1/daily-quotidien/181128/dq181128c-eng.pdf

The Conference Board of Canada. (2018b). Annual report card 2018: Advancing diverse leadership on Canada's corporate boards. Retrieved from https://phasenyne.com/wp-content/uploads/2019/03/ARC-Annual-Report-Card-2018.pdf

Turcotte, M. (2011). *Women and education*. Ottawa, ON: Statistics Canada. Catalogue no. 89-503-X. Retrieved from https://www150.statcan.gc.ca/n1/pub/89-503-x/2010001/article/11542-eng.pdf

Universities Canada. (2019). Equity, diversity and inclusion at Canadian Universities: Report on the 2019 National Survey. Retrieved from https://www.univcan.ca/wp-content/uploads/2019/11/Equity-diversity-and-inclusion-at-Canadian-universities-report-on-the-2019-national-survey-Nov-2019-1.pdf

Wall, K. (2019). *Persistence and representation of women in STEM programs*. Ottawa, ON: Statistics Canada. Catalogue no. 75-006-X. Retrieved from https://www150.statcan.gc.ca/n1/en/pub/75-006-x/2019001/article/00006 eng.pdf?st=Ru45CGUk

Walton, G. M., Logel, C., Peach, J. M., Spencer, S. J., & Zanna, M. P. (2004). Brief interventions to mitigate a "chilly climate" transform women's experience, relationships, and achievement in engineering. *Journal of Educational Psychology*, *107*(2), 468–485.

Wang, F. (2013). Educational equity in the access to post-secondary education: A comparison of ethnic minorities in China with aboriginals in Canada. *Interchange*, *44*(1–2), 45–62.

Zarifa, D. (2012). Choosing fields in an expansionary era: Comparing Canada and the United States. *Research in Social Stratification and Mobility*, *30*(3), 328–351.

Index